D1523340

ENGLAND'S TIME OF CRISIS: FROM SHAKESPEARE TO MILTON

England's Time of Crisis: From Shakespeare to Milton

A Cultural History

DAVID MORSE

Lecturer in English and American Studies
University of Sussex

St. Martin's Press   New York

First published in the United States of America in 1989

Printed in Hong Kong

ISBN 0–312–02413–4

Library of Congress Cataloging-in-Publication Data
Morse, David.
    England's time of crisis: from Shakespeare to Milton: a cultural
history/David Morse.
        p.   cm.
    Bibliography: p.
    Includes index.
    ISBN 0–312–02413–4: $35.00 (est.)
    1. English literature—Early modern, 1500–1700—History and
criticism.   2. Literature and society—England.   3. England—
Civilization—16th century.   4. England—Civilization—17th
century.   5. Shakespeare, William, 1564–1616—Contemporary England.
6. Milton, John, 1608–1674—Contemporary England.   7. Great Britain—
History—Civil War, 1642–1649—Literature and the war.   I. Title.
PR408.S64M67   1989
820′.9—dc 19
                                                                88–18292
                                                                      CIP

Contents

For Allon

Preface

Like a rambling and draughty Jacobean manor house, English culture in the late sixteenth and early seventeenth centuries has been made the more comfortable by partitioning it up with a variety of tall, ponderous and heavily ornamented screens. In writing this book I have reflected that not the least advantage of screens is that, no matter how cumbersome or how well established they may be, there are times when they may be advantageously folded away – and I have been encouraged by the thought that such students of the period as Christopher Hill, Lawrence Stone and Keith Thomas appear to share this belief. I have learnt much from my colleagues at Sussex and I should like to thank Jonathan Dollimore, Michael Hawkins, Angus Ross, Alan Sinfield, Peter Stallybrass and Allon White for commenting so helpfully on sections of the manuscript. Wherever possible and within the restrictions imposed by modern typography I have tried to reproduce texts in their original spelling.

D. M.

Part One

Part One

1
England's Time of Crisis

The century of English history from the coronation of Elizabeth in 1559 to the end of the Commonwealth in 1660 was, for those who lived through it, a period fraught with fear, tension and anxiety. The world seemed such a desperately insecure and unstable place, beset by alterations and imminent possibilities of further change, that it became hard to adopt a balanced attitude towards it. Indeed, in an atmosphere of crisis such a response might seem altogether inadequate to the circumstances. This book is an attempt to pursue this shifting yet cumulative sense of crisis from Elizabethan to Civil War England as it is articulated in literature and other printed sources, in the belief that the characteristic energies of English writing of this time are better grasped as a response to the social and political tensions of the Reformation than through the aestheticised perspectives that a notion of 'Renaissance' has tended to impose. Although those who put pen to paper may well have been both more critical and more pessimistic than the majority of the population and although their sense of cultural crisis may not have always found an echo, they nevertheless shaped a climate of opinion which contributed to the Civil War. For cultural crises are as much a matter of attitude as of historical fact. A crisis exists when enough people believe that there is one. So it may well have been the case in the 1640s that war could have been avoided if all the different parties had been able to put their fears and suspicions behind them. Yet they were unable to do so because their sense of crisis was so intense, because it seemed that absolutely everything was at stake, from political freedom to the existence of a Protestant Church. It was generated as much as anything by the prospect of unprecedented change, and because it seemed the crystallisation of all the anxieties of an age of discord.

The most fundamental cause for English concern was the threat posed to her religious and political independence by the opposition of the Pope and the Catholic powers of Europe led by Spain, whether it took the form of external attack by the Spanish Armada or internal subversion in the form of the Gunpowder Plot. So real was this menace under Elizabeth that there was a great eagerness, verging on desperation, to put the best face on things and to claim that things had never been better. It was an age of shameless, if understandable, propaganda yet those who were most inclined to believe it were those who lived afterwards under James I and Charles I and who looked back nostalgically to a bygone age when, it seemed, everything had been comparatively rosy. The kind of deceptive evidence that they might light on is exemplified by Foxe's celebratory rhetoric in the second edition of his *Actes and Monuments of these latter and perilous dayes touching matters of the Church*, otherwise his *Book of Martyrs* (1571). Here Foxe goes a long way to contradict the spirit of his title and speaks enthusiastically of

> the long tranquillity, the great plenty, the peaceable liberty, which the Lord in his mercy hath bestowed upon this land during all the reign hitherto of this our sovereign and most happy queen Elizabeth, in such sort as the like example of God's abundant mercies is not to be seen in any nation about us during these halcyon days.[1]

Yet in 1569 there had been a Northern uprising under Northumberland and Westmorland. In 1570 the Pope published a bull excommunicating Elizabeth and releasing her Catholic subjects from their oath of allegiance to her, a move which promised, and provoked, disruptive consequences, since in March 1571 a plot was discovered, organised by the Florentine banker Ridolfi, in which an internal rebellion led by the Duke of Norfolk was to be reinforced by a Spanish expeditionary force, landing on the East coast. Yet Foxe was not being insincere. After the nightmare of the Marian persecutions English Protestantism had emerged once more into the sunlight and was still holding its ground. That in itself was miracle enough. So under the circumstances there was every reason to think positively and to clutch at every hopeful straw. In the same way John of Gaunt's invocation of England, in Shakespeare's *Richard II*, as

> This fortress built by Nature for herself
> Against infection and the hand of war

rings somewhat oddly in the light of the fact that the play was written in the immediate aftermath of the narrowly averted invasion of 1588, when a further attempt was regarded as imminent. Moreover, there had been a major epidemic of the plague in London in 1578. Although it had been traditionally believed that the English Channel was a guarantee of security from invasion, it was just that belief that was now being put in question. Robert Greene wrote more truthfully in his *Spanish Masquerado*: 'seeing how secure we slept, careless, reposing our selves in that our owne strength, for that wee were hedged in with the sea'.[2] It was precisely because England was in danger that an impregnable England needed to be invoked. For a long while a further cause of political anxiety was the fact that, so long as Elizabeth remained unmarried, there must be uncertainty about the succession to the throne. This was the more worrying because arguments about legitimacy and struggles over the throne had been a bloodstained thread running through English history from Richard II to Henry VII, yet this prolonged episode had barely been brought to a close when Henry VIII's attempts to produce a son and heir laid the basis for further conflict, which was now complexly intertwined with religious controversy and claims to a right of rebellion.

A further dissonant note is struck by print culture itself. From the Martin Marprelate controversy there develops a tradition of abusive, inflammatory and sharply critical writing which, despite censorship, can never be altogether damped down. Censorship exerts a constant pressure on what can overtly be said from Elizabeth to James and Charles I, yet even in the 1630s when Archbishop Laud made enormous efforts to ensure that censorship would work, even attempting to stamp out banned books in Holland itself, it was never really effective. Political corruption could be obliquely exposed in dramatic allegories. The Bible itself could be mobilised as an offensive weapon. The regular practice of Bible reading among sections of the population, especially those thought of as Puritan, and the typological thinking that that encouraged meant that the Bible came to be seen as a key with which to interpret contemporary events. The most powerful of all these keys was the Book of Revelations whose prophecies, many Protestants believed, were now on the point of being fulfilled. Bad harvests, outbreaks of the plague, the appearance of comets and other portents could be seen as expressing God's disfavour and as harbingers of still greater punishments to come. Moreover, it was through the printed word itself that people became better informed about wars and other disasters. So the more they knew the more they feared. In disseminating a dizzying tumult of knowledge, prophecy and opinion the book both reflected cultural unease and exacerbated it. The book was a multiplier.

The city of London itself was an important source of unease. The possibility of anarchy and disorder always simmered beneath the surface as its narrow streets became ever more crammed with work- and pleasure-seeking vagrants from all over England. It was in London that great fortunes were made by money-lenders, merchants, lawyers and courtiers who had been granted monopolies and the right to levy duties. London was where fashions and manners continually metamorphosed and where many went bankrupt in the struggle to keep up. It was in London that the plague and venereal disease made their most dramatic impact. Though life might continue in time-honoured ways elsewhere, in London the pace of change was unsettling. The enormous power of London as a centre simultaneously of commerce, political power and popular disturbance makes itself felt in many diverse ways from the anathemas directed against it in the 1590s to the role it played in the Civil War right through to the Glorious Revolution of 1688. London itself was a massive innovation.

For the Puritan minority it was the state of the Church that aroused their deepest anxiety and concern. They were shocked at the way in which superstitious practices contrary to the spirit of the Reformation still persisted. They were shocked at the corrupt worldliness of bishops and at the sloth and ignorance of the clergy, who were often absent from their parishes and who neglected their duty of preaching against sin. For a long time they remained isolated and were unable to bring effective pressure to bear on Elizabeth, James or Charles. But when Laud began his reforms, an important goal of which was to strengthen the role of bishops still further, even the Puritans appeared as guardians of tradition. Their warnings against bishops and the corrupting consequences of having a powerful Church hierarchy were now vindicated. If there was one thing all parties in 1640, whether Royalist or Parliamentarian, were agreed on, it was the necessity of putting the clock back and of bringing an age of discord to an end. But everyone had a different idea of what harmony would be.

2

This Luckless Kingdom

A significant development in the second half of the sixteenth century was the rediscovery of the English past and its presentation in the form of a detailed linear narrative. The trend was inaugurated by the Italian scholar Polydore Vergil, whose history first appeared in 1534 but which he continued right up to the present in a later edition of 1555. Polydore was followed by Edward Hall, whose chronicles of the Wars of the Roses followed in 1548 and this in turn stimulated the subsequent chronicles of Holinshead, Grafton and Stow, as well as *The Mirror for Magistrates* (1559) and the historical plays of Shakespeare. What emerged was a compelling tale of conflict and division, treachery and usurpation, murder and revenge, which could not but hold the attention but which also seemed to point a sinister moral: that of all the nations it was England that had the most bloodstained and continuously disastrous history. When the more recent acts of Bloody Mary were thrown into the balance it seemed that any considered, retrospective glance at the national record could only take the form of an act of mourning. Indeed, in this light, the phrase used by Clifford in Shakespeare's *Henry VI, Part III*, which I have taken for the title of this chapter, might even seem like a careful understatement. In any event, it could not but serve as a daunting reminder of the problems and pressures that would face any English ruler, especially when the legitimacy of the English crown was under further challenge from Rome. England, as it seemed, had always been up against it. Edward Hall began his *Union of the Two Noble and Illustre Families of Lancastre and Yorke* by insisting on England's status as the paramount instance in world history of a land afflicted by discord and division:

What mischief hath insurged in realmes by intestine divion, what depopulacion hath ensued in countries by civill discension, what detestable murder hath been committed in citees by separate faccions, and what calamitee hath ensued in famous regions by domestical dischord & unnatural controversy: Rome hath felt, Italy can testifie, Fraunce can bere witnes, Beame can tell, Scotlande maie write, Denmarke can shewe, and especially this noble realme of Englande can apparently declare and make demostracion.[1]

Hall then goes on to suggest, somewhat melodramatically, that although it is possible to set forth in words the struggle between Caesar and Pompey, Burgundy and Orleans, Guelf and Ghibelline, the England narrative is so horrendous as to be virtually beyond the power of articulate utterance:

> But what miserie, what murder, and what execrable plagues this famous region hath suffered by the devision and discencion of the renoumed houses of Lancastre and Yorke, my witte cannot comprehende nor my toung declare nether yet my penne fully set furthe.[2]

Hall does indeed overcome all restraint in order to do just that; but at the commencement of a work of some 868 substantial pages he asks the reader to begin in a chastened and apprehensive frame of mind. Here we also encounter a paradox that recurs in all such meditations on the national identity: England, whose history is uniquely bloodthirsty, is nevertheless 'a noble realme' and although the kings who fought out the struggle may well have been ruthless, treacherous and cruel, it is nevertheless all part of a tale of glory and renown, involving two noble and illustrious families. The same contradiction appears in Samuel Daniel's poem *The Civil Wars Between the Two Houses of Lancaster and York*, the first four books of which appeared in 1595 and which was subsequently completed by 1723. In the sixth book Daniel presents the figure of Pandora, whose mission it is to bring discord and confusion to the European nations and who, therefore, begins her task in England, as the land that is fairest of all:

> And first begin, with factions, to divide,
> The fairest Land; that from her thrusts the rest,
> As if she car'd not for the world beside;
> A world within her selfe, with wonders blest:
> Raise such a strife as time shall not decide,
> Till the deare blood of most of all her best

> Be poured foorth, and all her people tost
> With unkinde tumults, and almost all lost
>
> Let her be made the sable Stage, whereon
> Shall first be acted bloodie Tragedies;
> That all the neighbour States, gazing thereon,
> May make ther profits, by her miseries.

But a complex dialectic is at work; for England, sunk from the highest to the lowest, will eventually be restored to her former pre-eminence and having, as it were, supped full of horrors, she will finally be able to enjoy a peace and tranquillity that will be the envy of other nations:

> And, from the Rockes of Safetie, shall descrie
> The wondrous wracks, that Wrath layes ruined;
> All round about her, blood and miserie,
> Powres betray'd, Princes slaine, kings massacred,
> States all-confused, brought to calamitee,
> And all the face of kingdomes altered:
> Yet, she the same inviolable stands,
> Deare to her owne, wonder to other Lands

It seems that England has been marked out for special destiny in which unparalleled sufferings and unequalled blessings go hand in hand. This was also the view of John Foxe. Although Foxe approached English history from a completely different point of view, since his focus was on the history of the Church construed above all in terms of the Protestant martyrs who had been persecuted and burned for their beliefs, he could nevertheless agree both with Daniel that England was a uniquely privileged nation, and with Hall that the root of it all was in the reign of Henry IV. For Hall, this was because Henry had usurped the throne from Richard II, the last king before more recent times to hold the office with a clear title. For Foxe it was because it was in the reign of Henry IV that the persecution of Protestant martyrs began; it was he who began 'the unmerciful burning of Christ's saints for standing against the pope'.[3] Foxe could also agree that English history had been uniquely bloodthirsty, for it was on native grounds above all that martyrs had been made – an ambiguous sign of depravity, or of God's special favour:

There hath been no region or country more fertile or fruitful for martyrs, than our only region of England. Whether it happeneth or cometh by the singular gift or privilege of God's divine grace, or else through the barbarous and foolish cruelty of such as at that time ruled and governed the church, it is uncertain.[4]

Although kings were always implicated in these acts of persecution, Foxe was disposed to lay the responsibility at the door of corrupt and intolerant bishops. It was they who, time and time again, had stained the land with the blood of innocent men, who sought to do nothing more than practise the religion of Christ:

> During this business among the bishops beyond the sea, in the mean time our bishops here also in England were not unoccupied. Whether it be the nature of the country that so giveth, or whether the great livings and wealthy promotions of the clergy do draw with them a more insensible untowardness in God's religion, hard it is to say: this is manifest to all them who will read and mark our stories from time to time, that in England is more burning and slaying for religion and for all other matters; more bloodshed among us, than in any other land or nation in Christendom besides.[5]

Yet Foxe nevertheless believed in the unique destiny of England, which, as the one nation to stand out against the papal Antichrist in 'these latter and perilous days', had inaugurated the final phase of world history. England's status as elect nation was grounded in a long and honourable tradition of Protestant martyrdom.

In *The Faerie Queene* Spenser has an equally catastrophic tale to tell, though one which is protracted over a very much longer period of time. In Book III, Canto III the magician Merlin unfolds to Britomart, the legendary foundress of the British race, his prophetic account of what the future holds for them, from the earliest times until far beyond the Norman conquest. The luckless Britons will be subject to repeated foreign invasions and will be forced to endure the humiliation of alien rule – what Foxe had referred to as 'the woeful captivity of this nation'.[6] Of the period of Saxon domination Merlin exclaims in patriotic anguish and despair:

Then woe, and woe, and everlasting woe,
Be to the Briton babe that shal be borne
To live in thraldome of his fathers foe!
Late king, now captive; late lord, now forlorne;
The worlds reproch; the cruell victors scorne;
Banisht from princely bowre to wastefull wood!
O! who shal helpe me to lament and mourne
The royall seed, the antique Trojan blood,
Whose empire lenger here than ever stood?

Britomart is equally distraught at having to ensure such a relentless catalogue of national disasters and she responds to Merlin by asking:

Ah! but will hevens fury never slake,
Nor vengeaunce huge relent it selfe at last?
Will not long misery late mercy make,
But shall their name for every be defaste,
And quite from off the earth their memory be raste?

Such a query implicitly acknowledges the perspectives of the new history, which, in setting forth a narrative of English misfortunes in demoralisingly circumstantial detail, nevertheless holds out the promise of a rainbow at the end, in which suffering may reap its belated reward in the conferring of 'late mercy'. Merlin is happy to confirm Britomart's anxious expectation. The foreign yoke will only last about another 800 years! The Britons will finally reclaim their heritage through Henry VII, who, in addition to uniting the Houses of York and Lancaster, was also able to trace his ancestry back to the native British kings. This consummation will itself be crowned by the successful reign of Elizabeth, the Virgin Queen, and the defeat of the Spanish Armada. But at precisely this moment Merlin abruptly breaks off:

'But yet the end is not.' – there Merlin stayd,
As overcomen of the spirits powre,
Or other ghastly spectacle dismayd,
That secretly he saw, yet note discoure:
Which suddein fitt, and halfe exstatick stoure,
When the two fearful wemen saw, they grew
Greatly confused in behaveoure.

It is perhaps not surprising that Merlin, after reeling off nearly half a millennium of English history, should suddenly become baffled when attempting to look beyond the 1590s, and it may be that Spenser here intends an oblique reference to the coming struggle between Christ and Antichrist in the last days of the world as outlined in Foxe and the Book of Revelations, but what is more significant is that it shows that the very attempt to impose a optimistic closure on the nightmare of English history is itself problematic. History and life go on and there can be no guarantee that peace and harmony will prevail, especially when Protestantism and Catholicism are so deeply at odds. Even Edward Hall, writing in the reign of Henry VIII, could not fail to recognise that sedition had not ceased with the restoration of legitimacy and that Henry VIII himself had had more than his share of problems – though he did try to distract attention from them by launching into lavish descriptions of Henry's pomp and ceremonial. But those who came later could only be conscious that the reign of Edward VI, which Hall had hoped would be long and prosperous, had, on the contrary, been extremely short and had opened the door to the persecution of Protestants by Mary. Moreover, as Samuel Daniel was forced to admit, the passing of the conflict between York and Lancaster offered no secure basis for optimism, since it had been supplanted by new grounds for the shaking of kingdoms – the conflict between Catholic and Protestant. So the desire to hypothesise an end to England's troubles is always more of an earnest hope than a confident conviction and one that is prompted by the shock of exposure to the uniquely bloodstained annals of English history.

England stands perennially poised between misfortune and bliss, marked out for a fate that cannot be other than exceptional. Holinshead's *Chronicle* recounts how Brightwold, a monk of Glastonbury, who is deeply concerned about the fate of England after Edward the Confessor, has a dream in which he sees St Peter and communicates his anxieties to him. St Peter tells him that he has no grounds for concern as England is a country under God's special protection – a statement which, for Holinshead, is confirmed by the subsequent course of English history:

And as he thought he did demand of saint Peter, who should succeed the saint Edward? Whereunto answer was made by the apostle Have thou no care for such matters, for the kingdom of

England is Gods kingdome. which suerlie in good earnest may appear by manie great arguments to be full true unto such as shall well consider the state of this realme from time to time, how there hath beene ever governors raised up to maintaine the majestie of the Kingdome, and to reduce the same to the former dignitie, when by anie infortunate mishap it hath been brought into danger.[7]

Indeed, the existence of England's special destiny is actually confirmed by the fact that salvation flies so evidently in the teeth of historical probability. In Shakespeare's *King John*, for example, the fourth act ends ominously as the Bastard Faulconbridge sees dangers looming on every side:

> Now powers from home and discontents at home
> Meet in one line; and vast confusion waits,
> As doth a raven on a sick-fall'n beast

yet the play ends soon afterwards on a triumphantly patriotic note:

> Come the three corners of the world in arms
> And we shall shock them! Nought else shall make us rue
> If England to itself do rest but true.

This final line has a double implication: England must avoid internal division but equally she must avoid compromising her integrity through involvement with doubtful and unreliable foreign powers. In *King John*, where both King Philip of France and the Pope are seeking to influence English affairs, the moral is patent, but similar conclusions were drawn about other historical periods. For Hall, Henry VI's marriage to a French queen, Margaret, was the source of virtually all the disasters of his reign. The English Channel itself is taken as a peculiar sign from God, and not one to be taken lightly, that God has willed it that England shall have a special destiny apart from the other nations. In the longer term a patriotic ideology articulated in the last decade of Elizabeth's reign in *The Faerie Queene*, Daniel's poetry and Shakespeare's *King John* and *Henry V* has complex repercussions. For no later monarch was able to serve as the symbolic articulation of Englishness in the way that Elizabeth had. Elizabeth was not only native born but had even declined to take a foreign husband. She had proved uniquely able to keep England in a state of proud isolation; whereas James, in addition to being Scottish, devoted many years of his reign to the abortive project of marrying his son and heir to a Spanish princess – a most unpopular move in the country at large. Charles's eventual marriage to Henriette Maria, who was both French and Catholic, stored up further problems, as many believed that he was being unduly influenced by the Queen and her entourage of Jesuit priests. So it seemed that if the role of representing Englishness could no longer be assumed by the monarch it must necessarily devolve on the people and their representatives in Parliament. In the 1640s many Members of Parliament, as well as Puritan ministers, were conscious of England as a nation uniquely suspended between triumph and disaster and they looked for one final desperate heave in which England's glory would finally be secure. The message of sermon after sermon preached to that anxious assembly was that the fate of England was suspended on a knife-edge and that the issue could only be resolved by the forceful action of Parliament itself, which held the fate of the nation in its hands. As Herbert Palmer put it in his sermon of 1643, *The Necessity and Encouragement of Utmost Venturing*:

> I would hope, we are upon the borders of that promised blessing, which we at least have made to our selves many a time: And I do hope we are not now in the worse temper that ever we were. Though, on the other side, it is altogether apparent, we are still upon the borders of ruine, and of one of the wofullest curses, that ever befel a Nation professing Gods name.[8]

One of the principal reasons why the reign of Elizabeth, both early and late, has been so extensively glamourised is that it has been crucial to all attempts to present English history in the form of a progressive narrative, and because the temptation to present it as some kind of culminating or redemptive moment has been irresistible. The end of Elizabeth's reign provides a convenient point of historical closure, a still point from which it is possible to look back over the sixteenth century and estimate the progress that has been made. The decisive ending that Spenser wanted to supply but could not quite manage has been inserted all the same. It is hard to think of Elizabethan England without an imaginary full stop. Yet although the nostalgia began early, those who came immediately after were still conscious of the nail-biting, cliff-hanging tensions that persisted through her lengthy reign. In his *Britain's Remembrancer*, inspired by the suffering of the plague of 1625 – Charles I's coronation year – it would have been natural for George Wither to cast a romantic glow over the earlier times, but instead, though anxious to extol the virtues of 'blest Eliza', he chose rather to emphasise the difficulties she had faced:

> When she within her Kingdome had a swarme
> Of *Hornets*, which did howrly threaten harme
> Both to her State and person. When their pow'r
> And fury, was more likely to devoure,
> Than at this present it appeares to be.
> When her owne Court from traytors was not free,
> When she had *Irish* Rebels to correct;
> Oppressed *Netherlanders* to protect;
> And France to umpire: ev'n when all these,
> And other troubles did her State disease.
> What glory, wealth, and safety has thou got,
> That she, amid those dangers, purchast not?
> Religion in her dayes did still encrease:
> At home she had both *plentiousnesse* and *peace*;
> Abroad she was renown'd . . .

The stability of Elizabethan England was always a retrospective and relative concept – it had been a moment of precarious balance, that was somehow maintained in the face of desperate odds and against the background of England's turbulent history.

I would therefore want to argue that the whole tradition that has grown up of interpreting Elizabethan literature in terms of ideas of harmony, order and degree involves a whole series of complex misrecognitions both of the culture itself and of the way in which these concepts are articulated within it. I simply cannot accept that it would have been either easy or natural for men and women of the time to predicate order as a normal state of affairs. Indeed, all the evidence suggests that the exact opposite is true. For many years the definitive expression of these views has been contained in the writings of E. M. W. Tillyard and especially in two books, *Shakespeare's History Plays* (1944) and *The Elizabethan*

World Picture (1958). Although there has been a massive reaction against Tillyard's views in recent years – exemplified by the work of such critics as Robert Ornstein, S. C. Sen Gupta, Wilbur Sanders and John Wilders,[9] whose primary thrust has been to acknowledge the existence of these ideas as Tudor commonplaces but to deny that Shakespeare merely reiterates them – in my view it has still not gone far enough since it has left the commonplace themselves pretty well intact. Although Tillyard's canvas has been heavily overpainted, the 'picture' that it offers still continues to subtly condition the whole way in which theoretical problems are posed. Yet Tillyard's case, as I hope to show, was never adequately developed or argued, but from the outset depended heavily on categorical assertion, reiteration and the unhesitating manipulation of texts. My focus will be primarily on *Shakespeare's History Plays*, both because the explanatory framework of *The Elizabethan World Picture* is essentially foreshadowed there and because it rests on an alternative reading of many of the texts that have entered into discussion here. In this work Tillyard is concerned to argue the case for Edward Hall both as a seminal Tudor historian and as *the* formative influence on the writing of Shakespeare's history plays. Tillyard is not just concerned to show how Hall has influenced particular Shakespearean passages, since this has already been done by lesser lights, but to see him as the figure who decisively epitomises 'the new moralising of history',[10] which is demonstrated by his treatment of an 'organic' stretch of English history, in which the dissension and disorder inaugurated by the deposing of Richard II by Bolingbroke 'has been healed for ever by the union of Henry VII and Elizabeth and by the issue of that union in Henry VIII'.[11]

Before examining in greater detail what Tillyard has to say about Hall it would not be inappropriate to ask why it was that he needed to show that Hall was 'very important'.[12] In his preface to *The Elizabethan World Picture* Tillyard subsequently wrote: 'This small book has come out of an attempt to write a larger one on Shakespeare's Histories. In studying these I concluded that the picture of civil war and disorder they present had no meaning apart from a background of order to judge them by.'[13] This formulation is suggestive in itself. On Tillyard's own reading what comes across in the Histories is an impression of confusion and there seems to be little in the plays themselves that can contradict it, but this cannot be what the plays are about, so they need to be illuminated by placing them in a context that will reveal their true meaning. Tillyard's main problem is that the Ulysses' speech in *Troilus and Cressida*, which he invokes as a vision of the anarchy and discord that would ensue if order and degree were shaken and which is the touchstone for his whole approach, does not actually occur in the history plays; worse still, there is nothing in any of the nine plays that remotely resembles it. He asks the reader to have a copy of *Troilus and Cressida* open at the appropriate page and to study the text carefully. However, Tillyard has not yet acquired the confidence to present this speech as the entire key to world history, so he has to cast around for something corresponding to it elsewhere and what he hits upon is Henry VI's speech, beginning

> O God! methinks it were a happy life
> To be no better than a homely swain.

This, allegedly (but perhaps truly), is 'the most effective statement of the principle of order'.[14] Such a naïve idyll can scarcely bear all the metaphysical freight that Tillyard would burden it with, but he nevertheless does his best: 'This ordered life of the shepherd is a pitifully small thing compared with the majestic order he as a king should have been able to impose. Yet it stands for the great principle of degree.'[15] So Tillyard needs some other means of demonstrating the prevalence of order in the history plays and he finds this, or purports to find it, in the work of Edward Hall. According to Tillyard, Edward Hall had seen being worked out in English history a providential pattern, in which discord and division are finally overcome, when Henry VII is at last able to rule with an unchallengeable title. This is echoed in the closing speech of *Richard III* when Richmond, the new king, sees the passing of a time of violence:

> England hath long been mad, and scarr'd herself:
> The brother blindly sheds the brother's blood;
> The father rashly slaughter's his own son;
> The son compell'd, been butcher to the sire.

and the coming of a better age, when his heirs, if God permits, will

> Enrich the time to come with smooth-fac'd peace,
> With smiling plenty, and fair prosperous days.

Richmond's speech is to be taken not just as the culmination of
Richard III but of the three plays dealing with the reign of Henry
VI as well. It is here that their governing, but largely submerged,
theme finally surfaces. Shakespeare, according to Tillyard, at this
point 'comes out with his full declaration of the principle of order,
thus giving final and unmistakable shape to what, though largely
implicit, had been all along the animating principle of the
tetralogy'.[16] Really the argument has a certain audacity, for now
that Tillyard has enclosed the first 'tetralogy' within this
formulation he can extend it effortlessly to cover all the other
history plays as well since Richard III comes sequentially, if not
chronologically, last. Has any critic ever made a handful of
treasured quotations go further? At all events, Tillyard now has
all nine plays marching to the simple and rousing tune of these
twenty lines and the justification for this prodigious feat of
reductiveness is, of course, 'Hall'.

Unfortunately, Hall's *Chronicle* cannot be used as an instant
vade-mecum to Shakespeare in the way that Tillyard supposes,
even if we assume that Tudor history is the monolith that he takes
it to be and pass over the fact that Foxe's *Actes and Monuments* is
not so much as mentioned. Tillyard's presentation of Hall
irresistibly recalls the one-time fashion of alluding to the 'simple
faith' of the Middle Ages; thus rather notably overlooking the fact
that the medieval period produced such figures as Duns Scotus,
Peter Abelard, Thomas Aquinas and William of Ockham, whose
faith, whatever it may have been, was scarcely simple. There is,
in fact, a definite continuity between the nostalgia of Chesterbelloc
and Eliot's subsequent and ostensibly more sophisticated antithesis
between the harmonious world of Dante and the disassociated
sensibility of modern man. It is from Eliot that Tillyard's disposition
to discuss Elizabethan literature in terms of order comes. However,
Tillyard's engaging picture of Hall, the sage old moralist who
pertinaciously elaborates a moral tale over the centuries and
whose triumph it is 'to impose so powerful a pattern on this
theme',[17] can scarcely survive a reading of the *Chronicle* itself, as
distinct from the title-page and the first two or three pages.
Significantly, Tillyard scarcely quotes from Hall at all outside of
his brief introductory section. He is content to reiterate his claim

that Shakespeare, the grateful pupil, has completely absorbed the 'lessons' of Hall. So we have: 'his loyalty to Hall', 'Shakespeare fulfilling his old debt to Hall', 'Shakespeare adopts the whole teaching of Hall', 'his own main teacher of the philosophy of history of history, Hall', 'Hall's ideas had by this time become a part of his mind', and so on.[18] Tillyard makes great play with Hall's chapter headings which he takes to demonstrate the clarity and dramatic nature of the overall conception. These are:

i   The unquiet time of King Henry the Fourth
ii   The victorious acts of King Henry the Fifth
iii The troublous season of King Henry the Sixth
iv   The prosperous reign of King Edward the Fourth
v   The pitiful life of King Edward the Fifth
vi   The tragical doings of King Richard the Third
vii The politic governance of King Henry the Seventh
viii The triumphant reign of King Henry the Eighth

In practice, however, these chapters often correspond very imperfectly to the description in the brochure. The 'prosperous reign' of Edward IV is a clear case in point. Hall begins by describing Edward's marriage to Elizabeth Grey, which he sees as being almost as disastrous as that of his predecessor, Henry VI, to Margaret, and he comments: 'Yet who so will marke the sequele of this story, shall manifestly perceyve, what murther, what miserie and what trobe ensued by reason of this marriage.'[19] Hall subsequently goes on to describe the catastrophic consequences of the rebellion led by the Earl of Warwick and the Duke of Clarence:

> by the sedicious rebellinge of these persons, the state of the Realme was broght to great miserie, for churches and Temples – were every where robbed & spoiled, houses burnt and men slayne in every place, all the Realme was replenished with bloud, slaughter, sorow & lamentacion, Cornefeldes were destroied, cities and Townes were made desolate and languished with famyn & dearthe besyde many other thinges, which happen by the cruetie and fury of warre and rebellion.[20]

All this is hardly the average person's idea of a prosperous reign. Hall's title is justified by the relative stability and a concurrent economic upturn that existed in the latter part of Edward's reign. But it should also be added that amongst Hall's diverse explanatory principles is a general propensity to blame England's misfortunes on treacherous, conniving, deceitful, oath-breaking foreigners, especially the Scottish and the French. Since the loss, in the reign of Henry VI, of all of England's French possessions save Calais weighed heavily on Hall's patriotic mind he viewed Edward's journey to France with an army – which then earned Edward a subsidy from Louis XI to take it back home – with quiet satisfaction. It was a partial restoration of England's pride. But the purchase of Hall's ostensible scheme on the detail of the overall narrative is very imperfect, to say the least, which Tillyard in his discussion should certainly have acknowledged, instead of indicating precisely the contrary. Moreover, as Henry A. Kelly has persuasively argued and comprehensively documented, such constancy and coherence would have been most unlikely given the disparate nature of the sources which Hall used.[21] If Hall had been able to achieve this it would have called for a sophistication in narrative organisation and the treatment of sources far beyond the attitudes and assumptions of his time and Tillyard is being quite unhistorical in suggesting it. In Tillyard's account Hall becomes a kind of sixteenth-century Gibbon, tracing not so much the decline and fall of the Roman Empire as the ascent of Tudor man.

A further awkwardness in Tillyard's attempt to present Edward Hall as the unequivocal exponent of order and degree is that this concern for hierarchy is seldom explicit in the *Chronicle*. When it does make its appearance it does so very strikingly, and very unpropitiously, as one of the 'flagicious facts' connected with that evil prince, Richard III: it is Richard, addressing his troops at Bosworth Field, who insists:

> I doubt not but you in hart will thinke and with mouth confesse, that yf ever bond of allegians obliged the vassal to loue and serue his naturall-sovereigne-lorde, or yf euer obligation of dewtie bound any prince to ayde and to defende his subjectes? All these loues, bondes and deuties of necessitie are this daie to be experimented, shewed and put in experience.[22]

And it is Richard who says of the redeemer, Henry VII:

I dought not but you know, howe, the deuil continuall enemie to humane nature, disturber of concord and sower of sedicion, hath entered into the harte of an unknowen welshman.[23]

It would be hard for the Elizabethan reader to respond to these words in the spirit of the Homilies, which insisted on a subject's duty of obedience. Richard III is hardly the most convincing exponent of this particular doctrine.

Tillyard also assumes that references to Providence can be introduced as if the question of providential determination is completely unproblematic. But the action of Providence, as Hall well recognised, is always a matter of human interpretation, so that it is always possible to advance this or that version or disagree with any, since ultimately God's purposes must always remain obscure. Thus, on the one hand, Hall categorically denies that the outbreak of plague at the beginning of the reign of Henry VII was a sign that he would be troubled by many rebellions – 'These were the phantasticall judgements of the unlettred persons which I ouerpasse, and retourne to my purpose'[24] – yet only a couple of pages later he concludes, without batting an eyelid, that Edward IV's desire to marry his own niece had 'provoked the Ire of God and the swoorde of vengeaunce agaynste hym'.[25] Fortune, the uncertain action of divine providence, cause and effect, personal rivalry and foreign malice – Hall juggles a whole set of explanatory principles as the occasion suits or a source suggests and the upshot of it all is not so much the clear daylight suggested by Tillyard, as of a man peering through obscurity and gloom in search of some conjectural reason. If Shakespeare was as thoroughly saturated in Hall's *Chronicle* as Tillyard intimates, then the sense of history that he derived from it could scarcely have been such as simply to instil a faith in happy historical endings.

There is a conspicuous lacuna in *Shakespeare's History Plays* in that it never makes any reference to the multiplicity of ways in which rebellion had historically been validated. Tillyard's account of the 'doctrine of rebellion'[26] has the familiar univocal flavour: he simply asserts that rebellion is universally condemned and deplored. Tillyard bases his case once more on the Homilies and assumes that the arguments against rebellion commanded as total an assent as ever Big Brother received in Orwell's *Nineteen Eighty-Four*. Yet there were many arguments on the other side.

There was a long and popular tradition of revolt against unjust kings and the fact that this was in no way part of establishment thinking does not make it any the less real. Moreover, Hall, though generally deploring discord and division, nevertheless implicitly accepted that a king such as Henry VI, who was incompetent and unfit to rule, could reasonably be displaced. Tillyard conveniently manages to gloss over the fact that if the Homilies are to be taken seriously then both Richard III and Macbeth must be obeyed. *Macbeth* is a key text for Tillyard and the only tragedy to be discussed in *Shakespeare's History Plays*, yet Tillyard manages to quote Malcolm's words:

> Macbeth
> Is ripe for shaking, and the powers above
> Put on their instruments

without so much as recognising that they put forward the traditional argument that tumult and disorder may be God's way of punishing an unjust king. Tillyard's very one-sided and deliberately blinkered method of arguing is particularly evident in his discussion of *The Mirror for Magistrates*. He quotes this injunction that follows the story of Jack Cade: 'And therefore whosoever rebelleth against any ruler either good or bad rebelleth against God and shall be sure of a wretched end, for God cannot but maintain his deputy',[27] and links this with the Calvinist doctrine that even wicked rulers are to be obeyed. But what this omits is that a distinction was always made between a general popular uprising and disciplined revolt lead by a prince or body of noblemen – the difference, in fact, between Magna Charta and Jack Cade. Moreover, Calvin himself left the door open for resistance led by an inferior magistrate. By cutting the quotation off at this point Tillyard also omits the following:

> Yet this I note by the wa_ concernyng rebelles and rebellion. Although the devyll rayse *l*em, yet God alwayes useth them to his glory, as a parte of his Justice. For whan Kynges and chiefe rulers, suffer theyr under officers to mysuse theyr subjectes, and wil not heare nor remedye theyr peoples wronges whan they complayne, than suffreth GOD the Rebell to rage, and to execute that parte of his justice, which the parcyall prince would not.[28]

Here we find not only the belief that rebellion may ultimately serve divine purposes, but the argument that was to figure so prominently in justification of the struggle against Charles I: that it may be necessary to rescue a king from the harmful influence of his corrupt and self-serving flatterers and subordinates. The great division between Protestant and Catholic rendered all questions of obedience problematic. Tillyard should be setting the homilies in their historical context as a strategy of containment, instead of using them, in conjunction with Ulysses' degree speech, as a covenient 'framework' into which everything else can be neatly fitted.

Tillyard's *The Elizabethan World Picture* attempts to present medieval cosmology with its revolving spheres and chain of being from ant to angel as a master discourse that cannot be problematised. But, as I have already indicated, such a cosmological perspective cannot finally suppress or cancel the urgent questions raised by a reading of English history. For in this context the ideal synchronic order lies so far beyond the diachronic confusion that its existence is almost mocking. It certainly can be no source of consolation. Striking evidence of this is furnished by Michael Drayton's poem *The Barons Warres* (completed 1603) which also addresses itself to the issue of England's violent past and which deals with events in the reign of Edward II. Drayton moves from an indictment of the horrors of the age to an invocation of the harmonious spheres that presumably govern the universe, yet the contradiction between the two is an evident source of perplexity:

> Inglorious Age, of whom it should be sayd,
> That all these Mischiefes should abound in thee,
> That all these Sinnes should to thy charge be layd,
> From no calamnious or vile Action free!
> O let not Time, us with those ills upbrayd,
> Lest feare what hath been, argue what may be,
> And fashioning so a habit in the mind,
> Make us the Haters of our Kind!
>
> O' pow'rfull Heaven, in whose most Sov'raigne Raigne,
> All thy pure Bodies move in Harmonie,
> By thee, in an inviolable Cheyne
> Together link'd; so ty'd in unitie,
> That they therein continually remayne

Sway'd in one certaine course eternally;
Why, his true motion keepeth ev'ry starre,
Yet what they governe, so irregular.

Drayton is so deeply worried about the possible course of English history that he can scarcely connect it to the regularities of the universe. Rather, what he fears is that there may actually be something unnatural about the English people, since they have for so long struggled against one another, and that a destructive cycle of violence established in the past may continue to shape events both now and in the future. The norm is not order but disorder. This sense of man as apart from an overarching pattern of order in the cosmos was reinforced by the Calvinist antithesis between a just and all-powerful God and weak, sinful and unregenerate man. God's universe might indeed be stable and harmonious but the human world, equally predictably, would bear all the marks of man's inherent wickedness and depravity. But there were also grounds for not expecting harmony in the universe either. For some, tempests, plagues and other disasters could be expected to occur more frequently because the world itself was now manifesting signs of progressive decay and deterioration. For others it was inevitable that, as the world entered its last days in the final struggle between Christ and Antichrist, God would intervene more and more directly in human affairs with signs of his judgement and wrath. In truth the harmonious, ordered cosmos was as much an object of nostalgia in Elizabethan times as ever it was for Tillyard or Eliot.

3
The Corrupted Church

Once the optimism and euphoria produced by the succession of Elizabeth to Mary and the consequent establishment of a Protestant Church had gradually subsided, those English Puritans who sought more far-reaching changes were faced with an extraordinarily recalcitrant and potentially demoralising situation. For it now suddenly became all too apparent that the English Church, for no very explicit set of doctrinal reasons, had resolved to pitch camp indefinitely, while the Celestial City of a truly reformed religion still beckoned tantalisingly on the horizon. Their best hope for more purposive action came in 1575 when Edward Grindal, who was sympathetic to their aims, was appointed Archbishop of Canterbury; but Grindal was rapidly shunted aside by Elizabeth once his attitudes became apparent and subsequently they were persecuted and pursued first by Whitgift and then, with still greater ruthlessness and severity, by Archbishop Bancroft. If it were at all possible they would have preferred to avoid a confrontation with the Queen herself, proclaiming in the 'Second Admonition to Parliament' of 1572: 'her Majestie shall not finde better subjectes, in her land, than those that desire a righte reformation',[1] but, on the other hand, they insisted, in the same document, 'we say the worde is above the church',[2] which, of course, is also to say that the authority of the Bible must take precedence over earthly rulers, over bishops and monarchs alike. Against the charge that they are being unduly polemical at a time when the threat from papism is serious enough, their argument is that it would be positively impious to temporise. There can be no tarrying or dallying in the face of the explicit commandments of God:

Againe wheras some men (& that good men to) will say these treatises be too hotte for this time, I wish to know wherin? whether in the matters which we handle? or in the handling of the matters? The matters are Gods, wherein we may not minse him. And the deformities have continued long, and are

25

manifestly intollerable, where against we are commaunded to
cry out. Crye out and cease not, lift up thy voice like a trumpet,
& tell my people their wicknesse, and the house of Jacob their
sinnes, saith the Lord to his Prophet, which saying and the
verse following, doth so belong to us, that we shall hardly
answer it to God, if we doe the contrary, & scarse wel answere
it, that we have forborne so long.[3]

The Bible positively requires the faithful to be difficult. In the face
of accretions to the Christian faith and practice that have
accumulated through centuries of corruption under the papal
Antichrist there can be no possibility of acquiescing in compromises
or further makeshift arrangements. For such temporising places
the entire reform movement in jeopardy and makes it appear that
the principles on which it has been founded are less than absolute.
In these last days of the world, reform is now a matter of the
utmost urgency. The Puritans employed a powerful rhetorical
distinction between 'reformation' and 'deformation' in order to
suggest that anything which fell short of their absolute demands
was not so much half the truth as a capitulation in the face of evil.
The struggles of the faithful against corrupt bishops, says Thomas
Cartwright, the Puritan leader, in this 'Second Admonition', will
have been justified because,

> they which have these many ways and times bene hampered
> and ill handled by them, they still offer themselves to al their
> extremities, and therefore put forthe their treatises, because
> they passe not howe deare they bought it, so they might
> redeme our state out of this deformed reformation, to a righte
> platforme drawne out of the scriptures.[4]

Initially Puritan discontent was directed against such 'heathenish
practises'[5] as the wearing of surplices and costly vestments, the
use of the wedding ring in marriage and of the sign of the cross in
baptism, and other matters of a ritual or ceremonial nature; but
increasingly their criticism came to be focused on two targets in
particular: the prayer book and the institution of bishops. They
objected to bishops because they found no authority for the office
in the Bible and because they were convinced that bishops were
both the source of all corruption in the Church and the command

posts from which all resistance to their proposals were directed. They objected to the prayer book in part because they felt that it was improper to assign canonical status to a latterday work 'in deede culled out of the vile popish service booke'[6] yet impiously placed on a par with the Bible in status and authority; but more importantly because they felt that the length and complexity of the services laid down left insufficient time for the vital work of ministers – the preaching against sin. It seemed to them that the assumption that such an agglomeration of practices was all that was needed to constitute the religious life all too easily blended into pagan superstition and magic, especially when, as so often, this was linked with indifference to the power of the biblical word and with a lack of determination to lead a truly Christian life based on a strict fidelity to its teachings. Consequently, much Puritan effort went into the task of consciousness-raising, whether this took the form of preaching or private Bible reading or whether, more dramatically it was channelled into such communal events as public 'prophesying' and 'night conventicles', through which the faithful could become more conscious of their solidarity as a group and more concerned to raise the general level of their commitment and awareness. In the face of a largely illiterate, uneducated and uncomprehending mass of the people, still sunk in the depths of pagan idolatry, the Puritan ministers felt that it was incumbent upon them to do all in their power to promote the true religion. Moreover, if they were to reclaim individual souls for Christ they knew that this could not be carried out by the old methods or with the aid of the old corrupt practices. Before all else they had a mission to educate.

Symptomatic of the evangelic and militant spirit was a sermon preached by Edward Dering before Queen Elizabeth in 1569 or 1570. Instead of striking the complaisant and desperately grateful note of a John Foxe, which had become almost a ritual for English Protestants, Dering was sharply critical, indeed positively insulting. He did not merely point the finger at corrupt bishops and priests but pursued the accusation as far as the person of the Queen herself, since it was under *her* auspices that these sins were committed:

> If I would declare unto your Majesty all the great abuses that
> are in our ministry, I should lead you along in the spirit as God

the prophet Ezekiel. And after many intolerable evils, yet I shall still say unto you, behold you shall see more abominations than these [cf. Ezekiel 8].

I would lead you to your beneficies, and behold, some are defiled with impropriations, some with sequestrations, some loaded with pensions, some robbed of their commodities. And yet behold, more abominations than these. . . . Look upon your ministry, and there are some of one occupation, some of another, some shake bucklers, some ruffians, some hawkers and hunters, some dicers and carders, some blind guides and cannot see, some dumb dogs and will not bark, and yet a thousand more iniquities have now covered the priesthood, and yet you, in the meanwhile that all these whoredoms are committed, you at whose hand God will require it, you sit still and are careless.[7]

It is difficult not to perceive this as a crucial turning point in the history of the Elizabethan Church. For it demonstrated to the Queen, with shattering clarity, that the Puritans would continue to be utterly uncompromising in their principles and that even a monarch instrumental in restoring the Reformation could not be exempted from their critique. Faced with their non-negotiable demands it seemed to make more sense to reject them outright than to imagine that it would ever be possible to strike some kind of deal that would leave all parties contented. So the Church of England, half-way house itself, became immutable and non-negotiable. Dering was also more ruthless and implacable than Foxe in his reading of signs and portents. What became apparent was that the implicit analogy between England and Israel was a treacherous one; since if England was indeed peculiarly favoured amongst nations this might also signify that she would be subject to especially terrible manifestations of the divine wrath if she were once to depart from the path of righteousness. Dering turns Foxe's argument on its head. Instead of rejoicing in God's favour Englishmen should rather tremble:

Let us behold ourselves how plentifully at this day are God's mercies and benefits poured out upon us, both upon our Queen and upon her people. How mightily doth he defend us in so many dangers? How sit we here in safety, when all the world is in an uproar? And is this, think you, of our deserving, or rather of God's mercy? Now surely, surely, we are very blind if we will not all confess with the prophet Jeremiah that it is God's mercy that we be not consumed [cf. Lamentations 3:22]. So much disobedience both in prince and subject, so little care of duty, so deep forgetfulness of God, what doth it else deserve but heavy judgement? . . . It is no good argument that our estate is sure because God hath delivered us out of a great many troubles. Nay, let us the rather fear and be the more circumspect.[8]

Dering's questions are in any event rhetorical since in Calvinist theology man deserves nothing anyway but may nevertheless receive the miraculous gifts of divine grace. So Dering, like his Puritan successors, imposes a deadly double bind. Wars, plagues, famines and other disasters are the inescapable signs of God's wrath and constitute an unimpeachable call to righteousness and reformation. But, contrariwise, serene and prosperous times are only evidence of God's infinite mercy in the face of endless provocations, which may be brusquely brought to a halt if evidence of contrition and repentence is not speedily forthcoming. To lead the Christian life is necessarily to live in fear.

Striking evidence of this new-found Puritan concern to accentuate the negative is provided by Thomas Cartwright's *The Holy Exercise of a True Fast* (1579–80). Puritans were disposed to stress the importance of fasting, both in rebuttal of Catholic claims that this was an aspect of Christian discipline that Protestants neglected and because fasts were a way of publicising issues and grievances. In Cartwright's account we are a long way from the 'halcyon days' of Foxe. Disasters loom on every side. Far from rejoicing that England has been so mercifully and continually spared he concludes that it is time for Englishmen to awaken from their spiritual torpor and recognise that the waters of God's wrath are now lapping ominously close around their feet:

Now the churches round about vs, being fallen into great decay, partly by the spirituall miseries, as well of the heresies of *Papistes, Arrians, Anabaptistes,* the *Families of loue,* &c, as also the schisme of *Lutheranisme,* dayly preuailing, partly by bodily plagues of the Pestilence, almost in all places: of the sworde in our neighbour countries, and of the Famine, which waiteth commonly upon the same: It is euident that thereby groweth one cause of humbling our selves before our God. . . . And among bodily punishmentes, the Plague hath indifferently fedde, and yet doth feede vpon us, The Sword hath been shaken at vs both in the North by Traytors, and in the South by disorderly wicked persons. And shold it not strike vs, that her Maiestie was of late in danger of her life by a Shotte? Which that it was not meant towardes her, ought not to abate our care for her maiestue, but rather encrease it: as that which was more neerely directed against her of the Lord, to make her and vs, to cry for his gratious couer and protection ouer her. And if we consider the wrath that hangeth ouer our heads, the notes thereof are taken by the example of the people of God, the first of *Ezra*, who understanding that the people had married strange women, fasted: wherevpon wee haue this note of the wrath to come, that considering how that sinne is committed openly in the land in diuers sortes, that therefore anger is at hand.[9]

All the signs of national favour have been eroded. There are no grounds for complacency or self-congratulation since evils abroad have their counterparts at home. God will only extend his favour and protection to those who are truly his and the moment when the life of the Queen was placed in danger (in 1571, the Northern Rebellion was in 1569) should be interpreted rather as a warning than as a merciful deliverance. The land can only continue to be looked favourably upon by God if it assiduously perseveres in the path of righteousness. In a similar vein Laurence Chaderton, whose role as sponsor of puritan trends while master of Emmanuel College, Cambridge from 1584 to 1622 led Patrick Collinson to dub him 'the Pope of Cambridge puritanism',[10] was moved to utter dire warnings in his Paul's Cross sermon of 1680. While Chaderton acknowledged that England was indeed a 'peaceable land flowing with milk and honey'[11] it was nevertheless the case that true repentence was still lacking. God was beginning to grow impatient with his people as was evident from any unlooked for manifestations:

Not four years ago the Lord did as it were with his own hand set a star in the heavens, whereof the wisest astronomer that liveth can give no reason. Since then we have been admonished by a great and strange comet in the air, by earthquakes, inundations of waters, all which signs and forerunners of God's wrath are returned to him again as being unable to mollify our stoney hearts that we might turn to the Lord.[12]

The plague in London was an equally menacing sign. Although God's privileged treatment of England had been freely given, he could not be expected to maintain it without stronger evidence of a desire on the part of Englishmen to submit themselves wholeheartedly to His will. By admonishing England with such diverse portents God was putting the country on notice that this bounty which she had enjoyed had not been granted in perpetuity and what it might abruptly be withdrawn if she persisted in her indifferent course.

That the Puritans should have been prophets of disaster is perhaps not altogether surprising. It was very much in their interest to paint a dark picture of the times and suggest that all this was to be attributed to a tarrying in reformation, to the fact that a corrupt ecclesiastical establishment continued to preside over a lax and spiritually moribund Church. What is distinctly more puzzling and incongruous is the fact that their opponents should have taken an almost equally gloomy and apocalyptic view of things. Even they, in the aftermath of Armada, had grown apprehensive and it no longer seemed appropriate to strike the euphoric note that had once seemed so uncontentious. What the Martin Marprelate controversy demonstrates is not only that the Puritans were violent, scurrilous and abusive and that their opponents answered in kind, so that in the furore all distinctions of status were undermined – undoubtledly a significant portent of things to come – but also the way in which they were able completely to dominate and control the assumptions on which the debate was conducted. To their credit, or shame, scarcely anyone in the ecclesiastical establishment is prepared to argue that everything in the garden is rosy; their predicable note is to reproach those who have dared to strike such a brazen and culturally dissonant note at a time when England herself is in danger. In his reply to the Marprelate attack, Thomas Cooper, Bishop of Winchester, deplored the untimely hour of its launching: 'when the view of the mighty Nauie of the *Spaniards* is scant passed out of our sight: when the terrible sound of their shot ringeth, as it were yet in our eares'.[13] Thomas Cooper is beginning to feel quite shell-shocked. But his appeal to patriotic unity got short shrift from the Marprelate quarter, for in their reply 'Hay any work for Cooper' they deliberately transvalued the significance of the Armada and presented it not as an alien threat mercifully averted but as God's warning to impious men of power:

> You are then the men by whome our estate is most likely to be overthrowne, you are those that shal answer for our blood which the Spaniard, or any other enemies are like to spill, without the Lords great mercy: you are the persecutors of your brethren, (if you may be accounted brethren) you and your hirelings are not only the wound, but the very plague and pestilence of our church.[14]

Thomas Cooper, needless to say, could not accept that all responsibility for evil and ungodliness should be laid at the bishops' door but he did admit that they were genuinely and alarmingly there. He simply felt that the Puritans had got the wrong target. It was unreasonable to make the episcopacy both scapegoat and cause of such a pervasive sinfulness, when, in the final analysis, each individual must answer personally to God for his own sins:

> If right zeale, with conscience and detestation of evil, were the roote of these invectives, which so boyle in loathesome choller and bitter gall against the Bishops and other of the Clergie: surely, the same spirit would mooue them to breake out into like vehement lamentations against the euils and vices, which shew themselves in a great number of this Realme: I meane, the deepe ignorance and contempt of God in the midst of the light of the Gospell, the heathenish securities in sinne and wickednesse, the monstrous pride in apparell, the voluptuous riot and sensualitie, the excessive buildings and needelesse nestes of mens treasures, which bee as cankers consuming the riches of the realme.[15]

Cooper is, of course, declaring his opponents hypocrites, so a little moral righteousness does not come amiss, especially from a bishop, but even he is conscious that all is not well. What the conduct of the controversy reveals is that the attempt to fix the Elizabethan settlement was storing up problems in the longer term, since the justice of the criticism could not be denied, even if the vehemence of it could be deplored. Only three decades after the passing of Mary it was only to be expected that there would still be many for whom religion meant an eclectic mixture of Catholic ritual and pagan superstition. Many of the merchants and gentry were rejecting a life of sobriety in favour of extravagance and conspicuous consumption. The financial affairs of the Church were in a terrible mess. The fact that the whole settlement was based on compromise and muddle meant that there was very little in the way of a consistent policy in the Church, apart, that is, from a desire to harass Puritans. Under Elizabeth, in the face of a clear Catholic threat, everything had to be subordinated to the need for political stability. James I's general neglect of the Church did not seem to matter so much because he had at least shown himself to be a good Protestant. But under Charles I and Laud it had become clear that the issues would finally have to be clarified. Unexpectedly, in Laud's vigorous drive for centralised control and in his campaign to extirpate puritanism once and for all, all the old arguments about the dangers of innovation that had once seemed so powerful blew back in their faces. It was now the Puritans who could claim to speak for tradition and who were able to mobilise the nation's anxieties about the dangerous and unpredictable nature of change.

In the 1590s it was not only the critics of the Church who saw doom looming up on the horizon. The expectation of apocalyptic events was common ground. The fact that the mathematician Regiomontanus had predicted long before the Armada that the year 1588 would be a year of great upheavals gave genuine grounds for anxiety. It seemed that Foxe's reading of Church history was further confirmed by the astronomical evidence. Yet is could be argued that if disaster threatened, the Puritans were as likely to be its effective cause as a righteous prophylactic. In 'An Almond for a Parrat', Thomas Nashe, the presumed author, issued them with this warning: 'Amend, amend, and glorie no more in your hipocrisies, least your pride and vaine glory betray our prosperitie to our enimies, and procure the Lords vengeance to dwell in the gates of our citie'.[16] Even more desperately apocalyptic and anxious was the tone adopted by Thomas Cooper, though doubtless he has his own good reasons for not wishing to be outflanked by the Marprelaters. In the face of 'schismaticall factions and curious doctrines'[17] he repeated the by now familiar consolation that 'God hath dealt as mercifully with this land, as euer he did with any',[18] but he nevertheless insisted that the hour was late and that this was England's last chance to reform and mend her ways:

> I beseech him, that in time we may repent with *Niniue*, and turne to him in sackcloth and ashes, while hee may bee founde, and while hee stretcheth vnto vs the hands of his gratious goodnesse, least when it is too late, and hee hath turned his face from vs, wee crie vnto him with vaine gronings, and mourne with unprofitable sighing.[19]

One consequence of the more widespread practice of Bible reading was that people developed a more powerful sense of a jealous and ever-watchful God, whose presence loomed alarmingly over their every action, and who in full cognizance of their many sins of omission and commission would now chastise his people into obedience and repentence. In the coming decades the contrary instances of Nineveh and Babylon were very much on people's minds. The former had been restored to God's mercy and grace in the nick of time, but Babylon, in its pride and obduracy, had met the full might of his religious wrath. The only question was: which one was England to be?

Of all those figures in the Elizabethan Church who played a part in rallying it against the determined assaults of the Puritans, none has achieved a more lasting reputation than Richard Hooker, whose *Of the Laws of Ecclesiastical Polity* (Books I–IV, 1593, Book V, 1597) offered such a comprehensive and authoritative defence of its doctrines and practices that it was to become definitive of the Church of England. To his credit Hooker did not shirk any of the issues – except in so far as he chose to argue on the high theoretical ground for the need for Church government rather than to offer a detailed defence of the ruling ecclesiastical establishment – and his claim that the ways of the Church were sensible and reasonable gained credibility from the sensible and reasonable way in which he argued his case. Yet Hooker shared many assumptions with his opponents. In the first book he acquiesced to their pessimistic view of the state of the nation: 'We all make complaint of the iniquity of the times: not unjustly; for the days are evil'[20] though he did try to draw the sting from this by suggesting that the times before the existence of any civil society (what Hobbes was subsequently to call 'the state of nature') had been even worse. Hooker never completely spells out why it is that he has such a gloomy view of his own times but in so far as he declares his hand it would seem that what chiefly concerns him is the threat to stability and order posed by radical Protestantism. Hooker is concerned at the effectiveness of the puritan technique that would 'impute all faults and corruption, wherewith the world aboundeth, unto the kind of ecclesiastical government established',[21] especially when they are able to win popular sympathy when 'the faults especially of higher callings are ripped up with marvellous exceeding severity and sharpness of reproof'.[22] The reason why Hooker is so desperately anxious to validate traditional practices wherever possible is that he can see that the whole process of challenging existing structures and of finding them wanting when weighed against the authority of the Bible could acquire such an irresistible momentum that there could be no stopping it until the entire fabric of social legitimacy had been liquidated. Hooker is alarmed by those who urge the truth of their proposals so emphatically that they are not even prepared to consider what the social cost would be: that 'it must be received although the world by receiving it should be clean turned upside down; herein lieth the greatest danger of all'.[23]

Hooker envisages an apocalypse of his own in which the determination to insist on the truth of 'bare and naked scripture' will actually have the effect of abolishing the Christian Church as an institution and which will have the further consequence, implicit in the whole argument of the work, of depriving kings of political legitimation and the means of social control. It is precisely the political chaos in Europe that makes all such initiatives especially dangerous:

> For the scope of all their pleading against man's authority is, to overthrow such orders, laws, and constitutions in the Church, as depending thereupon if they should therefore be taken away, would peradventure leave neither face nor memory of the Church to continue long in the world, the world especially being such as it now is.[24]

The paradox which Hooker recognises, but which was to have far more intricate consequences than he could ever have forseen, is that reform of the Church would be possible in a general context of political stability; but it is the very pressure for reform that undermines political stability and makes reform impossible.

Hooker's call for moderation was strengthened by the circumstances of his own time and, subsequently, by the experience of Civil War, but the argument itself, when scrutinised more closely, is riddled with contradictions. Hooker objects to those who 'by following the law of private reason, where the law of the public should take place, they breed disturbance',[25] yet if pressed he would have to concede that Luther, by obeying his private conscience, had unleashed the discord of the Reformation. Hooker is generally opposed to innovation yet in justifying the existence of bishops he is obliged to defend it. He believes that gradual and moderate reform is to be preferred to rapid change, but why then should not reform steadily and purposively continue? Why must it now come to a halt? Why has the Elizabethan settlement become undiscussable even in the discussion of it? Moreover, if Hooker objects to those Protestant extremists who justify themselves by claiming that they are the new Jerusalem and the chosen people of God, why does Hooker make God's apparent favour the clinching argument for a more moderate course: claiming that God has used 'the bridle of his provident restraining hand, to stay those eager affections in some, and to settle their resolution upon a course more calm and moderate',[26] that the Church of England 'the thing which he blesseth, defendeth, and keepeth so strangely, cannot choose but be of him'?[27]

The knives that Hooker was using were dangerously double-edged. The appeal to tradition is one that can be made in a diversity of ways. England, in crisis, all too eagerly drank in the Elizabethan anathema directed against innovators and those who otherwise rock the boat. Forty years later it was Charles I and Laud who appeared as terrible shakers of the stability of the kingdom.

4

London: the Corrupted City

If there was any one place that could be confidently singled out as the focus of iniquity in the kingdom that place was London. The sheer size of London made it an unprecedented and altogether overwhelming phenomenon. With a population of some 200,000 inhabitants in 1600, London was thirteen times greater than Norwich, its closest rival, yet the rapidity of urban growth was such that Norwich with a population of 15,000 was rapidly approaching the size that had made Cologne, with its 20,000 inhabitants, by far the largest city in Germany in the fifteenth century. Fernand Braudel suggests that 'Before 1500, 90% to 95% of the towns known in the West had fewer than 2000 inhabitants',[1] yet A. L. Beier has estimated that the population of London rose from approximately 120,000 in 1550 to no less than 375,000 in 1650.[2] London was the only place in England with an unquestionable right to be called a city, yet this might well have seemed a dubious honour to some contemporaries since it would tend to rank it with all those places of ill-repute in the Bible, from Babylon to Tyre, which had mostly met with some disastrous fate. London was a place of bewildering diversity, which acted like a magnet to attract people into its orbit from all parts of the country, whether they were gentry bent on legal business, place-seeking or pleasure, or the hordes of migrants, beggars and vagabonds who came thronging there seeking work, alms or easy money. Like many present-day cities of the Third World there was an absolute break between the standards and amenities of the prosperous central areas and the ramifying, higgledy-piggledy suburbs beyond. The majestic structure of the cathedral of Old St Paul's and the tall, well-built houses of merchants and money-lenders that lined the wide, well-paved streets in the Strand and Cheapside were surrounded by a maze of narrow, tortuous alleys, crammed with people, merchandise, stray dogs, mendicants, carriages and carts, always muddy and strewn with refuse, inescapably putrefying to the nostrils, at night dangerous and menacingly dark. Finding your way was never an easy task. Since London attracted so many migrants – A. L. Beier suggests that London 'must have been attracting an average of over 7000 migrants each year from 1605 to 1660 and this figure takes no account of persons who came and left again, which might raise the total by 50 per cent'[3] – it was difficult to find somewhere to stay and as a result there was overcrowding on a scale and in a manner which it is difficult for us to imagine, conditions which necessarily contributed to the rapid spread of infectious diseases. Paul Slack in *The Impact of the Plague in Tudor and Stuart England* cites an instance given by the Recorder of London in 1603 where 'there were 800 cases of plague in a single building, formerly one of four large mansions which now together housed 8000 people'.[4]

Yet the attractions of London were considerable, and although being a stranger in the city could be a risky and expensive business they came all the same. Then, as now, London was an unparalleled entertainment capital, offering pleasure and diversion in abundance. Here, if you had the money, you could have exquisite and costly garments tailored in the latest imported fashion, you could attend extravagant banquets and sample the most exotic foods and spices, you could take your pick of ostentatiously dressed courtesans. But even if your means were more limited there was an abundance of alehouses and theatres, there was cockfighting, bull- and bear-baiting, there was bowling and gambling at dice and cards. Southwark, on the wrong side of the river, as well as offering the Paris Garden with its animal entertainments, was a notorious red-light district and infamous for all kinds of licentiousness and immorality. It was in Southwark that the pious Puritan Nehemiah Wallington heard tell of a group of married men who for seven years had 'lived in the sin of buggery and were sworn brothers to it',[5] and who made a point of committing this sin on the Sabbath at sermon time. It was wickedness such as this, Wallington believed, that had caused God to burn London Bridge as a terrible warning on the night of 11 February in 1633 or 1634. In London it was absolutely certain that there were all kinds of disreputable goings-on.

London was a locus of forces that could scarcely be controlled. In the city, teeming with masterless men, new possibilities opened up for taking politics to the streets. Moreover, the growing financial power of city merchants and financiers meant that, particularly in times of crisis and when war threatened, their intervention could tip the scales. In the Civil War London decisively threw its weight behind the Puritan cause, yet its influence in the political crises of the Restoration and in the Revolution of 1688 was no less crucial. London was not only the stage on which political events were acted out, it was itself a powerful determinant of the direction which they would take. In London nothing could be taken for granted any longer; everything was negotiable.

In the urban scene of pleasure, commerce and power, gold was the lubricant that could grease all wheels. For actually possessing wealth in the form of lands and estates could seem merely notional so long as it could not be translated into the wherewithal necessary for conspicuous consumption. When faced with a choice of blessings, varying from beauty and strength to wisdom and longevity, Dekker's Fortunatus scarcely loses much sleep over his decision:

> Gold is the strength, the sinews of the world,
> The health, the soul, the beauty most divine,
> A mask of gold hides all deformities;
> Gold is Heaven's physic, life's restorative,
> Oh therefore make me rich.

Gold has become the quintessence of virtue and value, the standard against which everything else must be measured. A similar reverence for the sacred metal informs the opening of Ben Jonson's *Volpone*, where Volpone awakens to exclaim:

> Good morning to the day; and next, my gold!
> Open the shrine, that I may see my saint

as the curtain is drawn back to reveal huge piles of gold coins, Volpone, like Fortunatus, sees gold not simply as wealth but as the bearer of reputation:

> Who can get thee,
> He shall be noble, valiant, honest, wise

The pervasiveness of the new gold standard is ironically conveyed when Mosca concludes a panegyric to the beautiful Lady Would-be with the clinching affirmation 'Bright as your gold! and lovely as your gold!' References to 'gold' and 'golden' in the writing of the time are loaded with complex overtones, since gold is at once magical, valuable, deeply desired, yet at the same time fraught with implications of venality, baseness and corruption. Gold is a figure in which the romanticism and the cynicism of the age are paradoxically intertwined.

Whether engaged in gambling, ostentatious forms of social display, new commercial ventures or the costly and long drawn-out construction of country houses – or palaces as they were more appropriately known – there were few members of the aristocracy who did not experience cash-flow problems. The difficulties they encountered and the expedients they resorted to have been amply documented in Lawrence Stone's *The Crisis of the Aristocracy*, but in all their ambitious schemes or tight corners the services they were increasingly obliged to draw upon were those of the money-lender and the lawyer. There was a mutual dependency between these professions since the documents which the usurer depended on for his financial guarantees were drawn up by his legal confrères. The lawyers had much the best of it since their occupation involved less risk and no social stigma. Their activities incurred less resentment, while, as the careers of such men as Coke and Bacon demonstrated, they had far greater prospects for advancement. Their legal expertise could be put to a multiplicity of uses and they were in the advantageous position of being able to play both ends against the middle. Wherever there were bribes to be had, deals to be made or corrupt practices to be adopted, the lawyers were sure to have a hand in it, yet their services were necessarily called upon for the occasional drives against corruption that took place. Bacon was responsible for the downfall of Coke, yet he came to a sticky end himself when his extensive bribe-taking, which had paid for the construction of the magnificent Verulam House, became too extensive to be ignored. Of the iniquities of London, Thomas Nashe wrote in *Crists Teares over Jerusalem*: 'London, thou art the seeded Garden of sinne, the Sea that sucks in all the scummy chanels of the Realme. The honestest in thee (for the most) are eyther Lawyers or Vsurers',[6] but Nashe was here not so much paying tribute to their professional integrity as indicating, in the most hyperbolic manner, how desperately the ethical standards of London had fallen. Money-lenders and financial speculators were especially disliked – as their representation as Barrabas and Shylock would suggest. Their prosperity seemed as inexplicable as it was excessive. Barrabas, counting his hoard of gold – 'Infinite riches in a little room' – seemed as daunting a figure as today's computer expert, deploying a recondite expertise that baffles the understanding of ordinary men. Barrabas's rather absurd complaint, that counting his money involves too much exertion, foregrounds what is truly mysterious about lending money at interest: it totally cancels the biblical imperative to work:

> The needy groom, that never finger'd groat,
> Would make a miracle of this much coin;
> But he whose steel-barr'd coffers are cramm'd full,
> And all his life-time hath been tired,
> Wearying his fingers' ends with telling it,
> Would in his age be loathe to labour so,
> And for a pound to sweat himself to death.

All natural measures of value have disappeared. Yet lawyers could seem almost equally suspect because the complex documents they draw up seemed remote from the comprehension of the workaday world. In *A Knights Conjuring* (1607) Thomas Dekker suggests that the Devil himself, on his arrival in London, would be hard-pressed to lay his hands on a copyist, so engrossed were they in dubious legal business. Yet the Devil contrives to be sanguine about his difficulties, consoling himself with the reflection that they are, after all, engaged in the Devil's own work:

It troubled his mind where he should get a pen-man fit for his tooth to scribble for him, all the Scriveners i'th'towne he had at his becke, but they were so set at worke with making bonds between *Usurers* and *Unthrifty heyres*, between *Marchants Tradesmen*, (that to couzen and undoe others, turne Bankrowtes themselves, and defeate Creditours) and with drawing close conveyances between *Land-lordes* and *Bawdes*, that now sit no longer upon the Skyrtes of the Cittie, but jette up and downe, even in the cloake of the Cittie, and give more rent for a house, than the prowdest *London* occupyer of them all, that Don Lucifer was loath to take them from their *Noverints*, because in the ende he knewe they were but his Factors, and that he should be a part-owner in their lading, himselfe; Lawiers clarks were so durtied up to the hammes, with trudging up and downe to get pelfe, and with fishing for gudgeons, and so wrung poore ignorant Clyents purses, with exacting and unrasonable Fees, that the *Paye-maister of Perdition* would by no meanes take them from their wide lines, and bursten-bellied straggling ffs, but stroking them under their chinnes, called them his white boyes, and told them he would empty the ynke-pot of some others.[7]

The strict and unyielding nature of the new contractual agreements cast a long shadow over the age. Failure to meet repayments left the defaulter with a mountain of obstacles to climb, far outweighing that of the original debt and its interest, in which the starting point was the debtors' prison. From such a fate not even the highest were exempt. As a young man Francis Bacon, a future Lord Chancellor and himself son of Nicholas Bacon, Queen Elizabeth's Lord Keeper of the Great Seal, incurred this ignominy, along with such smaller fry as the writers Greene, Marlowe and Nashe. It seems symptomatic of the age that Shakespeare's *The Merchant of Venice* should be premissed on the conflict between a money-lender and a lawyer, in which the severity of the original contractual agreement can only be overturned by a still greater rigour and severity in the interpretation of the law. We may also note that alien power is overturned by native expertise and that in the process traditional values triumph. Love, beauty, friendship and honour are restored to the position from which avarice and the love of money seemed likely to evict them. Yet the lawyer's tools of trade could seem equally menacing. In Marlowe's *Doctor Faustus* much of the hero's trepidation stems from the inflexibility of the Devil's contractual agreements. Although Faustus protests that he has already risked much on the Devil's behalf, Mephistopheles insists that Faustus must sign a written agreement to give up his soul, with all the binding force which such a document is deemed to give:

> But now thou must bequeath it solemnly,
> And write a deed of gift with thine own blood,
> For that security craves great Lucifer.
> If thou deny it, I will back to hell.

Much of the power of the play stems from Faustus's strict contractual awareness of what precisely he is committing himself to when, despite the stoppage of blood in his veins, he finally puts his signature to the document, and on the strictness with which the contract is finally executed, on the very last stroke of twelve. Marlowe's medieval hero finally confronts the anxiety of the modern.

The contradictions of urban existence were acutely mirrored in the writings of Marlowe and his familiar associates Thomas Nashe and Robert Greene. Each of them achieved early recognition and notoriety, but as impecunious men of letters with no assured income their ability to live a sybaritic existence was severely hampered. Their shady reputations combined with their lack of patronage meant that they were always living from hand to mouth and that they were dependent on credit for their very existence. Like Aesop's fox they found the splendours and luxuries that they craved always dangled tantalising just out of reach, but they did not, therefore, conclude that they were not worth having. On the contrary they became that much more obsessional. They were simultaneously frustrated by the manifold restrictions on their existence, yet from their writings it would seem that they were nevertheless guilt-ridden and remorseful for the dissipated lives which they contrived to lead against the odds. The flavour of their circle is intriguingly conveyed by Dekker in his picture of them in the Elysian Fields:

> whils't *Marlow*, *Greene*, and *Peele* had got under the shades of a large *vyne*, laughing to see *Nash* (that was but newly come to their Colledge,) still haunted with the sharpe and *Satyricall spirit* that followed him heere upon *earth*: for *Nashe* inveyed bitter (as he was wont to do) against dry-fisted Patrons, accusing them of his untimely death, because if they had given his *Muse* that cherishment which shee most worthily deserved, hee had fed to his dying day on fat Capons, burnt sack and Suger, and not so desperately have ventur'de his life, and shortend his dayes by keeping company with pickle herrings.[8]

Be that as it may, neither Nashe, Marlowe nor Greene lived to see their thirty-fifth birthday and their sense of the transitoriness of life finds expression in diverse ways: in Greene's death-bed repentence, *A Groat'sworth of Wit*: in the dying agonies of Edward II and the climactic scene of *Faustus*; in Nashe's celebrated stanza:

> Beauty is but a flower,
> Which wrinkles will devour,
> Brightness falls from the air,
> Queens have died young and fair,
> Dust hath closed Helen's eye.
> I am sick, I must die:
> Lord, have mercy on us.

Despite Marlowe's reputation for frivolity a strong vein of moral earnestness runs through his work. Tamburlaine, the Scythian shepherd boy, becomes the scourge of God and is able to conquer more powerful, more complex and more decadent civilisations through the very simplicity and strenuousness of his upbringing. In *Dido, Queen of Carthage* Aeneas is impelled to break away from the luxurious Carthaginian environment that is beginning to weave its spell upon him before it is too late:

> Aeneas must away;
> Whose golden fortunes, clogged with courtly ease,
> Cannot ascend to Fame's immortal house,
> Or banquet in bright Honour's burnish'd hall,
> And cut a passage through his topless hills.

In the case of Faustus himself we recognise the seriousness with which he takes his pleasures, his frank determination to pay the ultimate price – if only he can live 'in all voluptuousness'. The difference between Faustus and the traditional Christian picture of the sinner is that Faustus does not plunge recklessly, forgetfully and heedlessly into a life of sensual dissipation, but rather goes against God in a conscious and calculating spirit, reckoning that the deal is worth it and that the pleasures gained now will more than compensate for any subsequent pains. Yet we also recognise the parodic spirit in *Faustus*, the way in which his powers are used to mock worldly reputation and dignity, so that the life of worldliness is simultaneously desired and made fun of, envied and condemned. In Faustus's appalling bargain the writer momentarily masters the world and himself and becomes the measure of all things. But it is as if the terror of his final damnation is finally the only sure remedy for the compulsive fascination of the attractions of the urban scene. *The Tragical History of Doctor Faustus* must be seen as an act of exorcism.

The 1590s saw the appearance of two impassioned religious tirades directed against the moral decadence and corruption of London: *A Looking Glasse for London and Englande* and *Crists Teares over Jerusalem*, in which its overpowering sinfulness was likened both to the city of Nineveh and to the ancient Jewish capital. Yet the objects of comparison could have been worse since both of these historic precursors presumed the possibility of reformation and repentance. The first of these was co-written by Robert Greene with Thomas Lodge, the second by Thomas Nashe. Since the reputation of Greene and Nashe was far from saintly it has sometimes been assumed that they were insincere, but clearly both men had a powerful interest in a project that might secure their own salvation along with, and perhaps ahead of, the rest. Certainly the case of London was disturbing enough to suggest that it might be of concern to God also. Moreover the medieval legacy of the Seven Deadly Sins, which is felt as much in Nashe's *Pierce Penniless* as in *Crists Teares*, was still such a powerful mode of perception that in contemplating the vices and follies of the London scene it was wellnigh impossible to offer a critique in a wholly satirical and secular fashion. A vision of the Last Judgement would always obtrude. Any attempt to transcend the immediacy of the moment would involve some imaginative reconstruction of how God would interpret the passing scene and would thus embrace the recognition that his anger and stern judgement could only be tempered by his infinite capacity for mercy. It is such a God's-eye view that *A Looking Glass* and *Crists Teares* adopt – literally so in the case of *Crists Teares* where Nashe, with astonishing boldness, writes from the point of view of the grieving Christ himself.

A Looking Glasse for London and Englande is a somewhat diagrammatic and schematic work, perhaps necessarily so through its point-by-point comparison of London with bibilical Nineveh, but for that very reason it sheds a clear light on the attitudes of the time. The play depicts episodes from the history of Nineveh that are interspersed with desperate appeals to contemporary London, imploring that the city should learn its lesson from this celebrated example. The authors depict the court of Rajni, King of Nineveh as a scene of erotic intrigue, adultery and murder, while the kingdom itself is a place where honest citizens are callously and unscrupulously exploited by the professional class of usurers, judges and lawyers. For a poor man his cow is his most cherished possession: 'Why sir alasse my Cow is a common-wealth to mee, for first sir, she allowes me, my wife and sonne, for to banket our selves withal, butter, cheese, whay, curds, creame, sod milke, raw milke, sower-milke, sweete-milke, and butter-milke', yet he is abruptly deprived of it by the ruthlessness of a usurer. At the same time the usurer cunningly delays acceptance of repayment from a gentleman until after the hour specified in his agreement is past so that his farm is forfeit. But when his victims take their grievances to court they get no satisfaction since the usurer bribes both their lawyer and the judge. By implication neither London nor England possess justice of any kind. Certainly, if Bacon's career is any guide, the bribing of judges was normal practice and the courts were scarcely the place where those with short pockets could expect to prevail. The play concludes with the following admonition to the city, which suggests that London has only been spared from punishment because of Queen Elizabeth's exemplary virtuousness:

> O London, mayden of the mistresse Ile,
> Wrapt in the foldes and swathing clothes of shame,
> In thee more sinnes than Ninivie containes.
> Contempt of God, despight of reverend age.
> Neglect of law, desire to wrong the poore:
> Corruption, whordome, drunkennesse, and pride.
> Swolne are thy brows with impudence and shame.
> O proud adulterous glorie of the West,
> Thy neighbors burn, yet doest thou feare no fire.
> Thy Preachers crie, yet doest thou stop thine eares
>
> The larum rings, yet sleepest thou secure.
> London awake, for feare the Lorde do frowne,
> I set a looking Glasse before thine eyes.
> O turne, O turne, with weeping to the Lord,
> And think the praiers and vertues of thy Queene,
> Defers the plague, which otherwise would fall.

It must, therefore, have seemed only fitting that England should have been afflicted by a virulent outbreak of the plague in 1603, the year of Elizabeth's death.

Though it is written in prose, *Crists Teares over Jerusalem* leaves *A Looking Glasse for London and Englande* plodding desperately in its wake, for its extraordinarily insistent, flamboyantly forceful and resolutely apocalyptic rhetoric is like nothing else in the English language. On the face of it Nashe's diatribe is unexpected since by attacking the corruption of London he seems to ally himself with the Puritans, whom he loathed and detested. But Nashe's hostility to the Puritans is based on the fact that he sees them as being socially subversive. Nashe is always the conservative, a man who respects wealth, rank and reputation even as he resents and envies it – indeed precisely because he resents and envies it. It was just because he was so deeply alienated that Nashe desperately desired to belong. Nashe insists on his pretensions as an ardent traditionalist; he is dismayed at the spectacle of England's sad decline from former standards, as her manners are progressively eroded by newfangled customs and foreign innovations. For Nashe social order and stability are essential. His Christ insists that coherence is a universal and omnipresent principle of God's universe: 'There is no perfect societie or Citty, but of a number of men *gathered* together. Geese (which are the simplest of al foules) *gather* themselves together, goe together, flie together. Bees in one Hiue holde their consistory *together*. The starres in Heaven doe shine *together*',[9] yet he laments of Jerusalem, and therefore by implication of London: 'They will not onely not *gather* themselves into order (which I their Captaine might exact at their hands), but scorne to be directed, mustered, and *gathered* by me, when with the myldest disciplines I offer to marshal them.'[10] The contemporary Elizabethan world is characterised by chaos, confusion and disorder. It goes both against Christ and against nature. In the struggle for position and the quest for novelty, in a refusal of the requirements of religion 'Every man heere in *London* is discontent with the state wherein hee liues.'[11] As Nashe sees it, a carefully structured, stable and law-abiding society based on rank, self-discipline and respect has been thrown into confusion through the desperate pursuit of extravagant display and conspicuous consumption, and if he is excluded so much the worse. Appearance becomes everything, yet this glittering appearance is the mask for a deep-seated moral corruption:

Decke our seues how we will, in all our royaltie, wee cannot
equalize one of the Lillies of the fields; as they wither, so shall
we wanze and decay, and our place no more be found. Though
our span-long youthly prime blossomes foorth eye-banquetting
flowers, though our delicious gleaming features make vs seeme
the Sonnes and the Daughters of the Graces, though we glister
it neuer so in our worme-spunne robes and golde-florisht
garments, yet in the graue shall we rotte: from our redolentest
refined compositions, ayre pestilenzing stincks and breath-
choking poysous vapours shall issue.

    England, the Players stage of gorgeous attyre, the Ape of all
Nations superfluities, the continuall Masquer in outlandish
habilements, great plenty-scanting calamities art thou to await,
for wanton disguising thy selfe against kind, and digressing
from the plainnesse of thine Auncestors. Scandalous and
shamefull is it, that not anie in thee (Fishermen & Husbandmen
set aside) but lyue aboue their ability and birth; That the
outwards habite (which in other Countries is the only distinction
of honour) shoulde yeelde in thee no difference of persons: that
all thy auncient Nobilities (almost), with the gorgeous
prodigalitie, should be deuoured and eaten vppe, and vp-starts
inhabit their stately Pallaces, who from farre haue fetcht in this
varietie of pride to entrappe and to spoyle them.[12]

In Nashe's strange gallimaufry of forceful plain speaking with
orotund and often incongruous phraseology – as in his brilliant
invention of 'worme-spunne' – it is tempting to perceive the
ambivalence of the age itself, poised between the simplicities of
rural existence and the dazzling, yet menacing complexities of the
city. Nashe himself, was forced to find some kind of counterweight
to London, in his panegyric to Great Yarmouth, *Lenten Stuff*.
Yarmouth, with its grave burghers, its straightforward, honest
citizens, its hard-working fishermen and its frank acceptance of a
culture based on the red herring, is a place with its feet firmly
planted on the ground, where you know exactly where you
stand. It is a place that can offer some sort of consolation to Nashe
when his fantasies of affluence have irreparably faded. In Nashe's
convoluted writing we can begin to glimpse just how unsettling
London could seem.

In his *Pierce Penniless* Nashe inserted an encomium to the
Puritan preacher Henry Smith, of whom he said: 'I never saw

abundant reading better mixed with delight, or sentences, which no man can challenge of profane affectation, sounding more melodious to the ear or piercing more deep to the heart'.[13] Such a response could not have been predicted from Nashe's view of the phenomenon of Puritanism in general, and it points to a widespread sense of cultural *malaise* that goes beyond such obvious polarisations. Henry Smith preached at St Clement Danes in the city from 1587 until his death in 1591 and in that short period won an enormous reputation as the 'silver-tongued preacher', both for his eloquence and for the frank and outspoken way in which he censured the rich and powerful. Indeed, Thomas Fuller, his earliest biographer, suggested that it was only because he enjoyed the protection of Burghley, chief minister to Elizabeth, that he was able to speak out as he did. Certainly Smith did not mince his words. At this time London was a city of startling contrasts in which the extremes of affluence and poverty daily passed before men's eyes, where it was not unusual to encounter the corpse of a vagrant who had starved to death while others gorged themselves to excess. Smith was not afraid to point the Christian moral or to rebuke the affluent for their reluctance to contribute to the welfare of the poor:

The rich worldling makes no conscience to have ten or twenty dishes of meat at his table, when in truth the one half might sufficiently satisfy nature, the rest run to the relief of the poor; and yet in the end he might depart better refreshed with one dish than commonly he is with twenty. Some will not stick to have twenty coats, twenty houses, twenty farms, yea; twenty lordships, and yet go by a poor person whom they see in great distress and never relieve him with one penny, but say, God help you; I have not for you. There are lawyers that will not stick to undo twenty poor men, and merchants that make no conscience to eat out twenty others, that have their hundreds out at usury, their chests crammed full of crowns, and their coffers full of golden gods, or glistering angels, that will go by twenty poor, miserable, hungry, impotent or distressed persons, and yet not bestow one penny on them.[14]

While some of the puritan preachers were particularly severe on the vagrants, vagabonds and masterless men who thronged the streets of London this was not the case with Henry Smith who laid the responsibility for their condition at the door of the well-to-do. Smith made no bones about regarding the 'great thieves' as a more significant social problem than the 'petty thieves' and he argued that when they ceased to find favour 'then, surely the commonwealth would soon be disburdened of that pestilential brood of caterpillars wherewith it is pestered'.[15] Smith's imagery suggests that there were some at least who found Elizabethan England quite as much an unweeded garden as the England of Richard II. For in the near-universal pursuit of short-term private advantage among the social élite there were few who gave much thought either to the wider implications of their actions or to the long-term consequences. Vagrancy was the symptom of social problems more complex and deep-seated than anyone at the time was prepared to realise. But the commonwealth, as Smith envisaged it, was a vanishing concept as the Court and its glittering prizes became the dominant reality. It would take a civil war to bring it back.

For Henry Smith the insatiable quest for splendour and prestige was a futile undertaking – 'look not for golden life in an iron world' was his stern and uncompromising message.[16] He was especially critical of the cult of the country house and the stately mansion, whereby the gentry sought to impress one another and lay the foundations for an enduring lineal greatness. In his sermon, 'The Pride of Nebuchadnezzar' he critically noted:

> These are the meditations of princes and noblemen when they behold their building, or open their coffers, or look upon their train swimming after them; they think as Nebuchadnezzar thought, Is not this great Babylon? Is not this great Glory? . . . knacks over their heads, they will say, Oh! he which built this was a great man, he bare a sway both in court and country: who but he while he lived? Although the king be dead and buried yet his pride is escaped and come to us.[17]

The irony of this, of course, is that the stately homes have achieved their object: they are taken so much for granted that the vainglory and financial malpractices that promoted their construction have long been forgotten. It is hard to recover the perspective from which, against a background of low and unpretentious wooden dwellings, these massive stone piles reared up as monstrous portents of a still more rapacious and inequitable future. In an age of transitory reputations they affirm the possibility of an enduring glory; in an age where the stakes were always high they were the ultimate wager.

At a time of plagues and other merciless epidemics, death was an omnipresent and ever-looming threat. Henry Smith, like other preachers of the day, was conscious that this was the strongest card he had to play in an attempt to humble the powerful. It is here we encounter the silver-tongued preacher in his most consummate rhetorical flights and in his most artfully constructed cadences:

> A hard thing for princes to remember death; they have no leisure to think of it, but chop into the earth before they be aware; like a man which walketh over a field covered with snow, and sees not his way, but when he thinketh to run on, suddenly falls into a pit; even so they which have all things at will, and swim in pleasure, which as snow covereth their way, and dazzleth their sight, while they think to live on, and rejoiceth still, suddenly rush on death, and make shipwreck in a calm sea.[18]

But despite, or even because of, such eloquence, Henry Smith could not but be aware that in the bustle and turbulence of the city the Christian message might well be expected to fall on stony ground. Amidst worldly distractions and enticing prospects for profit or advancement, repentance was an obligation that could be indefinitely postponed. Although the Puritan preachers were unceasing in their strictures on the fashionable world it often seemed that London was yet more obdurate than any of the fabled cities of wickness in the past. Smith exclaimed: 'Yet Nineveh, Jericho, Sodom, nor Rome have had half the preaching that we have had; yet we are unthankful too, then what have we to look for?'[19] His answer was predictable. Only the elect, the faithful would be spared, 'although they be but a remnant, like the gleaning after the harvest, or like a cluster of grapes on top of the vine after the vintage'.[20]

The plague of 1603 seemed to be that long-awaited and long-prophesied punishment. London, the proud, sinful and unregenerate city had finally got its come-uppance. For Thomas Dekker in his account of the plague year, *The Wonderful Yeere, 1603*, it was a verdict long overdue on so much careless hedonism:

And good reason had these time-catchers to be led into this fools paradise. For they saw mirth in every man's face; the streets were plumed with gallants; tobacconists filled up whole taverns; vintners hung out spick and span new ivy-bushes (because they wanted good wine) and their old rain-beaten lattices marched under other colours, having lost both company and colours before. London was never in the highway to preferment till now. Now, she is resolved to stand upon her pantofles. Now – and never till now – did she laugh to scorn that worm-eaten proverb of 'Lincoln was, London is, and York shall be' for she saw herself in better state than Jerusalem. She went more gallant than Antwerp; was more courted by amorous and lusty suitors than Venice, the minion of Italy; more lofty towers stood like a coronet or a spangled head-tire about her temples than ever did about the beautiful forehead of Rome; Tyre and Sidon were like two thatched houses to Theobalds, the Grand Cairo but a hogsty.

Hinc illae lacrimae – she wept her bellyful for all this.[21]

Nicholas Bownd, the Puritan minister whose *The Doctrine of the Sabbath* (1595) had called for strict observance of the Lord's Day, saw the outbreak as God's judgement on all pleasure-seeking sabbath-breakers. In his *Medecines for the Plague* (1604), which we should note did proffer remedies for sickness, he nevertheless expressed his conviction that the plague had carried the sinners away but left the faithful untouched:

And by this we might see, that as sinne is the cause of al plague, so in the middest of them, God will be merciful to those that are his, though they be mingled with the rest. In which respect wee must confesse, that it is no marvaile if this plague be so universal in the land, seeing that sin hath so long abounded in all places.[22]

He found it significant that in all the most morally polluted places, such as Shoreditch and the suburbs, the plague had acted with an especially virulent force, sweeping away whole families and streets 'like a devouring fire'.[23] It seemed as if the Elizabethan carnival was over. God's judgement had been passed on the corrupted city.

5

The Corrupted Court

In the first decade of the seventeenth century, broadly coinciding with the accession of James I, criticism became increasingly focused on the Court as a centre of social and political corruption. It is, therefore, rather too easy to jump to two separate, but equally erroneous conclusions: that the development of such a critique is to be explained by the profusion of largesse and patronage that the new Scottish king felt obliged to dispense as a way both of rewarding his own followers and of securing his position; or that it represents a more precise, more sharply focused awareness of the sources of contemporary corruption than can be winnowed from the religious lamentations of Greene, Lodge or Nashe. In fact, much of the representation of court corruption, on the stage or elsewhere, is based on Elizabethan rather than Jacobean events, specifically on the notorious overturning of Essex's position at Court, which led to his subsequent rebellion and execution. The emergence of such a critique, after the death of Elizabeth, was based on the assumption, largely mistaken as it turned out, that since the leading protagonists were no longer on the scene the events could be alluded to without risk of giving offence or of being construed as politically provocative. So while it may well have been the case that financial malpractice and corruption was more extensive under James than under his predecessor, the criticism of the Court that began to be heard was more a matter of breaking the silence than of responding to a wholly novel and unexpected set of circumstances. What makes the discourse of Court corruption difficult to analyse is that it stems not so much from indignant protesters without as from those who either move in Court circles or hover on the fringes and who are themselves participants in the game. For those who sought to influence the king and win his favour it was the most predictable gambit imaginable to suggest to him that his power, authority and finances were being undermined by disloyal servants, who were abusing their precious position of privilege and trust simply to line their own pockets. In any event, since it was generally recognised that those who enjoyed a prominent position at Court were entitled to be well rewarded, the issue was not so much whether certain individuals were benefiting as whether it could be shown that they were benefiting excessively, and that this was directly at the expense of the king. For those who held offices of profit under the crown would always protest their loyalty to the king and insist that it was only through their devoted service that the king was able to draw upon such substantial revenues. Those who sought to be awarded them would insinuate that the kings' servants skimmed off the cream for themselves, leaving his majesty with the curds and whey. In effect the argument was not about corruption or even about efficiency *per se*, but about loyalty. Those who served the king most faithfully would always be in a position to give him a better deal, since they would unhesitatingly make his own interests paramount, while not failing to secure their own interests at the same time. That such arguments could be plausibly urged even by blatantly self-serving individuals is evident from the case of Henry Howard, Earl of Northampton, who was widely regarded as being one of the most corrupt and venal members of the Jacobean Court. Under Elizabeth, Northampton had not only been relatively impoverished but had also been fatally compromised by his association with Essex. Since Cecil continued as chief minister under James it might have been expected that Northampton would necessarily be excluded from influence, but this was not the case since the political volte-face whereby he became the intermediary who helped promote this alliance between the old order and the new ensured him an important place in the regime. It was for such adroit manœvring and for the facility with which he changed sides that he was widely distrusted, but he was equally disliked for his extraordinary flattery and servility, which stood out even in an age where exaggerated deference to the monarch was regarded merely as common courtesy. Northampton was prominent in the moves against Catholics following the Gunpowder Plot, yet he was himself suspected of being a Catholic sympathiser, a charge that was not without foundation since he received a pension from the Spanish king and received the Catholic rites on his death-bed. Through his position at Court, Northampton rapidly enriched himself. He was able to build himself a magnificent palace in the Strand with funds largely derived from his hugely profitable starch monopoly. If anyone was corrupt then surely that man was Northampton.

Yet Northampton could speak the language of corruption as well as anyone. He was charged by the king with the task of reforming the Navy and the system whereby custom duties were administered, a system of which he himself was a major beneficiary. When accused of 'spleen' by other courtiers, whose own rake-offs were now threatened, Northampton responded as follows:

> It was a spleen that descried the false trick in the . . . ordnance, that sought to stop the leaks of the ships, that advised your Majesty to look to the gleanings and purloinings of the old Treasurer, that stops unworthy, dangerous and unjust demands at the Privy Seal, that seeks to reform the corruptions of the office of arms with a check to the purchasers of arms and gentility. . . . I am charged privily with spleen for moving my master in his wants rather to make use of springing profits to himself than to cram those that, in my knowledge, are full to the throat, and beg rather out of wantonness than necessity.[1]

In his own eyes it would seem that Northampton, like Fanny Price in Jane Austen's *Mansfield Park*, is alone in having acted with perfect rectitude, yet his very language points to the difficulty of drawing the distinctions that would point unmistakably to corruption. If gleanings are improper, purloinings are the more so and unjust demands are doubtless the more to be deplored than unworthy ones, but just what is it that can conceivably constitute 'wantonness' to one who is pretty well crammed himself? At court the pointing finger of accusation moves around in an endless and unrelenting circle yet it is never quite able to find an appropriate place to stop. The corrupt are those who become corrupt when they suddenly lose the royal favour, yet to their adversaries they were no less corrupt before. Paradoxically it is the very fear of excessive corruption that enables the ordinary, unassuming, workaday variety to continue unabated. Simply, scapegoats are needed from time to time in a system where all lines and boundaries have become impossibly blurred.

For the Court is nothing if it is not a system, at once social and symbolic. Effectively the power, authority and prestige of the monarch is greatly enhanced, since by assembling the nobility in a single place and by defining their status through the position that they occupy at Court rather than by the extent of their domains or the number of their retainers, he is able to imply that he alone is centre and source of everything. There can be no prestige that does not directly derive from his person or his favour. Indeed this favour is rather like a line of financial credit, which can be drawn upon almost inexhaustibly so long as it continues to be guaranteed. Favour can move mountains. It, was only the King's intervention that saved Buckingham from having his hand cut off shortly after he made his appearance at Court, which was the punishment stipulated for striking a blow in the royal presence. From that moment onward Buckingham's future was assured. This was his giant step up the glittering ladder of courtly eminence. If a monarch has favourites this is not simply because he needs advisers or because he is deeply attached to certain individuals, but also because it is the favourite who symbolically bodies forth the idea of unlimited, arbitrary power. For favourites can be both made and unmade at the ruler's whim. If the favourite, like Buckingham, or like his predecessor, Robert Carr, who was elevated by James to Viscount Rochester and Earl of Somerset, is initially a person of low status this may show the advantage to be gained from personal charm and attractiveness but, more significantly, the almost limitless blessings that can flow from the favour of a king. While the king must reckon with the existence of powerful factions at Court and endeavour to satisfy all of them to some degree, it is not in his interest to be the prisoner of any particular group. By operating through a favourite his own role becomes inscrutable. He seems to stand above the struggle, as the more or less disinterested dispenser of largesse that is distributed through negotiations and processes that must remain deeply obscure. To be in possession of accurate information at Court is crucial. The monarch is powerful both because his spies, sources and informers keep in him touch with all the latest developments and because that deepest of all court mysteries, that of his own motives, is the very one that need not exercise him. Admittedly he faces the difficulty as well as the delight of being continually flattered and it is not always easy to decide who should be a trusted and loyal servant and just what should be regarded as good or disinterested advice. His chief ministers face a similar problem. In *The Honestie of this Age* (1614) Barnabe Riche laments:

> In the Courts of Princes every great man (placed in authority) must be flattered in his follies, praysed in his pleasures, commended in his vanities, yea his very vices must be made virtues, or els they will say we forget our duties, wee malice his greatnes, we envy his fortunes.[2]

The deeper problem is that in this process of taking advice and listening to counsel the most urgent affairs of state will become strangely imbricated with petty personal motives. As Bacon notes:

> The referring of all to a man's self is more tolerable in a sovereign prince, because themselves are not only themselves, but their good and evil is at the peril of the public fortune. But it is a desperate evil in a servant to a prince, or a citizen in a republic. For whatsoever affairs pass such a man's hands, he crooketh them to his own ends; which must needs be often eccentric to the ends of his master or state . . . yet it is a greater extreme when a little good of the servant shall carry things against a great good of the master's. And yet that is the case of bad officers, treasurers, ambassadors, generals, and other false and corrupt servants, which set a bias upon their bowl, of their own petty ends and envies, to the overthrow of their master's great and important affairs.[3]

Mutual dependency exists as the ultimate law of the system, as the motive power that finally enables it to work. The monarch may appear to be outside this circulation of power, but he depends on his 'servants' just as much as his 'servants' depend on him. The paradox of the Court is that although it creates more and more elaborate gradations of rank and status, although it is nothing if not immensely hierarchical, it is at the same time a great leveller since the elaborate webs of intrigue that are spun within it catch up both high and low and create strange and improbable bedfellows. What made the murder of Sir Thomas Overbury so scandalous was that it could only have been prompted by the fact that Overbury was privy to dubious information about Robert Carr, the royal favourite, which he was threatening to reveal. It showed that apparently humble minions could threaten the position of the highest in the land who must necessarily trust those whom they employ to advance their ends, but who can never be sure if their confidence is justified. The monarch's particular strength is that he can continually cross-check his advisers against one another and subject them to repeated controlled tests of their loyalty. It was a generally acknowledged principle of sound government that a sovereign should cultivate a systematic distrust in order to assure his own position. Cornwallis wrote in his 'Discourse upon Seneca the Tragedian'

> Doubt belongs to Princes, but not by the name of doubt, but providence; this jogs him, if vaine pleasures lull him in sensualitie; this whispers in his eares, beware, & sharpneth his sight to look into the courses of his own life, and to amend his errors; this gardeth him from outward and inward invasions: both which strengthening and quickening his understanding, to penetrate into the most secret driftes of his adversaries, to conclude, this providence or doubt, is the mother of counsell, industry, and doing well.[4]

Cornwallis is disposed to suggest that the problem of whom to trust is manageable only because princes receive supernatural guidance which alerts them to any possible threat to their person. Consequently, his analysis is by no means conducted in the spirit of Machiavelli. But it does serve to demonstrate all the more forcibly just how daunting the task of unravelment and decipherment could seem in the tortuous labyrinths of Court – so inescapably realised in the tormented geography of Whitehall Palace.

Within the Court a person is what other people estimate him to be, no more and no less. The civility of the Court involves complex indicators of the degree of favour, admiration and respect that has been vouchsafed; yet the withdrawal, suspension, retardation and intermittance of favour is still more intricately signalled. Indeed, the difficulty of interpreting quite what one's standing is may itself be a sign that all is not quite as it should be. Neglect can assume a multiplicity of forms and those which are inadvertant are very nearly as hurtful as those which are calculated and deliberate. The world of favour is never static but constantly shifting and in motion. Favour is not simply a psychological matter but an actual state of grace, which can be translated into hard cash through the granting of patents, offices and annuities. As Norbert Elias has pointed out in his brilliant pioneering work *The Court Society*:

> But in court society reality inhered directly in the rank and esteem granted to a person by his own society and, above all, by the king. A person with little or no standing in society was more or less worthless in his own eyes. In such a society the chance of preceding another, or sitting while he had to stand, or the depth of the bow with which one was greeted, the amiability of one's reception by others, and so on, were not mere externals – they are that only when money or profession are taken as the reality of social existence. They were literal documentations of social existence, notations of the place one currently occupied in the court hierarchy. To rise or fall in the hierarchy meant as much to the courtier as profit and loss to a businessman. And the agitation of a courtier over an impending rise or fall in his rank or prestige was no less intense than that of a merchant over an imminent loss of capital, or of a manager or official over a threatened downturn in their career.[5]

At Court even the greatest can suffer from status anxiety. Just one miscalculation can have very serious consequences. In 1617 Francis Bacon was sufficiently ill-advised to counsel against the lucrative marriage which Lady Compton, Buckingham's mother, had arranged between her eldest son, Sir John Villiers, and Francis Coke, daughter of the Lord Chief Justice of England, Sir Edward Coke. There was a certain temerity, to say the least, in asking Buckingham and the King to frustrate the best interests of Buckingham's own family but Bacon felt compelled to do so because Coke was his deadly rival and he feared the development of a Buckingham–Coke axis that would operate at his expense. This bungling and foolish intervention instantly put Bacon in disfavour. Bacon backed down, grovelled and did everything he could to restore good relations with Buckingham. On the face of it he succeeded and in the following year he was appointed to the office of Lord Chancellor. But the fact remains that when accusations of bribery and corruption broke around Bacon's head in 1621 he found himself totally abandoned and isolated. His disgrace was so total and so utterly humiliating that it became a wonder of the age. Somewhere at the back of it all was that would-be statesman-like letter.

Reputation at Court is all important, yet its sources are often inscrutable. As eddies of gossip and innuendo swirl about him, and as unspoken implications pass him by, the seeker after position and status begins to doubt his own identity and the reality of the image that he wants to project. He seeks to reassure himself by the feedback he gets from others, but this only serves to intensify his sense that his reflection is more real than he is himself. At Court only the king is a self-sufficient and unquestionable presence. Everyone else is a shadow. Buckingham ensured his own position with James I by always insisting on his own derivative and subordinate status and by constantly acknowledging that he himself was nothing without this gracious and unremitting conferral of royal favour. When the King visited his favourite at his new country seat at Burley-on-the-Hill in Rutlandshire, Buckingham greeted him with the following lines, composed by his kinsman, Sir John Beaumont:

> Sir, you have ever shin'd upon me bright
> But now you strike and dazzle me with light,
> You, England's radiant Sunne, vouchsafe to grace
> My house, a spheare too little and too base.[6]

Buckingham's glory, like the moon, is only reflected and what the King encounters at Burley is not the place of Buckingham's proud independence but an enhancement and extension of his own feeling of power. It was impossible for the courtier to assume some transparent and unproblematic notion of personal identity. As Jonathan Dollimore observes, apropos *Troilus and Cressida* in *Radical Tragedy*: 'Identity is a function of position, and position of power; to be the object of power is also in part its effect.'[7] If there is anything that begins to be questioned it is the classical notion of virtue, as unshakeable and intrinsic moral rectitude, especially as that is conflated with the medieval and medicinal idea of 'vertue', as the inherent property of things. In his 'Discourses' Cornwallis laments the eclipse of ancient virtue which persists not so much as an actual quality of character but as something that people would like to be thought of as possessing: 'every one will wear her livery, though few do her service'.[8] Cornwallis betrays the

characteristic anxiety of the modern when he suggests that the
present age has lost the vitality, directness and energy of former
times, that it is vitiated by inauthenticity and impermanence: 'so
are most of these last ages; but painted with counterfeite colours,
which last no longer than themselves live, so long perhaps feare
of flattery make them hold'.[9] Virtue at Court is purely a matter of
rhetoric. However, it is not just that the idols of the Court are
praised and flattered beyond their true merits; the corollary is that
any true sense of worth must necessarily be lost and that those
who have instinctively acted on the assumption that they would
behave virtuously will begin to wonder why. For real virtue at
Court will simply not be recognised and will therefore, to all
intents and purposes, be non-existent. In Beaumont and Fletcher's
Philaster it is said of the hero, who is himself critical of the court,

> You are all of his faction; the whole court
> Is bold in praise of him; whilst I
> May live neglected, and do noble things,
> As fools in strife throw gold into the sea,
> Drowned in the doing.

In the Renaissance the idea of virtue comes to assume, all too
aptly, a 'quixotic' air.

Hardly surprisingly Latin literature, as one of the few available
sources for literary models, exerts a powerful influence on the
writing of the period, whether through the Roman satirists, the
epic and pastoral poetry of Virgil, the tragedy of Seneca or simply
the work of the Roman historians, and the employment of such
models has complex cultural effects since some kind of equivalence
is inescapably posited between London and Rome. A particularly
significant dimension to this structural zeugma is that much
Roman literature, Virgil aside, is obsessed with themes of
corruption, decadence and decline, and always prone to invoke
the heroic Roman republic as the benchmark against which the
subsequent decline under the Emperors can be measured. Now,
the adoption of a Latin manner by an Elizabethan writer can
(hypothetically at least) be regarded purely as an exercise in the
classical manner, which, as such, may be deemed to lack any
purchase on the present, other than, say, to point to the
enduring significance of virtue; but once some sort of analogy is
envisaged then the enterprise begins to acquire subversive

implications. One possible inference is that England is also losing touch with her time-honoured traditions – a theme which we have already encountered in Nashe but one more firmly grounded in native circumstances – while under James I there may always be the suggestion, warranted or not, that things were ordered better under Elizabeth. More dangerous still is the possible invocation of republican values: for although England may never have had a republican past, the example of Roman history may nevertheless serve to question the development of centralising power and correspondingly explain how it is that under emperors surrounded by ambitious, self-serving advisers, power can corrupt, truth be sacrificed, the general welfare neglected. The Roman analogy will tend to argue that rulers must not allow themselves, through the advice they receive, to become blinkered, short-sighted and arrogant. They must always remain in touch with the feelings of the people. Such was to be the persistently invoked sentiment in both Parliament and the country at the time of the proposed Spanish marriage under James, and it was to emerge as a still more sharply focused and pervasive critique of the government of Charles: to broach it in the theatre was always potentially inflammatory. To criticise the king's advisers is also to point the finger at the king himself. Significantly, of the two plays banned by the Privy Council, *Philotas* and *Sejanus*, *Sejanus* explicitly invokes this Roman theme, while *Philotas* transposes it to a Greek setting, the empire of Alexander, but remains within a Senecan tradition.

Samuel Daniel's *Philotas* is essentially a closet drama, both in that very little happens in it and because the events that do occur are offered primarily to develop a social critique. Character is not really Daniel's main interest. Like other writers of the period he sees social milieu as crucial for determining the behaviour of individuals. Philotas has long been the favourite of Alexander but he is now thought to have grown too proud and independent, having, amongst other things, criticised his emperor for assuming the title 'son of Jupiter'. Chalisthenes comes to Philotas and tells him of a plot against the throne that Dymnus, a hot-headed and overweening youth has revealed to his brother, Nichomachus. However, when Philotas fails to report this information to Alexander (thinking it no more than a fanciful and improbable scheme) he falls under suspicion of treason himself. At first Alexander is disposed to believe Philotas and to acquit him of harbouring any base or treacherous motive, but under the persistent and bitterly antagonistic urging of Craterus he becomes convinced beyond all doubt of Philotas's guilt and has him arrested. Philotas' trial is a mockery and consists of nothing more than a violent public defamation by a succession of his enemies, sanctioned by the emperor. Philotas initially refuses to confess but is eventually forced to do so, under repeated torture.

The obvious contemporary reference in *Philotas* is to the Earl of Essex, who was for a long time Elizabeth's favourite but who was finally ousted from power and influence because it was felt that he was seeking power in his own right. This imperilled Essex's status with his own followers since he could no longer satisfy their demands for patronage and for influence at Court. Essex rebelled but the rebellion was easily put down and Essex himself was executed. As Samuel Daniel had himself been a follower of Essex the allusion is that much more conspicuous. Daniel clearly invokes the eclipse of Essex's many supporters in the wake of their leader's disgrace when he writes:

> So much the fall of such a weighty Peere
> Doth shake the State, and with him tumble downe
> All whom his beames of favours did upbeare,
> All whom to rest upon his base were knowne:
> And none, that did bot touch upon his loue,
> Are free from feare to perish with his love.

The extravagant promises that Essex made to his dependents, which were the ultimate cause of his downfall, lie behind the charge that Craterus levels at Philotas:

> You promise mountaines, and you draw men on,
> With hopes of greater good than hath been seene.

Philotas/Essex unsettles the state by arrogating to himself sole power to dispense largesse and by offering more than the system itself can deliver. However, Daniel cannot accept that this charge is justified. The case against Essex, like that of his classical precursor, is composed of trumped-up charges brought by envious rivals. *Philotas* is a retrospective justification of Essex that portrays him as a proud but innocent, even naïve, figure, who is undone by the subtle and conniving machinations of his infinitely more unscrupulous rivals. Nevertheless, it is by no means evident that the play is seditious. In the first place, the analogy between Philotas and Essex is far from complete, if only because Philotas is more obviously the injured party than Essex was. Then, any contemporary application can either be passed over or dismissed by arguing that tragedy simply affords an opportunity to meditate on the perennial instability at the heart of human affairs and that there is no need to construe it as intending a particular allegorical reference. This was the line Daniel himself took, protesting

> And withall taking a subject that lay (as I thought), so farre from the time, and so remote a stranger from the climate of our present courses, I could not imagine that envy or Ignorance could possibly have made it, to take any particular acquaintance with us, but as it hath a generall alliance to the frailty of greatnesse, and the usuall workings of ambition, the perpetuall subjects of bookes and Tragedies.

But even if the universalist argument wouldn't wash – as it evidently didn't – it might still be felt that with the two implicit protagonists, Elizabeth and Essex, out of the way there might yet be more pragmatic grounds for thinking of the whole matter ancient history.

The deeper reason for the banning of *Philotas* was not so much the prosect of reading Philotas as Essex, as the barbed suggestion that Sir Robert Cecil, now Earl of Salisbury, was the model for the crafty and unscrupulous courtier, Craterus. It had been Cecil who had so skilfully outmanœuvred Essex in the Elizabethan corridors of power, despite the monarch's attachment to him, but of the original actors in the drama only Cecil remained. Cecil had managed to crown his former triumph by the feat of retaining the office of chief minister under James I – his reward for the adroitness with which he handled the problem of the succession. Moreover, by pointing the finger at Cecil, Daniel implied that James had shown very poor judgement in placing himself in the hands of such a crafty, self-serving and manipulative individual. *Philotas* was as much a portrait of Cecil the opportunist as it was of Essex, the proud and insufficiently devious favourite. In their speech at the end of Act II the Chorus do not mince words in their condemnation of Craterus/Cecil:

> See how these great men cloath their private hate
> In those faire colours of the publike good;
> And to effect their ends, pretend the State,
> As if the State by their affections stood:
> And arm'd with pow'r and Princes jealousies,
> Will put the least conceit of discontent
> Into the greatest ranke of treacheries,
> That no one action shall seeme innocent:
> Yea, valour, honour, bounty, shall be made
> As accessaries unto ends unjust:
> And even the service of the State must lade
> The needfull'st undertakings, with distrust.
> So that base villainy, idle luxury
> Seeme safer farre, than to do worthily.

Under this rubric *all* great men fall under suspicion for their selfish use of public office. The monarch becomes a helpless puppet, whose jealousy and suspicion make him the helpless plaything of his notional subordinates. At Court, as with Gresham's law, the debased currency drives out the good.

It is this critique of the Court as a social phenomenon that is conspicuous in *Philotas*. The Court so functions as to undermine each individual's confidence in his own judgement, even if that person is the Emperor himself. Alexander is convinced that Philotas is trustworthy, but instead of holding fast to the truth of this sound intuition he begins to doubt his perception of things and falls back on the evil counsel of Craterus, as his only guide. While, superficially considered, Philotas is a tragic hero, whose pride brings about his downfall, the more significant conclusion that Daniel is arguing is that integrity cannot hope to persist when surrounded by the duplicity of Court. Philotas is completely open and straightforward. He believes that virtue can speak for itself. He scorns

> to stand on any other feet
> Than these of my own worth

an admirable resolution but one which paradoxically seems as vainglorious as it is noble when even the Emperor himself is compelled to resort to deceit:

> And when he speakes to me, I see he strives
> To give a colour unto what is not:
> For he must think, that we, whose states, whose lives
> Depend upon his Grace, learne not by rote
> T'observe his actions, and to know his trym.
> And though indeed Princes be manifold,
> Yet have they still such eyes to wait on them,
> As are too piercing, that they can behold
> And penetrate the inwards of the heart,
> That no device can set so close a doore,
> Betwixt their shew and thoughts, but that their art
> Of shadowing it, makes it appear the more.

The Court is a world of seeming where even the monarch must struggle to retain his opacity if he is to remain in control. Deception reduces everyone to a common level. For each person must take part in the desperate game of decipherment in an attempt to ascertain the real situation, yet always conscious that there must be winners and losers, that there is no way of playing without risk. As Daniel sees it, the Emperor – far from being some sublime first cause and prime mover of the Court society – is rather in his actions the effect of innumerable smaller actions, so that Bacon's nightmare reversal of hierarchy is always realised:

> For this great emotion of a State we see
> Doth turn on many wheeles, and some (thogh smal)
> Do yet the greater moue, who in degree
> Stirre those who likewise turne the great'st of all.

Thus the whole idea of clear and authentic action is rendered problematic since no individual, not even Philotas, can resist the colossal pressures upon him. Even Philotas is forced to collude in the collective lie by confessing under torture to a crime he did not commit. But in any event resistance would be in vain since there is no action that can stand outside the process of interpretation: Philotas' behaviour will always be what the Emperor deems it to be. The sham trial of Philotas captures the arbitrariness of justice in Elizabethan and Jacobean England where what mattered above all was to secure a conviction, both as a warning to others and demonstration of power. The trial of Sir Walter Ralegh in 1618 was so manifestly unfair as to make *Philotas* seem prophetic of events to come and not simply retrospective. *Philotas* exposes the Court as an infernal machine.

On the face of it the banning of Ben Jonson's *Sejanus* (1603) is still more puzzling. Jonson was careful to base his play on the work of the Roman historians, primarily Tacitus, and because of this concern with strict fidelity and accuracy in the treatment of primary sources it becomes that much harder to foreground his interpretative strategies or to pick out contemporary allusions. *Sejanus* is far more difficult to decipher than *Philotas*. It has come to be assumed that the play was banned because of the parallel between the Earl of Essex and Sejanus, since both were powerful favourites who sought to displace their superiors; but the parallel remains on a fairly superficial level since Essex was an impetuous man of action, whereas Sejanus is a cunning and unscrupulous contriver of plots. Sejanus poisons the mind of the Emperor Tiberius against all possible rivals. His extraordinary powers of manipulation are demonstrated by the fact that he is even able to carry the day against Drusus, the Emperor's own son, whom he is able to murder with impunity. From this point of view Cecil is a more plausible candidate for the role, but again the correspondence is far from complete. *Sejanus* is seditious partly because its demoralising exposure of the power of favourites serves to undermine the authority of the king, but more importantly because of the ignominious part it assigns to Tiberius, who altogether lacks the dignity of an emperor and who is as vicious as he is gullible. *Sejanus* is a play without a hero, whose greatest crime is to undermine all distinctions of status and rank.

Sejanus is a tragedy in name only since the principal characters are so lacking in dignity and are so consistently repulsive that it is hard to discern any redeeming traits. Jonson's 'tragedies' are really his way of writing serious satire and of expressing a strongly felt moral indignation that will be unequivocally recognised as such. With Jonson's social comedy, no matter how caustic, it is always more difficult to decide quite how it is to be construed, and there can be no doubt that the equivocation on Jonson's part is quite deliberate. On the one hand, Jonson affects the the role of the detached and critical observer who will depict the cynicism, corruption and folly he sees in society without fear or favour. On the other hand, Jonson, as a man who in his middle years became well established at Court primarily through his role as purveyor of masques, sees himself as an insider whose work will express the high standards of conduct that are notionally to be associated with the courtly milieu, and reprimand those whose behaviour falls short of this. So when Jonson satirises the overblown ambitions, affected manners, narcissism, the grotesque money-making schemes, he contrives to have it both ways: to suggest to an audience that this is really quite representative and yet insinuate that it is nevertheless to be regarded as deviation from the norm. The assumption is that vices, genially mocked, will gladly stand corrected and thereby gradually be reformed – as the Prologue to *The Alchemist* has it,

> He hopes to find no spirit much diseased,
> But with such fair correctives be pleased.

Yet to straddle this gap is more difficult than many critics of Jonson have been prepared to acknowledge. With Molière's *Le Bourgeois Gentilhomme* and *Tartuffe* we can be in absolutely no doubt that what we encounter *is* a Court point of view in which the jumped-up bourgeois and the hypocritical priest are mocked both because they are not what they purport to be and because implicitly they fall far short of the high ideal of the courtier, in whose person there is thought to be no disjuncture between being and seeming. Jonson, on the other hand, knows at bottom both that his talk of correctives is empty and that the higher standards that he seeks to invoke are largely mythical, so that his own work is more powerful when, as in *Volpone*, *The Alchemist* and *Bartholomew Fair*, it honestly reflects the moral confusions of the age, instead of purporting to possess a privileged vantage-point from which to judge them. It is precisely this that constitutes the Jonsonian grotesque, but in *Sejanus* we are presented with a world that is virtually beyond laughter and where the absence of moral values can only evoke feelings of alienation and disgust. In *Sejanus* Jonson is genuinely censorious and deeply concerned. In the opening scenes of the play we are introduced to the familiar world of Court intrigue, where everybody makes it his business to be informed about everybody else, where the moths who cluster around the royal flame are sensitive to his every flickering whim, where anything is possible and everything is for sale. Sabinus and Silius are the dignified representatives of a worthier Roman past who concede that they are unsuited to the courtly world since they lack the requisite skills so abundantly displayed by the clients of Sejanus, the royal favourite:

> These can lie
> Flatter, and swear, forswear, deprave, inform,
> Smile, and betray; make guilty men; then beg
> The forfeit lives, to get the livings; cut
> Men's throats with whisp'rings; sell to gaping suitors
> The empty smoke that flies about the palace;
> Laugh when their patron laughs; sweat when he sweats;
> Be hot and cold with him; change every mood,
> Habit and garb, as often as he varies;
> Observe him, as his watch observes his clock;
> And, true as turquoise in the dear lord's ring,
> Look well or ill with him, ready to praise
> His lordship if he spit, or put piss fair,
> Have an indifferent stool, or break wind well –
> Nothing can scape their catch.

Jonson wants his audience to feel revulsion verging on physical nausea and he would hardly look for such a strong reaction if the subject-matter of the play really were confined to the distant Roman past. But what is alarming is not simply the oppressive atmosphere of obsequiousness but rather the fact such propitiation is not complete without attendant human sacrifices. Sejanus is able to eliminate all his rivals by playing on Tiberius' fears, and Tiberius, evil and stupid as he is, is only saved from his favourite's machinations by vestiges of low cunning. Jonson suggests that once favourites have the monarch's ear fundamental liberties will be swept away in an all-encompassing tide of fear and suspicion:

> The way to put
> A prince in blood, is to present the shapes
> Of dangers greater than they are, like late
> Or early shadows, and sometimes to feign
> Where there are none, only to make him fear.
> His fear will make him cruel, and once entered
> He doth not easily learn to stop, or spare
> Where he may doubt. This have I made my rule,
> To thrust Tiberius into tyranny.

Even Tiberius himself concedes that the Emperor himself can be reduced to a mere instrument in the hands of others since he is always put into the position of having to react to a favourite's initiative, as he says "tis the favourite hath the power to strike'. However, Tiberius is able to restore his position and regain command by using as a spy the infamous Macro – who, as he delightedly accepts this prestigious commission, frankly enunciates the credo of the times:

> It is the bliss
> Of courts to be employed, no matter how.

In this play Jonson is much less concerned with individual vices as such – though the affinity between Tiberius' erotic tastes and James I's own sexual proclivities may have been thought too close to the mark – than with the actual forms of power that produce such unscrupulous behaviour in the first place and with the manifest danger which they present to the State and to the people as a whole.

Jonson's theme is the relentless decline of Roman society from its high-water mark under the Roman republic, and we cannot but be conscious that, even with Tiberius, Rome has not yet touched bottom since Tiberius' minion Macro will prepare the way for the infinitely more criminal Caligula. But it may well be felt, and doubtless was felt even at the time to judge from *Sejanus*'s unfavourable reception, that such lurid happenings constitute rather too dreadful a warning when they seem so very far from the relatively staid atmosphere of the English Court. What can have been Jonson's motives in writing the play?

The most likely answer to this question is found in Jonson's personal circumstances at the time, as a Catholic writing from within a Catholic milieu and as a man who was himself under suspicion of being a possible enemy agent. English Catholics believed that it was possible for them to combine adherence to the Church of Rome with loyalty to any English sovereign, but they were becoming anxious at the way in which what seemed to them a perfectly tenable position was being eroded in an atmosphere of innuendo, suspicion and rumours of plots against the throne. For moderate Catholics there was the danger both that they might be tarred with the brush of more violent extremists, determined to restore England to the Catholic Church, and, equally, that they might quite unjustifiably be branded as traitors and dissidents on the evidence of undercover agents and spies. Such apprehensions were proved to be fully justified by the panic that gripped the kingdom following the discovery of the Gunpowder Plot only two years later. The insecurity of English Catholics at this time is reflected in the words of Sabinus:

> Every minist'ring spy
> That will accuse and swear, is lord of you,
> Of me, of all, our fortunes and our lives.
> Our looks are called to question, and our words,
> How innocent soever, are made crimes.
> We shall not shortly dare to tell our dreams
> Or think, but 'twill be treason.

Jonson is pointing to the dangers of a society in which guilt is presumed and a fair trial impossible, where freedom of expression and toleration are progressively eroded in a nightmare of fear and multiplying accusations. Jonson feared the coming of a terror, akin to the French Revolution, where the individual would be deprived of any possible defence and where only the most vicious and unscrupulous would prevail. *Sejanus* is offered in all seriousness as a warning.

Catiline (1611) can be seen as a retrospective apologia on Ben Jonson's part for the *lèse-majesté* of *Sejanus*. By this time Jonson had become firmly ensconced in the royal favour as a writer of Court masques and *Catiline* is clear an attempt to put distance between himself and the Catholic minority since the episode of Catiline in the history of the Roman republic represents a code, but wholly transparent, allusion to the circumstances of the Gunpowder Plot. If Cicero's rhetorical vehemence against Catiline, as articulated in countless tirades, seems somewhat excessive, it is to be explained or extenuated not so much on the grounds that Cicero himself was hardly one to hold the hyperbole, as that Jonson needed to demonstrate how utterly abhorrent he found any attempt to plot against the state. That the play espouses a doctrine of compliance conformism is evident from its revival in the Restoration period, where Catiline's rebellion could be seen as a type of the Puritan rebellion during the Civil War. Jonson's own personal and emotional involvement in the play is the more evident because of the parallels, of which he must have been

conscious, between Cicero and himself. Cicero, like Jonson, is a
man of humble birth, a 'new man', whose integrity is such that he
can be relied upon to devote himself wholeheartedly to the
defence of the realm:

> I have no urns; no dusty monuments;
> No broken images of ancestors,
> Wanting an ear or nose; no forged tables
> Of long descents, to boast false honours from:
> Or be my undertakers to you trust.
> But a new man (as I am styled in Rome)
> Whom you have dignified; and more, in whom
> You've cut a way, and left it ope for virtue.

Like Jonson, Cicero is accused of being self-important and of
taking himself too seriously, but his obsessiveness about the
safety of the republic is finally vindicated. Jonson insinuates that
such men are the salt of the earth, the saving remnant and the
only people who can be truly relied upon in corrupted times. Yet
Jonson's volte-face is conspicuous because in *Sejanus* he pointed
to the danger posed to individual freedom by such an all-
embracing suspicion, whereas in *Catiline* he praises Cicero for his
omniscience, his network of spies, his unceasing vigilence on
behalf of the State. Now the safety of the realm takes precedence
over everything else.

Nevertheless *Catiline* parades its continuity with the earlier play
by continuing to work the classical trope of decline from an
antique standard of virtue. If Catiline and his co-conspirators do
have grounds for dissatisfaction with the contemporary state of
affairs it is because it has become impossible to ignore the
ostentatious ways of those who have so flagrantly appropriate the
republic's prosperity to their private use:

> Whilst we
> Have not to give our bodies necessaries.
> They ha' their change of houses, manors, lordships;
> We scarce a fire, or poor household Lar!
> They buy rare Attic statutes, Tyrian hangings,
> Ephesian pictures, and Corinthian plate,
> Attalic garments, and now, newfound gems. . . .
> Their ancient habitations they neglect,

And set up new: then, if the echo like not
In such a room, they pluck down those build newer,
Alter them too: and, by all frantic ways,
Vex their wild wealth, as they molest the people,
From whom they force it!

These are, of course, the words of a malcontent, but they point the finger quite unmistakably at such figures as Cecil, Northampton and Suffolk (who built for himself the extravagant mansion of Audley End), who have subordinated all else to the cause of their own enrichment. Jonson now writes from within the establishment, but for that very reason he sees all the more need for restraint, all the more need for antique virtue:

Such as not seek to get the start
In state, by power, parts, or bribes,
Ambition's bawds: but move the tribes
By virtue, modesty, desert.
Such as to justice will adhere,
Whatever great one it offend:
And from the embraced truth not bend
For envy, hatred, gifts, or fear.

Jonson well knew that there were not too many of these around – indeed he could scarcely even number himself amongst them, new man or no, since *Catiline* was his own bid to erase the past and acquire legitimacy, so that in writing *Catiline* he was trying to have his cake and eat it. Nevertheless Jonson's brooding sense of a falling away from a simpler, nobler past was one that as time went by came to seem more and more plausible, and it was he, more than anyone, who set in motion the developing conviction that the world had been a far better place under Elizabeth. The Elizabethan myth began to acquire the status of fact.

The theme of British corruption was taken up by Beaumont and Fletcher in their play *Bonduca* (1613), a somewhat stereotyped tale of brave, simple, noble Britons who, led by Bonduca (Boudicca), their fearless Queen, are able to resist the decadent and luxurious Romans. By harking back to Boudicca it is possible to imagine a moment in British culture that symbolically corresponds to the age of Roman virtue and which is yet contemporaneous with Rome itself. Bonduca is defiant and proud. When Suetonius, the

Roman general, calls upon her to 'adore and fear the power of Rome', she answers:

> If Rome be earthly, why should any knee
> With bending adoration worship her?
> She's vicious; and, your partial selves confess,
> Aspires, the height of all impiety;
> Therefore 'tis fitter I should reverence
> The thatched houses where the Britons dwell
> In careless mirth; where the bless'd household gods
> See nought but chaste and simple purity.
> 'Tis not high power that makes a place divine,
> Nor that the men from gods derive their line;
> But sacred thoughts, in holy bosoms stored,
> Make people noble, and the place adored.

The implications of this speech are complex since the allusions to 'Rome' would have forcibly reminded a contemporary audience of the Rome of the papal Antichrist, with his morally indefensible demands for submission. But, equally, the thatched cottages of simple British folk are a standing reproach to the mansions of the great and powerful; their moral standards offer a pattern which those who fancy themselves more sophisticated would do well to emulate. The Jacobean Court, in giving way to luxury, has departed from the traditional and time-honoured path of virtue. This critique is paradoxically condensed in Bonduca's dying words, when she commands her adversaries:

> If you will keep your laws and empire whole,
> Place in your Roman flesh a Briton soul.

Rome can recover her ancient spirit by following the British example. But what this passage really argues is that the Court, which has become 'Roman' in its shameless pursuit of pleasure and luxury, should recover the antique British spirit!

Though the presentation of moral corruption in Jacobean drama is commonplace, the majority of plays – with *Philotas* and *Sejanus* in mind – are careful to skirt the possibility of being presumed to have ventured specific allusions. However, Massinger's *The Duke of Milan* (1622) is an exception. In Act III, Scene 2, the poet

That could indite forsooth, and make fine meeters
To tinckle in the eares of ignorant Madams,
That for defaming of great Men, was sent me
Thredbare and lowsie

is unmistakably the satirist George Wither, who was imprisoned
in the Marshalsea for his outspoken verses in *Wither's Motto*
(1621), having been imprisoned earlier for similar offences in
Abuses Stript and Whipt (1613). The fact that the Duke of Milan
endeavours to save himself by throwing himself on the mercy of
the Emperor, Charles V, can be seen as analogous, through the
Spanish connection, to James I's long-meditated project of
arranging a Spanish marriage for his son Charles. Moreover
Massinger introduces a deceitful Court favourite, Francisco, not
found in his sources – which clearly represents an attempt to
slander the royal favourite Buckingham. Nearly twenty years after
the banning of *Sejanus* it was still possible to see the court as a
place of ignominy, treachery and disrepute. Still later, as Anne
Barton has noted,[10] in *The Emperor of the East* (1631) Massinger
drew a pointed contrast between Pulcheria, the forceful princess
of Byzantium and her weak, ineffectual and gullible brother
Theodosius, who succeeds her. The decline from Elizabethan
greatness now looks irrefutable.

The pervasive belief that the Court could not serve as a theatre
for either virtue or greatness is unexpectedly confirmed by
Charles's and Buckingham's abortive attempt to clinch the whole
matter of the Spanish marriage by a personal visit to Spain. The
whole episode has baffled historians who have tended to fall back
on the rather half-hearted explanation that this was Buckingham's
bid to secure his future position by putting himself in the good
books of the heir apparent. But the problem is largely created by
the fact that historians tend to assume that events must always be
interpreted in terms of a generalised *raison d'état*, whereas it has to
be recognised that the imitation of historic and even literary
models may also be significant as a guide to action. In his
penetrating analysis of the radical Decembrist movement, *The
Semiotics of Russian Cultural History*, Iury Lotman has suggested
that much of the Decembrists' behaviour can best be understood
as imitating literary plots and stock literary situations.[11] The
enigma of the decision of Petr Chaadaev to retire at the very

height of his success, after he had been granted a meeting with
the Tsar in 1820, can only be clarified by grasping that Chaadaev's
behaviour is based on the example of the Marquis von Posa in
Schiller's play *Don Carlos*. A similar literariness characterised the
behaviour of Charles and Buckingham. Although they were the
most prominent individuals at court, after James I himself, they
nevertheless felt themselves diminished and overshadowed by
his overmastering presence. Though they were the greatest jewels
in the royal crown it was none the less galling to think that their
glory was always reflected and subject to their lord and master's
whim. Even Buckingham must have got tired of describing himself
as 'your humble slave and dog'. So the journey to Spain was to be
their bid for independence and autonomy, for glory and fame,
when for once they would be able to claim a triumph in their own
right. After many adventures and deeds of derring-do Charles
would win the heart of the lovely Spanish princess and bring her
back to England as his bride. In February 1623 Charles and
Buckingham set off on their historic mission, travelling incognito
and wearing false beards, and when they arrived in Paris piled on
further mystery by donning voluminous periwigs. The whole
enterprise was undoubtedly foolhardy and dangerous since they
could easily have been robbed or kidnapped by bandits, and
Charles was, in fact, nearly drowned in a barge off Santander on
the return journey. But this was, no doubt, just what they were
looking for. In the land of chivalry itself they would, like Don
Quixote, re-enact the *Mort d'Arthur* and *Amadis de Gaul*. Though
James I had vehemently opposed their plans he quickly entered
into the spirit of the thing and in words that must have given his
protégés great pleasure he addressed them in a letter as 'My
Sweet Boys, and Dear Venturous Knights, worthy to be put in a
new *romanso*',[12] and even turned to poetry to write:

> The wind was Love, which princes stout
> To pages turn; but who can doubt,
> Where equal fortune love procures,
> And equal love success assures,
> But venturous Jack will bring to Greece
> The best of prize, the golden fleece.[13]

The quest must succeed. Virtue and valour will necessarily be
rewarded. What Buckingham and Charles had rather overlooked

was that Spain was certain to use the marriage to drive a hard bargain over the position of Catholics in England, while this in turn was seen only as a preliminary to a full restoration of the authority of Rome. If England was desperate to conclude the match this would only make it easier for Spain to exert still greater leverage by protracting the negotiations. Matters dragged on and on. Buckingham turned against the marriage. Finally the ambassadors returned empty-handed to the great relief of the whole nation. Honour was salvaged by switching to a different symbolic mode. In St Paul's the 114th Psalm was sung: 'When shall I come out of Egypt, and the house of Jacob from among the barbarous people?' Yet the whole preposterous journey had been a covert protest, at the highest level, against the demoralising effects of life at Court.

6

The Corrupted World

In the latter part of the reign of James I a disillusionment with the corruptions of the Court began to be subsumed in a wider and more all-embracing disenchantment with the world. In part this stemmed from the Court's own confident proclamation of its importance. To all intents and purposes the Court was the world. Since it was the only possible context in which word or action could signify, since it was taken to be the theatre where every discourse must be uttered, many of those who rejected the Court were paradoxically compelled to acknowledge it – even in the gesture of dedicating their works to James I! Nevertheless, amongst those thwarted, disbarred or otherwise disillusioned, there is an increasing disposition to reject the Court as centre and to look for some antidote to the fashionable life in the simplicity of the country or to cultivate a more absolute religious perspective. Although Ben Jonson's celebrated poem 'To Penshurst' invokes the nobleman's country seat as the site of a rustic plenitude, a social harmony, where

> The blushing apricot, and woolly peach
> Hang on thy walls, that every child may reach.
> And though thy walls be of the country stone,
> They're reared with no mans ruine, no mans grone,
> There's none, that dwell about them, wish them downe;
> But all come in, the farmer, and the clowne.

Jonson in this very gesture can scarcely avoid the recognition of how anachronistic, not to say improbable, such a world has become. 'To the World', which closely follows in his collection *The Forrest* of 1616, strikes a much more intransigent note in its elegy for a virtuous and noble gentlewoman:

> False world, good-night: since thou hast brought
> That houre upon my morne of age,
> Hence-forth I quit thee from my thought,
> My part is ended on thy stage.

78

Doe not once hope, that thou canst tempt
A spirit so resolv'd to tread
Upon thy throate, and live exempt
From all the nets that thou canst spread.

The notion of an alternative moral space disappears.

If any one work makes visible this distinctive slide within the discourse of Jacobean culture it is Robert Burton's *The Anatomy of Melancholy* (1st edn, 1621). In developing the time-honoured topos of *contemptus mundi*, Burton, of course, was hardly an innovator, but by exposing himself so frankly as a reclusive and cantankerous scholar, wholly at odds with the world, and by adducing such bewilderingly diverse grounds for melancholy – God himself not excepted – Burton both became the spokesman for a diverse apolitical sense of *malaise* and, by his vast learning, gave it intellectual respectability and substance. Burton can, when he chooses, be a forceful social critic, who is notably ironic at the expense of the great and powerful: 'Princes, Magistrates, rich men, they are wise men born, all Politicians and Statesmen must needs be so, for who dare speak against them?'[1] and in so saying Burton breaks the silence of deference himself. When it comes to those that hover about the great and powerful, Burton is frankly contemptuous:

To see a man turn himself into all shapes like a Chameleon, or as Proteus transform himself into all that is monstrous; to act twenty parts and persons at once for his advantage, to temporize & vary like Mercury the planet, good with good, bad with bad; having a several face, garb, & character, for every one he meets.[2]

By contrast Burton will not mince words and makes it abundantly clear where he stands. Unlike his protean contemporaries he will engrave his own fixed identity deeply within the work even as his own progressive revisions bely it. The Burton who genuinely looks for a better society is progressively displaced in the ostentatious and undoubtedly theatrical pose of one who contemptuously turns aside from all the irritations and tribulations of the world, who leads 'a monastick life, a theatre to myself, sequestered from these tumults and troubles of the world', who becomes 'a mere spectator of other men's fortunes and adventures' and how hears 'new news every day, and those ordinary rumours of war, plagues, fires, inundations, thefts, murders, massacres, meteors, comets, spectrums, prodigies, apparitions, of towns taken, cities besieged in France, Germany, Turkey, Persia, Poland, &c., daily musters and preparations, and suchlike, which these tempestuous times afford'.[3] In his study Burton turns his whole century into a bad dream and in so doing he creates a new hero in his own likeness, who, though timorous, irascible and unsuccessful, may yet be wise.

George Wither, the poet and satirist, whom we have already encountered as a visitor to the Marshalsea prison, was both a man conspicuously involved in worldly affairs and a man who was considerably more courageous than Burton, yet he nevertheless came to share many of Burton's attitudes. In trying to chart the subterranean currents of thought and feeling that swerve and eddy from the splendour and arrogance of the Jacobean Court to the crisis of the Civil War, Wither is a particularly instructive instance of the way in which attitudes could come to be transformed. Like many others Wither sought advancement at Court. Like many others his hopes were frustrated and disappointed. He wrote world-wearily after the event, or non-event:

> I must confess, 'twas once a fault of mine
> At every misadventure to repine.
> I sought Preferment, and it fled me still,
> Wherat I griev'd, and thought my fortune ill.
> I vext to see some in prosperitee,
> Deride and scoffe at my adversity.
> But since, advis'd, and weighing in my minde
> The course of things, I soone began to finde
> The vainenesse of them. Those I saw of late
> In blisse (as I thought) scorning my estate,
> I see now ebbing, and the one full tide
> That over-flow'd the lofty bancks of pride,
> Hath left them like the sand-shoare, bare and dry,
> And almost in as poore a case as I.

This movement from worldly to anti-worldly attitudes is one commonly encountered. George Herbert, for example, became a minister after finding his path blocked at Court and in his

newfound vocation wrote the poems of *The Temple*. Herbert well
knew from his own experience that redemption was *not* to be
found 'In cities, theatres, gardens, parks, and courts', but could
only be won through a long and demanding process of personal
mediation, reflection and contrition. Poetry for Herbert is a way of
cancelling the world and of bringing him closer to God:

> My God, a verse is not a crown,
> No point of honour, or gay suit,
> No hawk, or banquet, or renown,
> Nor a good sword, nor yet a lute:
>
> It cannot vault, or dance, or play;
> It never was in *France* or *Spain*;
> Nor can it entertain the day
> With my great stable or demain:
>
> It is no office, art, or news,
> Nor the Exchange, or busie Hall;
> But it is that which while I use
> I am with thee, and *most take all*.

For Wither the rejection of the Court was a more complicated and
long-drawn out affair. He turned against it first in the satire of
Abuses Stript and Whipt, a work a good deal more garrulous and
less strenuous than its title might suggest, but which undoubtedly
rehearsed the familiar complaints against vanity, conspicuous
consumption, cupidity and corruption, hypocrisy and insincerity.
What made the work something of a hot potato was Wither's
readiness to be more specific – his allusions were so unmistakable
that they were tantamount to naming names. Although Robert
Cecil, for example, had recently died, Wither's allusion to his
physical deformity in a context of corruption was such as to throw
the Court into disrepute and create an ominous sense of shafts
thwanging steadily closer to the bull's-eye:

> But sure the World is now become a Gull,
> To thinke such scoundrels can be worshipfull.
> For, in these dayes, if men have gotten riches,
> Though they be Hangmen, Usurers, or Witches,
> Divels incarnate, such as have no shame,
> To act the thing that I should blush to name;

> Doth that disgrace them any whit? Fie no,
> The World ne'er meant to use her minions so.
> There is no shame for rich-men in these times,
> For wealth will serve to cover any crimes.
> Wert thou a crooke-backt dwarfe, deform's in shape,
> *Thersites* like, condition'd like an Ape;
> Didst never doe a deed a good man ought,
> Nor spake true word, nor hadst an honest thought.

Worked in together with the direct reference to Cecil is a more oblique allusion to James I's homosexuality and to his current favourite, Robert Carr. Wither speaks subsequently of princes who are

> Most bountiful to fools, too full of feare,
> And farre too credulous fo what they heare;
> So given to pleasure, as if in that thing
> Consisted all the Office of a King.

For Wither a king who is devoted to the hunt is as bad as a bishop like Abbott, with the same obsession. Wither's critique of the hedonism of Court has a strong Puritanical flavour and, significantly, he was prepared to praise Puritans for their commitment to the virtuous life at a time when it was unfashionable to do so, and when it was assumed that all their protestations of moral earnestness must necessarily be hypocritical. Wither was equally critical of worldly, self-seeking bishops in the Church of England and he singled them out for special criticism. But even in *Abuses Stript and Whipt* the satiric impulse is overlaid by a more general cultural pessimism. Wither is among those who believe that the world is in a state of decline; that modern man has become weak and enervated through luxurious living; that men who fall away from the path of righteousness so shamelessly are ripe for punishment:

> But what need I
> Recite examples of Antiquitie?
> Or thus to tax old ages of that crime,
> Sith there was nere a more presumptious time,
> Than this that's now. What dare not men to do,
> If they have any list or minde thereto?

Still, to put man's Faustian ambitions in perspective, one of the things that most men dare not do was to criticise the high and the mighty, and Wither, after his spells in prison, was rather more inclined to be obsequious to authority. There can be little doubt but that Wither was punished not simply for what he had done but to be a conspicuous example to others. In the world of the Court it was necessary to tread very, very carefully.

In the 1620s Wither's poetry becomes essentially devotional and it is characterised by the decision to reject a corrupt aristocratic way of life in which being for others totally overpowers any sense of being for one's self. As with Herbert, devotional poetry involves a search for personal authenticity; a discovery of God and the soul in a single endeavour. In Wither's song for John the Baptist in his *Hymns and Songs of the Church* (1623) (dedicated inexorably to his august majesty King James) it is difficult not to see an element of autobiography:

> Let us not gad to Pleasure's court,
> With fruitless toys to feed the mind;
> Nor to that wilderness resort,
> Where reeds are shaken with the wind:
> But tread the path he trod before,
> That both a Prophet was, and more.
>
> Let us hereafter feed upon
> The honey of thy Word divine;
> Let us the world's enticements shun,
> Her drugs, and her bewitching wine;
> And on our loins (so loose that are)
> The leather-belt of temperance wear.

Although John the Baptist is prototypically a man of the wilderness, Wither transposes the opposition in order to suggest that the real desert is to be found in Whitehall. Although Wither found it politic to mend his fences at Court he had become progressively estranged from it, and now was able to speak out against it without fear of rebuke since he was now functioning within a wholly unobjectionable form of discourse: religious poetry. Wither increasingly saw himself as a poet chosen by God to do his work and as one marked out for his calling by extraordinary signs: in *Britain's Remembrancer* he boldly insisted, 'I

have foretold what shall come upon such Transgressors, according
to the predictions of the *Prophets* . . . I have confirmed all my owne
Resolutions by the divine *Covenant*, and that working of the blessed
Spirit, which I have a feeling of in my own heart: And, if in these
things I be deceived, I know not who hath power to make me
confident of any thing in this life.'[4]

Wither thus indicated that he was a man enjoying the favour of
God and that he was now moving beyond the orbit of worldly
patronage amidst which he had earlier come to grief. Yet to others
the signs would have seemed more ambiguous. Since Wither still
looked for royal favour he could be construed as having mended his
rebellious ways. King and Court would have been disposed to
interpret his religious poetry as the expression of contrition and
remorse for his former behaviour. They would have been unlikely to
construe it as the defiant and unrepentant continuation of an
uncompromising moral critique, which was how Wither himself
would have preferred to regard it. In George Wither's career it is
possible to discern how, step by step, men could be brought from
conformity to dissent, from thence to quietism, and from quietism
and passivity to ultimate rebellion.

George Wither's most influential and enduring work was his *A
Collection of Emblemes* which appeared in 1635, a significant year
for the genre of the emblem book since it also saw the publication
of *Emblemes* by Francis Quarles. Time has conferred a certain irony
on the prefatory dedication to this work, addressed to 'the
illustrious King Charles' by 'his most loyal subject Geo. Wither':
within a decade Wither had been captured by Royalist forces,
fighting on the opposite side. The tension between Court and
Puritan culture is evident in other ways. Wither's poems
consistently rebuke the worldly life, yet the book is so organised
as to permit the playing of a game in which the emblems can be
selected by a lottery – thought the use of dice is explicitly
excluded. Such a 'morall Pastime'[5] manages to have the best of
both worlds, but we should not therefore conclude that the poet
is insincere. There has been a persistent tendency to undervalue
and misread the emblem books, primarily because the foremost
student of them, Rosemary Freeman, was less than responsive to
the nuances of the genre and, indeed, often ill at ease with it by
virtue of her allegiance to the credo of literary modernism. In the
modernist insistence on the supremacy of the word the parasitic
and derivative nature of the emblem poem seems self-evident. It

is in terms of the doctrine of the poem conceived of as an organic, self-sufficient entity that Quarles and his fellow practitioners are brought to book. For Freeman the continual possibility of pictorial allusion, the very existence of an external source, cripples the possibilities for poetic development and precludes a complexity that is internally generated:

> the picture supplies also the requirements of stricture and the poet can rely upon its support instead of having to create a support within the poem itself. . . . Each parallel fastens upon a single aspect of the central idea, and no attempt is made to develop that idea as a whole.[6]

The emblem poem is necessarily parasitic, creeping and proliferating across its subject like ivy across an old stone wall. Freeman seems determined to outlaw the interpretative elaboration and expansion of an image because it is so inescapably caught in secondariness. It always points to something beyond itself, the figure of a figure, yet it seems always tethered to its source, like a goat to a grazing post. Yet it is precisely this erratic process of circling that gives the emblem poem its fascination – as it seeks to demonstrate how naturally and spontaneously religious meanings can be drawn out of the simplest of representations. The idea is not to march unswervingly down some broad, rhetorical high road, but to make rapid twists and turns, to be copious, ingenious, allusive, unexpectedly aphoristic. The presence of the emblem by no means obliges the poet to be pedantically literal, as Rosemary Freeman is wont to suggest, but more often encourages him to be wayward and digressive, in the manner of Sir Thomas Browne. George Wither's emblem poems are genuinely dialogic, since he is far more likely to debate with his artist than endeavour to reflect the intended sense, which may often be hard to interpret. Wither candidly remarks

> little care I take
> Precisely to unfold our Authors minde.

Indeed, his quarrel with the artist (whom, of course, he respects sufficiently to produce suitable verses for 200 illustrations!) is instructive precisely because it shows just how determined he is to develop the *contemptus mundi* topos and how unwilling he is to concede at any point that those who seek to prosper in this world are justified in their endeavours. We may therefore also note that the Wither, though a Puritan sympathiser, is very far from endorsing the Protestant ethic as outlined by Max Weber. Particularly significant in this respect is the 32nd emblem of the Third Book, which shows two clasped hands superimposed on a cornucopia, and which bears the Latin motto *Fides Ditat Servata* which Wither renders as

> The safest riches, hee shall gaine
> Who alwayes Faithful doth remaine.

To the Puritan poet this line of argument is very far from carrying conviction:

> The *Horne-of-plenty*, which *Wealth* signifies,
> The *Hand-in hand*, which *plighted faith* implies,
> (Together being painted) seems to teach,
> That, such as will be *honest*, shall be *rich*.
> If this be so, why then, for *Lucre-sake*,
> Doe many breake the *Promises* they make?
> Why doe they cheat and couzen, lye, and sweare?
> Why practise they all Villainies that are?
> To compasse Wealth? And how doe such as they
> Inlarge their ill-got *Portions*, ev'ry day?
> Or, whence proceedes it, that sometimes we see,
> Those men grow poore, who faithfull seeme to bee?
>   Thus, oft it proves; and, therefore, *Falshood* can,
> In likelihood, much more inrich a man,
> Than blamelesse *Faith*, and, then, the *Motto* here
> Improper to this *Emblem*, doth appeare.

In Wither's hands the argument of this poem serves to reinforce that of the emblem on the facing page, where poor thieves are sent to the gallows while wealthy usurers and lawyers get off scot-free. Since he is not so much concerned with the intrinsic meaning of the emblem as with the extent to which it can signify and gain purchase on a real world, the discourse of the poem can function in the space between. Paradoxically the emblem can represent contradictory meanings simultaneously. In the poem above, Wither is able to retrieve the sense by suggesting that good men, though poor, nevertheless possess spiritual riches.

Such argumentative turns, redeploying the trope from the worldly to the heavenly, are a common rhetorical feature of the poems. For example, in his verses on Sisyphus, he points first to the ambitious or avaricious fools who are unappeasable in their pursuit of status and riches, but then uses the figure to suggest a characteristically Calvinist meaning: the inability of man to achieve salvation through his own unaided efforts:

> Yet, we are bound by *Faith*, with *Love* and *Hope*,
>   To roll the Stone of *Good-Endeavour*, still,
>   As neere as may be, to *Perfections top*,
>   Though backe againe it tumble downe the *Hill*.
>   So; What our *Workes* had never power to doe,
>   *God's* Grace, at last, shall freely bring us to.

Thus the poem intensifies the distinction between the Puritan elect and the unregenerate, who articulate the meaning of the Emblem in such dissimilar senses. There is no possibility of fudging or confusing the issue. The difference is absolute.

A constant theme in Wither's writing is the instability and changeableness of the world, which, he insists, can nevertheless be resisted through the steadfastness and unflinching integrity of the individual conscience. In both the Medieval period and the Renaissance such fickleness and unpredictability is characteristically embodied in the figure of a woman, the goddess Fortuna. To his credit, Wither is anxious to dissociate himself from this negative stereotype; against the grain of centuries of cultural conditioning he insists that he personally has never encountered an inconstant woman. He refuses to regard the emblem as part of a discourse about women and focuses rather on the winged ball on which Fortuna stands rather than on the goddess herself:

> The winged Ball, (whose tottering Foundation,
> Augments the causes of our *variation*)
> Meanes, here, those uselesse, and vaine *temp'rall things*,
> That come and goe, with never-staying *wings*,
> And, which (if thereupon our hearts we set)
> Make *Men*, and *Women*, the *Vertigo* get.
>   Hereafter, then, let neither *Sexe* accuse
> Each other; but, their best endeavours use.

To cure this *Maladie* in one another,
By living well, and loving one another.

Wither's disquiet at the instability of the world appears in his meditation on the emblem in which the world is represented as being carried backwards on the spine of a shellfish, a figure which permits him to move outwards from a candid acknowledgement of his own fallen fortunes and 'backward motions' to a disquisition on the familiar theme of the retrograde motion of the world. Wither's belief that authentic religious value are in eclipse, reflected in his plea that God should again restore the world to its true course, is echoed in a poem on the emblem of the waning moon. Since the light which the moon receives is reflected from the sun (God) this figure offers the hope and confident expectations that faith can be wholly restored, just as the crescent moon can become full. Again, there is always an element of paradox in these interpretations, since the moon has traditionally be regarded as a symbol of inconstancy. Wither takes the emblem of the elephant, caught by leaning against a cunningly half-sawn tree, as a sign of the treacherousness of the world. Though it may be factually inaccurate, it is nevertheless symbolically true:

Now, though the part *Historicall*, may erre,
The *Morall*, which this *Emblem*, doth inferre,
Is overtrue; and seemeth to imply,
The *World* to bee so full of Treacherie,
As, that, no corner of it, found can be,
In which, from Falshoods Engines, wee are free.
I have observ'd the Citie; and, I finde
The *Citizens*, are civill, grave and kinde;
Yet, many are deluded by their showes,
And, cheated, when they trust in them repose.
I have been oft at *Court*; where I have spent,
Some idle time, to heare them *Complement*:
But, I have seene in *Courtiers*, such deceit,
That, for their Favours, I could never wait.
I doe frequent the church; and I have heard
Gods judgements, by the Preachers, there, declar'd,
Against mens falshood; and, I gladly heare
Their zealous *Prayers*, and good *Counsells* there;
But, as I live, I finde some such as they,
Will watch to doe a mischiefe, if they may.

In all the great centres of influence and power, deceit is to be
expected. Appearances will necessarily not give the clue to men's
true motives. The half-sawn tree can stand as an emblem for the
differences between a world made by God in its original purity
and innocence and its latterday transformation into a place of
desperate uncertainty. The recurrent, fervently reiterated note of
Wither's *A Collection of Emblemes* is that of a call to the reader to
shun the lures and strategems of a corrupted world, to seek
refuge in the tranquillity of his own mind, to cultivate his own
inner resources. The power of a virtuous innocence can be
represented by Arion, riding on the back of a dolphin through
tempestuous waves, by a squirrel hoarding nuts for the winter,
by the tree that still continues to grow steadily upward even
when heavy weights have been placed upon it, by a cube that
remains ever the same. But perhaps the most apt symbol of a
Puritan self-sufficiency is the tortoise, which can be taken to
represent

> That man, who in himselfe, hath full contents;
> And (by the *Vertues* lodging in his minde)
> Can all things needful, in all places, finde.

The shell of the tortoise protects him from the hostility of the
world: it epitomises a virtue uncontaminated and unmoved by
worldly considerations, that seeks for nothing that it cannot find
within itself:

> Hee, always keepes and carries, that, within him,
> Which may, from those things, *ease* and *comfort*, win him.
> When, him uncloathed, or unhous'd, you see;
> His *Resolutions*, clothes and houses be,
> That keepe him safer; and, farre warmer too,
> Than *Palaces*, and princely *Robes*, can doe.

The inner world is enough.

A similar conflict between worldly ambition and otherworldly
spirituality runs through the career of the Scottish poet William
Drummond of Hawthornden, who might never have loomed up
on the fringes of courtly culture at all had it not been for the
Scottish connection. Drummond established himself with 'Forth
Feasting', a panegyric celebrating the visit of James I to Scotland
in 1617. In 1633, on the occasion of Charles I's belated coronation

in Edinburgh, it was again Drummond who supplied verses and speeches suited to the occasion. Yet much of Drummond's best poetry is devoted to a scornful and contemptuous rejection of the honours, vanities and ambitions of fashionable society. By contrast with George Wither's pugnacious amalgam of stoicism, moral indignation and faith in the future, Drummond seems a despairing, deeply isolated and introverted recluse, who can criticise the Court not so much because he, like Wither, knows it from the inside, but because he has never really been a part of it. Drummond was determined to maintain his personal integrity and to speak and act only as he saw fit, but like many unworldly individuals he became fatally confused and compromised by the pressure of events. With his loyalties desperately divided he somehow managed to be a supporter both of the covenanting cause in Scotland and of the Scottish invasion of England, and, at other times, a confirmed Royalist and supporter of Montrose, the commander of Charles's Scottish forces. The most plausible inference would be that his vocation as a poet made him sympathetic to the Court but that patriotism, pressure and his own undoubted moral earnestness led him into support for the Covenanters. But given the difficulty of his position as Scotland's leading poet and as a man beholden to royalty, it is impossible to arrive at any conclusive verdict on his motives. His own entanglements confirm that very distrust of the world which is articulated in his poetry.

Drummond's perpetual dilemma is his inability to reconcile his faith in the infinite power and goodness of God with the depressing and demoralising spectacle of the human world. Although Drummond often comes close to Calvinism he differs from the Covenanters in his clear conviction that man's eyes need not only be fixed on the next world, that God has placed man at the centre of a world that is itself glorious and which offers him the most magnificent opportunities. What gives grounds for despair is that despite such favourable circumstances the whole experiment seems to have gone disastrously wrong. So Drummond, like Milton, draws a sharp distinction between the nobility of God's scenario for man, and man's disastrously wilful and short-sighted failure to realise it. Drummond's writing, especially as evidenced in *A Cypress Grove* (1623), becomes a matter of incongruous juxtapositions, a titanic struggle of contraries in which the universe seems to be fought over in every successive sentence. The result is an extraordinary moral indignation:

> Fooles, which thinke that this faire and admirable Frame, so variouslie disposed, so rightly marshalled, so strongly maintained, enriched with so many excellencies, not only for necessity, but for ornament and delight, was by that Supreme Wisedome brought forth, that all things in a circularly course, should bee and not bee, arise and dissolve, and thus continue, (as if they were so many Shadowes careleslie cast out and caused by the encountring of those superiour celestiall Bodies, changing onlie their fashion and shape, or fantasticall Imageries, or shades of faces into Christall) But more They, which beleeve that Hee doth no other-wayes regard this his worke than as a Theater, raised for bloudy Sword-playeres, Wrastlers, chasers of timorous and combatters of terrible Beastes, delighting in the daily Torments, Sorrowes distresse and Miserie of Mankind. No, no, the Eternall wisedome, did make Man an excellent creature, though hee faine would, unmake himselfe, and returne unto nothing; and though hee seeke his felicity among the reasonlesse Wights, he hath fixed it above. Hee brought him into this world as a Master to a sumptuous well-ordered and furnished Inne, a Prince to a populous and rich Empirie, a Pilgrime and spectator to a Stage of delightful Wonders and wonderfull Delightes.[7]

For Drummond, men have too little faith, reverence and imagination. They immerse themselves in trivial and meaningless violence when they should respect both themselves and the world. It is too precious to be wasted.

In his most eloquent moments, as in *Flowres of Sion* which was published together with *A Cypress Grove*, Drummond is indisputably the poet of *contemptus mundi*. The contrast he draws between the gentleness, goodness and beauty of Christ and the harshness and corruption of the world becomes so intense as to be almost unbearable. It is as if the Crucifixion should be read rather as a verdict on mankind than as a promise of redemption. Drummond is attracted to the image of Christ as a pelican, who nourishes her children with her own blood, because it suggests what an extraordinary power is needed to redeem the world. His always latent misanthropy surfaces in his poem in praise of the solitary life, a poem which concludes with a characteristic antithesis, worthy of Burton:

> The World is full of Horrours, Troubles, Slights
> Woods harmless shades have only true Delightes.

Drummond's writing is suffused with a kind of neo-Platonism, in which man must constantly struggle to imagine, fix and retain images of God's goodness and power in the midst of many powerful and more palpable signs to the contrary. Faith is not so much to be seen as a steady and unwavering allegiance to the divine will as an insatiable striving after goodness that will break through all the veils of deceit that stand in its way. He seeks to awaken all those who are sunk in the torpor of worldliness before it is too late. If only his readers can for one revelatory moment be liberated from the grip of custom and habit they can rise to a disorientating recognition of the oddity of the purposes that typically have animated them:

> A Honour that more fickle is than wide,
> A Glorie at Opinions frowne that lowres,
> A Treasurie which Bankrout time devoures,
> A knowledge than grave Ignorance more blind:
> A vaine Delight our equalles to command,
> A stile of greatnesse, in effect a Dreame,
> A fabulous thought of holding Sea and Land,
> A servile Lot, deck with a pompous Name,
>   Are the strange endes wee toyle for heere below,
>   Till wisest Death make us our errores know.

They must make the imaginative breakthrough that will lead them from the temporal to the eternal.

The image of Francis Quarles, perhaps the most prolific and most widely read poet in the era preceding the Civil War, is equally riddled with contradictions. That Quarles had anything that smacked of the Puritan is resolutely denied by his Victorian memoralist, the Reverend Alexander B. Grosart:

the prevalent conception of our Worthy as 'a grim sour Puritan,' not to say 'of the vulgar,' is ludicrously mistaken. Throughout he was a man of cultured manners and habits and sensibilities, and to my vision stands out as the very type of 'the fine old English gentleman all of the olden time.'[8]

The engraving by Alain seems to confirm Grosart's judgement. Quarles's flowing, curly locks and slightly florid appearance would seem to intimate that he is scarcely one to deplore a little harmless amusement on the sabbath or overly anxious to endure a protracted sermon. Yet the persistent morbidity, preoccupation with death and contemptuous rejection of worldly vanities in his verse would seem to place him unmistakably in the Puritan camp. In Quarles we find an uncompromising severity of tone, a relentless chastising of moral viciousness that far surpasses anything in Wither, yet Quarles was a devoted Royalist, who, in the years preceding his death in 1644, produced several tracts on behalf of the King, which were collected as *The Profest Royalist* in 1645. In every setting he appears incongruous, a Cavalier among Puritans, or a starchy, censorious moralist, standing like a spectre before the pleasure-loving court. Quarles himself admitted as much, when, in the opening paragraphs of *The Loyall Convert*, the first of the tracts, he characterised himself, regarding the Civil War, as one 'who brought some Faggots to this *Combustion*'.[9]

Quarles was altogether justified in thus owning up, because his stern moralising verses played their part in firming up and sustaining a mood of popular disillusionment with royal counsellors, from Buckingham to Laud, that might otherwise have remained quiescent and half-hearted. There was no way in which Quarles's verse could have been subject to censorship because of its devotional nature; yet in the 1620s and 1630s Quarles was able to use this immunity to launch thinly veiled attacks on the national decadence and its source in corruption at Court. In *The History of Esther* he introduces the figure of Haman, the King's trusted minister, as a man 'cloking with publike good his private hate', and goes on to suggest what harmful consequences must follow from the decision to entrust so much power to a self-seeking and irresponsible favourite:

Even so the power from the Prince's hand,
Directs the subject with a sweet command,

But to perverse fantasticks if confer'd,
Whom wealth, or blinded Fortune hath prefer'd,
It spurres on wrong, and makes the right retire,
And sets the grumbling Common-wealth on fire:
Their foule intent, the common good pretends,
And with that good, they make their private ends,
Their glorie's dimme, and cannot b'understood,
Unlesse it shine in pride, or swimme in blood:
Their will's a Law, their mischiefe Policy,
Their frownes are Death, their power Tyranny:
Ill thrives the State, that harbours such a man,
That can, what e'r he wills, will what he can.

In 1621, despite or because of the royal dedication, Haman cannot be construed as anything other than a portrait of Buckingham, then at the very height of his power. Though Quarles maintained an unquestioning loyalty to the person of the King himself, he viewed with suspicion and a deep mistrust all those who advised the monarch. He believed that the commonwealth was in danger from their self-serving and ill-considered counsels. Quarles believed that the minister's role was to be Aristotle at the Court of Alexander, not to lead the King himself astray. His *Observations Concerning Princes and States* concludes with this admonition:

It is high wisedome in a Prince to weigh the several *actions* of his Counsellors: For the want whereof so many good Princes have both lost themselves, and ruined their Kingdomes: It is a common thing, to maske *private* ends under *publike* pretenses: It is better for a State to have a wicked Prince, of a *good nature*, than a good Prince, with such *Counsellors*.[10]

A wicked prince, who is not totally unregenerate may be brought to act properly with the help of sound advice, but even a good prince may be led astray when improperly influenced.

In his *Emblemes* (1st edn, 1635) Quarles develops a view of England and the modern world that is singularly bleak and comfortless. The golden days are past, the world has degenerated, the Seven Deadly Sins voraciously stalk the earth, Astraea has fled. Of course all this is familiar ground, but whereas others might be prepared to take the matter more philosophically Quarles is not. He writes in a tone of urgent indignation – clearly indicating his determination to do something about the situation before it is too late. Quarles assumes the fearsome demeanour of the old-time schoolmaster, who fixes his frightened pupils with an intimidating glance as he leans forward over the lectern and flexes a long, thin cane between his bony fingers. If Quarles's starting-point was *Pia Desideria*, with its naïve depictions of children, we rapidly discover that such a gay, unheeding innocence is not to be celebrated, but, on the contrary severely corrected and chastised. In Quarles, the sinner is invariably a sluggard, who must be roused from his state of torpor and lashed into earnest moral activity, a backslider who must be constantly brought up to the mark. Yet Quarles's strenuousness does have a point. Whereas for George Wither the moral universes of the elect and the worldly are utterly distinct and separated by an impassable gulf, Quarles posits a reader who is always suspended between the two and who must be recalled to the path of righteousness with all the seriousness and urgency that the poet can command. Quarles's *Emblemes* are the poetic equivalent of a Kitchener recruiting poster. The imperious finger positively gesticulates right out of the page. Quarles contrasts the reluctance of the soul to come to God:

> Lord, when we leave the world and come to Thee,
>   How dull, how slug are wee!
> How backward! how preposterous is the motion
>   Of our ungain devotion.
> Our thoughts are milstones, and our souls are lead,
>   And our desires are dead:
> Our vowes are fairly promis'd, faintly paid;
>   Or broken or not made:
> Our better work (if any good) attends
>   Upon our private ends;
> In whose performance one poore worldly scoff,
> Foyles us, or beats us off.

with the positive eagerness with which it responds to the lures of the world:

> So, so we cling to earth; we flie and puff,
>   Yet flie not fast enough.
> If pleasure beckon with her balmy hand,
>   Her beck's a strong command:

> If honour call us with her courtly breath,
>   An houre's delay is death:
> If profit's golden finger'd charms enveigle's,
>   We clip more swift then Eagles.

For Quarles the world is an insidious source of corruption and
moral infection, which is rendered all the more dangerous by the
enticing manner with which it seeks to enmesh the soul in a net
of delusive appearances:

> O what a Crocodilian world is this,
> Compos'd of treacheries, and ensnaring wiles!
> She cloaths destruction in a formal kisse,
> And lodges death in her deceitful smiles;
> She hugs the soul she hates; and there does prove
> The veriest tyrant where she vowes to love,
> And is a Serpent most, when most she seems a Dove.

The sheer relentlessness of Quarles's jeremiad, sustained through
five books of emblems, does make its impact. But although the
call for reformation ins strong and clear, the thrust of the collection
is nevertheless to suggest that there is something badly amiss
with the world. By lamenting the passing of the golden age and
the flight of Astraea, with their complexly codified identification
with the Elizabethan age, Quarles is able to imply that the evils
he depicts are relatively recent. In a particularly striking poem
that concludes the first book, prefaced by an epigraph from
Revelations, 'the Devil is come unto you, having great wrath,
because he knoweth he hath a short time', Quarles adopts a
desperate and strident tone and insists that England is now given
over into the hands of the Antichrist – an alarming accusation
indeed when levelled at Foxe's Elect Nation:

> Lord! canst thou see and suffer? is thy hand
> Still bound to th'peace? Shall earth's black Monarch take
> A full possession of thy wasted land?
> Till full'ag'd law-resisting Custom shake
> The pillours of thy right by false command?
> Unlock thy clouds, great Thund'rer, and come down:
> Behold whose Temples wear thy sacred Crown;
> Redresse, redresse our wrongs; revenge, revenge thy own.

See how the bold Usurper mounts the seat
Of royall Majesty; How overstrawing
Perils with pleasure, pointing ev'ry threat
With bugbear death, by torments over-awing
Thy frightened subjects; or by favours drawing
Their tempted hearts to his unjust retreat;

Lord, canst thou be so mild? and he so bold?
Or can thy flocks be thriving, when the fold
Is govern'd by a Fox? Lord, canst thou see and hold?

Quick-seeing *Faith* now blind and *Justice* see?
Has Justice now found wings and has Faith none?
What do we here? who would not wishe to be
Dissolv'd from earth, and with *Astraea* flee
From this blind dungeon to that sunne-bright Throne?
Lord, is thy Scepter lost, or laid aside?
Is hell broke loose, and all her Fiends untied?
Lord, rise and rowze, and rule and crush their furious pride.

Here Quarles gives voice to the mingled anger and demoralisation that affected Puritan sympathisers as they witnessed alarming new developments in Church and State, as Charles I gave William Laud, who held the posts of chief minister and Archbishop of Canterbury, a virtual *carte blanche* to drive them out of the Church of England, and even from the shores of England as well. But what is astonishing, given the temper of the times and Laud's own strong predilection for censorship and the implacable persecution of all offenders, is the boldness with which Quarles speaks out against England's 'wasted land', the confidence with which he speaks of usurpation, the frankness with which he alludes to Laud's reign of terror, which drove so many Englishmen across the seas. The poem virtually gives the signal for revolt – so it was not without good reason that Quarles was prepared to acknowledge his role in fanning the flames of revolution.

As we have already seen, at the back of many criticisms of the contemporary scene lay the more general argument that the world was in a process of decay and decline from some former flourishing state. There were of course sources for this belief both in the Classical and Christian traditions: in Latin literature the most important advocate of the organic decay of the universe is

Lucretius, whilst among the early Christian fathers St Cyprian could be cited as an authoritative exponent of the degenerative view. But the individual most responsible for reanimating these views and for disseminating them in the Jacobean period is Sir Walter Ralegh, whose *The History of the World* (1614) is thoroughly permeated by this pessimistic doctrine. According to Ralegh:

> And as all things under the sun have one time of strength and another of weakness, a youth and a beauty, and then age and deformity; so time itself (under the dutiful shade of whose wings all things decay and wither) hath wasted and worn out that lively virtue of nature in man, and beasts, and plants, yea the heavens themselves, being of a most pure and cleansed matter, shall *wax old as a garment*; and then much more the power generative in inferior creatures, who by the ordinance of God receive operative virtue from the superior.[11]

Such a view gains credence and authority through the diversity of the sources by which it is underwritten. Quite apart from the passage that Ralegh cites from the Psalms, there is the traditional belief that impure and mixed substances cannot last, a deference to those literary sources that present physically more imposing human predecessors, a respect and reverence for the classical tradition, a presumed homology between the life of man and the life of the universe and multifarious anxieties about a possible end to the world as foreseen in the Bible. Ralegh is so confident about the matter that he does not even bother to argue a case and simply presents it as an unchallengeable fact. The burden of actual justification fell on the rather unworthy shoulders of Godfrey Goodman, who presented his argument in *The Fall of Man* (1616). Goodman was at this time chaplain to Queen Anne but subsequently became Bishop of Gloucester. His book is so replete with curious anecdotes and disquisitions that it seems more like a collection of bric-à-brac than a seriously argued case, but in stating this it is also necessary to recognise that the name of the game was argument from authority: the author who could assemble the largest body of august witnesses from the past would be the one most likely to prevail. It is also rather difficult to enter wholeheartedly into the spirit of his wholesale condemnation of contemporary decadence, sinfulness and depravity since the knowledge that Goodman himself was notoriously one of the

most corrupt, worldly and unscrupulous churchmen of his time
will keep on intruding. Goodman was an artist in the multiplication
of emoluments and benefices. Even one bishopric was not enough
for him and he endeavoured to obtain another by bribery, but
was thwarted in the attempt by William Laud. For Goodman
everything is grist that comes to the mill, from theatres to bear-
baiting, from a deterioration in the coinage to a reluctance to
follow the Greeks and Romans in their pursuit of vigorous sports.
When Goodman is led to contemplate the woeful condition of
man he invites the reader to compare the dignified exit from the
world of a chicken with the more ignominious fate of man, who
far from being served up at a banquet, decays in the ground and
becomes food for worms. It is reflections such as this that create
an irresistible sense of the work as table-talk – Goodman evidently
found the good life and lamentation at the state of the world only
too compatible, though a reduction in the number of courses
served was not part of his evidence!

In fact Goodman is able to view the decay of the world with
equanimity: there is nothing that can be done. Since 'It is proper
to the corrupt nature of man, to turne all the best qualities into the
worst part, like a spider that turns the best substance into
poison',[12] post-lapserian man can be pretty well written off.
Goodman was a High Churchman, virtually Catholic in his love
of ornament and ritual, and he notably lacks that Protestant sense
of urgency: the sense of the world as the scene of a cosmic
struggle that continues to be fought out, where every single soul
finds itself in a desperate and precarious predicament, poised on
a knife-edge. It is on these grounds that he is explicitly, if not
directly, criticised by George Hakewill in his *An Apologie of the
Power and Providence of God* (1st edn, 1627; 3rd expanded edn with
comments and responses by Godfrey Goodman, 1635). Like
Goodman, Hakewill at one time occupied an influential position
at Court, as chaplain to Prince Charles, the future king, but his
opposition to the prince's projected Spanish marriage led to his
ignominious banishment from the Court. As a result of this
offence, and through his resistance to High Church ceremonial,
Hakewill never rose higher than an archdeacon. As he possessed
a large private income he was able to retain a degree of
independence but the importance of status in resolving arguments
at the time is clearly demonstrated by the tone of his replies to
Bishop Goodman in the edition of 1635. Goodman's tone is

haughty and peremptory. He virtually insists on Hakewill's
compliance, while Hakewill, though firm, is obliged to be
deferential and obsequious. So the struggle between the two men
is suggestive on many levels. Goodman and Hakewill are, on the
face of it, both members of the same Church, yet only one,
Hakewill, writes in the general spirit of the Reformation. When
Bishop Goodman writes in his world-weary way 'Religion is taken
wings, and is returned to heaven, from whence she descended'[13]
it is as if the Church has no meaningful role to play at all and that
it bears no responsibility for such a state of affairs. It is as if the
endeavours of Luther and Calvin had never been. So although
Hakewill is prepared to concede that the Church did indeed
depart from its original purity through greed, ambition, idleness,
luxury and ignorance, he nevertheless does believe that religion
can be restored to its 'primitive brightnes'.[14]

Hakewill's objection to the presumption of decay is that it
erodes God's power and justice quite as much as it undermines
human free will. For it consequently figures as some irreversible
organic process that lies beyond all possibility of action or
intervention, which neither God nor man can arrest. Moreover, it
induces laxity and complacency. As Hakewill sees it the many
and evident signs of God's righteous anger at human sinfulness
and recalcitrance will only be casually brushed aside as yet more
evidence that the celestial frame is grinding to a halt. Thunder,
lightning, tempest and earthquake are seen not as a call to
repentance but as the coughing fits of a world in its sick-bed. This
Hakewill cannot accept. The thrust of his own writing is always
activist and energising:

> If then we come short of our *Auncestors* in *knowledge*, let us not
> cast it upon the deficiencies of our wits in regard of the *Worlds
> decay*, but upon our own *sloth*, if we come short of them in
> *vertue*, let us not impute it to the *declination of the World*, but to
> the malice and faintnesse of our *owne will*; if we feele the
> scourges of God upon our hand by mortality, famine,
> unseasonable weather, or the like, let us not teach the people
> that they are occasioned by the *Worlds old age*, and thereby call
> into question the providence, or power, or wisedome, of justice,
> or goodnes of the Maker thereof; but by their and our *sins*,
> which is doubtless both the truer and more profitable doctrine,

and withal more consonant to the sermons of Christ and his Apostles, and the prophets of God in like case.[15]

In analysing bygone tales brimming with miraculous statistics, Hakewill brings a sharp critical intelligence to bear. Unlike Goodman he will not take his sources on trust. In general he is greatly impressed with recent, tangible evidence of human betterment in the form of such innovations as porcelain, paper, chimneys, watches, spectacles, guns and hats. Hakewill brings to his analysis of the past a supreme confidence in the moral superiority of a reformed Christianity to any previous form of society. He is scathing about the depravity and decadence of the ancient Romans: their massive banquets, their love of cruel spectacle, their love of luxury in clothing and building (a topic which he could well have illustrated with much contemporary material also), the multiplicity of their gods. So Hakewill is a modernist and he has been seen, quite justifiably, as representative of the new scientific spirit. Yet we must beware of presenting the confrontation between Goodman and Hakewill as a simple confrontation between ancient and modern since they have more than a little in common. Both men believe in the golden age and its loss, but Hakewill believes that it is possible to bring it back. Hakewill really accepts Goodman's sense of the senescence of the world but he sees it rather as a state of mind that that must be combated. What is needed is both faith in God and faith in the possibilities of the modern. In his Preface to the *Apologie* Hakewill speaks of how he has 'laboured to free the world from old age',[16] and he goes on to suggest that the good old days of England's prosperity and power (clearly the age of Astraea/Elizabeth) can be brought back if only the English people will undergo a moral reformation:

I nothing doubt but upon our returne to our God by humilation and newnesse of life, he would soone dissolve the cloud which hangs over us, and returne unto us with the comfortable beames of his favour, and make us returne each to other with mutual imbracements of affection and duety, and our Armies and Fleetes to returne with spoyle and victory, and reduce againe as golden and happy times, as ever wee or our forefathers saw.[17]

Implicitly good times are Protestant times. It is delay and dallying
in the work of bringing about a thorough reformation (as
evidenced no doubt by the successful careers of such impervious
and incorrigible souls as Bishop Goodman) that has brought the
nation into God's disfavour. If England continues in the path of
luxury and profaneness, Hakewill warns, there will inevitably be
trouble ahead. If Hakewill wants to rebut the argument for the
world's decay it is because he wishes to recall his readers to order
by insisting on the imminent terrors of the Last Judgement.
Hakewill concludes the *Apologie* with a stern warning to the high
and the mighty of society, to the nobility, gentry, military men,
courtiers, magistrates and counsellors that they should take heed
before it is too late. Hakewill also believes in a corrupted world,
but he believes that there is still time to do something about it.

7

A Great Hazard: the Coming of Civil War

In a famous speech, delivered in November 1640 before the House of Commons, when Parliament was reconvened after eleven years of personal rule by Charles I, Sir Benjamin Rudyerd said:

> I have often thought and said, that it must be some great extremity that would recover and rectify this State; and when that extremity did come, it would be a great hazard whether it might prove a Remedy or Ruin. We are now, Mr Speaker, upon that vertical turning point, and therefore it is no time to palliate, to foment our own undoing.[1]

In retrospect this was undoubtedly one of the critical moments in English history, on which the fate of King and Parliament alike depended, but, although the language of crisis is familiar, crises are rarely as obvious as it might seem: as I have already argued what makes for crisis is the widespread conviction that there is one, the sense that people have at particular historical moments that everything is at stake. My purpose is to explore the origins of this sense of crisis and to suggest that, in trying to understand the coming of civil war, we need to look more closely at the psychology of the participants and to consider more carefully the interpretative categories which they themselves used to focus and give meaning to events as they unfolded. The historiography of the Civil War is still caught between explanation in terms of long-term social and economic changes on the one hand, and, on the other, a more detailed and confused picture of actors and events, as it alters from year to year and from county to county. Yet it does need to be asked just how it was that the English people were brought to this 'great hazard' and why it was that the authority of the King came to be so directly challenged? Against the view that both sides were simply forced into a war that neither of them wanted, under the pressure of events, I would argue that, in intellectual terms, the gauntlet had been thrown down to the monarchy before Parliament even met. The very terms in which the discussion was being conducted were such that, at the very outset, the King was seen as an obstacle that stood in the way of England's realisation of a unique, divinely appointed destiny, rather than as a natural focus of loyalty and obedience. Ultimately the sacrifice of the King came to seem the only possible resolution of the national sense of crisis.

In considering the position of the King it is necessary to see the exercise of royal authority in the context of English history and more especially in terms of the mythology of Elizabeth as a focus for patriotic unity and as the hypothetical resolution of a catastrophic, turmoil-ridden past. The problem for her successors, James I and Charles I, was that this particular symbolic construction could not easily be repeated. James I's problem was that he was not English and that he could not be very plausibly identified with moral purity, but he partially made up for that by being indubitably Protestant and a knowledgeable theologian as well. However, the latter part of James's reign was dogged by the issue of a Spanish marriage for his son, Charles, which, so long as the proposal was on the table, suggested that England was in serious danger of compromising her purity and independence as the outstanding Protestant nation. Charles's eventual marriage to the French princess, Henrietta Maria, was less unacceptable than one with Spain, but it did have the immediate consequence that England was expected to come to the aid of France against Huguenot fellow-Protestants at La Rochelle. Although this policy was to be rapidly reversed by Buckingham, the consequences of the marriage in the longer term were a great deal more serious. It was Charles's misfortune that by this liaison, and through his unwise decision to maintain James's long-running favourite in office, he became associated from the outset with some of the most negative aspects of his father's regime. James had been able to use the operations of the Court to enhance his own position by virtue of his system of operating through a single, unchallenged favourite. James was able to give the impression that he was always behind Buckingham so that it seemed difficult, if not impossible, to contest his minister's position, yet there remained sufficient ambiguity in the position to allow James himself to remain essentially uncompromised. In any case, Charles had less incentive to play this system because there was so much less bounty to dispense and because such a lavish and largely uncontrolled dispensing of patronage had produced economic weakness in the King's position. Although in theory Charles's decision not to resort to Parliament should have strengthened his own position, in practice it did not do so because he himself no longer figured as the indisputable centre of power. Laud and Strafford were forceful personalities in their own right, who lacked either the temperament or the inclination to perform the intricate social manœuvres of a Buckingham and they did not try to dissimulate where power effectively lay. It was hard to think of them simply as minions of the King; if they acted on his behalf they nevertheless had a great deal of discretion. Moreover, there was Henrietta Maria, with her Catholic entourage, as a third centre of power. Charles contrived to have the worst of all worlds. He was directly associated with Strafford and Laud and thus had to feel the full force of the anger and resentment which they generated – which was considerable – yet critics could feel free to attack them while pretending that their only wish was to save the King from such evil counsels. The presence of Henrietta Maria at Court made it easy to insinuate that Laud and Strafford were dancing to the tune of Rome, a charge which could never have been made to stick if Charles had had a Protestant wife and thus been himself above suspicion. Worst of all, Charles no longer seemed to be at the axis of affairs, the unmoved centre of a moving world, but increasingly figured as the ineffective driver of a team of wildly galloping horses, who had got the bit far too firmly between their teeth for them ever to be brought back under control. Charles's Court began to seem less and less like the summit of English society and more and more like the outpost of some foreign empire, marked by outlandish tastes, unreformed religion and an alien style of autocratic government. Charles I was a convincing embodiment of neither Protestantism, England nor even the monarchy itself.

Puritan thinking continued to be deeply influenced by Foxe's suggestion that England was to play the leading role in the final struggle against the papal Antichrist and this belief was given a renewed stimulus by the publication in Amsterdam in 1615 of Thomas Brightman's *A Revelation of the Revelation*, which was the English version of a work first published in Latin in 1609. Brightman, who was born in 1562 and who died in 1607 before *A*

Revelation appeared in any form, belonged to that earlier generation of Puritans who had still hoped for great things from an English national Church. Most of their optimistic expectations concerning the abolition of surviving rituals and corrupt practices were knocked on the head by James I at the Hampton Court Conference of 1604, when he rejected their Millenary Petition and warned them that they would be driven out of the Church if they did not conform. So the belated publication of a work largely composed in the reign of Elizabeth, which is spoken of in the present tense, and which was filled with prophecies based on the book of Revelations, in which the downfall of Rome was envisaged as occurring before 1650, served to rekindle flickering hopes. Brightman was convinced that God had already shown extraordinary marks of favour towards England, but these in turn, in terms of Puritan dialectic, required yet further exertions from the faithful in order to deserve and justify blessings already received. There was always the risk that England might wear out her welcome with God and that he might then turn to some other nation to serve as his agent in the great work of ushering in the eternal kingdom. Brightman sincerely hoped and believed that England *was* so privileged but there were great risks and dangers in this should there be any risk of backsliding or any prospect of a return to the shameful practices of Rome. In the late 1620s – when Laud endeavoured to suppress preaching and to eliminate the alleged sedition caused by Puritan lecturers, reasserted the power of the ecclesiastical courts, insisted on placing the communion table at the east end of the church, and embarked on the installation of magnificent stained-glass windows – Brightman's words from an earlier era must have had an ominous ring:

And I hope that he who hath begun this everlasting Kingdome wil make our Queene also to be the Type of this eternall Kingdome. There is no good man that doth not desire with all his heart that it may be so. Onely we must take heed least that we suffer his truth to be corrupted, & his Majesty to be wronged and offended by bringing in Antichristian superstitions a fresh againe of whose power, love and faithfulness in defending us we have had such notable experience. We have made Christ angry against us already, in that we are so farrer of from coming to a full and due reformation, but if we shal returne unto our vomit, with what furye will he burne out against us?[2]

If England was determined to continue to enjoy favour in the sight of God it would not be enough to sit back complacently, she would have to intensify and renew her efforts. She would have to demonstrate unequivocally that her feet were firmly set on the path of righteousness. The Laudian 'innovations' aroused anger and dismay among Puritan ministers not simply because they were the principal victims of his policies but because they seemed to positively reverse what they had fondly imagined would be an irreversible, if all too gradual process of reformation. From being a beacon of enlightenment to the world, England was in danger of becoming a weak and flickering candle, finally to be snuffed out by the ruthless hand of Laud.

The prophecies of Foxe and Brightman created a sense of English identity that was at once strongly patriotic, and, at the same time, deeply concerned with the fate of Protestants in other lands. The Puritans were internationalists. In Foxe's *Actes and Monuments* events at home continually play second fiddle to the unfolding of the Reformation in Europe, where great world-historical events are being acted out, whether in Bohemia under John Hus or in Germany under Luther. One of the most striking and recurrent features of Puritan writings of the seventeenth century is the depth of their concern and the sincerity of their identification with the sufferings of co-religionists abroad as they faced persecution and even genocide. They were aghast at the violence directed against Protestants in Ireland and Germany, they feared for the fate of the Huguenots in France, they sympathised with the campaign of the Covenanters in Scotland and they were ever mindful of the situation of those fellow Puritans who had been led to choose exile and religious freedom in America. England's failure to render effective aid to the Elector Palatine came as a bitter disappointment. When Gustavus Adolphus went so triumphantly to the aid of German Protestants in the Thirty Years War it seemed that he had assumed the role of advancing the Protestant cause that rightfully should have been England's. For a while John Preston was one of the few Puritans to have influence at Court and he did what he could to discourage both the Spanish marriage and the collaboration with the French against fellow-Protestants at La Rochelle. From all these multifarious reverses for the Protestant cause Preston drew the lesson that they were to be regarded as God's punishment for the sin of lukewarmness. They had not prevailed because they had lacked determination and conviction:

What though the Candlestick bee removed out of the Palatinate,
because they were luke-warme and falne from their first love?
What if he should do it in France? What if in England? In the
Low Countries? should it seem strange to us? It is his manner
so to doe![3]

In this chastened mood reverses are even to be expected in the
work of reformation as God's rebuke to the faithful for becoming
too complacent and self-satisfied. But instead of being discouraged
they must recover the zealousness and determination of an earlier
generation. They must also strive and struggle to redeem
themselves in God's eyes without any immediate expectation of
reward.

Symptomatic of this newfound Puritan mood of resolution and
quiet determination is Richard Sibbes's *The Bruised Reed and the
Smoking Flax* (1630), which influenced men as diverse as John
Cotton, one of the leading lights of the settlement in New
England, Hugh Peter, who gained notoriety for presiding over
the execution of Charles I, and Richard Baxter, author of one of
the best-known of all Puritan autobiographies. Like John Preston,
Sibbes was deeply concerned about the fate of international
Protestantism. In his *The Saints Cordials* (1629) he deplored the
English insularity that made it possible to disregard the fate of
Protestants elsewhere: 'We forget the misery of the Church in
other places . . . they pray, and call upon us, as farre as Prague,
as farre as Heidelberg, as farre as France, that we would take
notice of their afflictions.'[4]

Sibbes was active in promoting the Protestant cause and from
1626, when he was elected to the Mastership of St Catherine's
Hall, Cambridge, he was able to exercise a wider influence. With
John Davenport and others he was one of twelve feofees who
established a fund for the support of Puritan ministers. He also
supported Davenport's efforts to raise money for the support of
distressed Protestant ministers in the Palatinate which was so
controversial that it led him to incur both the reprimand of a high
commission and the hostility of Laud. Yet, in a time of adversity,
Sibbes was better able to work the system than Davenport. He
was only driven out of Cambridge to Gray's Inn in London,
whereas Davenport was forced to resign his ministry in 1633 and
flee to Holland. But Laud pursued him even there so that he had

to make his escape to America and even from this Puritan refuge the implacable Laud still nourished hope of extracting him. Sibbes, from necessity, was more opportunistic than his writings would suggest, but his uncompromising words did much to harden the Puritan resolve.

The Bruised Reed and the Smoking Flax offers counsel and comfort in a dark time – and we may surmise that many Puritans read it in much the same frame of mind as the British people listened to Churchill's wartime speeches after Dunkirk. Its modulation of thought and feeling is complex as Sibbes moves carefully and steadily from reassurance to a prophetic optimism, articulated through a transition from the figure of the bruised reed, emblematic of the need to patiently endure suffering and persecution, to the figure of the smoking flax, which signifies the conviction that sooner or later Puritan spiritual fires will triumphantly blaze up again. What is equally remarkable is the skill with which Sibbes interweaves the development of an interior spirituality with a sense of how the spiritual life is to sustain itself and fight back in an uncompromisingly hostile world. At moments Sibbes's bitterness about the state of the Church flashes out when he refers to those 'such as raise temporal advantage to themselves out of the spiritual misery of others' or who 'count Preaching foolishness'[5] but his words are addressed to the Saints and it is their hearts which he seeks to infuse with fortitude and conviction that will prepare them for the long struggle that lies ahead. Like John Preston he insists that God's way is never simple and straightforward. Reverses are to be expected as part of the very process by which the faithful are to be educated:

That God often worketh by contrarie, when he meanes to give victory, he will suffer us to be foyled first, when he meanes to comfort us he wil terrifie first, when he meanes to justifie, he will condemne us first, whom he meanes to make glorious, he will abase first.[6]

The deeper implication of Sibbes's message is that the Puritans must never for one moment allow themselves to believe that they have been forsaken by God. These discouragements are simply a trial of their faith. God's mercy is infinite for those who have truly accepted Christ in their hearts. They must recognise that now is to be their period of testing and probation and that, despite their apparent vulnerability and isolation, they will be strong so long as Christ is with them. Knowledge of Christ is a 'transforming knowledge' which can give the Saints the ability to resist all the pressures that are brought to bear upon them; despite setbacks on the one hand and worldly inducements on the other, they will be able to maintain an unswerving course:

> Those that are under Christ's government, have the spirit of Revelation whereby they see and feele a divine power sweetly and strongly inabling them for to preserve faith when they feele the contrary, & hope in a state hopelesse, and love to GOD under signes of his displeasure, and heavenly mindednes in the midst of worldly affairs & allurements drawing a contrary way: they feel a power preserving patience, nay joy in the midst of causes of mourning, inward peace in the midst of assaults.[7]

With God on their side the Puritan elect have the courage to endure suffering, knowing both that this is his will and that they will ultimately be vindicated: 'And the Saints shall have their time, when they shall sit in judgement upon them that judge them now.'[8] The depth of present adversity must not be taken as a sign of long-continued persecution. On the contrary it should be taken as a sign that circumstances may rapidly change: 'Christ and his Church when they are at their lowest, are neerest rising: his enemies at their highest are neerest downfall.'[9]

Sibbes could not know how prophetic his words would prove. The Puritans seemed utterly defeated and driven from the field by an all-powerful Laud. All they could reasonably expect was more ruthless and uncompromising extensions of his power. Yet in one of the most astonishing and rapid reversals of fortune ever, William Prynne, who at Laud's behest had been sentenced in 1637 to have his ears cut off, the letters 'S.L.' – for seditious libeller – carved in his cheeks and to be imprisoned in the Tower, in 1641 found himself suddenly released on the order of Parliament to embark on the congenial task of searching through Laud's personal papers for incriminating evidence, while Laud was incarcerated in his place. In 1645 Laud was executed. So it was scarcely surprising that in the heyday of the 1640s, the Puritans, mindful of their former state of adversity, should have been acutely conscious of the many and diverse blessings from God which they had received. Although Sibbes does not labour over Apocalyptic prophecies, there can be little doubt but that the tone of his argument is shaped by a sense that the world is now embarked on its last days and that, therefore, violence, discord and division are to be expected. The Sainst must be ready for struggle and opposition since this is an inevitable part of the final battle with Antichrist:

> this then wee are always to expect, that wheresoever Christ cometh, there will be opposition: when Christ was borne all Jerusalem was troubled; so when Christ is borne in any man, the soule is in an uproare, and all because the heart is unwilling to yeeld up it self to Christ to rule it.
>
> Wheresoever Christ cometh, he breedeth division, not only 1, between man and himself, but 2, between man and man, and 3, between church and church.[10]

Here again Sibbes links the inner conflict with the wider conflict in the world. When he writes: 'It is therefore no sign of a good condition, to find all quiet and nothing at odds',[11] he suggests that true faith will always be a matter of desperate contention both in the Christian's relation to himself and to the world. The moment has come for all Puritans to steel themselves inwardly for the tasks that lie ahead.

One of the ways in which this hardening of Puritan resolve manifested itself was in the battle over cultural forms and especially in the attack on the theatre launched by William Prynne in his gargantuan work of anti-hedonist scholarship, *Histriomastix* (1633). Puritan preachers had for a long time been opposed to a whole spectrum of popular diversions, but their indignation was especially focused on the tendency for people to amuse themselves on the Lord's Day. This was not merely contrary to the Bible but was also a sign of disrespect to the Christian faith, since a day which should be given over in its entirety to pious meditation, Bible reading and prayer was commonly given over to popular entertainments, which, if anything, played into the hands of the Devil. This attack on pleasure had a clear class bias, since it struck at the common people who had to work during the week, rather than at the aristocracy who did not. Nevertheless the effect of Puritan preaching was to create a distinct segment of society which regarded the amusements of rich and poor alike with profound suspicion. Not the least significant aspect of Puritanism in this respect was the way in which it cut across class barriers to create a new type of social classification in which a person's deportment, bearing and general lifestyle were all important. As Patrick Collinson has pointed out:

> The effect on society of the religion of protestants and its moral values was to polarise communities between those who gadded to sermons and those who gadded to dances, sport and other pastimes; those whose speech was seasoned with godly salt and those who used the traditional oaths.[12]

With the formation of a distinct class of Puritan gentry it became possible to attack the idle and extravagant lifestyle of the aristocracy in ways which would formerly have been unacceptable. Of course, to be both a gentleman and a Puritan did involve reconciling a variety of cultural contradictions and some of them managed to combine piety with a liking for fine clothes, but it was nevertheless significant that it could no longer be automatically assumed that those who occupied a high position in society were exempt from the demands of holy living. In his popular allegory *The Isle of Man* (1st edn 1618, and many times reprinted) Richard Bernard introduced into his gallery of sinners one Wilfull Will, whose offence is precisely to have behave like an aristocrat of his day. But now he is repentent and ready to confess that he erred deeply in following not the principles of Captain *Reason*, but the dictates of lewd Mistress *Heart*:

> I also do freely acknowledge that I stood too much upon my birth, and Gentry, as too many at this day doe, having never a good quality besides to brag or boast off. I tooke it for granted, that my Gentrie stood in idlenesse, pleasurable delights, hawking, hunting, and haunting Tavernes, drinking of healths, whiffing the Tobaccopipe, putting on of new, and variety of fashions, in Hat and in hair, in cloathes and in shooe-ties, in bootes and in spurres, in boasting and bragging, in cracking of oathes, in big lookes, great words, and in some out bearing gestures of Gentry. . . .[13]

In response to this plea of guilty, Bernard's judge significantly redefines the notion of a gentleman so the implication that such a status is to be manifested in an idle and dissolute lifestyle is displaced by a significant emphasis on sobriety of conduct and useful employment:

> *Wilfull Will,* I am sorrie that thy deserts are no better, being so well-borne, and that thou hast so abused the Gentry to thy shame and confusion, through thy vaine mistake, and foule abuse of the conceit of *Gentry* which *consists of nobleness of spirit, honourable endowments of mind, praise-worthy qualities, & service-able imployments for the King and Country;* and not in such base conditions as thou has named, unfitting altogether true Gentrie . . .[14]

Bernard suggests that Wilfull Will has been misled into thinking that this irresponsible behaviour is appropriate for a person of his station, whereas he has in fact made a serious misjudgement as the result of mingling with the wrong sort of people – presumably fellow members of the élite. But Bernard insists such behaviour is no longer to be regarded as symptomatic but as a deviation from a higher norm, of which exemplars already exist. The true gentry, we are to take it from Bernard, are solid and sober Puritans.

In *Histriomastix* William Prynne goes much further, by carrying the battle right into the Court itself and by even daring to set his sights on the person of the King. *Histriomastix* is typically distorted as a cultural document by wrenching it out of context so that it appears nothing more than a blinkered, ponderous and humourousless attack on an perennial institution, which, thanks to the labours of Sophocles, Shakespeare and others, has placed itself beyond all possibility of criticism. But what this rejection of Prynne, the censorious Puritan, in the context of world literature rather overlooks is that Laud, his chief persecutor, was still more censorious, as his treatment of Prynne for his authorship of *Histriomastix* demonstrates. It was a censorious age. Prynne's indignation was aroused by the theatre as it functioned as a social institution in his own time and he objected to it both because he saw it as a rival to the pulpit and because it epitomised the hedonism of the Court. Even if we can hardly share Prynne's views we can surely recognise that he had grounds for dissatisfaction: Puritan preachers are persecuted and driven out of the country and yet it has become almost a sacred duty to defend the lifestyles of the great. Doubtless Laud was right to see this criticism as a threat to the social order, but if so then we should be prepared to take it as seriously as he. For what made Prynne's criticism so damaging was that every shaft of his invective, every one of his copious citations from the Christian fathers, ultimately pointed to Charles I and Henrietta Maria, who patronised the theatre, sponsored lavish masques and even appeared on stage themselves. After exposure to Prynne's massive bombardment of quotations any contemporary reader would have been hard put not to assume that the stage had been condemned by virtually every authority in antiquity, whether Christian or pagan, and that Charles in his addiction to such pernicious pastimes was fit only to be classed with such monstrous reprobates as Nero and Caligula. Prynne makes a particular point of insisting 'how infamous, how disgraceful a thing it is, for Kings or Emperours to turn Actors, Masquers, or Gladiators on a Stage, even in the very judgement of heathens, much more of Christians'.[15] Prynne, had he wanted to, could very easily have framed his argument in a more circumspect fashion that would have generally deplored the stage as a suitable diversion for pious Christians without trailing his coat any further. Instead he leans over backwards not merely to condemn the stage but to suggest that royal patronage, royal participation and the wasteful extravagance of the royal masque lie at the very heart of the evil. Prynne is scandalised at the colossal misallocation of resources by King and Court on such privileged entertainments at a time of general scarcity and hardship. He speaks of

> the over-prodigall disbursements upon Playes, and Masques of *late penurious times* which have beene welnigh as expensive as the Wars, and I dare say more chargeable to many then their soules, on which the most of us bestow least cost, least time and care[16]

and he goes on to exclaim:

> If we summe up all the prodigall vaine expenses which Play-houses and Playes occasion every way, we shall finde them almost infinite, wel-nigh incredible, altogether intollerable in any Christian frugall state.[17]

Doubtless England in the 1630s, despite Charles's attempts at economy, was very far from being such a Christian frugal state, which made Prynne's suggestion that it should be so very disconcerting. In questioning this central institution of the monarchy, Prynne questions the role of the King himself and the ceremonial that is used to validate it. The monarchy becomes stained with the implication of superfluity, of incurring expenses beyond the capacity of the nation to sustain.

Prynne was subsequently to turn his ever-ready pen to the subject of ship-money and clearly the King's right to levy such taxes on his hard-pressed subjects would seem that much more questionable in the light of such apparently untroubled wastefulness. So in focusing on the masque in this way, Prynne probed the Court at its most vulnerable point. What *Histriomastix* brings out clearly is that Puritans were no longer prepared to go on lying low or to remain silent. Many of them were now prepared to stand and fight. Since Charles supported Laud's persecution of the saints they recognised that they could temporise no longer. Superficially considered, *Histriomastix* is an unwieldy blunderbuss discharging shots in all directions but on closer analysis, as Laud could not fail to recognise, it appears rather as a musket shrewdly aimed. *Histriomastix* makes it clear that from now on, no one, not even the King, is above Puritan criticism. In its wake men became bolder despite the savage penalties imposed. For as William Gouge wrote in his *Commentary on the Hebrews* (published posthumously in 1655 but based on a lifetime of sermons preached at Blackfriars):

> Read the prophet's reproofs of such, and you shall find that they spared none, nor princes, nor priests, nor prophets, nor people.
> God is the master of all, all are his scholars; his instructions are given to all, all are bound to learn them; with whom is no respect of persons, to him King and beggar are alike.[18]

Through the medium of the printing press these injunctions could be passed on in the most categorical form.

On a symbolic level it was an important precondition for revolution, not only that the King should cease to be an expressive symbol of national identity in the way that Elizabeth had been, but also that it should be possible for the English people to think of themselves as an independent body in their own right. If

Englishmen increasingly came to think of themselves as a free and independent people such a conception was greatly facilitated by the myth that they had for long centuries suffered under a foreign yoke, whether Danish, Saxon or Norman. Since it appeared that England's kings had rarely been of truly native origin it thus began to seem inescapable that the burden of sustaining Englishness through seemingly endless periods of gloom had actually fallen on the common people themselves. They had, doubtless, endured the alien yoke with great fortitude but they had certainly never liked it and it was a matter for rejoicing when it finally came to an end. But as we have also seen, even in Edward Hall, the taking of a French wife by Henry VI was an event fraught with disaster for English politics for a century or more. Elizabeth had managed to remain an uncorrupted symbol by avoiding a foreign marriage, but Charles I was from the Scottish line of his father James, who, with his French wife, was apparently turning his court into a centre of foreign intrigue, where such papal agents as Panzini and Con were in a position to shape and influence policy. Moreover, under the aegis of Sir Edward Coke a view of the national history took shape in which the great fruit of the long struggle of the English people against foreign domination was the common law: a complex inheritance of traditional and often unwritten rights and customs, in which survived a tenaciously guarded propensity towards freedom. Coke wrote:

> No subject of this realm, being truly instructed by the good and plain evidence of his ancient and undoubted patrimony and birth-right (though he hath for some time by ignorance, false persuasion, or vague fear been deceived or dispossessed) but will consult with learned and faithful councillors for the recovery of the same. The ancient and excellent laws of England are the birth-right and the most ancient and best inheritance that the subjects of this realm have, for by them he enjoyeth not only his inheritance and goods in peace and quietness, but his life and his most dear country in safety.[19]

The common law was the one single and indisputable blessing that emerged from the otherwise doubtful saga of English history. In the decades before the Civil War it became a commonplace to contrast the people's Ancient Customs on the one hand with the

King's Innovations on the other. We might expect to encounter such terminology among the more critical parliamentarians and more radical preachers but it becomes so pervasive as to actually infiltrate the world of the court. In Richard Brome's *A Jovial Crew or the Merry Beggars* (1641), one of the last plays to be staged before the closing of the theatres in 1642, a group of aristocrats leaves the house of Oldrents, whose insatiable hospitality finally becomes intolerable, in order to mingle with the merry beggars. Oldrents's house clearly represents the enclosed but comfortable world of the Court, but what is particularly interesting about the beggars is that they do not merely suggest a carefree and irresponsible existence. The persistence of their way of life – one often seen as threatening to authority – is bound up with an insistence on traditional, customary rights. They are

> The onely Freemen of a Commonwealth;
> Free above Scot-free; that observe no Law,
> Obey no governour, use no religion,
> But what they draw from their own ancient custom,
> Or constitute themselves, yet are no Rebels.

At a time when a Scottish invasion of England had placed Charles in a position of extreme jeopardy, such a parenthetical reference to *Scot-free* was provocative indeed. Yet, ironically, the great virtue that Brome attributes to the community of beggar outlaws is stability. Their anarchic way of life evades all the perplexities of the modern state and of its attendant statecraft and persists not in spite of it but because of it. Significantly they are spared all innovation:

> With them there is no Grievance or Perplexity;
> No fear of war, or State Disturbances.
> No Alteration in a common-wealth,
> Or Innovation, shakes a thought of theirs.

This is humorously intended no doubt, but it nevertheless demonstrates how thoroughly the King had lost the propaganda battle, when even the dramatists of his own Court have implicitly accepted the terms of reference of the opposition: that is the King who is changing the established state of affairs and who is infringing the traditional rights of the people. Beyond the shifting, ever-changing world of the Court, an immemorial way of life goes on unaltered. It is here that you will find the real England.

But the English are not only a free people; they are also God's people. Separated from the rest of Europe by the English Channel they have been marked out by God for a special destiny. If their sufferings have been great this is in itself to be taken as a sign of election since God visited similar tribulations on the Jews, who were also his Chosen People. Like the Jews, the English people had been compelled to experience a history of marked contradictions, in which long periods of suffering and oppression were relieved by remarkable and unforeseen blessings. Puritan preachers were so constantly mindful of the Old Testament as a never-failing cornucopia of parallels and analogies that their appropriateness need scarcely be argued. The symmetry between the two nations as recipients of both divine wrath and divine favour becomes quite overt in George Wither's poem, *Britain's Remembrancer* (1627), inspired by the plague of 1625. The English, like the Jews, have been mercifully delivered from foreign bondage and they have been vouchsafed all the blessings of a land overflowing with milk and honey. On the one hand, says Wither addressing the English nation:

> Thou wert as often warn'd, and punished;
> As much befought; as largely promised,
> As *Judah* was

but, on the other

> The Jewish Commonwealth was never daigned
> More great Deliverances then thou hast gainèd.
> Nor was their help vouchsaf'd in better season;
> As *Eighty eight*, and our great *Powder-treason*,
> Can witnesse well.

It was, of course, the Puritan ministers who were particularly concerned to dramatise this sense of national crisis and to present the dramatic image of a nation poised on the knife-edge between catastrophe and triumph. From Cartwright and Perkins onward they were concerned to mark as auspicious moments either the punishments visited on England in the form of plagues, bad harvests and other disasters, or else miraculous deliverances from the forces of the Antichrist, like the defeat of the Armada, the Gunpowder Plot or Elizabeth's providential escape from an assassin's bullet. Their chosen instrument was the calling of a Fast and the consequent preaching of Fast Sermons. On such occasions Englishmen and women were admonished to return to the path of righteousness from which they had swerved or else were reminded how unworthy they were to receive such signal manifestations of God's favour. They were then issued with a timely reminder that England had been allotted the leading role in the great work of Reformation and that, to her shame, the task was still incomplete so long as many corrupt and heathenish practices persisted. From 1640 the preaching of such Fast Sermons to Parliament (and equally significantly the printing of them) became a way of intensifying Parliament's own sense of mission and of constituting it as both an instrument of God's will and the unimpeachable voice of the people. But it would be wrong to assume that this way of perceiving things was confined to the radical clergy. Much discussion of the political issues of the period by modern historians projects back into the past tacit distinctions between sacred and secular which would have been incomprehensible at the time. For example, in his essay on the Fast Sermons in *Religion: The Reformation and Social Change*, Trevor-Roper, following Clarendon, lays great emphasis on the way in which political leaders on the Parliamentary side would 'tune the pulpit' so that sermons were often used as a way of initiating a new course of political action.[20] I am not concerned to deny that sermons were used in this way, since politicians and clergy clearly did consult together, but I would want to resist Trevor-Roper's further implication that the Puritan preachers were simply the tools of their political masters. On the contrary, I would argue that this religious discourse had a power and a dynamism of its own and that, far from simply being a code in which to articulate political and proximate intentions, it became itself the mastercode in terms of which political events as they took shape were perceived and constructed. Members of Parliament themselves thought in terms of analogies between the Jews and Englishmen as the chosen people of God. For example, in the debate on religious grievances in the Parliament of 1628, the last called before Charles I's era of personal government, Sir Robert Phelips was moved to state, apropos the link which he perceived between Popery and Arminianism:

What misery befel the Jews when they broke their peace with
God. What hath blasted our designs since these heresies crept
in? Have we not still turned the back upon our enemies? I am
afraid that God sitteth in the council of our enemies against us.
Doth not God plague us with enemies abroad and destruction
at home? We are become the most contemptible nation in the
world: are not our miseries and our crosses daily increased.[21]

When the state of the nation was perceived in such biblical terms
the upshot was to make alterations in religion central to any
analysis of what had gone wrong and to suggest that the remedy
for all evils was that the English people should repent and reform;
reconfirming themselves as God's people by casting off all alien
ways and innovations of which God manifestly disapproved. The
inescapable conclusion, which had to be unblinkingly confronted
despite its explosive potential, was that if the King himself was
associated with such heresies then he would either have to be
rescued from them or cast out himself. While it is certainly
possible that Parliament itself might have been able to patch up
some kind of deal with Charles if religion had never been on the
agenda – itself an impossible hypothesis – it must nevertheless
be recognised that the Puritan ministers did not possess a
language of compromise. As far as they were concerned it was
now all or nothing. Temporising had already been their undoing.
Having faced the prospect of virtual extinction and extermination
under Laud they were convinced that there could be no true and
thorough Reformation of England so long as an arrogant, ruthless
and wholly self-regarding hierarchy of bishops stood in the way.
First the apparent half-way house of the Elizabethan settlement
had become a final solution, yet now this threatened to collapse
into a *rapprochement* with Rome. The Church of England was
Laodicea, luke-warm, easy-going, complacent. Only a new-found
zeal and determination to purge it of corruption and to create a
vigorous preaching ministry could ensure that the living word of
God really would reach out to the common people. The figure
introduced by Cornelius Burges, in the first of all the Fast Sermons
preached to Parliament, was that of Zorobabbel, who finally
brought the building of the temple to completion after many long
suspensions and delays. In the same way the reconstruction of
the Church of England must be finally brought about. Also
invoked by Burges, and by William Gouge in his sermon of 1642,

The Saint's Support, was the prophet Nehemiah, who had found Israel still labouring under a multiplicity of religious corruptions and who had struggled to eradicate them. In the Puritan emphasis on a covenant between God and his people, it was the prophet, as guardian of the covenant, rather than the King, who emerged as the vital link between God and his chosen people. But under this dispensation Parliament also had a role to play as, simultaneously, the embodiment of popular authority and the divine will. Gouge insisted that Members of Parliament had a mandate to redress the manifold grievances and injustices that had directly stemmed from the policies of the King. It was they, and they alone, who must be 'the great Judges of this land'.[22] In the same way William Greenhill, in his sermon *The Axe at the Root*, suggested that Parliament must act in defence of the people and free them from bondage. By invoking the familiar trope of Israel in Egypt he also suggested that the power to which they were subjected was essentially alien and that they could only be freed from it by their own popular leaders:

> You are a free Parliament, preserve your freedom, our Laws and Liberties are in your hands, let them not suffer: The being and livelihood of the kingdome depends much thereon. Leges terra & statuta regni, are the Sinewes and Bonds of the body politic, wound them and the kingdome bleeds, loose them and the life of it's gone. Arbitrary Government is a dangerous thing; a Comet that threatens destruction to the country, it's over: you tell us *that acts of will and Tyranny are the ingredients into it, that neither Parliament nor Kingdome can be safe with it*: let your convictions cause prevention, improve your power; let not England become a house of bondage a 2d Aegypt.[23]

In this emotional address Greenhill draws on Coke's arguments for the common law as the crucial guarantee of English freedom under foreign domination in order to create an interpretation in which the predicament of England is powerfully aligned with the biblical trope of Israel in Egypt creating a situation in which, far from it being natural to think of the King as a natural focus of loyalty and of patriotic identity, it actually becomes almost unthinkable that he could ever fulfil such a role. At best he could only hope to achieve it by making a strenuous effort to reunite himself with God and his people in a spirit of reconciliation and

atonement; by willingly and humbly agreeing to revert to the
well-established, traditional ways. In his preface to his sermon of
1642, *Israel's Petition in time of Trouble*, Edward Reynolds justified
the plain style of his address by observing 'The King of Nineveh
was a King as well in his Sackcloth as in his Robes',[24] but since its
purpose was to attack arbitrary government and to make the
radical claim that 'no power, no malice, no policies should stand
between us and Gods Mercies',[25] he clearly had more than a
figural meaning in mind. If sackcloth is right for the King of
Nineveh and Reynolds it is even more apt for Charles who should
confess his errors instead of standing on his dignity. He should
admit his own responsibility for the plight of the land and put an
end to the innovations that have caused so much havoc. With the
end to arbitrary government England could once more be restored
to her former, Elizabethan, glory: 'this Nation would continue to
be as it hath been, like the Garden of Eden, a mirrour of
prosperity and happinesse to other people'.[26] This sense of a
people somehow beyond the monarchy and outside political
institutions enabled Cromwell to think of the New Model Army
as an instrument of popular feeling and of God's purposes and to
validate his construction of the 'Barebones' Parliament as
'representative of the people of England, sifted, winnowed, and
brought to a handful'.[27] The very fact that the English were God's
people and that England was God's land meant that, like their
Jewish predecessors, they could pursue their destiny under divine
guidance without benefit of kings. In a speech to Parliament of
1657, Cromwell described the English people as

> A People of the blessing of God, a People under his safety and
> protection. A People calling upon the Name of the Lord; which
> the Heathen do not. A People knowing God; and a People
> (according to ordinary expressions) fearing God. And you have
> of this no parallel, no, not in all the world! You have in the
> midst of you glorious things.[28]

Without a king, God's people could finally realise their appointed
destiny. The execution of Charles I had finally marked England's
exit from the secular into a truly sacred history and opened the
way to Zion.

A milestone on this road was the publication in 1636 of Henry
Burton's two sermons, which, despite its ostensibly loyalist title,

was not unreasonably regarded by Laud as a seditious work. It earned Burton the honour of appearing in the great show trial staged by the government in 1637 along with John Bastwick and William Prynne. In characteristic Puritan fashion Burton elected to preach these sermons on 5 November, so that, as he inveighed against present and imminent dangers from Popery against the historic background of gunpowder treason, his word would carry a staunchly patriotic and defensive ring. At first sight *For God and the King* is a notably casuistical work in which Burton endeavours to combine tortuously worded protestations of loyalty to the crown with vituperative attacks on the ecclesiastical hierarchy as exemplified by Laud and his henchmen and on papistical influences at Court. But more than hypocrisy is involved. Burton doubtless had to maintain a veneer of deference in his attacks. It would have been impolitic to suggest anything other than that the King had been mislead by evil counsellors. Yet Burton goes out of his way to accentuate the patriotic theme, as his title itself suggests, and it is this comprehensive reworking of the significance of the phrase 'For God and the King' that gives these sermons an enduring ideological significance. By the time Burton has finished he has sundered Charles from all the authority that such an utterance ostensibly attributes to him. For in Burton's argument God, king and people must remain linked together in an indissoluble unity; so he can argue with perfect sincerity that he is against discord and division. Burton says that men must learn 'to keep this knot of the feare of the Lord, and of the King, inviolable. For to separate them destroyeth both',[29] so in theory he is advancing the familiar argument of the obligation of absolute loyalty to the Christian magistrate. However, since Burton also argues that the Christian's loyalty is to God first and foremost, before the King, what he is really suggesting is that they should only obey the King in so far as the King himself obeys God and that they should be prepared to resist both him and his appointed ministers if they seek to impose papistical Antichristian teaching. Moreover, in defending the King or office of King, Burton strikes at those who both infringe his sovereignty and separate him from his Protestant people. Laud and his bishops usurp the King's authority while claiming to speak in his name; Henrietta Maria and her Catholic advisers seek to bring him under the influence of the Pope. So that to speak in the King's name is to speak for an ideal of truly patriotic and Christian kingship that is already under erasure; it also claims to be an attempt to save the King in his authentic majesty from the covert and illegitimate forces that have obtained such a hold over him. Just as it was felt that Rasputin exerted a malign influence over the last of the Tsars so Burton discerns a sinister conspiracy at Court that imperils the safety of the kingdom itself. Burton's most compelling and influential argument is to suggest that 'division or heart-burnings between the King and his subjects, are most perillous'.[30] Since such divisions are invariably the consequence of the fact that the King has been misled by evil counsels it follows that all that is needed to restore the situation is that the King should once more place himself in harmony with the sentiments of the people. Division no longer suggests rebellion or subversion against the monarch, but the abandonment of a loyal, God-fearing and trusting people by a wilful, misguided King. Burton skilfully links the High Church mannerisms of Laud and his bishops with the obsequious gestures of the Court. Just as true religion is not to be found in those who counterfeit it with elaborate rituals and ceremonial bowing, so true patriotism is not to be found in those who flatter and fawn over the King:

> Doe not these novellers honour, love, feare the King? Who seems more True? Yet (as was shewed before) these are the most dangerous enemies of the King, who under a pretence of honor and love, doe machinate the overthrow of his Kingdom and State, as by altering the State of religion, and by that meanes alienating and unsettling the hearts of his Subjects, by filling them with feares and suspicions, as if the King gave these novellers authority soe to doe; which farrer bee it from every good subjects heart once to imagine. For the King and novellers here doe stand in opposition one against the other. Can those be the Kings friends, that goe about to divide him betweene him and his good Subjects? Or to expose his kingdome to Gods displeasure by corrupting his worship, and oppressing his truth? Its impossible.[31]

The King necessarily cannot be in favour of innovation since this would be to cut himself off from all that which itself sanctions his power and authority. So in the King's name the King must be saved from himself. The King has become a hypothetical construction, a model to which the King manifestly is failing to correspond, but Burton would rather disbelieve in the actual King than in his hypothetical model. And the deeper implication is that a King who is not in harmony with his people is not a King at all. Burton's argument places Charles I in a double bind: to prove himself a true King he must abandon the policies with which he has become identified. He must wear a hollow crown.

Part Two

8

Shakespeare and the Crisis of Authority

Running through Shakespeare's history plays as much as through his tragedies is an acute consciousness of the degree to which all authority is problematic. Behind his celebrated description of man as 'dressed in a little brief authority' is a recognition not simply of the fragility and arbitrariness of power, but also of the degree to which its exercise depends on the deliberate maintenance of appearances. Kings are invested with pomp and majesty precisely to legitimate their role and to enable them to project themselves as the mythic centre on which everything must converge. It was scarcely accidental that Henry VIII, a king greatly agitated by the problem of maintaining the succession and simultaneously open to foreign destabilisation through his conflict with the Pope, should have been a monarch deeply concerned with conspicuous consumption and display. To 'be a king' involves complex forms of self-projection where all that finally matters is that the person who symbolically embodies and represents kingship should have his claims accepted by others. At the intersection of medieval and Renaissance worlds Shakespeare recognises the peculiar dilemma of power: that the more impossible legitimacy is, the more urgently is it required. As a dramatist who had early concerned himself with the bloody, confused and seemingly interminable political struggles of English history, Shakespeare was peculiarly well placed to grasp that in the struggles between York and Lancaster there was actually never a moment when the case was clear or when authority was unchallenged. Indeed there is a certain absurdity in asserting incontrovertible claims to political power and legitimacy when it is perfectly clear that such claims are precisely in question and needs must be – or they would not be made! Such is the predicament of Richard II. By comparison with the long line of his successors – and just as Milton's Eve is the fairest of her daughters – Richard's title to the English throne is indisputably the clearest. But that is only evident with hindsight.

The fact of the matter is that, despite this, Richard is not accepted as king by significant sections of English society and if he cannot gain this recognition then he is effectively not a king. Richard's failure to project himself as king and inability to impose his authority produces a situation in which he has only the notional status without the effective power that should go with it. He is a shadow king who can be relegated to the margins precisely because he has failed to embody this sense of a centre. The consequences of Richard's failure go deep: authority in England is always problematic from that time until Shakespeare's own. Tillyard's unfortunate influence once led many to believe that all this chaos and confusion ended with the election of Henry VII as a king with a clear title, but of course what Tillyard omits is that political authority was almost immediately reproblematised through the struggle between Catholic and Protestant. In the sixteenth century England was a byword throughout Europe for the political and religious dislocation that resulted from the alternation of Catholic and Protestant rulers. In his 'Apologie of Raymond Sebond' Montaigne writes:

> Nothing is more subject unto a continuall agitation than the lawes. I have since I was borne, seene those of our neighbours the English-men changed and rechanged three or foure times, not only in politike subjects, which is that some will dispense of constancy, but in the most important subject, that possibly can be, that is to say, in religion; whereof I am so much the more both grieved and ashamed, because it is a nation with which my countriemen have heretofore had so inward and familiar acquaintance, that even to this day, there remaine in my house some ancient monuments of our former aliance. Nay I have seene amongst our selves some things become lawfull, which erst were deemed capitall: and we that hold some others, are likewise in possibilitie, according to the uncertainty of warring fortune, one day or other, to be offendors against the Majestie both of God and man, if our justice chance to fall under the mercy of justice; and in the space of few yeares possession, taking a contrary essence.[1]

England represents a peculiarly modern form of infidelity that Montaigne fears and distrusts. If religion for men be 'but a peece of their owne invention, fit to combine their societie',[2] then it is, in his eyes, nevertheless quite indispensable that it *should* serve to promote social cohesion and harmony rather than become a force for political destabilisation. With undoubted prescience Montaigne sees England as a country embarked on a frantically zigzagging and politically erratic course that other nations may be expected to follow. He fears the possibility of contamination, that France may come to see marks of an English presence less endearing than the old. Montaigne would prefer to think of England in terms of the good old days rather than associate her with the uncertain and ever-changeable new. Shakespeare was equally conscious of this dilemma of authority and in his work it became an ever-growing, ever-intensifying theme. Shakespeare's pessimism and his sense of the tragic, I would argue, grows out of his meditation on the course of English history, and becomes more philosophically complex as it is fed by a sense of the problematic nature of human action as that is articulated in the pages of Plutarch. Shakespeare's history plays represent the predicament of a whole society, with the Roman plays primarily the tragedies of particular individuals, but in Shakespeare's greatest plays, above all in *Hamlet*, *Macbeth* and *Lear*, a more complex sense of an all-pervasive crisis that affects every aspect of individual and collective lives is enunciated with spectacular force.

Shakespeare's three plays dealing with the troublesome reign of Henry VI can be assigned with some confidence to the years 1590–1 but what seems puzzling at first sight is that Shakespeare, in the period immediately succeeding the defeat of the Spanish Armada, should have embarked on such an ambitious sequence that takes as its subject one of the darkest and most demoralising periods in English history. Furthermore, the extreme popularity of these plays enabled Shakespeare to make a name for himself so rapidly that he was already to incur Robert Greene's resentment as the 'upstart crow'. If such a confusing and convoluted narrative found an echo it was precisely because contemporary Englishmen also felt themselves to be living through a troubled and confusing time, when England was subject to both internal and external threats and the legitimacy of political authority was very much in question. If there is one thing that we cannot afford to lose sight of in Shakespeare's history plays it is that the anxieties displayed by Henry VI, Henry IV and Henry V about the validity of their claims to the throne had an immediate contemporary relevance since Elizabeth's retention of the throne was imperilled and undermined by the existence of Mary, Queen of Scots, who was regarded in continental Europe as having a legitimate claim. In 1586, just prior to the writing of the trilogy, Sir Anthony Babington and others had plotted a Catholic uprising in which Elizabeth was to be assassinated and Mary placed on the throne. Documents were discovered which provided incontrovertible evidence that Mary had been a willing party to this conspiracy. Thus Elizabeth herself was exposed to the contradiction that runs through *Henry VI* as to whether, in the struggle for political authority, it is appropriate to be guided by a Christian sense of tolerance and forbearance, or whether, in accordance with the doctrines of Machiavelli, it is necessary to act firmly and ruthlessly against a threat to the stability of the State. Elizabeth's initial response to this dilemma was to refrain from the use of violence against Mary – even though Mary's execution would pre-empt the possibility of yet more conspiracies in her name. But in 1587, when Mary proclaimed Philip of Spain to be her rightful heir, Elizabeth finally succumbed to the overwhelming pressure of opinion and political logic. There was now no alternative but to have Mary tried and executed. Shakespeare's plays reflect the uncertainties and vacillations of this time. It is worth noting the parallel between Henry VI's concession, in *Part III*, that York has a legitimate title to the throne and that therefore York rather than his own son should succeed him, and the fact that Elizabeth, although she strongly resisted Mary's own claims, was nevertheless compelled to recognise that Mary's son, James, was the obvious candidate to succeed her. This sense of a land in a state of continual crisis, of the national destiny suspended on a knife-edge as claims to authority are advanced that seem to be always beyond arbitration or compromise, can, without much difficulty, be projected back into an equally troubled past.

In any encounter with Shakespeare's history plays we will be hard-pressed to evade the recognition that the ideal of kingship in which they are grounded is something of a chimera. In theory all any king needs to perform his role is a clear title and a certain minimal competence, yet the relentlessly unfurling scroll of English history seems to record remarkably few incumbents who possessed either one or the other, let alone both. Like a peasant stumbling across some interminable quagmire in pursuit of a will-o'-the-wisp, English history stumbles ever forward inspired by the desperate faith that surely, somewhere, there must be solid ground. Yet the moment of stabilisation never comes – or if when it seemingly does come it almost immediately slips away. It is certainly possible to believe that the reign of Henry V, for instance, was one such clear, untroubled moment, when the power and the confidence of the monarch was reflected in unity at home and impressive conquests abroad. The spirit of such optimism is caught in the very first lines of *Henry VI, Part I* when Gloucester says 'England ne'er had a king until his time'. But what is depressing is that such a vision of full and complete kingship, like the Holy Grail, manifests itself only to disappear, for what has prompted Gloucester's encomium is the news from France of Henry's death. Moreover, as Shakespeare was subsequently forced to acknowledge in that most patriotic of plays, *Henry V*, Henry – as the son of a usurper – had no clear title to the throne of England, let alone to any territories in France, and who, far from ruling over a contented and united kingdom, was actually betrayed by his own most trusted advisers. From the ecstasy of victory over the French at Agincourt, England is immediately plunged into the depths of internal discord. Henry leaves only a baby son as king, which reopens the struggle for the throne and creates a power vacuum, which in turn leads to a rapid loss of virtually all the French territories. *Henry VI* articulates a nostalgic dream of returning to the 'norm' of perfect kingship momentarily embodied in Henry V, coupled with the gloomy *de facto* recognition that the norm is an impossibility.

The fascination of the sequence of plays from *Henry VI, Part I* to *Richard III* lies in its depiction of a seemingly remorseless succession of lurid and bloody events. Although the course of English history through the Wars of the Roses is full of unpredictable twists and turns and although the plays confound this confusion by their abrupt shifts of tone and perspective from act to act and from scene to scene – reflecting in part an incoherence in Shakespeare's narrative sources, Hall and Foxe – they nevertheless maintain a clear narrative focus by a process in which the subtext of each play becomes the main text of its successor. Thus, in *Henry VI, Part I* the main action centres on Talbot's resistance to the efforts of the French to regain their territory under Joan Pucelle against the background of the rivalry between York and Somerset, which undermines the English efforts, and Suffolk's plans to make Margaret both his mistress and Queen. In *Part II* these ambitions take centre stage as

Margaret and Suffolk plot Duke Humphrey's downfall and death. York, after masking his intentions behind Jack Cade's rebellion, is finally led to an assertion of his claim to the throne in open rebellion. *Henry VI, Part III* is built around the fluctuating fortunes of the Houses of York and Lancaster as Warwick changes sides, yet it announces a new subtext, the ambitions of Richard Crookback, which will be brought to fulfilment in *Richard III*. Yet the same plays set in motion a counter-narrative that will eventually prevail: as Henry VI, in a benediction over young Henry, Earl of Richmond and the future Henry VII, says

> If secret powers
> Suggest but truth to my divining thoughts,
> This pretty lad will prove our country's bliss,
> His looks are full of peaceful majesty;
> His head by nature fram'd to wear a crown,
> His hand to wield a sceptre; and himself
> Likely in time to bless a regal throne.

This language also suggests a future in which sanctity and political effectiveness, separated in *Henry VI*, will be providentially recombined. The succession is thus passed on across the confused historical events that seemingly intervene. As authorised by the saintly King Henry, acting under the power of divine inspiration, this becomes the new master-narrative in which all others will be incorporated and subsumed. This also figures as a particularly satisfying reversal since up till now, in a fictive Gresham's law, the bad narratives have driven out the good. Now, after the loss of the French possessions, the death of good Duke Humphrey and a progressive descent from the anarchy of Jack Cade's rebellion into the full horrors of civil war – which itself only opens the door to the uninhibited criminality of Richard III – there is now a possibility of reversing the tide. What is more doubtful is whether a mere restoration of order and legitimacy can cancel out the cumulative disintegration of moral values that the dramatic sequence powerfully depicts. To pass from Henry VI to Richard III is to cross the threshold from medieval to modern. Henry VI as a king still tries to act in the spirit of Christ, to be gentle, conciliatory and honest, but Elizabethans must have wondered if such a course of action was any longer possible, or whether it had been even then. The trajectory of English history simultaneously calls for some kind of overarching perspective that will render it bearable, yet in its recalcitrance mocks the vanity of all attempts to bring it to heel. The ideal is that of the mythical Henry V, who is a sign both of integrity and national unity, but after his death these become uncoupled – it is not possible to speak with confidence of either or to imagine that they are necessarily connected. In Talbot in *Henry VI, Part I* we have a striking emblem of the patriotic spirit; in 'good' Duke Humphrey, after Foxe, we have a man who endlessly studied his country's good, who is 'The map of Honour, truth and Loyalty', but such men are progressively and relentlessly marginalised. After Duke Humphrey's death there is no one who can represent 'England'. In *King John* Shakespeare faced a similar problem and created the character of the Bastard Faulconbridge to fill the gap. But Faulconbridge's famous lines that conclude the play:

> Nought shall make us rue
> If England to herself do rest but true

only create a further puzzle. For Shakespeare's audience could not fail to be aware that England nevertheless *had* had many occasions to rue its internal divisions over the succeeding centuries and so presumably had not remained true to itself. So the Bastard's well-intentioned advice is counsel that England has never actually been able to take, and this idea of such effortless self-transparency as legitimacy, unity, fidelity and morality figures as a 'natural' state that perennially evades all attempts to realise it. In an Elizabethan world divided, if unequally, between Protestant and Catholic, and faced with the constant possibility of internal subversion, the dream of restoring England to wholeness must have been a powerful one and Shakespeare's history plays continually return to it. But this yearning for 'England' as a validating transcendental principle, as a unity that must be deemed to persist through discord and division, only serves to demonstrate the more powerfully the absence of such an unproblematic and confidently centred entity. Even Elizabeth I, who was made the focus of a powerful propaganda effort to establish her as the definitive symbol of the country she ruled, could not but be conscious of a lack when her own position was subject to an interrogation that made so much propagandising necessary. Indeed Elizabeth must *be* England because it is only in such synechdochal terms that unity could be constructed.

True authority would bring with it an unquestioning loyalty that would preclude even the thought of treason, which in turn would generate an effortless social harmony; but such a symmetrical and circular set of conditions can only figure as a mirage that irresistibly beckons from the beyond the actuality of an unstable and unpredictable world. The crisis of authority in Shakespeare's drama affects the incumbent of the throne quite as much as his usurper double, for both would like to rule unchallenged; yet they are compelled to live with a situation in which they are tormented by insecurity and bad faith, where even the smallest cloud on the horizon can be rapidly transformed into a tempest that will wreck the commonwealth. So Henry IV's confession, 'Uneasy lies the head that wears the crown', seems not merely a personal statement but to invoke a more general state of affairs. That the role of the monarch was peculiarly onerous was, of course, a Renaissance commonplace – Montaigne suggests that 'the sharpest and most dificile profession of the world, is (in mine opinion) worthily to act and play the king'.[3] Montaigne suggests that the particular problem of being a king is that his actual personal qualities become altogether lost in the role, so that he can be nothing but the wearer of a crown. A king, surrounded by flatterers, is the last man in the world who will hear the truth. More intriguingly still, and almost in passing, Montaigne seems to prefigure Hegel in suggesting that there is a complementarity and possibility of resistance inherent in the master–servant relationship that makes it impossible for mastery to remain uncontested: 'Superiority and inferiority, maistry and subjection, are joyntly tied unto a naturall kind of envy and contestation; they must perpetually entre-spoile one another.'[4] Certainly, the Renaissance produces a much greater sophistication in an analysis of the effects of power, and Shakespeare progressively goes far beyond such pious acknowledgements of the burden of kingly office, as in Henry V's speech in Act IV, Scene I of that play, to a profounder recognition that the whole notion of authority itself is fatally flawed.

The paradox of *Henry VI* is that the ideal of a full and morally authoritative kingship is simultaneously asserted and put in question. In *Henry VI, Part II*, in particular, King Henry, though doubtless lacking the cynicism, ruthlessness and *savoir-faire* that would undoubtedly be helpful to him in combating so many unscrupulous contenders for power, appears as the model of a Christian king, who on the departure of Duke Humphrey, who has been acting as Protector, announces

> Henry will to himself
> Protector be; and God shall be my hope,
> My stay, my guide, and lantern to my feet.

Henry VI still belongs to a world that acknowledges no distinction between the sacred and the secular. He always believes the best of people and is reluctant to condemn – since judgement is the prerogative of God alone. Henry has a touching faith in the power of goodness and innocence to triumph: 'What stronger breastplate than a heart untainted!' In the face of reverses in France he is prepared to accept that this must be God's will. When his very throne is in jeopardy from the rebellion of Jack Cade that has been instigated by the Duke of York, Henry's primary concern is that there should be no unnecessary suffering:

> I'll send some holy bishop to entreat;
> For God forbid so many simple souls
> Should perish by the sword! And I myself,
> Rather than bloody war should cut them short,
> Will parley with Jack Cade their general.

At the back of this is still some notion of general welfare that must not be sacrificed to political and personal self-interest, which is, of course, the first casualty of the Wars of the Roses. Immediately there comes news that Cade with his ragged multitude has already reached Southwark and then London Bridge, which only elicits from Henry the Christ-like response 'O graceless men! they know not what they do', and a readiness to put himself in the hands of God. Thus Henry, by his conduct, supplies ammunition for the charge levelled at him by the Duke of York:

> No, thou art not king;
> Not fit to govern and rule multitudes

so that, perversely, by his treachery, York's position at the end of the play seems more convincing that it ever was at the beginning. Nevertheless Henry VI, ineffectual as he is, continues to represent the possibility of ethical behaviour in politics, albeit subject to the severest pressure.

However, in *Henry VI, Part III*, a consoling faith in the possibility of a benign authority no longer seems possible. The cruel scene in which Queen Margaret, Henry's wife, taunts and humiliates the Duke of York by crowning him with a paper crown before stabbing him in tandem with her supporter, Clifford, produces a transvaluation of all values as the result of which even a Richard Crookback can seem like an avenging angel, while Henry's position, as effectively complicit in such evil acts, is fatally compromised. When the young Richard in *Henry VI, Part II* looks down on the body of Somerset, whom he has just killed, and coolly observes 'Priests pray for enemies, but princes kill' he seems to inhabit a different universe from Henry VI, who in the preceding scene, exclaims in shocked disbelief, when Warwick and Salisbury turn against him: 'O! where is faith! O! where is loyalty?' Such incommensurability no longer exists. Now they are both compromised individuals moving across a desolate scene of civil strife. Once Henry admits that his claim to the throne is weak and concedes the substance of the Yorkist claims he is reduced to an empty cipher, who can only watch as the impotent spectator of catastrophe. Henry's helplessness is strangely echoed and counterpointed by that of Richard. Henry is a king who wishes to be a subject, Richard a subject who would be king, yet both feel oppressed and demoralised by the power of the historical forces that are set against them. Henry's comment on his own position, 'things evil got had ever bad success', has a prophetic significance where Richard is concerned. At the battle of Towton, Henry speaks nostalgically of the simplicity of the shepherd's life as the conflict sways to and fro about him. It is as if he has no purchase on reality and therefore no option other than to acquiesce in what he sees as the will of God. Richard, on the other hand, is a tormented, driven personality who seeks to compensate for his physical deformity by attaining the crown which he believes will serve to make him complete. Yet Richard feels similarly impotent, for the obstacles that bar his path seem incredibly daunting. The Machiavellian, the modern – one might even add, the Calvinist – difference is that Richard, instead of resigning himself to passivity, resolves to intensify his efforts and thereby makes himself the master and not the victim of circumstance:

> And yet I know not how to get the crown,
> For many lives stand between me and home:
> And I, – like one lost in a thorny wood,
> That rents the thorns and is rent with the thorns,
> Seeking a way, and straying from the way;
> Not knowing how to find the open air,
> But toiling desperately to find it out –
> Torment myself to catch the English crown:
> And from this torment I will free myself,
> Or hew my way out with a bloody axe.
> Why, I can smile, and murder while I smile,
> And cry 'Content!' to that that grieves my heart,
> And wet my cheeks with artificial tears,
> And frame my face to all occasions.

Richard will *be* the monster he is already presumed to be. If he is already hunchbacked, crippled and has a withered arm he will make these into signs of his election and cancel all deformity in the very fervour with which he pursues the crown, as symbol of wholeness and perfection. The irony of the situation is that he believes the crown will bring him peace and contentment when it has brought nothing but disquiet and misery to those that have actually worn it. As Henry VI says in the preceding scene:

> My crown is in my heart, not on my head;
> Not deck'd with diamonds, and Indian stones,
> Nor to be seen: my crown is call'd content;
> A crown it is that seldom kings enjoy.

Richard's symbolic role in *Henry VI* and *Richard III* is to reassert the principle of male authority which, as Hall would have it, has been undermined by Henry's unwise marriage to Margaret, and Edward IV's equally imprudent match with Lady Jane Grey. In each case a king, besotted with feminine beauty, not only causes widespread offence but allows himself to be ruled by his wife's self-regarding and injudicious counsels. Even 'good' Duke Humphrey is humiliated and driven from office through the schemes of his ambitious wife. So Richard is resolved, above all, to be a conqueror of women, as his wooing of Anne by her father's coffin demonstrates. When Clarence explains that his imprisonment has been brought about by witchcraft, Richard exlaims: 'Why, this is it, when men are rul'd by women.' Richard subsequently attributes his own misfortunes to female machinations:

> See how I am bewitched! Behold, mine arm
> Is like a blasted sapling wither'd up!
> And this is Edward's wife that monstrous witch,
> Consorted with the harlot, strumpet Shore,
> That by their witchcraft thus have marked me.

Women, symbolically and literally, are the source of all pollution, disease, imperfection and corruption. The invocation of prostitution here hints at the well-known ravages of veneral disease of which woman is deemed the bearer. So in his perverse way Richard is seeking to be a principle of health. Since he fears no one and need obey no one, he is, it would seem, uniquely fitted to be that focus of authority that a divided England lacks. Yet the irony of the situation is apparent in the incongruous language with which Buckingham purports to persuade a reluctant Richard to assume the throne:

> This noble isle doth want her proper limbs;
> Her face defac'd with scars of infamy,
> Her royal stock graft with ignoble plants,
> And almost shoulder'd in the swallowing gulf
> Of dark forgetfulness and deep oblivion;
> Which to recur, we heartily solicit
> Your gracious self to take on you the charge
> And kingly government of this your land.

Here Buckingham presents an England that is damaged and deformed, and Richard as the principle of wholeness that can make all good: he must cure England as he would have the crown cure him. Richard's deformity is no longer an accident of birth but has become the comprehensive figure through which the state of England can be represented. His hunchbacked shadow broods

over the land as the marker of a malign new Machiavellian order
that is also represented by the sign of the hog.

Nevertheless in the final scenes Richard does acquire both
pathos and grandeur. His determination to make his way
regardless and to resist all contrary portent, as when he exclaims
'Be opposite, all planets of good luck', proclaims a courageous
and unquenchable spirit, but beneath it all he is a fatally split
personality. When it comes to the last his self-created identity is
vulnerable and cracks under the pressure of extreme moral
isolation. Richard constitutes himself under his own gaze, but,
since he prides himself on a relentless capacity to interrogate and
unmask he can never finally live in peace with himself:

> What do I fear? Myself? There's none else by;
> Richard loves Richard, that is, I and I.
> Is there a murderer here? No. Yes, I am!
> They fly. What, from myself? Great reason why,
> Lest I revenge? What, myself upon myself?
> Alack, I love myself. Wherefore? For any good
> That I myself have done unto myself?
> O no, alas, I rather hate myself
> For hateful deeds committed by myself.
> I am a villain – yet I lie, I am not!
> Fool, of thyself speak well! Fool, do not flatter.

Shakespeare makes Richard into a moralistic emblem of false
consciousness, which, in its doubleness has the effect of
humanising him since he is shown to be capable of guilt and
remorse. Yet there is a psychological truth here nevertheless
which is that, despite his protestations, Richard actually is unable
to love himself and thus always imperils the mastery he seeks. He
is destroyed by the scepticism and cynicism that he himself
embodies and which his own 'I' is uanble to resist. His identity is
perpetually destabilised by his own relentless self-interrogation.
Richard can never truly be that principle of authority, despite
being a consummate actor on the stage of the world, because he
lacks the inner certitude it calls for.

The paradox of a special authority that is presumed to be
invested in the role of a king, but which is in practice everywhere
denied, is nowhere more evident than in *Richard II* (1595). For it
was the displacement of Richard by Bolingbroke that inaugurated

the whole ritual of challenge and counter-challenge by the Houses of York and Lancaster that affected English political life for 200 years and made kingship an essentially contested concept. Yet Richard is a king whose legitimacy, uniquely, is never in dispute, but who is nevertheless able to exert so little political, authority that he scarcely needs to be actually overthrown. So the question as to what actually makes for royal authority is once more thrown open to debate, without any of the implicit guidelines that had previously governed it. Of all Shakespeare's plays *Richard II* is the one most fraught with contemporary implications, the one that gestures most pointedly at actual political circumstances of the time. Its pertinence is attested to by the fact that a play on this subject was performed at the Globe on 7 February 1601, the night before Essex's abortive rebellion against the Queen. Whether or not this play was by Shakespeare the circumstances surrounding the deposition of Richard II did afford both precedent and historic justification for rebellion against a ruling monarch. This is not to say that *Richard II* is *ipso facto* seditious since it is full of warnings about the dangers of overthrowing a legitimate ruler. Critics of the claim that the play is an explicit contemporary allegory have rightly emphasised that the political situation at the original time of writing was very different from that in 1601, when Essex, completely excluded from power, felt that he had no alternative but to rebel. Nevertheless it is hard to resist the conclusion that the play *does* directly address questions of moment in the 1590s. For one thing the first act of *Richard II* is strangely irrelevant and obscure. The charges made by Bolingbroke against Mowbray are couched in a rhetoric as opaque and nebulous as Mowbray's own protestations of innocence. The one fact that would make matters clear – that Richard himself instigated Mowbray's murder of the Duke of Gloucester – is never brought out into the open. One way of dealing with the problem, proposed by A. P. Rossitter, is to suggest that an audience would have known of Richard's complicity from the earlier *Woodstock*,[5] and that therefore they would have been fully conscious of the irony of a situation in which Richard pretended to adjudicate between Bolingbroke and his henchman, while Bolingbroke masks a deliberate challenge to the authority of the King behind indignant and altogether insincere protestations of treason. I would want to argue that Shakespeare was not greatly concerned with the pros and cons of the matter and simply began the play here because it afforded an opportunity to present Richard exercising his power as king in a dramatic and spectacular way. It is not the source or origin of later troubles, for if it were it would need to be more legible than it is. Rather it is a decoy, an apparent attempt to pull the play back into the obscure context of medieval chivalry which thus deflects attention away from the full force of the criticisms levelled at Richard by John of Gaunt on his death-bed, since these are, simultaneously, cogent objections to the Elizabethan style of government. Yet even Gaunt's rhetoric is slippery and evasive. How few citations of his famous apostrophe to England manage to acknowledge that this greatness lies in the past or get to the heart of the matter, which is that

> This land of such dear souls, this dear dear land,
> Dear for her reputation through the world,
> Is now leas'd out – I die pronouncing it –
> Like to a tenement or pelting farm

that England, once 'bound in with the triumphant sea'

> is now bound in with shame,
> With inky blots and rotten parchment bonds.

In part this is because the obliquity of the language and its context as the speech of an old and dying man seems to suggest nothing more than a general nostalgia for the good old days, combined with some vague implication of corruption and improper influence. Nevertheless this scene, when taken in conjunction with other allusions in the play, presents a fairly comprehensive indictment of Richard, which also corresponds closely to the continuing critique of the abuse of royal power as it develops through the reign of Elizabeth and her Jacobean successors:

(a) Richard is charged with innovation and of having departed from the old, customary ways.

(b) He has surrounded himself with evil, self-serving, flattering counsellors in the form of Bushy, Bagot and Greene.

(c) Acting under their false advice he has infringed the law and denied traditional rights by appropriating Bolingbroke's lands and by imposing heavy taxes without consent.

(d) Instead of ruling in the best interests of all his subjects he has turned England into a source of personal profit for himself and his favourites, to whom he offers colossal and wholly unjustified tax-farming privileges that must be paid for by the people.

(e) The law, instead of being the safeguard of individual rights, is transformed into an instrument of oppression.

(f) Through this abuse of royal power he has forfeited all right to be regarded as the legitimate king as his legitimacy is grounded in his relationship with the people: 'Landlord of England art thou now, not king.'

Although the granting of monopolies and tax-farming privileges was still at a comparatively undeveloped stage, and was very far from approaching the excesses that were to become routine under James I, it was already the subject of adverse comment and audiences of the time would have been conscious of contemporary equivalents of such 'caterpillars of the commonwealth' as Bushy, Bagot and Greene. It is not unreasonable to surmise that *Richard II* was by nature of a veiled warning against undue favouritism and the abuse of royal power by a writer who was aligned with the cause of Essex. In its oblique way the play comes across with what was very much the Essex line: that the monarchy needs to be sustained by a broad spectrum of popular support and that this can easily be forfeited either through an over-indulgence of particular favourites, or through the arbitrary exercise of power against those who are correspondingly out of favour, such as Bolingbroke or Essex. The ruler is morally obliged to be even-handed and to maintain a balance. The argument *Richard II* presses home is not so much that Bolingbroke is to be copied – even though Essex was eventually to do just that with disastrous consequences – as that, to avert the possibility of dissention and discontent within the realm, the example of Richard is one to be studiously avoided.

Nevertheless *Richard II* manages to combine this critical intention with a more complex exploration of the problem of authority. In the acutely aware yet abject figure of Richard II, Shakespeare brings into sharp focus the contradiction that had been present all through *Henry VI* and *Richard III*: the royal authority which should be full is actually always empty. The crown, far from being the esteemed prize and 'sweet fruition' that Tamburlaine spoke of, is always experienced by its possessor as a lack, since the very set of circumstances that enabled it to be gained makes inescapable the possibility that it can be lost. Kingship, far from being a repository of stability and security that it ostensibly should be, is, even in Richard's own account of it, perpetually encompassed by violence and anxiety:

> For God's sake let us sit upon the ground
> And tell sad stories of the death of kings:
> How some have been depos'd, some slain in war,
> Some haunted by the ghosts they have deposed,
> Some poisoned by their wives, somme sleeping kill'd
> All murthered – for within the hollow crown
> That round the mortal temples of a king
> Keeps death his court, and there the antic sits,
> Scoffing his state and grinning at his pomp,
> Allowing him a breath, a little scene,
> To monarchise, be fear'd, and kill with looks.

The very word 'monarchise' is shocking. It suggests that kingship is not a firm and enduring social function but a transitory theatre, where the gestures are as empty as the part that is being played. What makes this doubly disturbing is that this comes from the lips of a man who profoundly believes that the sources of royal authority are divine. Richard's pathos is generated by the discrepancy between this faith and the actual circumstances that falsify it: by the fact that he who actually *is* king nevertheless only *seems* to be so. The rights and wrongs of Bolingbroke's *coup* are already beyond discussion and debate since their *de facto* power sets things up in a certain way and makes them judge and jury in their own case with the anointed monarch their helpless victim. Northumberland and John of Gaunt appeal to a myth of immaculate kingship in terms of which Richard is found wanting, but Richard well knows that such a thing is impossible since no king can be deemed beyond judgement unless he is sole judge himself. Northumberland is determined to restore the truth and integrity by supporting the usurper, Bolingbroke:

> If then we shall shake off our slavish yoke,
> Imp out our drooping country's broken wing,
> Redeem from broking pawn the blemish'd crown,
> Wipe off the dust that hides our sceptre's gilt,
> And make high majesty look like itself.

Yet this single purifying act by which authentic kingship is to be restored only produces a deep sense of anxiety in Henry IV about his own tenure of the throne, which leads to the murder of Richard and his own departure in penance to the Holy Land. Having purged the land Henry now vainly seeks to purge himself of the guilt that that purgation itself created. The crown is yet more blemished than before. The dream of 'high majesty' beyond all such contingencies remains elusive.

In *Richard II* the brittle nature of authority is made all too evident. After the opening scenes Bolingbroke and his supporters consistently refuse to accept that Richard is actually king and withhold all recognition from him. Even John of Gaunt's suggestion to his son that exile will be the more tolerable if only he will

> Think not the king did banish thee,
> But thou the king

proves prophetic, for it is just this reversal of roles that is the psychological precondition for successful rebellion. Richard himself grasps that Bolingbroke has already put himself in the position of a future king and that he no longer thinks of himself as a subject:

> Off goes his bonnet to an oyster-wench;
> A brace of draymen bid God speed him well,
> And had the tribute of his supple knee,
> With 'Thanks, my countrymen, my loyal friends' –
> As were our England in reversion his,
> And he our subjects' next degree in hope.

The ambiguity of this 'supple knee' recurs when Bolingbroke once more kneels before Richard, although he is now wholly within his power, so that in receiving such 'deference' Richard is conscious that he does not possess it and that he is indeed only 'monarchising'. What remains momentarily is only the name of king. The transvaluation of values that occurs in the seizure of power is brought out in York's reference to 'plume-plucked Richard' – an allusion to Aesop's story in which the crow is detected in stolen plumage, which the other birds pluck away. The metaphor transforms Richard into an imposter and suggests that he can be deprived as easily of his authority as of his royal robes; there is no indissoluble connection between man and king. Richard's impossible task is to maintain such a powerful representation of kingly being that he will continue to validate his divine commission in the face of a world that refuses to acknowledge it:

> God save the king! Will no man say amen?
> Am I both priest and clerk? Well then, amen.
> God save the king! although I be not he;
> And, yet amen, if heaven do think him me.

Richard is psychologically unnerved by the fact that his kingly 'pretensions' find no echo. He is demoralised by the extent of the popular revolt against him and fears that – *vox populi* – this may be a sign that God has licensed the revolt against him:

> Strives Bolingbroke to be as great as we?
> Greater he shall not be. If he serve God,
> We'll serve Him too, and be his fellow so.
> Revolt our subjects? that we cannot mend;
> They break their faith to God as well as us.

In this convoluted utterance Richard both insists on his divinely sanctioned authority and concedes that God may actually be on the opposite side – that it may indeed be, as York subsequently says, that 'heaven hath a hand in these events'. The agony of Richard is not just that he is deprived of the throne but that it is humiliatingly implied that he never truly possessed it, that he has always been 'a mockery king of snow'. In smashing the mirror in which he sees his face, Richard symbolically demonstrates that his whole identity has been an illusion. If Richard himself seems insubstantial so does the God whom he so ineffectually calls upon, even though the Bishop of Carlisle speaks prophetically of massive retribution to come. The world of the play is ominously secular which is why, for Richard, it is so unnerving.

By comparison with *Richard II, Julius Caesar* seems closed off from the possibility of contemporary reference. Of all Shakespeare's plays it seems the easiest to overinterpret because of its fidelity to the circumstances narrated in Plutarch and because it seems content to remain within the parameters of the Roman world. The play is a discourse on Roman virtue as exemplified by Brutus, where Brutus seems like an antique statue: noble and heroic without doubt, yet frozen into an attitude that seems altogether alien to the plasticity of the Elizabethan present. In Plutarch's version of things, great men fall because they eventually lose the Fortune, conceived of as a beneficent power or form of vital energy, that had hitherto favoured them. For a while the hero's ambitions are in harmony with the world but suddenly and unexpectedly he finds himself out of phase with it, his downfall heralded by ominous signs and portents that annouce a change in the political weather. This sense of the arbitrariness and the obscurity of events in *Julius Caesar* is echoed in *Henry V*, written at about the same time (1599), where Fluellen deliberately interrupts Pistol's rather ridiculous alliterations on the subject of blinded fortune in order to draw out the full significance of the figure:

> By your patience, Ensign Pistol: Fortune is painted blind, with a muffler afore her eyes, to signify to you that fortune is blind. And she is painted also with a wheel, to signify to you – which is the moral of it – that she is turning and inconstant and mutability and variation. And her foot, look you, is fixed upon a sperical stone, which rolls and rolls and rolls. In good truth, the poet makes a most excellent description of it. Fortune is an excellent moral.

The contemporary spectators would have found much in *Julius Caesar* that corresponded to their own sense of an uncertain world and they were as much preoccupied with signs, auguries and portents as ever the Romans were. They were also living in what seemed a 'strange-disposed time', marked by 'strange eruptions' and untoward events. There had been the comet of 1577, the earthquake of 1580, the plague of 1592 and a run of disastrous harvests from 1594 to 1597. Their significance was heightened by England's precarious isolation from a hostile Catholic Europe, by the threat of renewed invasion and by the threat of internal subversion. Puritan ministers were as eager as Roman soothsayers to decipher these auguries and to interpret them both as warnings not to tarry in the work of Reformation and as evidence that the world was entering the last days. Moreover, London with its motley crowds of idlers, vagabonds and masterless men, with its pleasure-loving citizenry thronging the theatres, bear-pits and taverns, must have seemed just such a bloated metropolis as imperial Rome. Again, what *Julius Caesar* depicts is a progressive loss of power and autonomy on the part of the Roman élite as Caesar, surrounded by an army of sycophants and flatterers, is pressed toward the assumption of an untrammelled imperial authority. As Cassius says:

> Why, man, he doth bestride the narrow world
> Like a Colossus, and we petty men
> Walk under his huge legs and peep about
> To find ourselves dishonourable graves.

In the same way many members of the aristocracy at the court of Elizabeth were becoming increasingly discontented at their own inability to influence patronage and policy as the threads of power were being increasingly drawn together into the hands of one favoured minister. This had already taken place under Burghley, but on his death in 1598 it rapidly became clear that, far from there being any prospect of the 'out' group being restored to grace and favour, they were, in anything, going to find it even harder-going under his son, Robert Cecil. From this perspective Rome, like England, seems irresistibly set on a steeply descending curve, and Brutus, as the man who tries to stop it, is therefore a figure of more than passing interest.

The most significant difference between *Julius Caesar* and the Plutarch of Thomas North is that whereas North is in absolutely no doubt that Plutarch's heroes are noble – to the point of leaning over backwards in his translation to intensify their greatness – Shakespeare is a good deal more disenchanted. In *Julius Caesar* the very idea of nobility seems to fall under a cloud. Caesar is simultaneously timorous, greedy and overbearing. Antony is obsequious, insincere and manipulative. Cassius is self-centred, envious and full of bad faith. So when Antony, in paying tribute to Brutus at the end of the play calls him 'the noblest Roman of them all', the encomium may well seem less enthusiastic than its clarity would suggest. Antony is hardly the stalwart fellow portrayed by Thomas North and there are many other inglorious roles. So in his integrity and unwavering rectitude Brutus is unique. Rome itself, instead of being a natural amphitheatre of human greatness, figures rather as a scene of ignominy that calls for the most determined and spirited resistance. So it is as if Shakespeare has recast Plutarch in terms of Seneca's *Octavia*, for while the Rome of Caesar is not yet that of Nero, the writing is already on the wall. What Shakespeare intensifies in his presentation of these figures is their alienation. Caesar is so conscious of the widespread resentment that his rise to power has provoked and of the consequent precariousness of his own position that he must needs distrust everyone. Yet the conspirators arrayed against him fear betrayal from within their own ranks. Brutus himself, though unfailingly honest and direct in all his dealings, is nevertheless compelled to bottle up his feelings so intensely within him that his wife Portia stabs her thigh in frustration at having to sleep with a man who will not communicate his fears and anxieties to her. It is symptomatic of Caesar's rise and the atmosphere that has been created that open communication, grounded in democratic values, is no longer possible. After Caesar's murder Brutus' speech, uncompromising, blunt and straightforward goes down like a lead brick, while Antony's artful rhetoric, interwoven with the prospect of bribes, provokes the crowd to hysteria and violence. Liberty is already little more than an empty word. The pressure of the time is such as to produce more complex forms of interiority. When Cassius taxes Brutus at the beginning of the play for being unduly reserved and distant, Brutus responds by saying

> Cassius,
> Be not deceived: if I have veiled my look,
> I turn the trouble of my countenance
> Merely upon myself. Vexed I am
> Of late with passions of some difference,
> Conceptions only proper to myself.

so that, with hindsight, we can already discern the germination of *Hamlet* and that paradoxical mode of articulation whereby the individual is most completely himself only in that which cannot be socially spoken. The dilemma of Brutus, in the face of the disintegration of the Roman Republic and the ambitions of Caesar, is that in arrogating to himself the exclusive right to represent the moral authority of the Republic he cancels the values in the name of which he would speak. Yet he does seem justified since no one else shares his sense of the urgency of the hour or can grasp that the spirit which should sustain it has already vanished. Brutus meets only with apathy, narcissism and self-serving ambition.

The wider perspective has been lost. But as Rome collapses around him Brutus endeavours to remain true to himself and his principles. Despite everything Brutus is at one with himself, a man unbending and implacable in his refusal of 'this age's yoke'. Brutus, truly, is cast in bronze. Never again will Shakespeare be able to present the hero in this way.

The equivocal and troubling status of Brutus, the classical hero who offers to the modern age a pattern which it knows it cannot follow, emerges with particular clarity in *Hamlet*. The very possibility of nobility in ancient Rome rested on a very specific social formation. The traditional class conflict between patrician and plebeian could be moderated by the emergence of leaders who could command more broadly based support through their personal charisma, military success and political adroitness. There was always a popular dimension to the wielding of power under the Roman Republic. Those who sought political authority knew they had to be able to deliver the goods. But equally they knew that there could be no arguing with success. The Roman people would hail in rapturous acclamation anyone who enhanced the power and influence of Rome. Under Elizabeth, however, this was very far from being the case. Essex and Ralegh, to cite two obvious names, were not invariably successful; but their grievance was both that they had received insufficient credit for what they had done and that there was no guarantee that the most triumphant general or conquistador would receive any acknowledgement at all. Success abroad could be cancelled out by a whispering campaign at home. Obviously, as England was a monarchy and not a republic on the Roman model, what a ruler looked for was good and faithful servants, who could be relied upon to be cautious, discreet and business-like, not flashy and flamboyant military superstars who might even overshadow the monarch in popular favour and whose extravagant demands for reward consorted ill with the overriding need for retrenchment and financial cutbacks. Elizabeth maintained and consolidated her power at Court by playing off different figures against one another and by perennially dangling before them the prospect of a future felicity for all who would perform meritorious deeds in her service – without in any way feeling called upon to deliver. It was a try-your-strength machine where no amount of effort could guarantee ringing the bell. No claims were self-evident. England, from Elizabeth to James, is a society where esteem is no longer based on birth, the profession of arms or a large body of retainers, but on influence at Court. The arts of war are driven out by the more devious arts of peace. In *Hamlet* this is reflected in the fact that while Hamlet's father was an energetic and forceful military leader, who 'in an angry parle . . . smote the sledded Polacks on the ice', and who by his valoriousness in single-handed combat was able to extend his realm, Hamlet himself is no more than a hanger-on at Court. Much of the glamour that attaches itself to Fortinbras in Hamlet's eyes stems from the fact that he comes from a simpler, more war-like culture, where the pursuit of greatness is still a possibility. Before the example of Fortinbras Hamlet feels rebuked as if he is incapable of dispelling the ignominy of the Court by killing Claudius he cuts an even more ignominious figure himself:

> Examples gross as earth exhort me,
> Witness this army of such mass and charge,
> Led by a delicate and tender prince,
> Whose spirit, with divine ambition puff'd,
> Makes mouths at the invisible event,
> Exposing what is mortal and unsure
> To all that fortune, death, and danger dare,
> Even for an eggshell.

The Court of Elizabeth, like that of Elsinore, does not produce risk-takers so much as people like Polonius. The pertinence of this analysis seems confirmed by the fact that subsequently it was not to be England that took the lead in defending Protestantism in Europe but Sweden under the bold, not to say reckless, generalship of Gustavus Adolphus. For in England this was a style that had already gone out of fashion.

   Hamlet epitomises the dilemma of authority in the age of Renaissance and Reformation. Although Claudius is a murderous usurper, whose authority is wholly illegitimate, Hamlet is either incapable or unwilling to assume the authority that could righteously overthrow him. Despite the urgency and compelling detail of the Ghost's narration Hamlet is reluctant to proceed. The Ghost may be a malignant spirit. The familiar injunction to revenge flies in the face of Christian doctrine. The story itself is doubtful. Hamlet asks for incontrovertible evidence of Claudius guilt. Yet *Hamlet* is the product of an age that knows how little there is that cannot be controverted or called into question. In the age of the book, in the polyphonic confusion of competing voices, authorities no longer seem harmonising and mutually supportive, but serve to promote doubt and uncertainty as they are rallied under different flags. Can man be both the glory of God's universe *and* utterly worthless without God's saving grace? Is the Pope the Vicar of God or the Whore of Babylon? Can suicide be the definitive act of a noble spirit as with Brutus, or must it rather be seen as a mortal sin, as Augustine insisted. For Montaigne such an exposure to so many distinctive viewpoints – expressive as they are of the diversity of human culture – could only lead to scepticism and a humbled recognition of human limitation. The strange fruit of a more searching intellectual inquiry is to perceive the frailty of the very enterprise: Montaigne withdraws from the blank skies and parching heat of the desert to sit beneath the expansive and cooling shade of custom. Calvin, contrariwise, sees the Bible as the one book that can give unshakeable authority, the sole text in a corrupted world that can confidently be relied upon as a guide to action. Or, in fictional terms, is man to be Hamlet or Don Quixote? In his *Our Lord, Don Quixote* Unamuno compares Don Quixote with Ignatius Loyola, the founder of the Jesuits, and points out that in their passion for righteousness and their self-authorising self-confidence they are strangely alike:

And how indeed was it possible that Ignatius dared speak of virtue and vice when he had no licence, nor title, nor degree conferred by any tribunal whatsoever? And who gave Don Quixote permission to call himself a knight-errant, or what licence did he have to go about righting wrongs and correcting abuses, even those abuses not corrected by the grave ecclesiastics for doing do?[6]

Loyola and Don Quixote enter a world that has become dangerously unsettled and reassert the possibility of authority in a world that lacks it – even though they themselves have no 'authority' to do so. They have confidence in their ability to restore order, in their power to reverse what seems to others like an irresistible tide that is sweeping men away from the rock of fidelity and truth. Don Quixote proclaims to his faithful squire:

Sancho, my friend, you must know that, by the will of Heaven,

I was born in this iron age of ours to revive the age of gold or, as it is generally called, the golden age. It is for me that are reserved perils, mighty feats, and valorious exploits.[7]

As Don Quixote knows that he is going against the grain of the time he is not at all surprised to encounter problems or difficulties, or to find himself in deeply unsettling circumstances that seem to contradict all that he has read in the chivalric romances. On the contrary, it was just what he had expected. The romances are such an indispensable and unshakeable guide to a world that bears no relation to them because they can equip him with a psychological armature that is altogether impervious to its blandishments, wiles and deceptions. They have the power to convey truth in a world that lacks it. The knight errant is his own principle of legitimacy. Don Quixote categorically refuses to acknowledge either the impositions or the authority of the modern state with a bravado that the imprisoned Cervantes must certainly have envied:

> Tell me, who was the dolt who signed a warrant of arrest against such a knight as I am? Who was it who did not know that knights errant are exempt from all jurisdiction, that their law is their sword, their charters their statutes their own will? Who was the idiot, I repeat, who does not know that there is no patent of nobility with so many privileges and immunities as a knight errant receives on the day when he is knighted and undertakes the stern practice of chivalry? What knight errant has ever paid tax, duty, queen's pattern, money, customs, or toll?[8]

Don Quixote seeks to carry on as if the struggle to impose a centralised authority was not already well under way and refuses to accept that it could have any legitimacy anyway. Cervantes, as a not very successful tax collector for the Spanish government, must have relished the irony of this also. Don Quixote pointedly contrasts the free, unbounded and self-determining existence of the knight errant with the constricted horizons of the courtier:

> For the courtiers do not stir from their rooms or beyond the threshold of their court, but travel over the whole world merely by looking at a map, without a farthing's cost or suffering heat

or cold, hunger, or thirst. But we, the true knights errant, measure the whole earth with our own feet, in sun, in cold, and beneath the sky, exposed to the inclemencies of the heavens by night and day, on foot and on horse.[9]

Hamlet finds Denmark and the Court just such a prison. He suffocates in an atmosphere where every word and thought is subject to royal surveillance and where honesty and openness are necessarily precluded. The possibility of radically contradicting the world which Cervantes so ironically asserts, Shakespeare, with equal irony, denies. Hamlet cannot summon up the intellectual and moral clarity which would enable him to purge the Court of the evil that inhabits it and even if he could he would continue to doubt whether there would be any point to it. At bottom the enterprise can only seem – 'quixotic'.

Unlike Don Quixote, Hamlet is unable to insulate himself from the degraded world in which he finds himself. He is conscious of the all-encompassing moral pollution at Court as something that threatens to invade every aspect of his being. Hamlet wears black for so long not only to proclaim his grief for his dead father but to demonstrate his resistance to the new order, his determination to stand apart from it. But in practice this is not so easy. To all appearances the Court of Claudius is calm, well ordered and decorous. At the centre of it is Hamlet's own mother. As Roland Mushat Frye has pointed out in *The Renaissance Hamlet*, the circumstances of *Hamlet*, far from seeming fictitious or remote, would have brought to mind the hasty remarriage of Mary, Queen of Scots, only three months after the death of her husband Darnley, to the man who was known to be his murderer, the Earl of Bothwell.[10] This episode and its parallel in *Hamlet* emphasises the frank and utterly shameless espousal of violence in the political world of the Renaissance, where crime could itself mark its perpetrator as the bearer of the new legitimacy. Although Claudius's crime is ostensibly veiled, the impropriety of his remarriage and the ambiguity of the circumstances that surround it creates a wall of silence at Court that cannot be breached. In rebuking Hamlet for his unduly protracted grief, Claudius hypocritically pretends that his own brutal action must be taken as the will of God and death, no matter how violent, as simply part of the order of nature:

> Fie, 'tis a fault to heaven,
> A fault against the dead, a fault to nature,
> To reason most absurd, whose common theme
> Is death of fathers, and who still hath cried
> From the first corse till he that died today,
> 'This must be so.'

For Hamlet the evil in Claudius' action is not simply a matter of murder and incest, scandalous as that may be, but even more that it transforms every single person at Court, from Hamlet's mother to Hamlet himself, into his guilty and wholly tainted accomplice. So wherever Hamlet looks, whether it is at Rosenkrantz and Guildenstern, at Polonius or Laertes, at Gertrude or Ophelia, it is this contagion that he sees. So long as Claudius possesses power and authority all moral values are turned upside down. As Hamlet says to his mother when he rebukes her for the betrayal of his father;

> Forgive my this my virtue;
> For in the fatness of these pursy times
> Virtue itself of vice must pardon beg.

Hamlet himself is infected by the corruption because he well knows that for him to perform the cleansing act of killing Claudius would be simultaneously to cause his mother considerable grief and, at the same time, to expose her as a figure of public scandal. Yet to do nothing can only intensify his disillusionment and self-disgust and indefinitely protract an already intolerable state of affairs. The Court is nothing more than a mechanism for perpetuating itself and legitimating itself. It enforces compliance through peer-group pressure and the expectation of reward, backed up by the use of informers against dissident elements and the systematic practice of monitoring and surveillance. In this world of distorted communication and deceit the King must always know more. He should never be in the position of wishing to be better informed. The deck is eternally stacked in his favour. Claudius can manipulate to such good purpose that he can use Laertes as a tool to get rid of Hamlet and then set up the duel in such a way that Hamlet cannot win. The Court is a world of masquerade where nothing is ever quite what it appears to be and where even the noblest and most honourable action will be rendered ignominious by the base setting in which it so desperately figures. Hamlet is noble, against all the odds, but he may not necessarily appear to be so. It is therefore quite crucial that Horatio should not take poison in the antique style, in order finally to lay bare what would otherwise be an inglorious and indecipherable pattern of events:

> O God, Horatio, what a wounded name,
> Things standing thus unknown, shall I leave behind me.
> If thou didst ever hold me in thy heart,
> Absent thee from felicity a while,
> And in this harsh world draw thy breath in pain
> To tell my story.

At Court, truth is the first casualty.

Although classical antiquity is everywhere invoked in *Hamlet* the similitude is invariably ironic. For little Denmark can never be mightly Rome, and Elsinore is worlds away from the ponderous heroics of a Senecan Troy that acquires such exemplary significance in 'The Mousetrap'. If the supernatural visitations of the ghost recall the time when

> In the most high and palmy state of Rome,
> A little ere the mightest Julius fell,
> The graves stood tenantless and the sheeted dead
> did squeak and gibber in the Roman streets

Claudius is scarcely Caesar and even the Ghost is more than a little bathetic. We learn that Polonius once played the part of Julius on the stage, so that Hamlet, in accidentally killing him, figures as a kind of maladroit, pasteboard Brutus. While it might seem entirely fitting that Macbeth should introduce the figure of 'Tarquin's ravishing strides' before his assassination of Duncan, it seems preposterous for Hamlet to disclaim any ambition of being a Nero. Violence is out of place at Elsinore – the death of Polonius is shocking just because it is so little expected or intended and we might almost expect Judge Brach to pop up from Ibsen's *Hedda Gabler* to exclaim 'People don't do such things.' After the performance of 'The Mousetrap' on which Hamlet sets so much store and which is intended to hold up the mirror to Claudius' crime, Gertrude can only offer the anti-climactic and all too genteel response: 'The lady doth protest too much, methinks.' Nothing must disrupt the tyranny of decorum or bring the courtly spectacle to a halt. There is simply no space for high seriousness or heroic action in such a banal environment. In his famous soliloquy 'To be or not to be', Hamlet is not simply hesitating between alternatives, he is endeavouring to reconstitute the sense of possibility in which action and the moment of decision could be laden with significance. Hamlet suggests that under the pitiless gaze of introspection

> enterprises of great pitch and moment
> With this regard their currents turn awry
> And lose the name of action

but it is also the case that at Court such enterprises become problematic by definition. Claudius, 'a king of shreds and patches', has surrounded himself with such ridiculous figures as Osric, Rosenkrantz and Guildenstern, Polonius. The Court demands to be parodied in order to restore a sense of perspective, so that the mockery of Hamlet's feigned madness is the most effective assault upon it. Hamlet's sustained mockery drains the Court of all dignity and significance, but correspondingly diminishes the scale of Hamlet's task which is the more baffling because it is at once inconsequential and vast. Hamlet seeks not so much to change things as to disturb and unsettle. Claudius impatiently asks

> And can you by no drift of conference
> Get from him why he puts on this confusion,
> Grating so harshly all his days of quiet
> With turbulent and dangerous lunacy?

He seeks mischief rather than vengeance; to question authority rather than assume it. In *Hamlet* all moral certainties dissolve. Action appears simply as a vain attempt to resolve the irresolvable and to replace one conundrum by another, so that what Plutarch perceived as greatness may have been nothing more than a frantic, impetuous blindness. Hamlet does not seek authority because it has become synonymous with infamy.

In *Troilus and Cressida* Shakespeare projected this disillusionment back into the legendary past of classical tradition. The archetypal heroes of Western culture are displayed as petulant, narcissistic figures whose 'greatness' is self-consciously fabricated into the myths which will put an oppressive curse on all the generations to come. As 'The princes orgulous their high blood chafed' strut up and down outside Troy it is hard to detect any dignity in their conduct, let alone nobility or valour, and Ulysses' unavailing attempt to call them to order invokes a system of ideal values that proves to have been conspicuous only by its absence even at the very beginning of narrative time. The Shakespearean conservatives are certainly right in thinking that Ulysses' great speech on order shows that Shakespeare was anxious about the course of contemporary events; but what he was actually preoccupied with was the de-stabilising impact of the struggle between Catholicism and Protestantism with its terrible premonition of the last days:

> But when the planets
> In evil mixture to disorder wander,
> What plagues and what portents, what mutiny,
> What raging of the sea, shaking of earth,
> Commotion in the winds, frights, changes, horrors,
> Divert and crack, rend and deracinate
> The unity and married calm of states
> Quite from their fixture!

It is *this* that is undermining the position of European monarchs. Where they themselves wander in disorder is in imagining that Shakespeare believed that there could be any simple answers. In his exploration of history he finds conflict and division at every moment. Even the eternal, marmoreal, classical frieze proves – when restored to living motion – as chaotic and transitory as anything else. There has never been any secure authority. What *Troilus and Cressida* disquietingly confirms is that order needs always to be invoked because it is so exasperatingly and perennially absent. Hector here is the main of principle with his unimpeachable fidelity, his insistence on his own consistency

> I must not break my faith.
> You know me dutiful

leads only to an ignominious death at the hands of Achilles and his accomplices. Hector strives to preserve the ideal of heroism in a world that cannot sustain it. Even he comes after. Shakespeare insists that the immemorial world of Troy was in reality as evanescent, fugitive and opportunist as any other, but that Western man has been unable to come to terms with such an irresistible vacancy and has therefore endlessly struggled to adorn a sordid tale in the hope of also pointing a moral.

This spectre of absent authority haunts *Measure for Measure,* a play in which authority is nevertheless forcibly asserted. For as long as the Duke actually remains at the head of affairs in Vienna the laws are widely disregarded and he is incapable of maintaining control. Paradoxically he can only regain control by leaving the city and assigning his powers to his deputy, Angelo. Like many a Renaissance despot the Duke discovers that the great advantage of delegated authority is that it becomes possible to surround his magisterial clarity in a penumbra of deep ambiguity. For behind a law that seems always arbitrary, prejudicial and unfair, it is always possible to infer the existence of a higher justice that is capable of mercy, honesty and truth. The Duke can only serve to embody this transcendental justice by being elsewhere, while Angelo is able to expose the true face of justice as cruel, hypocritical and indifferent to human suffering because the authority he wields is allegedly inauthentic. The possibility opens up of questioning power and of exposing its irrationality, of recognising that

> man, proud man,
> Dress'd in a little brief authority,
> Most ignorant of what he's most assur'd –
> His glassy essence – like an angry ape
> Plays such fantastic tricks before high heaven
> As makes the angels weep –

because, by the very fact that Angelo is an imposter, the deeper imposture of authority itself can be obliquely acknowledged. Angelo's falsity both stands for and covers up for the Duke who, like the 'Lady' in the three-card trick, is the figure who is always there but never actually gets exposed. The Duke's hypocrisy differs from that of Angelo in that he, by purporting to resign his power, can distance himself from the guilt and bad faith that is actually endemic in the system, just as 'justice' is always outside it. What the play cannot evade recognising is that exemplary authority must always be displaced from the centre where it notionally belongs because it is precisely there that its existence comes into question. The Duke can only represent moral authority when he is cut off from the exercise of power. In the face of this dilemma only a botched together, *ad hoc* resolution is possible.

Like *Hamlet, Othello* (1603) is essentially a modern play which focuses on the instability and fragility of authority in the context of Renaissance culture, even though, as we have already seen, Shakespeare was well aware that analogues could be found in a variety of historical contexts. Nevertheless Othello's tragedy is produced by a world which altogether lacks legitimate forms of authority and where loyalty can never be taken for granted. Othello as a Moor in the employ of the Venetian government has achieved his position by his proven effectiveness as a military leader. As Venice needs victories to maintain her supremacy in the Mediterranean she is prepared to reward a soldier of fortune such as Othello accordingly. But Othello as a foreigner and a black man can never feel entirely confident of his position. To the disgruntled Iago, who looks for preferment and does not get it, that such a man as Othello can be placed in a position of authority and that he can appoint the intellectual Cassio as his deputy is symptomatic of the way in which rank is determined by opportunism and influence rather than by long service and tradition:

> Preferment goes by letter and affection
> And not by old gradation, where each second
> Stood loyal to th' first.

Iago, it would seem, belongs to this bygone world of established hierarchy and unquestioning obedience, yet despite this he devotes himself wholeheartedly to its converse, an unscrupulous, self-serving opportunism. Paradoxically it is Othello, the new man, who actually is honest, straightforward and trustworthy, whereas Iago gains influence rather by the artifice with which he contrives to represent it:

> For when my outward action doth demonstrate
> The native act and figure of my heart
> In compliment extern, 'tis not long after
> But I will wear my heart upon my sleeve
> For daws to peck at – I am not what I am.

So that although Othello seems capable of mastering this shifting and unstable world of the modern by his own integrity and personal forcefulness, Iago graps that he can equally well be its victim. Othello must learn to doubt. Othello's authority as a commanding presence on the public stage of Venice, which manifests itself as much in his defence of his marriage before the Senate as in the way in which his mere appearance can halt a brawl, is more tenuous than it seems, for his self-image is ultimately grounded in the respect and confidence that he receives from others. Iago slyly suggests that Othello's triumph in winning Desdemona against all the prejudices of the culture is hollow. He invites Othello to see it rather as a victory for Desdemona, whose direct repudiation of her father's wishes in a shameless display of sexual passion is subversive of all patriarchal authority. If she can make her own father into a public laughing-stock she can do the same to Othello. Although Desdemona is thus transformed in Othello's mind into an archetypal symbol of treacherous, voluptuous, unstable woman, she nevertheless is also a blank screen on to which he projects all his complex and contradictory feelings towards his adopted state of Venice. Othello is confronted with the mask of an alien culture which he is unable to look behind, which torments him with its enigmatic mockery. This insecurity in his personal relationships is so directly related to his insecurity in his profession that Iago plausibly extenuates his pathological jealousy to Desdemona by alluding to his replacement in command by Cassio:

> I pray you, be content; 'tis but his humour,
> This business of the state does him offence,
> And he doth chide with you.

Desdemona becomes a signifier of an ungraspable Venetian other than perennially haunts him and which he must finally confront with violence. When Iago reveals to Othello the secret of her 'infidelity' this threatens absolutely every aspect of his identity so that he can no longer believe in himself as a military leader:

> O, now for ever
> Farewell the tranquil mind! farewell content!
> Farewell the plumèd troops, and the big wars
> That make ambition virtue – O, farewell!

Farewell the neighing steed and the shrill trump,
The spirit-stirring drum, th'ear-piercing fife,
The royal banner, and all quality,
Pride, pomp, and circumstance, of glorious war!
And you, O you mortal engines, whose rude throats
Th' immortal Jove's dread clamours counterfeit,
Farewell! Othello's occupation's gone.

What makes it possible for Othello to lead Venetian troops into battle is a sense of identification with the culture that has now broken down at the most fundamental level. Now that he can no longer believe in Desdemona or imagine that she has confidence in him he feels his whole being to be utterly extinguished, which is what gives his act of smothering her on the bed such a horrifying and ironic symmetry. For in this way the honour and identity of both can finally be restored. In this way Othello proclaims himself master of the spectres that have been menacing them, but the moment of truth and clarity he seeks eludes him once more. In his final gesture of stabbing himself Othello summons up his former decisive and untroubled self as the exemplary servant of the Venetian state:

And say besides, that in Aleppo once,
When a malignant and a turbaned Turk
Beat a Venetian and traduced the state,
I took by th'throat the circumcisèd dog
And smote him thus

and thus authoritatively despatches the self which, invaded by anxiety and doubt, can no longer be a figure of authority. Paradoxically Othello's suicide shows neither stoic resignation or weakness but is a tremendous assertion of power.

With *King Lear* (1605) Shakespeare returns to the disquieting but familiar ground of English history. Many scenes are reminiscent of *Henry VI* and *Richard III*. The blinding of Gloucester at the hands of Goneril and Regan recalls the cold-blooded murder of York by Clifford and Queen Margaret. Edmund, like Richard, is the unscrupulous villain who, for the moment, is condemned to stand on the sidelines but who is determined eventually to command the centre. Civil war and civil disorder are articulated through the strife of son against father and brother against brother. The crucial difference is that *King Lear* is set in such a remote period as to be virtually beyond any sense of historical time. According to Holinshead, Lear ruled over England in the year of the world, 3105, at a date before the founding of Rome and before the reign of Jereboam in the Old Testament. On such an epoch it is hard to gain any decisive purchase. *King Lear* expresses the symbolic truth of English history as a record of division, violence and injustice, but in such a manner as to free it not simply from narrative closure but from the teleologcial thrust of narrative altogether. In Shakespeare's earlier history plays, no matter how shocking the events depicted may be, there is always the possibility of a narrativity that will seem to endow them with meaning or a culmination that may finally validate them. Merely by naming them we assign the Wars of the Roses to the historical and comprehensible past and invoke a structure, the conflict between the Houses of York and Lancaster, that can explain and exhaust them. Such events still have the power to disturb, despite their obvious pastness, because we can only imperfectly grasp the forces that lie behind them. How could they have engaged the emotions of men and women with such intensity and for so long? Yet there remains the sense that the struggle *did* have a meaning and that its significance persists as protracted prolegomena to the present. But in the case of *King Lear* it is hard to make the connection. The world of Lear lacks chronology and its events seem near instantaneous. It lacks identifiable places apart from Dover, which serves to establish the scene as England. Yet Dover itself is a kind of illusion, a fiction of Doverness without topographical mooring. We have no sense at all of the historical continuum into which all these disparate events are inserted. We can scarcely get our bearings. We are asked to think of a time when Lear ruled over a united kingdom, when Cordelia was his favourite daughter and when he preferred the Duke of Albany to the Duke of Cornwall, yet we know that it is as futile to think of this as it is to ask what happened to Lear's or Gloucester's wife. The world of Lear is as abrupt and disconcerting as a mechanical toy that suddenly springs into motion and, equally suddenly, stops.

There is a disturbing elasticity to the England of Lear that is marked at the very outset. With no more than a casual glance at the map and a perfunctory solicitation of flattery from his daughters – since he knows well that Cordelia loves him most –

he plans to liquidate his kingdom and take retirement. We must believe that his kingdom is of an amplitude that defies all measurement and that, having disposed of a generous third of 'plenteous and wide-skirted meads' to both Goneril and Regan, there will be a yet more superabundant segment remaining for his favourite, Cordelia. It is impossible to reconcile this invocation of plenitude and fertility with the extremes of poverty and deprivation that the play actually presents. Clearly, in the language of myth, it is Lear himself who squanders all this in the reckless act of dividing his kingdom. England can never again be thus complete. What the fairy-tale calls for, what will indeed make it a fairy-tale, is a symmetrically balancing return to abundance at the end, when all wrongs will be righted, and when Lear, restored to the power he so foolishly dispersed, can lavish on the daughter he misconstrued all the blessings and more which she deserves and to which in a fairy-tale she is entitled. Since the lack so dissonantly introduced into the scene by Cordelia's refusal of inflated rhetoric was imaginary its menace can only be dispelled by a happiness in which the cup is filled to overflowing. So it is just because *Lear* invites us into a world where all things are possible and where our sense of the plausible is stretched to the uttermost limit that we are suddenly brought up short by the frightening recalcitrance of *Lear*'s last scene. All pretensions to dignity, status and importance have been so utterly deflated that we are quite unprepared for the strangely simple nobility of Lear as he stands with Cordelia dead in his arms. We leave *Lear* not in the abundance that was expected, but like Lear himself, desperately grasping at vacancy:

> Do you see this? Look on her, look, her lips,
> Look there, look there!

In *King Lear* authority is always absent. Here, the game of abdicating power only to opportunely and sagely reclaim it as practised by the Duke in *Measure for Measure*, is subjected to an altogether more rigorous scrutiny. Lear, like the Duke, gives up the official exercise of power but seeks to retain the substance. Though his daughters will rule he will nevertheless continue as master of all three – a lord of lords. He will be the unshakeable and irreplaceable representation of patriarchal authority which can never be theirs both because they are women and because the kingdom has been divided. Although Kent at least acknowledges the image of authority in Lear's glance and devotedly follows him, the fact remains that Lear on the heath can only figure as a pathetic simulacrum of the majesty he would embody. As the play progresses it is not just Lear's ability to be a figure of authority that is put in question but the forms of domination themselves and the identities that that domination constructs. It is authority itself that goes walkabout. Trials, tests and other impromptu arraignments loom large in *Lear*, but no juxtaposition is more inexorable than that the blinding of Gloucester, introduced by Cornwall's statement:

> Though well we may not pass upon his life
> without the form of justice

should be directly preceded by this:

LEAR.   I'll see their trial first. Bring in their evidence. (*To Edgar*)
Thou robed man of justice, take thy place; (*To the Fool*) And
thou, his yoke-fellow of equity, bench by his side. (*To Kent*) You
are o'th'commission, sit you too.
EDGAR.   Let us deal justly.

> Sleepest or wakest thou, jolly shepherd?
> Thy sheep be in the corn;
> And for one blast of thy minikin mouth,
> Thy sheep shall take no harm.

Purr, the cat is grey.
LEAR.   Arraign her first; 'tis Goneril. I here take my oath before
this honourable assembly, she kick'd the poor King her father.
FOOL.   Come hither mistress. Is your name Goneril?
LEAR.   She cannot deny it.
FOOL.   Cry you mercy, I took you for a joint-stool.
LEAR.   And here's another, whose warp'd looks proclaim what
store her heart is made on. Stop her there! Arms, arms, sword,
fire! Corruption in the place! False justicer, why hast thou let
her 'scape?
EDGAR.   Bless thy five wits!

In this higgledy-piggledy mixing together of scraps of folklore, humorous colloquialisms and legal jargon the effect is not simply to demonstrate that Lear is as whimsical in his proceedings when he lacks the crown as when he possessed it, but to show how language is saturated with the implications of power even when it has been broken down into tiny fragments. Lear's speech, disconnected from the authority that would otherwise validate it, always borders on madness since by the very nature of its address it invokes subjects who do not exist. *King Lear* forces us to recognise what a complex thing authority is; to acknowledge that its exercise is bound up with such things as a serious manner, specific locutions, suitably dignified clothing, a context where some persons are raised and others lowered, where the open and public nature of the proceedings is taken to give them a prescriptive and binding character. Social morality is enacted as a powerful set of appearances. What Lear calls 'The great image of authority' is indeed an image, in which justice is made manifest through ritual rather than through actual ethical demands:

> Through tatter'd clothes small vices do appear;
> Robes and furr'd gowns hide all.

So many of the manifestations of authority in *Lear* are incongruous because they are partial, because they have been torn from any context that could endow them with significance and meaning; although, paradoxically, the presence of this full context would only mask more deeply the arbitrariness of the proceedings from us because we would lose our sense of puzzlement and incongruity before the inexorable spectacle. For example, when Kent is put in the stocks there is no sense at all that this is an authorised procedure, not so much because it is unjust, as that the episode takes place before Gloucester's castle, as a site of power, yet it is Gloucester himself who argues against it. Moreover, Kent's moment of punishment, interspersed as it is with a scene in which the fugitive Edgar wanders at large, seems disconnected from anything else. It is the oddity of the punishment that strikes us even more than the unfairness.

In exile and in madness Lear still attempts to act as if he were the natural focus of authority, as if authority were somehow not dependent on actual structures of power but received its sanction in the very constitution of the universe. On the heath he purports to orchestrate thunder and lightning as extensions of his baleful mood, but he reluctantly concedes that far from doing his bidding they are as far beyond his control as anything else:

> Rumble thy bellyfull! Spit, fire! spout, rain!
> Nor rain, wind, thunder, fire, are my daughters:
> I tax you not, you elements, with unkindness;
> I never gave you kingdom, call'd you children,
> You owe me no subscription: then let it fall
> Your horrible pleasure; here I stand, your slave,
> A poor, infirm, weak, and despis'd old man.

With this admission comes another: that Lear, far from abdicating his authority, was only seeking to strengthen it – hoping to infuse his daughters with a still greater sense of reverence for his patriarchal authority through their very sense of obligation at having the kingdom conferred on them. Lear gives up the kingdom early because he expects to benefit. Lear as king has always had things too easy. He has enjoyed the wielding of power and the deference he has unfailingly received and this has altogether blinded him to the feelings of others and to the resentments he has provoked. It is only in face of the resistance and indifference of the heath that he begins to grasp what has been going on:

> they flattered he like a dog, and told me I had white hairs in my beard ere the black ones were there. To say 'ay' and 'no' to every thing that I said! 'Ay' and 'no' too was no good divinity. When the rain came to wet me once and the wind to make me chatter, when the thunder would not peace at my bidding, then I found 'em, there I smelt 'em out.

But even as Lear is saying this he is still asserting his pretensions to be the pivot around which the whole world turns. Wilson Knight emphasises: 'Lear is the centre of our attention, and as the world shakes with tempest and unreason, we endure something of the shaking and the tempest of his mind.'[11]

But it might be more pertinent to insist that what the play rather exposes is Lear's persistent delusion that he can be such a centre even when he is now utterly marginalised and indeed barely conscious of what is actually going on. When Hamlet soliloquises, the plot moves forward – even in his indecisions –

but Lear's rhetorical outbursts seem like endeavours to suspend the processes that he has already set in motion. Yet Lear always commands the stage even if he is never in command of events. Lear, like Richard II, must play the part of the king with such intensity that the loss of that authority will be invested with a terrible pathos. For the spectacle of kingship remains. It is scarcely possible to imagine Lear without a whole arsenal of histrionic gestures that will seem to give substance to his empty but linguistically overwhelming threats. Somehow the imperious patriarch is able to construct a court around him out of the most incongruous elements. Just as spells are rendered effectual within the orbit of a magic circle, so Lear weaves a spell of power around himself, even when powerless, as much a witch-doctor or shaman as king. Through his incantations, conjurations and curses, Lear endeavours to impose on others both his own perception of things and his sense of his own centrality in that perception, even though this continually threatens to topple over into absurdity:

> Blasts and fogs upon thee!
> Th'untented woundings of a father's curse
> Pierce every sense about thee! Old fond eyes,
> Beweep this cause again, I'll pluck ye out,
> And cast you, with the waters that you loose,
> To temper clay. Yea, is't come to this?
> Ha! Let it be so: I have another daughter,
> Who, I am sure is kind and comfortable:
> When she shall hear this of thee, with her nails
> She'll flay thy wolvish visage. Thou shalt find
> That I'll resume the shape which thou dost think
> I have cast off for ever.

Such a moment was implicit in Lear's original pretence at abdication. For he always imagined that he could maintain his authority by the threat of returning to the full plenipotentiary power that he originally wielded. Less would be more. But Lear discovers that authority is always less than it should be, otherwise it would not strive to be more. It is a bottle that always needs topping up. But Lear's habit of command persists even in a world that will not recognise it and he becomes completely baffled when he does not receive the signals he expects. After the rebuff by Goneril and the humiliation of his messenger, Kent, in the stocks,

Lear is provoked to the very height of indignation by the fact that
Regan and the Duke of Cornwall will not speak to him. There
surely must be some mistake! The following exchange takes place
with Gloucester:

> LEAR.   Deny to speak with me! They are sick! They are weary!
>   They have travell'd all the night! Mere fetches, ay,
>   The images of revolt and flying off.
>   Fetch me a better answer.
> GLOUCESTER.   My dear Lord,
>   You know the fiery quality of the duke;
>   How unremovable and fix'd he is
>   In his own course.
> LEAR.   Vengeance! plague! death! confusion!
>   Fiery! what quality! why, Gloucester, Gloucester,
>   I'd speak with the Duke of Cornwall and his wife.
> GLOUCESTER.   Well, my good lord, I have inform'd them so.
> LEAR.   Inform'd them! Dost thou understand me, man?
> GLOUCESTER.   Ay, my good Lord.
> LEAR.   The King would speak with Cornwall; the dear father
>   Would with his daughter speak, commands, tends service:
>   Are they inform'd of this? My breath and blood!
>   Fiery! the fiery duke! Tell the hot Duke that –
>   No, but not yet; may be he is not well.

Lear's perplexity is caused by the fact that he now finds himself
on the wrong side of the language of power. For the Duke's 'fiery
quality' and his alleged immovability are not *sui generis* – indeed,
as king, Lear could never have perceived the Duke as being such.
So long as Lear ruled it was his prerogative to be choleric,
unshakeable and unreasonable, and he even tries to continue to
be so when out of office. But those who are endowed with
authority can afford to be imperious and arbitrary because this is
what they are expected to be. Fieriness and fixity are not universal
human traits but are a function of power. As Lear tries to come to
terms with this new situation his language expresses his confusion
as he is by turns angry, indignant, ironic, confused and
supplicating. He both pleads and orders and is scarcely conscious
of the contradiction between these modes of address so desperately
anxious is he to receive some sort of attention. But the cognitive
dissonance he experiences is acute as he has to learn both how to

listen and respond to the cues he receives from others. If Lear is brought to ask 'Who is it that can tell me what I am?' this is because his whole identity has been constructed in terms of the kingly role and he had never ever thought in terms of reciprocity. He was indifferent to the feelings of his flattering and apparently devoted entourage to the point of being scarcely conscious of what was passing through their minds. Now vulnerable, he is disorientated by the complexity of the signals to which he is exposed, like someone spinning the dial on a shortwave radio. As the Fool points out:

> Thous wast a pretty fellow when thou hadst no need to care for her frowning; now thou art an O without a figure. I am better than thou art now; I am a Fool, thou art nothing.

What *King Lear* throws into sharp relief is the extraordinary nature of the demands and expectations that we seek to impose on others. Lear is not alone in his narcissistic blindness to the needs of those whom he claims to love or in his craving for total dedication and adulation. Coredlia's response to her father may have the merit of being honest and of refusing to indulge in flattery, but it is nevertheless cruel in the way in which it foregrounds limitations in life that we would prefer not to dwell upon. For love always has to be divided in three ways: between husband, wife or lover, parents and children. But like the division of Lear's kingdom we must believe that love has such an amplitude that more love for one person does not mean there will be any the less for another. In *King Lear* we see the impossibility of all this, especially when it is bound up with deference to patriarchal authority, for love which is not freely given cannot be love at all. Yet there are those like Edgar, Kent and Cordelia who give without condition and without expectation of reciprocity so that the dissolution of authority brings unexpected gains along with the losses. After *Lear* it is hard to believe in the naturalness of authority or to think of it as anything other than destructive.

In *Macbeth* (1606) there is no originary moment of dissolution, we are immediately plunged into a world of confusion and unpredictable violence. Macdonwald's rebellion against Duncan aided both by an external enemy, Sweno, King of Norway, and an internal traitor, the Thane of Cawdor, comes very close to succeeding. For a moment all seems lost as

> Fortune, on his damned quarrel smiling,
> Showed like a rebel's whore

a figure which already announces what is to be a recurrent motif: the linking of the unpredictability of fate with the fickleness and subversiveness of woman. In this hurly-burly world there is no way of knowing what unexpected turn of events may follow, what realignment of loyalties may take place. The Scots are presented as being the treacherous, unreliable and unscrupulous nation that Edward Hall had always insisted they were and that Englishmen had always known them to be. Despite James I it would be hard to underestimate the degree of hostility and suspicion with which Scotland continued to be regarded and such reactions would necessarily have coloured contemporary reactions to the play. The moment when the witches hail Macbeth as Thane of Cawdor in a parodic travesty of sanctioned ritual is one which has complex reverberations, for it is already here that authority is being questioned. Macbeth promises to be Cawdor's double in his disloyalty to Duncan; yet Macbeth is to be haunted by his own double, Banquo, who will always represent a threat of substitution beyond substitution that even his most desperate and ruthless efforts can never suppress. In the witches' prophecies all legitimacy is abolished. So when Duncan speaks of binding Macbeth further to him and Banquo speaks of being connected to Macbeth with 'a most indissoluble tie' such language invokes a context of feudal loyalty that is already being superseded. There is no longer any sense of unity or common purpose in Scotland and even Malcolm and Macduff in desperate exile scarcely know whether to trust one another or in what language they could speak it. In *Macbeth* the fateful pattern of English history during the Wars of the Roses is repeated. A weak king such as Duncan cannot effectively wield authority, yet a powerful usurper such as Macbeth is thwarted by the fact that no one will acknowledge him as a legitimate ruler. But in a Scottish context it becomes impossible to contain and valorise these destructive episodes by distributing them within a progressive narrative. James I's alleged descent from Banquo notwithstanding, Scotland becomes analogous to the Italy of Marston and Webster, an imaginary space in which can be realised all the dark dreams of the Renaissance spirit.

Macbeth has been a crucial text in establishing an affording anchorage for a politically conservative interpretation of

Shakespeare's plays that would read them as offering an uncritical celebration of stability and order. *Macbeth*, significantly, was introduced into *Shakespeare's History Plays* by Tillyard despite being outside the canon, because he saw it as a yet more 'culminating version' of 'the most solemn and most deeply felt of all Shakespeare's political motives: the working out of a crime, the punishment of the villain and the establishment of the Tudors'.[12] Banality, surely, could go no further. But what rather needs to be stressed is the way in which such an overtly political interpretation of the play actually works by suppressing its actual political implications. Tillyard is at pains to emphasise that Macbeth's 'vain conflict with an overruling Providence' and 'the pervading cosmic theme of disorder seeking to upset the divine order of nature' are more significant than 'the actual political theme'.[13] Such an emphasis permits Tillyard to make some argumentative moves that are somewhat surprising in the light of his earlier discussion of the history plays. There Tillyard had insisted, in the light of the Homilies that rebellion was always wrong, whereas here he quotes Malcolm

> Macbeth
> Is ripe for shaking, and the powers above
> Put on their instruments

without apparently noticing what an unequivocal endorsement this offers of the view that some rebellions can be regarded as a divinely inspired means of getting rid of unjust rulers.[14] The repeated characterisation of Macbeth as a 'tyrant' not only justifies the struggle against Macbeth more powerfully than the charge that he is a usurper but it also serves to validate rebellion against tyranny itself – quite a radical position and one from which Calvin and others had specifically disassociated themselves. Moreover, the issue is hardly academic when we consider that such a performance before James I justifies the position that Milton was to urge against his son, Charles I, in *Eikonoclastes*, that he deserved to be overthrown because he was a tyrant. Thus *Macbeth* is not just a moral essay in black and white, but an altogether more unsettling text when its actual implications are pondered. However, Tillyard's simplistic reductions are reinforced by L. C. Knights' apparently subtle and certainly more influential reading, which finds in Banquo's apostrophe to the 'temple-haunting martlet' in Act I, Scene 6 nothing less than an italicised 'natural and wholesome *order*', and beyond that, in the play as a whole, the creed that 'moral law', whatever that may be, is nothing less than the 'law of life'.[15] Knights writes from within the tradition of the New Criticism, which sought to replace the discussion of Shakespeare's plays in terms of character with a more sensitive attention to poetic texture and an awareness of the way in which this could lead to the apprehension of pervasive metaphysical 'themes'. Yet what such an approach produces in practice is an opportunistic fastening on any verbal detail that serves to corroborate easy assumptions about what Shakespeare meant and a deliberate glossing over of anything that might contradict or undermine the Elizabethan commonplaces which they take Shakespeare's wisdom to be. The turbulent and unstable world of *Macbeth* can be treated as a photographic negative, which when suitably reversed, yields a positive image of order and harmony.

Nevertheless, it cannot be denied that any interpretation of *Macbeth* must take as its starting-point Shakespeare's insistence on the terrible nature of Macbeth's crime as a wilful repudiation of every humane and social impulse:

> He's here in double trust;
> First, as I am his kinsman and his subject,
> Strong both against the deed; then, as his host,
> Who should against his murderer shut the door,
> Not bear the knife himself.

Macbeth's sense of wrongdoing is infinitely greater than it could have been either in the Scotland that Holinshead describes or in the contemporary world of Renaissance politics. His murder of Duncan is a political primal scene, a violation of taboo, a deadly initiation into the modern that is fraught with incalculable consequences. Elizabeth I stepped across a similar threshold when she agreed to the execution of Mary, Queen of Scots, for in so doing she placed political expediency before the sanctity of royal blood and also undermined her own claim to rule by divine right. So what *Macbeth* symbolises is the passing of an actually always absent, if always imaginable, legitimacy of authority from which Renaissance man now seems as absolutely barred as if by the blazing sword that blocks the return to Paradise. It is by no means certain that Machiavellian policy strengthens a ruler's position since it weakens the force of custom and a prince who has broken the rules may find that he no longer has any traditions which he can appeal to. He finds others as incalculable as he necessarily is himself. We should note that what shocks Malcolm about Macbeth's deed is that it is so entirely unexpected and out of character:

> This tyrant, whose sole name blisters our tongues,
> Was once thought honest.

In *Macbeth* the witches are sinister signifiers of the modern, who herald an era of ambition, ruthlessness and political uncertainty, by suggesting that anything and everything is possible. Macbeth is a Faustian figure, tortured by the gap between this possibility and its realisation, who in energetically grasping at the opportunity that the age seems to offer, finds that even his most desperate and determined efforts only end in futility. In seeking to master his time he is mastered by it; his dream of power turns to ashes because he has unleashed forces beyond his control –

> though the treasure
> Of Nature's germens tumble all together,
> Even till destruction sicken.

His attempts to discern a significant pattern in events are unable to contend with the endless multiplication of possible scenarios. It is this continually shifting, incalculable nature of Renaissance politics that is the nightmare of Macbeth.

What is notable about *Macbeth*, especially when we compare it with the backward glance of the history plays, is its obsessional orientation towards an unfolding future. In this sense Macbeth is the authentic representation of an age of discord, in which religious conflict is delegitimising rulers and unsettling the basis of states. Moreover, there was a clear contemporary connection between prophecy and the incidence of rebellion. As Keith Thomas has shown, prophetic rumours inspired many sixteenth-century revolts – Ket's rebellion of 1549, Wyatt's rebellion against Mary Tudor, and in the Catholic Ridolphi plot of 1572 the Duke of Norfolk was misled by 'a prophecy about a lion (Norfolk) and a lioness (Mary, Queen of Scots) who would overthrow a lion (Elizabeth I)'.[16]

So in his fatal addiction to the predictions of witches Macbeth was in the company of many others who were seduced by siren voices *guaranteeing* success to any who would challenge the existing order. Prophecy itself had become more respectable through the reading and interpretation of the Book of Revelations, which, as the divinely inspired word of God, could scarcely be dismissed as dangerous or trivial nonsense. If the Day of Judgement really were imminent and if the final struggle against the Antichrist really were at hand, then not to be concerned about the future was to cultivate an irresponsible ignorance and to bury one's head in the sand. Uncertainties over the succession from Henry VIII to Elizabeth meant that political continuity could never be taken for granted at any time during the sixteenth century. This would offer grounds for anxiety, but England, like Duncan, faced the ever-present possibility of being overthrown by a combination of enemies without and enemies within. So, equally, the fact that Macbeth seems more concerned that Banquo's descendants will rule in the distant future than he is about his own immediate prospects would have been understandable at a time when guaranteeing the succession was the key to political stability. With religion everywhere acting as a powerful destabilising force, the future had seldom seemed more menacing or more urgent than it did to the embattled generations of the Reformation. The ability to 'look into the seeds of time' was eagerly cultivated and still more eagerly attended to, as the influence of Foxe, Brightman and Mede demonstrated. In unsettled times prophecy offered a prospect of certainty that was eagerly grasped. It is just because Macbeth is fearful

> Letting 'I dare not' wait upon 'I would,'
> like the poor cat i'th'adage

that he hangs onto every word of the witches and progressively sheds his inhibitions.

While Lear goes on trying to be every inch a king even when he ceases to be one, Macbeth is never able to project a royal authority even when he officially is one. No one can respect him. No one would willingly serve under him. As Malcolm, Donalbain, Ross and Macduff flee not only from Court but from Scotland itself, they leave Macbeth as the lord of vacancy, as if his domain were as desolate as the blasted heath on which he first met the witches. Although, of all Shakespeare's plays there is scarcely one, even *Coriolanus*, that centres so fixedly on its protagonist, so that even in England there is no escaping him, Macbeth nevertheless fails to project himself as an effective centre. Although he is forceful and violent after his initial hesitations, Macbeth nevertheless seems ineffectual, more acted upon than acting. His inability to be king is not simply a function of his illegitimacy, but derives more fundamentally from the fact that his guilt and bad faith make it impossible for him to truly be the authority figure even within the confines of his tortured mind. Even for him the office seems like a giant's robe, for what Macbeth has murdered in Duncan is the possibility of kingship itself. In England the notion of the monarchy as a sacred office still survives through Edward the Confessor but once the role itself has been diminished it is questionable whether it can ever again achieve such respect. Macbeth is tortured by the sense of his own transitoriness. Never for one moment does Shakespeare allow him to savour his success. He is haunted by phantoms that seem more tangible than he is himself. Lear is a nullity without the crown. Macbeth is a cipher with it – for the symbolic dimension of kingship is denied him. We are never shown Macbeth being crowned or granted allegiance. Even at the great banquet that should finally legitimise him he imagines that he is excluded – the only person to be denied a seat. If, as Richard Marienstras has persuasively suggested in *New Perspectives on the Shakespearean World* (in French *Le proche et le lointain*), it was the customary role of a king to be master of forests[17] then the very movement of Birnam wood to Dunsinane represents the return of a legitimacy that Macbeth, the usurper, cannot deny. Yet this movement, this imposture, also serves to signify how problematic the idea of authority has become. As Macbeth becomes still more hopelessly isolated, deprived of his wife's moral support through madness and backed only by reluctant conscripts – 'constrained things / Whose hearts are absent too' – he becomes obsessed with the fiction that he bears a 'charmed life', since this would supply a charisma that could replace the sanctity of kingly office. But even this is denied him. Shakespeare suggests that Machiavellian statecraft will destroy the very authority which it seeks to intensify. In a resort to absolute coercion old loyalties fall away and wheels frantically whirring at the centre find themselves disengaged from the processes of society as a whole. So Charles I was to discover, so, too, Macbeth.

The liquidation of the very possibility of centre, so prominent in *Macbeth*, is a preoccupation that runs through all of Shakespeare's later plays. Indeed the themes of exile, alienation and exclusion are so recurrent, the sense of disillusionment so strong, that critics of an older school not implausibly hypothesised a connection with Shakespeare's own decision to quit city and Court and return to Stratford. The belief that honesty, virtue and integrity are to be found on the periphery rather than at the centre emerges with particular clarity in *Cymbeline*. There is no one at Cymbeline's Court, a provincial setting by Roman standards, not even the Queen, who can match the ruthlessness and unscrupulous cunning of Iachimo; yet there is no space here for the personal authenticity of Belarius, Guiderius and Arviragus, so that virtue, like the ripples in a pond, is displaced outwards from periphery to periphery. It is only through the intervention of Belarius and his adopted sons that Britain is saved. But what is equally significant is that the centre as a locus of power, authority and truth is progressively demystified. *Antony and Cleopatra* is a notable instance of this. Of all the classical Roman heroes whom Plutarch memorialised in his classic work, which Shakespeare read in Thomas North's translation, Mark Antony is the one whom Plutarch regards most critically. Plutarch never questions Antony's heroic status, which is after all the reason for writing about him in the first place, but he nevertheless regards the whole course of his career as catastrophic. Antony's great offence, in Plutarch's eyes, was that he slighted the greatness of Rome, the imperial city, and repeatedly manifested his disregard, not to say contempt, for this uniquely authoritative centre. In Plutarch's case such an emphasis might seem more than a little odd, given he was a citizen of Chaerenia in Greece, which was very definitely part of the Eastern periphery and Greece had been a country where both Antony and Cleopatra were held in high esteem. It was from Athens that Antony set off for his Parthian campaign bearing an olive wreath from the Acropolis. But, of course, Plutarch eventually gained high office in the Roman Empire under Hadrian so that his project of writing the lives of the Greeks and Romans can be seen as a way of working through this conflict of loyalties. What is above all disquieting to Plutarch in Antony's career, far exceeding his disposition to wassailing and lasciviousness, is his determination to think of Alexandria in Egypt as a centre. Indeed the very naming of Cleopatra becomes a kind of complex shorthand for Antony's inexplicable failure to return to Rome, for his construction of an Eastern empire, for every aspect of his behaviour which seems aberrant when viewed from the proud but anxious watchtower of the metropolis. When Antony defeated the King of Armenia it was to Alexandria not Rome that he returned in triumph, of which Plutarch writes (North's translation): 'This greatly offended the Romanes, and made them much to mislike it: when they saw that for Cleopatra's sake he deprived his country of her due honor and glory, onely to gratifie the Aegyptians.'[18]

What was even more serious from the Roman point of view was that it was in Alexandria, amidst great pomp, seated on thrones of gold and silver, that Antony chose to hold the ceremony in which he divided his empire between his sons: 'And to confesse a troth, it was too arrogant and insolent, and done (as a man would say) in derision and contempt of the Romanes.'[19] For whether or not this was Antony's motive this was certainly how it appeared from the vantage point of Rome. He acted as if Rome did not exist and as if he could arrogate all decisions to himself, without deferring in any way, even on a symbolic level, to Senatus Populusque Romanus. Octavius as Augustus became supreme ruler of the Roman empire, in the process extinguishing all popular rights and liberties, but he was careful never to slight the people he sought to master. Indeed he successfully discredited Antony by reading out the will he had made in which 'he willed that his bodie, though he dyed at Rome, should be brought in funerall pompe through the middest of the market place, and that it should be sent into Alexandria unto Cleopatra'.[20] In Antony's alarming scheme of things it is Rome herself that is consigned to the periphery.

What is surprising in *Antony and Cleopatra* is the way in which the play so insistently reiterates the Roman perspective and yet manages to contradict it quite comprehensively. For the censorious moralism that emanates from Rome loses all its pretensions of dignity when it is so evidently founded on envy, malice and gossip. In Philo's opening speech the claim that Antony has been reduced from the 'triple pillar of the world' into 'a strumpet's fool' defines greatness in terms of service and subordination to Rome, but as Antony will point out the terms of such recognition are always opportunistic:

> our slippery people,
> Whose love is never linked to the deserver
> Till his deserts are past.

Public opinion in the capital is fickle and easily swayed by those who proclaim their unswerving allegiance to a 'Rome' that is itself being constantly redefined. Yet the insidious power of this Roman critique of Antony is that Antony himself cannot altogether shake it off. Although Antony's initial proud rejection of everything that Rome represents – 'Let Rome in Tiber melt' – reverberates through the play it is nevertheless a note that he finds impossible to sustain. Since his whole identity is bound up with his role as a leader honoured by Rome for military prowess he finds it impossible to make the break that his desire for personal fulfilment requires. Antony's is a deeply split personality; when he says

> These strong Egyptian fetters I must break,
> Or lose myself in dotage

he reveals how comprehensively he has internalised an unquestioning loyalty to Rome and everything it represents, which only constitutes fetters of another kind. Antony always seems to be in a state of bad faith. When in Rome it seems he should be in Egypt, when in Egypt in Rome. Antony is made to feel that through his divided allegiance he deserves to fail, since an unflinching commitment to either one or the other would lead to a more decisive course of action. His belated decision for Egypt is taken when it can only bring about the collapse of his political affairs. Contrariwise, his earlier return to Rome and marriage to Octavia, far from rectifying the situation as he fondly imagines, only provides Octavius with the rope with which to hang him. Antony is unable fully to grasp Alexandria as a creative and fructifying centre only because of the self-distrust that the Roman ideology induces.

Unlike *Macbeth*, the moment of defeat in *Antony and Cleopatra* is infinitely protracted – stretching over nineteen scenes. Antony's refusal of the sober, calculating Roman values is reflected in his determination to give himself up to 'chance and hazard', to fight a sea battle which he can be expected to lose. In defeat Antony suddenly feels his powerlessness: 'Authority melts from me', and in moment he appears to have lost all the moral grandeur that is his prerogative as a Roman hero. But, in a subtle transvaluation of values, Rome itself no longer seems to represent anything significant and Caesar's triumph seems completely hollow since the Roman virtue it should vindicate has already been destroyed in the Byzantine intrigues through which Caesar rises to total power. In death, Antony and Cleopatra strive not only to assert their love as a significant value but to deny the metropolitan desire to diminish them. Their consuming passion will also burn to ashes Rome's arrogant claim not only to rule but to be life's final arbiter on every point. So Cleopatra goes to her death with Antony in a deliberate assertion of the incommensurability of their passion with everything that Rome either is or can be and in the sure knowledge that this action will itself be devalued:

> Nay, 'tis most certain, Iras: saucy lictors
> Will catch at us like strumpets, and scald rhymers
> Ballad us out o'tune: the quick comedians
> Extemporally will stage us and present
> Our Alexandrian revels; Antony
> Shall be brought drunken forth, and I shall see
> Some squeaking Cleopatra boy my greatness
> I'th' posture of a whore.

The play itself becomes a gesture of defiance at the public world – a secret narrative of all that it finds it impossible to incorporate. What it represents and celebrates is the exotic, the taboo, the forbidden.

A crucial unmasking scene in the play takes place when Caesar, Lepidus, Antony and Pompey meet together on Pompey's galley, off Misenum. The drunken dancing and revels of these 'world-sharers, these competitors' cuts them all down to size and exposes Caesar's earlier criticism of Antony as the sanctimonious, self-serving attitudinising it is. Yet undignified though it may be, it is also a display of mutual trust. Pompey, albeit reluctantly, passes up this unique opportunity to dispose of his rivals at a single blow. It is Caesar who is the first to break the accord and make his bid for supremacy, by renewing the war against Pompey and disparaging his main rival, Antony. The byplay in this scene has

more than a passing significance. When Lepidus asks Antony
what kind of creature the crocodile is, Antony ironically replies:

> . . . It is shaped, sir, like itself, and it as broad as it has breadth:
> it is just so high as it is, and moves with its own organs: it lives
> by that which nourisheth it, and the elements once out of it, it
> transmigrates.
>
> LEPIDUS.   What colour is it of?
> ANTONY.   Of its own colour too.

In this way he obliquely speaks of himself and mockingly creates
an identification with an exotic, Egyptian creature. Antony is
unwilling to be judged by Roman standards or to be brought into
conformity with them. He is determined to live by that which
nourishes him – his relationship with Cleopatra and the hedonistic
world in which she moves – so his response to Lepidus is to
refuse to undertake the task of cultural translation and
accommodation which Lepidus seeks. Antony, like the crocodile,
is *sui generis*. Even the meaning of 'virtue' is altered. When
Cleopatra addresses Antony as

> O infinite virtue, comest thou smiling from
> The world's great snare uncaught?

virtue is no longer identified with some notion of a golden mean
or prudent conduct, but on the contrary is identified with an
excessiveness that the world cannot tolerate and which it strives
to reduce and constrain. Antony's own reference to 'Egyptian
fetters' is now metaphorically surpassed. In this play Shakespeare
endorses the ideal of a private world of integrity that is at odds
with all notions of public esteem and reputation in a way that
aligns him with what becomes a major trend in seventeenth-century
writing and which I discuss in a subsequent chapter. In Cleopatra's
final eulogy, Antony is endowed with a transcendent value that
cannot be reduced to a Plutarchian recital of memorable action,
but is concentrated in the nature of the man himself and in that
most un-Roman word, 'delights'.

Yet a contemporary audience would have perceived in *Antony
and Cleopatra* rather more than a tale of antique virtue. As with
Philotas and *Sejanus* they would have caught more than a glacing
allusion to the tragic fate of the Earl of Essex, executed for

treason in 1601. Like Antony, Essex was impetuous, romantic, spontaneous, generous and, equally, he lacked the self-discipline and capacity for negotiation and intrigue that might have preserved his career. Like Antony, Essex was a bright star who began to be eclipsed by others and who might also have exclaimed with Antony;

> Authority melts from me. Of late when I cried 'Ho,!'
> Like boys unto a muss, kings would start forth,
> And cry 'your will?'

and equally, as Antony exclaims 'I am Antony yet', so Essex proclaimed his own defiance by his desperate gesture of rebellion. Antony is never more reminiscent than when he laments the desertion of his faithful band of followers:

> The hearts
> That spanieled me at heels, to whom I gave
> Their wishes, do discandy, melt their sweets
> On blossoming Caesar

and even Caesar's own tribute:

> The death of Antony
> Is not a single doom; in that name lay
> A moiety of the world

suggests the large number of followers of Essex who went down to destruction with him in the comprehensive wreck of his fortunes. In retrospect, at least, Essex had come to seem the noblest Elizabethan of them all.

By comparison with the somewhat idealised and romantic presentation of Antony, *Coriolanus* (1608) is harsh and disenchanted and its subject-matter relates still more directly to the contemporary political scene. Indeed it is the most overtly political of Shakespeare's plays, *Richard II* not excepted. When the play was first performed James I had only been King of England for five years and the shock of this invasion by a Scottish monarch and his retinue was still being absorbed and assimilated. One of James I's earliest and most strongly urged proposals after he became king was for a Union of England with Scotland. Almost certainly

James underestimated the English distrust of the Scottish and the deep-seated fears which this innovatory proposal aroused. In his opening speech to Parliament in 1604 James pressed this ungrateful topic on the assembly and in November 1606, at the beginning of the third session, he returned to the subject, insisting that it was 'the greatest and weightiest matter of all' and beseeched Parliament to 'embrace it, that we may all enjoy it'.[21]

To James this idea of Union may have seemed relatively uncontentious since he ruled both kingdoms already. All he was asking for what that this arrangement should continue with his successors, as it almost certainly would. But English Members of Parliament, who were already concerned about the extent of Scottish infiltration and influence, were anxious that their sanctioning of such an arrangement might effectively lead to the consolidation and perpetuation of alien rule. Instead of Scotland being absorbed into England, England might rather be subordinated to Scotland and in the process forfeit many traditional rights. This proposal can be seen as one of the earliest moments at which Parliament became anxious about the possibility of an abridgement of its powers and privileges, a feeling which was to intensify over the coming years until it finally came to a head under Charles I. The parallels between Coriolanus and James I are many and striking. James I's triumphant entry into London on his accession aroused the same enormous interest on the part of the general public as the return of Coriolanus to Rome, after his victory at Corioli:

> All tongues speak of him, and the bleared sights
> Are spectacled to see him. Your prattling nurse
> Into a rapture lets her baby cry
> While she chats him: the kitchen malkin pins
> Her richest lockram 'bout her reechy neck,
> Clam'bring the walls to eye him: stalls, bulks, windows,
> Are smothered up, leads filled and ridges horsed
> With variable complexions, all agreeing
> In earnestness to see him.

But since James was also accompanied by a multitude of Scottish followers, all eager for knighthoods and subventions from the royal purse, this would also give rise to the fear that James's arrival might soon take on a more threatening character, like

Coriolanus at the head of a band of uncouth Volscians, and pave the way for alien domination. James, although welcome as a king who would safeguard the Protestant succession, might easily be led to forget that it was to England, the English Parliament and the English people that he owed his position. Since James asserted his position as king by divine right and claimed that monarchical authority preceded any other, he might well desire, like Coriolanus, to be beholden to no one,

> Affecting one sole throne
> Without assistance.

In *Coriolanus*, significantly, it is Coriolanus and the senators who are seen as the innovators, while it is the plebeians who insist on their traditional and customary rights. They expect Coriolanus to exhibit his wounds to the people in the market-place and to canvas for their support before he can be confirmed in the office of consul. After Coriolanus has been banished Sicinius suggests to Brutus that he should disperse the crowd:

> Bid them home:
> Say their great enemy is gone, and they
> Stand in their ancient strength.

This anxiety on the part of the plebeians that their traditional role in Roman public affairs shall not be weakened parallels the anxiety amongst Members of Parliament about innovations that will weaken their voice in the counsels of the nation. *Coriolanus* denies the validity of a purely personal authority of the sort that James I was claiming for himself. All power ultimately derives from the people – as Milton was later to argue.

In the Rome of *Coriolanus* the city is only able to maintain such fragile cohesion as it has through the pursuit of aggressive policies against such neighbouring peoples as the Volscians. In this way the resentment of the plebeians against social injustice at home can be deflected, while the patrician class can reassert its claim to dominance, based on military prowess. Yet all that is possible is an uneasy truce, since the patricians want to curb and throw back the plebeians, while the plebeians seek to extend their own power and to capitalise on their newfound potential for political mobilisation. There is therefore no real possibility of stability or

political legitimacy since there is no constitutional arrangement
that both sides could accept. Coriolanus acknowledges that the
problem of political authority has become acute:

> They choose their magistrate;
> And such a one as he, who puts his 'shall,'
> His popular 'shall,' against a graver bench
> Than ever frowned in Greece. By Jove himself,
> It makes the consuls base! and my soul aches
> To know, when two authorities are up,
> Neither supreme, how soon confusion
> May enter 'twixt the gap of both and take
> The one by th'other.

Coriolanus believes that he alone can resolve this crisis in the
state by exercising a purely personal authority, based on his own
charisma as an extraordinary military hero. Weakness, discord
and division will be replaced by unity and strength. The difficulty
with this, however, is that Coriolanus does not transcend these
divisions at all, but is rightly perceived by the plebeians as being
at the sharp end of a patrician thrust against them. In fact the
plebeians, rather like the English House of Commons, see
themselves as being on the defensive. It is they who have been
effectively excluded from the system. What they are looking for is
a place in the sun – some acknowledgement, such as Coriolanus
will not give, that they will be able to make their influence felt.
Until this becomes a reality they will continue to act negatively,
invoking their ancient rights and producing a stalemate. However,
Coriolanus refuses political negotiation and dialogue since this
would have precisely the effect of cancelling the transcendental
role he has mapped out for himself which is to bring the era of
conflict to an end. Coriolanus is thus both a would-be Augustus
and an exiled and excluded Antony. Coriolanus criticises the
plebeians for their instability –

> you are surer, no,
> Than is the coal of fire upon the ice,
> Or hailstone in the sun

and rails against the world's 'slippery turns', by virtue of which
he has been betrayed and banished. Yet Coriolanus' belief in his

own marmorial rectitude and consistency is hardly borne out by
his own behaviour in going over to the Volscians. As Jonathan
Dollimore has pointed out, this play, of all Shakespeare's tragedies,
is 'the least amenable to the perspective of essentialist humanism'.[22]

Shakespeare offers us no grounds for believing in Coriolanus'
integrity; on the contrary what is stressed is his inner emptiness
as he attempts to repudiate all cultural supports and mediations,
to be a man who will be beholden to no one. Thwarted in Rome,
Coriolanus imagines that he can simply start all over again in
Corioli, 'a world elsewhere', which will once again be a blank
sheet of paper on which he can inscribe his name, which already
seems his through the name he has won. If there was ever a time
when a purely individual greatness was possible it was surely
this, yet even here the political is relentlessly present. Coriolanus'
attempt to use Aufidius and his followers for a purely private and
personal project of revenge in which his own will will be more
powerful than that of a city, collapses in futility when his own
mother calls upon him to desist. Coriolanus sees exile primarily as
a possibility of return. What he really seeks is to be revered and
respected in Rome and to have his name immortalised in the
Roman chronicles, so that the centre still exercises its power over
him even as he desperately resists it. He now refuses to go under
the name of 'Coriolanus':

> 'Coriolanus'
> He would not answer to; forbade all names;
> Till he had forged himself a name i'th'fire
> Of burning Rome.

The very idea of such a name has become an impossibility since
Coriolanus denies the authority by which it was conferred – only
by cancelling Rome, he believes, can he reclaim his own lost
identity – yet this would be an empty gesture, like Napoleon
placing the crown upon his own head. In his claim for absolute
authority Coriolanus is brought to recognise what a desperately
uncertain thing authority is. Authority is never *sui generis* but
rests on complex and never unclouded processes of legitimation.
It can never rise above the social context that sustains it and gives
it meaning. Authority is necessarily problematic.

Though intimations of finality are always dangerous *The Tempest*
(1611) can reasonably be regarded as Shakespeare's definitive

attempt to resolve the problem of authority once and for all and
therewith to exorcise all the demons that had haunted it. *The
Tempest* is perhaps the one play of Shakespeare that fully reflects
the altered circumstances of the Stuart Court, in which the power
and status of the monarch is affirmed on a symbolic level through
divine right and the ceremonial of the masque, yet is in practice
undermined through his massive dependence on a single favourite
or chief minister. There is no need to insist on an identification of
James I with Prospero in order to grasp that his position is
nevertheless obliquely reflected in the play. For although Robert
Cecil, now Earl of Salisbury, continued under James as the leading
counsellor and adviser to the monarch, the relationship between
King and servant was greatly altered. Elizabeth had certainly
depended on Cecil to manage her affairs but his position, though
secure, was never wholly unassailable so long as Essex was
waiting in the wings. He was always dependent on the Queen's
favour. With James I the position was subtly altered. As a Scottish
monarch and a foreigner, James needed Cecil to ensure continuity
and to provide him with an understanding of how the system
worked. Moreover, James I was beholden to Cecil for his crucial
role in the secret negotiations that led to a smooth transference of
power, despite the fact that Elizabeth had made no provision for a
successor. Cecil himself may have been responsible for the story
that Elizabeth assigned the succession to James with her dying
breath. So James I had no alternative but to rely on Cecil and
permit him to retain the strings of power in his own hands, very
much as Prospero allows his brother Antonio the right of
patronage:

> Being once perfected how to grant suits,
> How to deny them, who t'advance, and who
> To trash for overtopping, now created
> The creatures that were mine, I say, or chang'd 'em,
> Or else new form'd 'em; having both the key
> Of officer and office, set all heart's i'th'state
> To what tune pleas'd his ear; that now he was
> The ivy which had hid my princely trunk,
> And suck'd my verdure out on't.

As an authority figure, Prospero is doubly displaced – first from
his kingly role and then from Milan itself – through intrigues

which typify the unstable jurisdiction of the Renaissance Court.
But what has been lost must now be restored.

On the periphery, on a remote and virtually uninhabited island
in the New World, Prospero seeks, through his magical powers,
to regain command of the centre, to re-establish the power and
authority he has lost. Now he has the opportunity to start afresh.
On the island the principle of political legitimacy that in Europe is
everywhere being undermined can be re-established on a sound
basis. The idea of mastery, as Prospero sees it, will never be put
in question here. There is a certain inevitability, in every sense, to
Prospero's confession:

> know for certain
> That I am Prospero, and that very duke
> Which was thrust forth of Milan: who most strangely
> Upon this shore, where you were wrack'd, was landed,
> To be the lord on't.

For what else could Prospero do there but be a lord, and what
was the island for if not to replace what he had already lost? A
largely deserted island is an unlikely spot for the magisterial
exercise of power but Prospero must be able to rule in order to
substantiate his pretensions to rulership. The island is a locus of
symbolic substitutions whereby Prospero's legitimacy can be
validated. His magical powers replace the equally magical principle
of divine right. His mastery of Caliban proclaims the original
relation of bondage between master and servant. His power over
Ariel suggests the angels that should always hover over the
throne of legitimate kings. In this white space Prospero works to
reconstitute the tradition of heriditary rule that in his own case
has been so treacherously set aside. Ferdinand and Miranda, as
the royal equivalent of Adam and Eve, can re-establish the
principle of authority in an exemplary fashion that will provide a
pattern for the world. Prospero, through his magical powers, will
be able to thwart the now seemingly omnipresent tendency to
usurpation, whether it takes the serious form of Sebastian's
attempt to replace his brother as King of Naples, or its comic
double, the dream of Stephano to be 'King o'the isle'. It is as if the
pulsating musical energies that permeate the island world are a
sign of a cosmic harmony that has elsewhere been violently
disrupted and disturbed. Yet even under such special

circumstances Prospero's powers seem questionable. For no matter how base Caliban may be it is hard to deny that there is some substance to his claim that it is Prospero who is the intruder and the usurper: 'I am subject to a tyrant, a sorcerer, that by his cunning hath cheated me of the island.' In this way Caliban also emphasises that Prospero's use of magic is an illegitimate form of power. Similarly it is by no means certain that Ariel has profited so very much from Prospero's gesture of releasing her from a knotty pine if she is continually made to serve under the threat of being reincarcerated within a knotty oak. Prospero's authority, like all authority, is whimsical, tyrannical, arbitrary. Far from strengthening our conception of authority Prospero's behaviour leads us to doubt it.

In the course of the play the honest old counsellor Gonzalo reminds us that remote islands offer the possibility of sanctioning altogether different models of how society could be constituted. Significantly he invokes a world that is characterised by the absence of domination:

> I'th' commonwealth I would by contraries
> Execute all things; for no kind of traffic
> Would I admit; no name of magistrate;
> Letters should not be known; riches, poverty,
> And use of service, none; contract, succession,
> Bourn, bound of land, tilth, vineyard, none;
> No use of metal, corn, or wine, or oil;
> No occupation; all men idle, all;
> And women too, but innocent and pure:
> No sovereignty.

This is, of course, as problematic as anything else in *The Tempest* and it is immediately ironised by Sebastian's retort, 'Yet he would be king on't.' To realise the Golden Age Gonzalo would have to be a Prospero himself. The dilemma of authority would be repeated. Rather the significance of the speech, like Montaigne's essay 'Of the Caniballes' to which it alludes, is that it serves to demonstrate how the discovery of the New World served to further problematise traditions that were already being called into question. When Trinculo exclaims: 'they say there's but five upon this island: we are three of them: if th'other two be brain's like us, the state totters' all the elaborate mental partitions the play has erected cannot distract from our recognition of how easily a state totters in any case. Many a true word is spoken in jest just as Caliban's preposterous worship of Stephano, his desire to be 'For aye thy footlicker' points to the danger in any uncritical reverence before authority. It is as if in the white space of the New World, far from the confusion and discord of contemporary Europe, we can bid a fond farewell to the dream of authority, which is exerted only in order to bring about its abolition. Prospero's definitive gesture is to *renounce* power – to break his staff and bury his book. Legitimacy is restored through a series of systematic displacements which simultaneously disclose how uncertain a matter authority is. The question that has agitated the surface of so many Shakespeare plays remains unsettling to the very last.

9

Counterfeit Representations: Tragedy at the Stuart Court

As the sound and fury of twentieth-century avant-garde movements recede into an almost infinite distance and the shock value of abstract art and absurd theatre is seemingly dissipated for ever, it becomes even harder to grasp the contrary: that in the Renaissance, representation was charged with anxiety and danger, precisely because it appeared so lifelike. Art undoubtedly proclaimed its pretensions to truth, but not so much in the sober spirit of the court-room as in the fabulous and flamboyant manner of the conjuror or magician. The highest art was endowed with all the power of magic. The counterfeit was charged with so much energy that it was not only able to usurp the place of reality, but to give the force of actuality to things purely imaginative. The spectator of sculpture, painting or spectacle would be so overwhelmed by the sheer presence of the representation, so transfixed by the vividness of the illusion before him, that he would respond to it as if it were utterly real. A story which Vasari tells of the buckler, which Leonardo da Vinci painted for his father, Piero, epitomises the ambitions of Renaissance art. Leonardo took the buckler, which Piero himself had made from a fig tree, and, after getting it straightened and the surface smoothed, decided to paint on it something that would be as terrifyingly real as the head of Medusa. To achieve this effect Leonardo entered the world of the alchemist. He took lizards, bats, snakes and other disturbing creatures into a totally secluded workroom and laboured so long over the creation of a composite monster, that, according to Vasari, he even failed to notice the terrible stench of the putrefying animals around him, so absorbed was he in his grandiose project. Leonardo was literally creating life out of death. On the buckler he painted a grotesque monster emerging from a dark cleft of rock, belching forth fire from its

192

eyes, smoke from its nostrils and venom from its throat, which was calculated to achieve the most horrific impact. Leonardo was not disappointed. When Piero's eyes fell on the buckler he started away in such terror that Leonardo is supposed to have said: 'This work certainly served its purpose. It has produced right reaction, so now you can take it away.'[1] The task of artistic representation is to cross and recross the borders of animate and inanimate, to counterfeit so cunningly that the very idea of illusion is driven from the field. When Benvenuto Cellini wanted to impress the King of France with his skill as a sculptor he had his assistant give his statue of Jupiter a very slight push in the King's direction, since Cellini believed that his sculpture was so convincing that even this small element of movement would be enough to make it seem to come alive. Cellini also describes how when a young girl hid in the head of his great statue of Mars some ignorant people were led to believe that they had seen a ghost by the flashing eyes which they glimpsed within. In such context the moment of transformation in *The Winter's Tale* from statue to living person begins to seem entirely plausible. Of course this magical power attributed to images was by no means a new phenomenon. The medieval Church had developed wonder-working statues and images – in order to impress the faithful and create centres for pilgrimage – which were also designed to give signs of life, by shedding tears or drops of blood. The Reformation objection to idols is both that such representations have supplanted God as an object of veneration and that through their dissemination religion is debased to the level of magic and becomes nothing more than a way of imposing upon the credulous and the simple-minded. In his *Astrologaster* (1620) John Melton writes:

And since the time of Poperie, there have beene found in Churches Images that have had eyes put in by Art, that would weepe, and let drops of bloud trickle down their faces, sweat bloud, and would twinkle with their eyes to the people by the helpe of instruments, and would wry their heads and neckes backward and forward, according to the will of the Priests that invented them, to beguile the people, and to enrich themselves. These Puppets had no tongue, but onely moved and stirred, making signes to the people, many of which, the Cardinalls, erected, and adorned, and commended, to instruct the people: which were nothing but deceits and tricks of these holy and religious Fathers, still to detaine the people in ignorance, and that they should not smell out their knaverie.[2]

This dependence on the counterfeit can be made to serve as decisive testimony that the Roman Church itself offers only a counterfeit faith, that there is nothing in it that is authentic, that the Pope himself is the Antichrist. Yet over and above the wickedness of Catholicism itself Protestants are impressed and deeply disturbed by the power of art to lie – to present things that are *not* in such a plausible way that it seems scarcely possible to doubt them. Richard Carpenter, for example, was an Englishman who entered holy orders in Rome but who subsequently became reconciled to the Church of England and who wrote of these vicissitudes in his *Experience, Historie and Divinitie* (1642). Whilst in Italy, Carpenter was disquieted by much that he experienced. He found it especially shocking that

> those eminent Princes, the Cardinals, should behave themselves with such open curtesie towards noted women, noted onely for their publike profession of wickedness: or cover one nakednesse with another, the naked wals of their Palaces, with pictures, moving to lust, and venery.[3]

But what he found even more disorientating was a mural which he was shown in a church, depicting Catholic martyrs in England, which involved such complex misrepresentations of English history that he was moved to anger and rebellion by its unscrupulous bias. With hindsight Carpenter saw this moment as prefiguring his subsequent apostasy:

> When I came within halfe a dayes journey of *Rome*, and beheld part of Saint Peters Church, I was taken presently, (and I have often wondered at it) with a strange rising of spirit against the City and Churth of *Rome*: By which, I did as it were, presage what I should afterwards know. The Church of this Colledge is all painted in the inward. And the pictures counterfeit men and women, that were hang'd or beheaded in *England* (as they speake) either in the profession of faith, or the defence of vertue. And the painter played the counterfeit too. For, he hath cunningly mingled old stories with these of late dayes; the more

to deceive the beholder; and to passe them all under the same cause.[4]

Here we see a characteristic movement, the idea of counterfeit is doubled: it is through counterfeit representation that counterfeit religion gains its hold. So to attain truth and freedom it is necessary to destroy the power of these representations, just as in Spenser's *Faerie Queene* Sir Guyon hacks down and defaces the Bower of Blisse. Those who are in the thrall of such counterfeit representations are always the spiritually lost.

In his *Pseudodoxia Epidemica* Sir Thomas Browne also voices his warnings against the power of the picture to mislead. The work is devoted to the exposure of a multiplicity of popular errors and Browne insists that one of the most fundamental sources of confusion is a tendency to rest at the level of the sign without interrogating it further:

By the same fallacy we proceed, when we conclude from the sign unto the thing signified. By this incroachment Idolatry first crept in, men converting the symbolical use of Idols into their proper worship, and receiving the representation of things as the substance and thing itself.[5]

In Protestant eyes this is, of course, the more general error of Catholicism: to take the communion wafer and the wine for the thing itself instead of recognising that they are only symbols of Christ's body and blood. Browne finds something analogous to idolatry in the general disposition to take images on trust. He points out that the imaginary or symbolic depictions that appear in maps, emblem books, travel literature and so forth are widely assumed to be accurate even though they may be nothing of the kind. So Browne is made indignant by the pictorial representation of sea-horses. According to Browne the whole concept rests on a complete mistake. He argues – and who am I to disagree with him – that 'that which is commonly called a Sea-horse is properly called a Morse', and that the pictorial representation of sea-horses bears no relation to reality: 'they are bot Grotesco deliniations, which fill up empty spaces in Maps, and meer pictorial inventions, not any Physical shapes'.[6] They are literally a nothing and it is only the power of the image that makes us think otherwise. Implicitly only the written word can be truthful and full; the picture is most likely to be false and hollow to the core. An extensive section of *Pseudodoxia Epidemica* is devoted to the exposure of such images that can mislead. So there are certainly grounds for discerning a Reformation spirit in the seventeenth-century advancement of science, especially when Thomas Sprat likens the Royal Society to the Church of England, since they

> may lay equal claim to the word Reformation; the one having compassed it in Religion, the other purposing it in Philosophy. . . . They both have taken a like course to bring this about; each of them passing by the corrupt copies, and referring themselves to the perfect Originals for their instruction, the one to the Scripture the other to the huger volume of Creatures.[7]

It is precisely this same project that lies behind Locke's proposals for the reform of language. In every case it is counterfeit representation that bars the way to reality and truth. This view is expressed as early as 1582 in Edward Worsop's *A Discoverie of sundrie errours* in which he writes:

> In the time of Poperie moste singular knowledges were shut up. A Ciceronian was accounted a heretike. They could not abide the opening of learned knowledges. They made darkenes, and ignorance, two of their pillars. They fedde the people with scumme and dross, as well in humane sciences, as in divine. For as in stead of divinitie, they brought in superstition and idolatry: so in stead of the pure Mathmatical knowledges, they used conjurations, sorceries, invocations of spirits, enchauntments, and other unlawfull practises, under the names of Divinatorie and Judiciall Astrologie.[8]

In a similar vein Bacon linked the Reformation, in which God called the Roman Church to account for its 'degenerate manners and ceremonies', with 'A renovation and new spring of all other knowledges',[9] and Henry Power, in his *Experimental Philosophy* (1664), envisioned a tide of progressive thought which would be powerful enough to carry all the old rotten buildings away. The cleansing of the Augean stables, created by centuries of decadent popery, would also involve ridding the world of deceitful counterfeits.

Sir Thomas Browne seems to have had fewer objections to the

theatre than many of his contemporaries – they were, after all, closed in the very year in which *Religio Medici* first appeared – but he was nevertheless acutely conscious of the uncanny power of counterfeit representation and of the moral dilemmas to which it gave rise. It is in the second part of that work that Browne makes his astounding claim:

> There is I thinke no man that apprehends his owne miseries less than my selfe, and no man so neerely apprehends anothers. I could lose an arme without a teare, and with a few groans, mee thinkes, be quartered into pieces; yet can I weepe most seriously at a Play, and receive with a true passion, the counterfeit griefes of those knowne and professed impostures.[10]

It is hard to take this as anything more than a towering hyperbole by which Browne seeks to dramatise his sense of the power of sympathy in human affairs – and it was as well for him that the Civil War did not put this doctrine to the proof – but what is interesting is the way in which Browne almost seems to glory in his capacity to be moved to tears by that which he well knows to be imaginary. It both parallels and reinforces his famous confession that

> even that vulgar Taverne Musicke, which makes one man merry, another mad, strikes in mee a deepe fit of devotion, and a profound contemplation of the first Composer, there is something in it of Divinity more than the eare discovers.[11]

It would seem that Browne is here staking out his claim to be considered what the eighteenth century would call 'the man of feeling'. But what is significant for Browne is more that every experience points to another, that the microcosm always signals the macrocosm, so that true piety, in a process of meditation and contemplation, will always be brought to an awareness of higher things. Yet many people in the seventeenth century were alarmed by the counterfeit and although Browne is sanguine here, he could himself be concerned when matters of learning were at stake. His diverse responses indicate just how perplexing an issue the counterfeit had become.

Although this exploration of the idea of the counterfeit in English culture from Elizabeth I to the Civil War will eventually work its way to an analysis of the concern with counterfeit representation as it is articulated in the tragic drama from Chapman and Marston to Middleton and Ford, I want first to show that there is in Elizabethan and Jacobean culture a complex and pervasive discourse centring on the idea of the 'counterfeit'. The figure itself, of course, derives from coinage. The counterfeiting of coins was a genuine problem at the time, and as coins varied so much in appearance and quality they were not, as they are now, mere unnoticed and indistinguished tokens, but each and every one presented problems of evaluation. It is also worth bearing in mind that since most coins were clipped and badly worn, counterfeit coins in their simulated newness would have been relatively glamorous in appearance and possibly the more conspicuous for that very reason. However, what gave the notion of the counterfeit such a fearful moral urgency was the pressure of the Reformation and the consequent rejection of a whole range of ritual practices associated with the Roman Church. It is in the struggle against Rome and the papacy that this discourse of the counterfeit is elaborated. The starting-point is a deep mistrust of the way in which the medieval and Renaissance Church had developed its patronage of the arts in a commitment to conspicuous consumption and display. Protestants objected to the multiplication of saints and shrines, to stained-glass windows, to elaborate vestments and, indeed, to all forms of adornment. They equally objected to complex forms of liturgical music and to imposing, mystifying rituals, designed not so much to create a reverence before God as before the Church hierarchy. These counterfeit forms of representation are seen as decisive evidence of a corrupted religion that denies the possibility of a comprehensive living faith, but rather seeks to manipulate the masses through incomprehensible Latin incantations and dramatic spectacle. For Protestants this is nothing more than magic and superstition. It is absolutely crucial to this view to assert that by such means Christianity is transformed into its very opposite, that what should be for the service of God has become an instrument of the Devil. When, for example, Andrew Willett, in his *Tetrastylon Papisticum* (1593), protests against the Jesuit view that representations of the scourging of Christ or the Nativity should be accorded reverence, he exclaims 'So in the Jesuits judgement everie alehouse painted cloath, shewing any such picture, must be adored and worshipped.'[12] What is at stake here is more than an objection to the reverencing of pictures. Willett suggests that the Catholic mind scarcely knows where the house of God ends and the alehouse begins, that, despite their protestations of piety, they are heretics who are kneeling down in adoration of the Golden Calf. What purports to be one thing has become its very antithesis. The art of the papacy, as the domain of the Antichrist, has been to obliterate crucial moral distinctions and to erase vital spiritual truths, which Protestantism must once again reassert even in the face of accusations that it is the bearer of heresy itself. This worry about falsity and imposture becomes more and more pervasive until it affects almost every aspect of life. It becomes the great issue of the age. As the status landscape rapidly changes with the ennoblement of many new peers, the cultivation of Court favourites with their army of dependants, the social advancement of lawyers and merchants; where ostentatious and stylish clothing becomes a decisive signifier of an individual's importance; the conviction grows that the Court is itself a theatre of counterfeit. In *The Anatomy of Melancholy* Burton suggests that the parading and posturing courtier, who proclaims his identity through a battery of essentially deceitful semiotic indicators is the characteristic phenomenon of the age:

> If Democritus were alive now, he should see strange alterations, a new company of counterfeit vizards, whifflers, Cumane asses, maskers, mummers, painted puppets, outsides, phantastic shadows, gulls, monsters, giddyheads, butterflies.[13]

If there was any one place that could be regarded as the source of all contemporary evils that place was Italy, which figured as the baleful site of the modern very much as the United States does today. Italy was the source of corruption in religion. It was in Italy that the institution of the Court, with all its lavish patronage and extravagant manners, was reaching its apogee. It was Italy that was pouring forth a torrent of paintings, sculptures, entertainments, masques, that was producing all kinds of innovation in art and architecture. Italy was the seedbed of the amoral, unscrupulous and altogether deceitful new politics, of Machiavellian 'policy'. Italy was a land of ruthless despots, vicious cardinals and dangerous charlatans. Italy was not just corrupt, more than that, it was a land where you simply no longer knew where you were.

The discourse of the counterfeit establishes a complex set of homologies between religion, politics and the arts. The counterfeit designates a whole series of practices that seek to manipulate, captivate and entrance. Those who have been ensnared by such maligant arts are like the followers of Odysseus on the island of Circe, or Catholics beneath an alehouse sign, they have become so stupefied, so utterly mesmerised, that they have become incapable of discrimination. It is this state of trance and bemusement induced by the counterfeit, the sense of a total moral disorientation which it imposes, that becomes so very alarming to the Protestant imagination. I want to illustrate the pervasiveness of this discourse of the counterfeit and its association with Italy in the popular mind, by initially citing not a Jacobean tragedy, but a slightly less obvious instance – *Othello*. Not the least striking aspect of *Othello* is the way in which themes of love and jealousy are articulated in terms of black magic and false religion. Othello and Desdemona, who have fallen in love with a person of a different race and colour, are seen as individuals who have recklessly abased themselves before alien idols under the influence of a naked sexual passion. Each has bewitched the other. Iago cannot believe that Desdemona's love for Othello is either durable or genuine because it is based, as Othello himself seems to admit, on 'bragging and telling her fantastical lies'. Othello's dubious 'pilgrimage', which enables him to regale Desdemona with innumerable outlandish anecdotes of cannibals and Anthropophagi, represents a world of pagan legend and credulity of which a reformed Christianity must purge itself, and Desdemona, by believing it, has given herself up to an alien power. Brabantio, her father, finds it impossible to imagine that Othello could have won her affection in any way other than through love philtres and witchcraft. For the relationship is altogether against nature:

> It is a judgement maimed and most imperfect
> That will confess perfection so could err
> Against all rules of nature, and must be driven
> To find out practices of cunning hell
> Why this should be. I therefore vouch again
> That with some mixtures powerful o'er the blood,
> Or with some dram conjured to this effect,
> He wrought upon her.

But, if Desdemona has been magically captivated by Othello the reverse is no less true. Othello is perceived by Iago as a man who has been totally enthralled by Desdemona's beauty, who worships her with a religious adoration. Othello's passion for Desdemona is so great as to banish all other thoughts from his mind. It is literally idolatrous:

> And then for her
> To win the Moor, were't to renounce his baptism,
> All seals and symbols of redeemèd sin,
> His soul is so enfettered to her love
> That she may make, unmake, do what she list,
> Even as her appetite shall play the god
> With his weak function.

Yet this is only from Iago's perspective. From another, it is Othello who is honest, Desdemona who is virtuous and Venice itself the universe of counterfeit in which such figures as Iago are able to effect a transvaluation of values. With conspicuous innuendo Iago defines Venice as a world of subterfuge and of essentially deceitful appearances:

> I know our country disposition well;
> In Venice they do let heaven see the pranks
> They dare not show their husbands; their best conscience
> Is not to leave't undone, but keep't unknown.

It is on this sense of the custom of the country tht Iago relies to inflame Othello's jealousy. But it is Iago himself, not Desdemona, who epitomises the Venetian counterfeit; a man who is everywhere known to represent honesty, even though his actual disposition is the absolute antithesis of this. In theory, Iago's cunning Renaissance policy is the acme of rational calculation and therefore to be seen as the very reverse of witchcraft and black magic – 'we work by wit and not by witchcraft' – yet this very denial signals a deeper identification. Iago ensnares Othello by manœuvres and insinuations that work to disrupt his sense of reality. They capture him in a network of the magical where it is no longer possible to be confident of anything. Othello's fits, his frenzy, are induced by the cognitive dissonance he experiences as things are transformed into their opposite. Iago is the master magician of the counterfeit, who feigns virtuousness:

> Divinity of hell!
> When devils will the blackest sins put on,
> They do suggest at first with heavenly shows,
> As I do now

only to disable Othello's confidence in his own judgement and to insinuate into his consciousness intimations of Desdemona's duplicity:

> So will I turn her virtue into pitch,
> And out of her own goodness make the net
> That shall enmesh them all.

Yet, while Iago is never anything other than the villain, the play proposes, in true Protestant fashion, that Iago's counterfeit discourse could never impose itself were it not for the fact that Othello and Desdemona, like the Church of Rome, have allowed fetishistic representations to stand for the thing itself. Their love can only be destroyed for the reason that, as Catholics become fixated in such symbols as the cross or the communion wafer, so do they superstitiously allow their love to be embodied in the token of the handkerchief. The handkerchief is the first thing that Othello ever gives Desdemona and he insists that she must make it the emblem of their mutual dedication – as Emilia says:

> but she so loves the token,
> For he conjured her that she should ever keep it,
> That she reserves it evermore about her
> To kiss and talk to.

The handkerchief takes the place of her often absent husband. For his part Othello believes that the handkerchief has supernatural powers: 'There's magic in the web of it.' Since the Egyptian who gave it to his mother could decipher the thoughts of others, he doubtless imagines that it has talismanic powers that can ward off all the evils of his new environment. The handkerchief will both preserve Desdemona from harm and serve to detect the hidden malevolence of the Venetian counterfeit. The loss of the handkerchief is simultaneously the loss of a token, a guardian angel and a deliberate betrayal, since Othello has said to Desdemona:

> to lose't or give't away were such perdition
> As nothing else could match.

It is Othello's idolatrous fetishisation of the signifier that enables evil to triumph. For once the counterfeit has gained entry it can never be mastered.

The link between this falsity of appearances and the artifice of painting is made explicit in Shakespeare's poem *The Rape of Lucrece*. For Tarquin, in committing his terrible crime against Lucrece, belies his own reputation and has allowed the demonic other of erotic 'will' to assume control:

> In Tarquin's likeness I did entertain thee:
> Hast thou put on his shape to do him shame

In this brutal act both identities are effaced but reconstituted as perpetual signs, in which Lucrece will always represent victimised innocence, Tarquin the violent betrayer. After the rape Lucrece is led to meditate on the Trojan war, the original narrative of capture and betrayal in which the seizure of Helen by Paris is figuratively answered by the introduction of the wooden horse into Troy by Sinon, a gesture of peace that masks the secret violence. For Lucrece this painting of the siege of Troy focuses in her mind all the terror of the counterfeit that she has so recently undergone; for the artfulness of the representation is such that its cunning is ingeniously concealed. The power of the image is such that it is able to confer honesty on deceit and to withstand even the most searching interrogation, so that for Lucrece to gaze upon it is to repeat her own experience:

> This picture she advisedly perused,
> And chid the painter for his wondrous skill,
> Saying, some shape in Sinon's was abused:
> So fair a form lodged not a mind so ill.
> And still on him she gazed, and gazing still,
>   Such signs of truth in his plain face she spied
>   that she concludes the picture was belied.
>
> 'It cannot be,' quoth she, 'that so much guile' –
> She would have said 'can lurk in such a look';
> But Tarquin's shape came in her mind the while,

And from her tongue 'can lurk' from 'cannot' took:
'It cannot be' she in that sense forsook,
    And turned it thus: 'It cannot be, I find,
    But such a face should bear a wicked mind.

'For even as subtle Sinon is here painted,
    So sober-sad, so weary, and so mild,
As if with grief or travel he had fainted,
    To me came Tarquin armed to beguiled
    With outward honesty, but yet defiled
    With inward vice. As Priam him did cherish,
    So did I Tarquin; so my Troy did perish.

In her confusion, anger and distress Lucrece tears the representation with her nails not merely because Sinon is a prefiguring figure of Tarquin but because in this gesture she seeks to cancel finally the destructive potential of the counterfeit itself.

Opposition to counterfeit forms of representation in Elizabethan and Jacobean culture involves a desperate engagement with a hydra-headed monster which looms up menacingly on every side. It can take the form of a struggle against Roman Catholicism as a counterfeit religion, a critique of the shams and impostures of popular witchcraft, or condemnation by Puritans of the seductive and sexually disorientating world of the theatre, in which the parts of women are played by boys. What is most striking is that each of these activities is perceived in terms of the other. The papacy is involved in the practice of witchcraft. Witchcraft itself is little more than an extension of Roman religion. Catholic rituals and exorcism are a form of theatre. Theatre itself can be a kind of witchcraft. The starting-point for all this is the startling claim that many of the popes had actually practised witchcraft, which most anti-Catholic polemicists, following Foxe, regarded as a matter of sober and well-documented fact. There was some disagreement as to how many popes had been involved. The most frequently cited name is that of Sylvester II, but Richard Bernard, in his *A Guide to Grandjurymen* (1627), also mentions Benedict the 8th, Alexander the 6th, John the 20th and 21st. Edwin Sandys, Archbishop of York under Elizabeth, believed that the popes, in addition to the political intrigue which they habitually practised, were fully prepared to sell themselves to the Devil if necessary to attain their ends:

When these practices will not serve, then they sell themselves to Satan, as did Pope Sylvester: they enter into an execrable league with the devil; and labor by incantation, conjuration, magic, sorcery, and witchcraft, to consume, kill, and destroy the Lord's anointed by picturing.[14]

An embattled England, before the Armada, faces a multiplicity of unscrupulous practices which her enemies will not hesitate to use. Andrew Willett, following Benno, writes in a similar vein of Pope Sylvester: 'that hee poisoned six Popes his predecessors to make himselfe a way to the popedom: that he was a conjuror, a raiser of Divels, and in his rage he cast the sacrament into the fier'.[15] With men such as this at the helm the position of the Christian faith in the world could not be more precarious. As far as Edwin Sandys was concerned, the Pope was endeavouring to deceive mankind by selling pardons and remissions of sin like a merchant, when they were not his to deliver: '"Eternal life is the gift of God." The pope therefore selleth but wind and smoke for fire, shadows for truths: he deceiveth the buyers with false sleights, false measures, false weights.'[16] The very existence of such commercial activity furnishes unmistakable proof that the papacy is only an imposture of true religion:

Thus you see a manifest difference between Christ and Antichrist, the doctrine of God, and the learning of man, sound and counterfeited religion. The one offereth true bread freely: the other, that which is no bread for bread, and that not freely either, but for money.[17]

On a symbolic level the allusion to money itself validates the charge that Roman religion is counterfeit – it is rewoven into a metaphorical system of coinage and trade where short measure and cheating are to be expected. But the argument against Rome can be extended further: by suggesting that, just as the Devil is the father of lies, so Rome, counterfeit herself, has served to generate the multiplicity of false religions. Rome represents the initial falling away from truth that makes all the others possible. This is the charge levelled at Roman Catholicism by William Wilkinson in his polemic against the Anabaptists in his *A Confutation of Certayne Articles delivered unto the Familye of Loue* (1579), where he writes:

For hereupon it ensued that the romanistes so cloyed the church with their fond festivals, lewd legendes, and so stuffed into the service of God such store of idle revelations, and unnecessary visions, that by the reading of them openly in the congregation, the holy and canonical wrightings of the holy ghost were wholly abandoned and cleane cast out of the dores. And this was that which the anabaptists and others heretiques have practised, which they had not witnes nor warrant from the written word and approved truth of God, they forged straunge evidence, and that which with blasphemy they invented, they bitered with untruth.[18]

Catholicism initiates the dangerous process by which the true word of canonical writings is progressively supplemented and systematically supplanted by illegitimate texts, which in turn are the seedbed from which innumerable heresies spring. So in struggling against the Family of Love, Wilkinson does not see himself as engaged in a controversy with fellow Protestants, but, rather, as participating in a much larger struggle against counterfeit religion, for which Rome offers both a precedent and a model. He finds it significant that the Family of Love have kept their affairs so much in the dark, for 'whosoever intendeth to broach any new and straunge doctrine, (as false coiners use to doe) he counterfaiteth in secret'.[19] The very darkness from which their word emerges is evidence that whatever it is it cannot be the light and word of God. Wilkinson consistently uses the rhetoric of the counterfeit to discredit their ideas and to marginalise their significance. In referring to the arguments of his opponent he describes them as 'vayne paintings of the margent', and dismisses the plethora of Biblical quotations which he marshalls in support of his case by describing them as 'Mutes upon a stage called forth to fill up a roome and make a show, depart not utterynge any word at all.'[20] But what is most significant is this nightmare of multiplication. Rome has spawned doctrines, saints, miracles, legends. It has served to infinitely multiply heretical sects of all kinds that themselves depend on the proliferation of false precedents, on innumerable apocryphal and innovatory texts. The process of supplementation becomes more and more difficult to arrest and control. It is precisely this exponential increase in the counterfeit that makes it so incredibly elusive and powerful, and

correspondingly makes the task of those who would defend the
true faith all the more difficult.

In his recent work *Treason in Tudor England* Lacey Baldwin
Smith has focused on the paranoia and anxiety that the very idea
of treason was capable of producing and the evident absurdity of
many of the alleged attempts at sedition. As he perceptively
insists, to explain such episodes solely in terms of deliberate
scaremongering will underestimate the panic and fear of betrayal
on the part of all those involved as they frantically tried to pierce
the all-enveloping fog of conspiracy that surrounded them. Under
such circumstances it was wellnigh impossible to remain
dispassionate.

> If care is maintained in selecting the evidence, it is quite
> possible to maintain that such plots as the Lopez, Moody,
> Squire, and Stanley schemes to assassinate Elizabeth by a
> variety of unlikely means – including deadly perfumes, balls of
> fatal incense, poisoned potions and silver bullets – were
> carefully orchestrated trumperies in which relatively innocent,
> albeit not overly bright, political small-fries fell victim either to
> deliberate government efforts to demonstrate the existence of
> treason or to the political machinations of Court factions.
> Nevertheless to dismiss such performances as calculated
> fabrications is to misunderstand the pressures under which
> traitors themselves operated, the hysterical response their
> treason generated and the mentality that could translate real or
> imagined sedition into a fundamental threat to all good order
> on earth and throughout the universe.[21]

In the light of a discourse of the counterfeit as presented here the
suggestion that conspirators were resorting to the black arts, far
from making them appear ludicrous, would, on the contrary,
make them appear at once the more threatening and the more
guilty. If we ask how treason was supposed to spread at this time
then it seems clear that treason, like false religion, was endowed
with an extraordinary capacity for multiplication. Treason could
spread with incredible rapidity both through its elusive and
clandestine nature and because it was sponsored by infernal
powers.

For Protestants, witchcraft became a matter of acute concern because it was so complexly bound up with religious issues. In effect those writers who criticised witchcraft were equally convinced that the rituals and forms of imposture performed by witches and conjurors were essentially analogous to the equally superstitious practices of the Roman Church. Reginald Scot's *The Discoverie of Witchcraft* (1584) might equally be termed 'The Discovery of Roman Catholicism' since his intention is to disclose and subject to analysis a pattern of resemblances between witchcraft and Catholic ritual in order to show that the one is parasitic on the other. Witchcraft is a further dangerous supplement. As Sydney Anglo points out what is at stake is far more than witchcraft *per se*:

> For Scot the study of demonology meant much more than mere haggling over the verities of witchcraft: over whether witches could work wonders, charm people, fly through the air, attend sabbats, or copulate with devils, the whole problem of magic was involved. . . . And this, in turn, involved the entire question of scriptural interpretation: a patristic accretion *versus* biblical fundamentalism; allegory *versus* literality; myth *versus* historicity; orthodox Catholicism *versus* Protestantism. Moreover, the Catholic Church still had its own magic; and it maintained the possibility of miraculous occurrences, but what were these miracles, and how did they differ from the wonders attributed to witchcraft, against which the church had itself instituted an inquisition?[22]

The overall thrust of Scot's writing is to suggest that the superstitious practices of the Papists are the worst of all. For the pagan soothsayers knew no better and witches are somewhat pathetic figures, both superstitous and ignorant, who ply their trade amongst those who are even more simple than they are themselves; whereas those who perpetuate magical beliefs within the Catholic Church are educated people who should know better and who do so in full knowledge and deliberate defiance of divine revelation. The Catholic attack on witchcraft, in Scot's eyes, was hypocritical since it could draw no meaningful distinction between its own magical practices and those of the witches it persecuted. Moreover, it could be demonstrated historically that the Catholic Church had invariably had the effect of promoting witchcraft as a social practice. In *The Discoverie of Witchcraft* the word 'papist' is often inserted into a string of terms such as 'witch', 'cousener', 'conjuror' and 'juggler' in order to mark what little respect he has for them and how little credence he gives to their protestations of religious piety. To believe in magic is to refuse to acknowledge the omnipotence of Almighty God. It is to proclaim, contrary to scripture, that the age of miracles is not past and to permit the corruption of faith with blind credulity. As Scot sees it, witchcraft has always been an integral part of Catholicism. He insists that 'In all ages moonks and preests have abused and bewitched the world with counterfeit visions.'[23] It is such ministers of the Church who have in the past conjured up walking souls and spirits in order to mystify the people. But where are they now, Scot asks ironically – 'Are they all gone into *Italie*, bicause masses are growne deere here in *England*? Marke well this illusion, and see how contrarie it is unto the word of God.'[24] In the wake of Scot, Richard Bernard asserts such a connection still more emphatically: 'healing witches doe use many of their superstitious ceremonies, lip-prayers, Ave-Maries, Creeds, and Paternosters by set numbers',[25] and 'when Poperie beare sway heere, the Divels and Spirits often appeared, and at that time were many more witches than now'.[26]

For Protestant opponents of Rome, such homologies and transpositions, far from posing a problem, are on the contrary to be expected. For once the belief in God as the sovereign power in the universe is diffused and attenuated, once it is conceded that popes, cardinals, priests and monks are endowed with special powers by their employment of specific rites and verbal formulae, then this process can no longer be arrested. In consequence a comparable efficacity will be attributed to the spells and incantations of witchcraft. The nightmare of Catholicism to the Protestant mind lies in the fact that a religion that is in itself feigning and counterfeit no longer possesses truth, authority or powers of discrimination. The Roman faith has become so confused, so blurred, so adulterated by a multiplicity of accretions over the centuries that it has lost all sense of what it is. It can no longer condemn when it has sinned so deeply itself. Catholicism is itself incapable of controlling the dizzying proliferation of counterfeit representations that it has set in motion. Only Protestants have the integrity and clarity of conscience, the moral energy, that will enable them to cleanse the world of deceit and restore the true faith. So the struggle against witchcraft is a uniquely Protestant mission – as Scot insists when he impugns the credibility of Roman inquisitions and points to the mutual complicity of all such idealogical constructions.

In the Protestant consciousness the dangers of the counterfeit are epitomised in the idea of theatre and the project of dramatic performance. Just as for Richard Carpenter the frescoes in an Italian church were characterised by an extraordinary power to lie and *mis*represent, so a play was an open invitation to idolatry, where the audience, bemused by the spectacle, would become entangled in pagan rituals and heretical beliefs. The development of a secular theatre in Elizabethan times coincided with a determined and successful attempt to stamp out the performance of Mystery plays within the Church, which were now seen as the corrupt survivals of earlier, less scrupulous days. Puritan ministers could not accept the idea of a secular theatre either, since to their eyes anything that was not directly from God or the Bible must necessarily be contrary to them or inspired by the Devil. In a sermon of 1607 William Crashaw exclaimed:

> The ungodly Playes and Enterludes so rife in this nation; what are they but a bastard of Babylon, a daughter of error and confusion, a hellish device, (the divels owne recreation to mock at holy things) by him delivered to the Heathen, from them to the Papists, and from them to us?[27]

We may note that Crashaw's objection to plays is not based solely and simply on their content, though there can be little doubt that from this point of view they offered multitudinous grounds for alarm, but also because they are bound up with the whole insidious process by which the Roman Church has effaced the boundaries between Christian and pagan, and, ultimately, good and evil. To turn a blind eye to the theatre is thus to remain indifferent to the work of Reformation itself, it is to remain unconcerned about all corruptions of faith instead of zealously combating them, it is to refuse the divinely inspired either/or that must affect every conceivable aspect of life. Thus Crashaw will not allow actors to attend communion. Contrariwise true religion will exclude the possibility of theatrical performance. *The Directory of Church-government* of 1644 warns against the expressive gesture: 'let the gesture be grave, modest and seemly, not utterly none, nor too much neither like the gestures of Players or Fencers'.[28]

The Church must never allow itself to merge into a social continuum that also embraces the theatre, the market-place and the tavern. Such differences must be marked absolutely.

The counterfeit is always hollow, transitory, ephemeral. The danger of dramatic representation is that it consists solely of externals. The mind is dazed, bemused and distracted when it should be firmly and devoutly concentrated on higher things. In succumbing to the lure of the sensual, man forgets his spiritual nature and swerves away from the path of righteousness. As Protestants see it, Catholicism obliterates the true symbolic significance of the Christian service, which should by its very lack of elaboration remind the worshipper of the Last Supper, and transforms it into an incomprehensible pagan ritual. Tyrer objects

> The Sacrament of the supper, they make as it were a maske or mummerie by their massings, yea they use it as heathenish sacrifice by their manifest Idolatrie, yea like a plaie or pageant by their goulden shewes, by their bendings and bowinges, mockings and mowinges, windings and turnings.[29]

Peter Smart in *The Vanities and Downe-Fall of Superstitious Popish Ceremonies* (1628) similarly protests at the way in which theatrical representation serves to nullify the authenticity of what should, by rights, be a profound religious experience:

> Nay the Sacrament it self is turned well neare into a theatricall stage play, that when mens minds should be occupied about heavenly meditations of Christs bitter death and passion, of their owne sinnes, of faith and repentence, of the joyes of heaven, and the torments of hell: At that very season, very unseasonably, their ears are possest with pleasant tunes, and their eyes fed with pompous spectacles, of glittering pictures, and histrionic gestures.[30]

If the service aims to be entertaining and all-engrossing to the eye it will for that very reason be rendered spiritually meaningless. In a like fashion Samuel Harsnett waxes indignant at the wicked imposture of Catholic exorcism, which not only seeks to use theatre to manipulate the ignorant, but, in so doing, reduces religion to the most utterly debased level – that is to the level of theatre itself. As Stephen Greenblatt points out in his important article, 'Shakespeare and the Exorcists' (which draws attention to many of the connections made here):

> The spectators do not know that they are responding to a powerful if sleazy tragicomedy; hence their tears and joy, their transports of 'commiseration and compassion,' are rendered up, not to a troupe of acknowledged players, but to seditious Puritans or to the supremely dangerous Catholic church. The theatrical seduction is not, for Harsnett, merely a Jesuitical strategy; it is the essence of the church itself: Catholicism is a 'Mimick superstition.'[31]

For Harsnett exorcism is essentially sacrilegious for it reduces the sublime to the ridiculous. It is to play

> at *bo peepe* with Almighty God, our blessed Saviour, his holy Angels, and blessed Saints in heaven, presenting them in this feigned theater, and making them to squeale, pype, & tumble, like puppits in a pageant.[32]

Catholicism, theatre, exorcism and witchcraft can be coupled together as forms of a counterfeit and essentially degraded representation. They are defined by an inescapable lack and they vainly simulate that which they can never be. In the complex analogical system in which they are inscribed each can be exposed and denigrated simply by being expressed in terms of another. They are bound together in a burning circle of infamy. Even witchcraft seems the more questionable when it can be shown to be associated with Papists. The play suffers by association with the Roman mass, yet no more serious charge can be levelled at the mass than to say that it is no more than theatre. Stephen Gossen supplies more links to the chain, when, in his notorious attack on the stage, *The School of Abuse*, he compares play-going as a distraction for the mind with the counterfeit remedies dispensed by witches:

> Being pensive at home, if you go to Theaters to drive away fancies, it is as good phisicke as for the ache of your head to knock out your brains, or when you are stung with a waspe to rub the sore with a nettle. When you are Greeved, pass the time with your neighboures in sober conference, or if you

canne reade, let bookes bee your comforte. Do not imitate those foolishe paitientes, which having sought all meanes of recovery and are never the neere, run unto witchcraft. If your greefe be such that you may not disclose it, and your sorrowe so great that you loth to utter it, looke for no salve at playes or Theaters, lest laboring to shun Silla, you light on Charibdis; to forsake the depe, you perish in sands; to warde a light stripe, you take a deathes wound, and to leave physike you flee to inchaunting.[33]

To embrace the counterfeit is to cast discretion to the winds and to court damnation. Spectacle is not the completion but the negation of the word. While the book offers integrity, spiritual comfort and truth, theatrical representation is fraudulent through and through.

Yet if the theatre, in Puritan eyes, is counterfeit it nevertheless offers its own critique of the counterfeit through its representation of the Court. Although there was opposition to the intrigues and favoritism at Court even under Elizabeth, much of this remained muted and it only really began to surface after her death, in such diverse plays as *Sejanus* (1603), Chapman's *Bussy D'Ambois* and Marston's *The Malcontent* (both probably 1604). *Bussy D'Ambois* places some forceful and quite explicit criticisms of the style of Elizabeth's Court into the mouth of Guise:

> I like not their Court fashion; it is too crestfall'n
> In all observance, making demigods
> Of their great nobles, and of their old queen
> An ever-young and most immortal goddess.

The play extends this exposure of 'greatness' although in ways that suggest that Chapman was simply using the occasion to vent his opinions, without attempting to correlate them too closely to the development of the action. *Sejanus* is ostensibly more oblique in its fidelity to classical themes but the disguise was transparent enough for it to fall foul of the censorship. However, a *modus vivendi* was quickly established, whereby Jacobean (and Caroline) dramatists were allowed to display the corruption and decadence of the courtly world on the basis that this was always and everywhere of a Catholic provenance, whether French, Spanish, or, most often, Italian. The tacit assumption was that such foreign excesses could scarcely be paralleled at home – though even this was called into question by the notorious poisoning in 1613 of Sir Thomas Overbury whilst he was imprisoned in the Tower, which was clearly intended to prevent some unpalatable information about prominent people getting out. The theatre is an especially powerful medium for criticising the Court because the possibility of local allusion can never be altogether excluded. The play inescapably constructs an interface with the specific social context in which it is performed. No representation can ever be altogether without resonance. It is a shiny surface that necessarily gives back reflections no matter how fragmentary, or distorted. Moreover, in the theatre, role-playing at Court can be both mimicked and ironised through its representation on stage. Disguise is highly significant. The behaviour of Altofront, sometime Duke of Genoa, in his role as Malevole, the malcontent, is very different from his demeanour when restored to office. *Bussy D'Ambois* contains no less than three friars, one of whom is the aristocrat Montsurry in disguise, whom Bussy, perhaps understandably, confuses with another friar whom he believed was dead. In consequence, the role of friar necessarily becomes problematic; so that to be a friar is inescapably to be a 'friar'. Disguise disrupts all the complex protocols by which the Court is able, ordinarily, to function smoothly. It undermines all behavioural codes and draws attention to the hypocrisy and dishonesty that such compliance involves. In George Chapman's play *The Widow's Tears*, based on a famous episode in Petronius' *Satyricon* in which a widow grieving over her husband's tomb soon finds comfort in the arms of a passing soldier, Chapman has the husband pretend to die and then impersonate the soldier in order to put his wife to the test. The counterfeited role will itself be a method of laying bare the truth:

> Come, my borrow'd disguise, let me once more
> Be reconcil'd to thee, my trustiest friend.
> Thou that in truest shape hast let me see
> That which my truer self hath hid from me,
> Help me to take revenge on a disguise
> Ten times more false and counterfeit than thou.
> Thou, false in show, hast been most true to me;
> The seeming true hath prov'd more false than thee.

The convention in Jacobean tragedy, whereby the denouement is often effected through a deadly masque that becomes the means for retribution and revenge, is endowed with great dramatic energy because of its potent suggestion that those who live by the counterfeit shall die by it. The courtly world becomes a house of cards in which illusion is piled on top of illusion until the whole rickety and perilous structure necessarily collapses. It is as if the play seeks to demonstrate with axiomatic rigour that the Court is inherently unstable when it depends for its very existence on the fraudulent and the false. The Court is obsessed with the idea of an absolute centre of power yet at that centre there is a vacuum which events will necessarily disclose. The King and his Court are strong – but only for so long as they are believed to be so. They rely on the power of representation.

Chapman's *Bussy D'Ambois* is a protest against the values of the Court in the name of antique virtue, which oscillates violently between a tenuous optimism and downright cynicism, as the possibilities that Bussy is supposed to embody are progressively extinguished. The play's dilemma is epitomised in the very first line of the play, when Bussy announces: 'Fortune, not Reason, rules the state of things' for it is never clear whether this is a state of affairs that Bussy is determined to struggle against, or whether it is simply a fact of life that he will have to come to terms with. Bussy might have been more convincing had he persisted in the role of outsider and malcontent, since, paradoxically, the more Chapman insists that he is a shining beacon of exemplary virtue at Court the less admirable he seems. Bussy's first great speech overshadows the whole play. He launches a forceful condemnation of that contemporary 'greatness' which does not rest on genuine personal qualities, but which is constructed out of the expectation of deference, an overbearing manner and the ruthlessly self-aggrandising exercise of power. For Chapman, the translator of Homer, this is a paltry simulacrum the real thing:

> so men merely great
> In their affected gravity of voice,
> Sourness of countenance, manner's cruelty,
> Authority, wealth, and all the spawn of Fortune,
> Think they bear all the kingdom's worth before them;
> Yet differ not from those colossic statues,
> Which, with heroic forms without o'er-spread,
> Within are nought but mortar, flint, and lead.

If Bussy is tempted to return to the Court of Henry III by his brother, Monsieur, who plans to make use of him to gain the throne for himself, this is not just because he has been bribed with a thousand crowns, but also because he is attracted by Monsieur's insidious suggestion that such great heroes from the past as Themistocles, Epaminondas and Achilles would never have allowed their merits to languish in obscurity. Yet what is precisely in question is whether the Court is a possible stage on which great parts can be acted out. It is 'greatness' above all that rules. Far closer to reality than this initial prompting is the subsequent appearance of his steward, Maffe, with the money. Maffe can only imagine that Bussy has been engaged as a pamphleteer, soldier or jester so he estimates his worth at the more frugal figure of one hundred crowns. Though Bussy aspires to the free and independent greatness of the classical hero, he is fatally compromised at the very start. He must expect to be used and, subsequently, to be discarded.

Reborn in a new suit, Bussy attracts attention at Court by the impetuousness and insolence of his manner and by the courage with which he vanquishes Barrisor, L'Anou and Pyrrhoy. Bussy is determined to stand up for himself. He is no respecter of persons. He speaks his mind. Momentarily it seems that genuine independence at Court is still possible and that a man who has the courage of his convictions can outface corruption, duplicity and intrigue. Bussy is that cherished, but largely imaginary icon of the Renaissance, the courtier who does not flatter, who by telling the king honestly what he thinks thereby protects him from the self-serving counsel of those who dare not utter unpalatable truths. Henry III encourages him as follows:

> Speak home, Bussy! Thy impartial words
> Are like brave falcons that dare truss a fowl
> Much greater than themselves; flatterers are kites
> That check at sparrows; thou shalt be my eagle,
> And bear my thunder underneath thy wings;
> Truth's words, like jewels, hang in the ears of kings.

Bussy responds by launching an attack on ambitious ministers, corrupt clergy and unscrupulous lawyers but the speech itself is something of a set piece and a hero thus indulged is no longer the oppositional figure that Chapman had envisaged. The minute he becomes just another figure angling for influence he can no longer expose the system itself.

In the earlier part of the play Chapman delivers a few 'home' truths, but as it progresses, as if conscious of the danger, he plunges deeper and deeper into a miasma of exoteric evil and moral confusion that has a distinctively Catholic flavour. In the process some of the ideological circuits that I have already described are activated: in addition to the counterfeit representation of sculpture, we encounter exorcism that is indistinguishable from magical conjuration and Monsieur's policy presented as yet another black art. Monsieur himself compares his action in summoning Bussy, an outsider, to assist him with a conjuror who summons a spirit that he is unable to control:

> I fear him strangely, his advanced valour
> Is like a spirit rais'd without a circle,
> Endangering him who ignorantly rais'd him,
> And for whose fury he hath learnt no limit.

The circle symbolises the ideal of both courtly and magical power that is always at risk because the circle is a limit that is continually transgressed. Moreover, policy is akin to magic in its use of fear, mystery and intimidation to achieve its effects. It is primarily a mode of psychological conditioning that seeks to keep individuals in a state of abject subjection and to intensify their feelings of powerlessness. In his adulterous affair with Tamyra, the wife of Montsurry, which eventually brings about his downfall, Bussy proves himself as much an amoralist as a moralist, when in response to her confession of the guilt and anxiety she experiences in their illicit relationship, he responds:

> Sin is a coward, madam, and insults
> But on our weakness, in his truest valour:
> And so our ignorance tames us, that we let
> His shadow fright us: and like empty clous,
> In which our faulty apprehensions forge
> The forms of dragons, lions, elephants,
> When they hold no proportion, the sly charms
> Of the witch Policy make him like a monster
> Kept only to show men for servile money:
> That false hag often paints him in her cloth
> Ten times more monstrous than he is in troth.

From this point of view the honest passion of Bussy and Tamyra flies in the face of Court hypocrisy and the discipline imposed by Monsieur, unsettling the complex structures of hierarchy and deference – it is taken for granted that Monsieur, as brother to the king, has the right to proposition the wives of courtiers simply because of his status. In this way their love can become heroic. Yet despite Chapman's special pleading and the romantic valuation he places on his hero, it is hard to see practically how it differs from other clandestine liaisons at Court, like Tamyra's earlier affair with Barrisor, or how Bussy can point the finger at Monsieur when he is so deeply engaged in intrigue himself – as their preposterous slanging-match in Act III, Scene 2 seems to confirm. For Bussy's behaviour is informed more by cynicism than by idealism. One of the most provocative aspects of *Bussy D'Ambois* is that Chapman has a Friar act as intermediary between Bussy and Tamyra and has him perform magical conjurations passed off as acts of exorcism, without in any way indicating that this is morally wrong or referring to him as anything other than 'most honoured father' and 'kind worthy man'. Such episodes give greater substance to Puritan objections to the stage. However, it must be borne in mind that for an English audience a friar would automatically be a morally dubious figure and they would not be greatly surprised to find him involved in either immorality or black magic. In the troubled times of the Reformation Montsurry's entrance disguised as a Friar and accompanied by murderers would not necessarily be thought to involve incongruity. Indeed it would be just the sort of thing that a Samuel Harsnett would expect. This disguise spells out the moral dubiety of Roman Catholicism and the pervasiveness of the imposture in which evil palms itself off as good. On a symbolic level Bussy's resort to evil spirits is validated because it is only in this way that he can hope to penetrate the deadly machinations of Monsieur. One form of black magic must be set against another. But this only serves to show how utterly hopeless Bussy's dream of purging the Court of infamy in order to restore true greatness has become.

In the final act Monsieur invokes a world of meaningless repetition that is seen to be strictly analogous with the emptiness of Catholic ritual:

> And as illiterate men say Latin prayers
> By rote of heart and daily iteration,

Not knowing what they say, so Nature lays
A deal of stuff together, and by use,
Or by the mere necessity of matter,
Ends such a work, fills it, or leaves it empty
Of strength or virtue, error or clear truth,
Not knowing what she does.

So Chapman announces a dark vision of things in which the hollowness of religion corresponds all too closely to a felt lack of meaning in the world, and the fact that these words are placed in the mouth of a villain by no means deprives them of cogency. For Bussy's 'Protestant' struggle to restore clarity, faith and meaning fails as he reels 'Before the frantic puffs of blind-born chance'. So the play returns to a negative enunciation of a world that is controlled by inscrutable Fortune which Bussy had originally proposed to defy. Bussy, wounded, proclaims

Here like a Roman statue I will stand
Till death hath made me marble

in his last-ditch attempt to impersonate the antique virtues, yet even he must incur the suspicion of counterfeit. Virtue must always lie beyond the circle of the Court.

It is a paradox that Marston's *The Malcontent*, a far more cynical play than *Bussy D'Ambois*, should nevertheless conclude, as *Bussy* does not, with a general righting of wrongs and the restoration of Altofront, the deposed Duke of Genoa, to his former position. What the plays have in common is a disposition to represent the duplicity of the Court through sexual intrigue and to make women the malign source of all counterfeit representations. Women are dangerous because they are inscrutable and unpredictable. They conceal beneath a virtuous exterior a nature that is, in reality, lustful and recklessly bent on pleasure. In the *Malcontent* Mendoza characterises women as

extreme in desiring, slaves unto appetite, mistresses in dissembling, only constant in inconstancy, only perfect in counterfeiting: their words are fained, their eyes forg'd, their sights dissembled, their looks counterfeit, their hair false, their given hopes deceitful, their very breath artificial: their blood is their only God while in *Bussy D'Ambois* Monsieur observes:

> Oh, the unsounded sea of women's bloods,
> That when 'tis calmest, is most dangerous!
> Not any wrinkle creaming in their faces,
> When in their hearts are Scylla and Charybdis,
> Which still are hid in dark and standing fogs,
> Where never day shines, nothing ever grows,
> But weeds and poisons that no statesman knows:
> Not Cerberus ever saw the damned nooks
> Hid with the veil of women's virtuous looks.

Here the feminine body itself becomes a signifier of female deviousness. It is as if the myth of virtuous woman serves only to conceal a scandal too deep for masculine culture to acknowledge. For woman, far from living up to the high ideal that man has imposed upon her has rather used it as the impenetrable mask for her own lascivious purposes. Marriage has become simply the cover for a string of adulterous liaisons in which every male is either a cuckold or a dupe. Woman, in her use of mysterious arts to enchant and captivate men, is always implicitly a witch. Like Roman Catholicism she uses painted appearances to keep her followers in a state of subjection. Marston makes the connection between Catholicism, witchcraft and woman explicit in the eighth satire of *The Scourge of Villanie* (1599):

> *Publius* hates vainely to idolatries,
> And laughs that Papaists honour Images,
> And yet (o madnes) these mine eyes did see
> Him melt in mouing plaints, obsequiously
> Imploring fauour, twining his kinde armes,
> Vsing inchauntments, exorcismes, charmes.
> The oyle of Sonnets, wanton blandishment,
> The force of teares, & seeming languishment,
> Vnto the picture of a painted lasse:
> I saw him court his mistres looking-glasse,
> Worship a busk-poynt, (which in secrecie
> I feare was conscius of strange villainy.)
> I saw him crouch, deuote his liuelihood,
> Sweare, protest, vow pesant seruitude
> Vnto a painted puppet, to her eyes

> I heard him sweare his sighs to sacrifice.
> But if he get her itch-allaying pinne,
> O sacred relique.

Fetishism and idolatry are one. Both lose sight of their true object and are captured in a web of symbolic substitutions from which they are unable to escape. The Papist and Publius in his debased eroticism inhabit a world of counterfeit representations that has become an end in itself but which is nevertheless perversely satisfying. This language extends into *The Malcontent* which displays a curious obsession with the details of a woman's toilet. Passarello further extends the implications of fetishism by observing 'what a natural fool is he that would be a pair of bodies to a woman's petticoat, to be trusst and pointed to them'. When male desire takes the form of servitude then it is at the mercy of a female desire that is anarchic and unstable. Running through *The Malcontent* is the persistent insinuation that at Court the natural order of male domination is overthrown and, under the sign of Venus, woman is able to impose her will – in all the contemporary significances of that word. With Maquerelle, 'an old Pandress' continually hovering in the background, the Court of Genoa seems little more than a high-class bawdy house, as Malevole admits when he says 'I would sooner leave my lady singled in a bordello than in a Genoa palace.' He then goes on to invoke the 'powerful incitements to immodesy' the courtly context offers. Sex here is infinitely more erotic and provocative precisely because it is so elaborately masked – 'sin it self gilt o'er'.

At Court such guardianship as exists operates in reverse. Its purpose is to protect those who participate in its erotic delights from the consequences of their indiscretions. But this situation has only been brought about through the power of a woman, Aurelia, the wife of the usurping duke, Pietro Jacomo. Aurelia, a daughter of the influential Medici family, uses her connections there to oust Altofront and replace him with Pietro. But no sooner is he installed than she embarks on affairs with Mendoza, the Court favourite and with Ferneze, a handsome young courtier. Altofront, in his disguise as Malevole, the malcontent, reveals her infidelity with Mendoza to Duke Pietro, but Mendoza is able to escape the imputation by exposing Ferneze. Aurelia and Mendoza then plot to overthrow Pietro. It is thus Aurelia who sets in motion a chain of usurpations, which, in turn, are only symptomatic of the way in which male authority has been undermined. Malevole makes the homology between adultery and political action explicit when he says to Pietro:

> thou, closely yielding
> Egress and regress to her, madest him heir,
> Whose hot unquiet lust straight tous'd thy sheets,
> And now would seize thy state.

It is through a woman that the state becomes subject to disorder. It is Aurelia who makes Mendoza possible.

Nevertheless it is Mendoza who is at the heart of the corruption that afflicts the Genoan state and it is Mendoza who epitomises the Machiavellian arts that have seemingly become indispensable to the conduct of public affairs. In narrating to Celso the story of his expulsion from the dukedom, Malevole explains:

> I wanted those old instruments of state,
> Dissemblance, and suspect.

Under the new dispensation loyalty and openness are not even to be looked for, let alone expected. It has become essential for anyone who seeks to dominate that he should be as adept in concealing his own motives as he is at penetrating the disguises of others. The Court is a perennial masked ball, but a masked ball transposed: where the art is not so much to detect the familiar behind the unfamiliar as to detect alien and subversive intentions as they flicker behind the customary, familiar masks. Mendoza is always a consummate actor, a veritable master of counterfeit, who can turn every situation to his advantage yet always convince others that he has nothing but their own best interests at heart. In the pivotal scene, Act II, Scene 5, where Mendoza lies in wait for Ferneze with his master the Duke, Marston has Mendoza stab Ferneze on his hasty exit from the duchess's bedroom, and then, when Aurelia appears, he 'bestrides the wounded body of Ferneze and seems to save him'. Through the art of such counterfeit representation Mendoza can simultaneously demonstrate his loyalty both to Duke Pietro and to Aurelia, since he has apparently risked his own position by such a flamboyant gesture of defiance. But of course, nothing is ever quite what it seems. It is therefore symbolically appropriate that Mendoza should be destroyed by a masquerade still more elaborate than his own. It is only by purporting to be Mendoza's passive and subservient tools, as malcontent and hermit, that Altofront and Pietro can beat him at his own game. It is through the counterfeit of the masque that the tables are turned in what is, after all, only one further imposture. Pietro, a usurper himself, is placed in a position where he must choose whether he will recognise Altofront or Mendoza as his spiritual brother. In choosing legitimacy he must delegitimise himself. So in presenting both a humbled Pietro and, in Maria, Altofront's wife, a figure of unshakeable virtue, Marston seems to reassert traditional values and the importance of respect for authority. Yet this consorts oddly with the actual disrespect for authority which Malevole shows and which Marston, in the Induction, actually identifies with his own position, by having Burbage say:

> No sir, such vices as stand not accountable to law should
> be cured as men heal tetters, by casting ink upon them.

The importance of policy and subterfuge in affairs of state is actually confirmed by the action of the play. Altofront can only regain his dukedom by posing as a Malcontent and by securing his position with the aid of the undoubtedly corrupt regime in Florence. Marston like Chapman, is a pessimist striving to be an optimist but in envisaging the restoration of Altofront the manner in which this is achieved casts doubt on the significance of the event itself. It is hard not to feel that it is Mendoza who has the last word when he says 'Mischief that prospers men do virtue call', and that what Marston is really saying is although we may rail against the status quo, like the Malcontent, our determination to do so is a sign that we have already learned to live with it.

If Marston seems finally to pull his punches the same cannot be said of *The Revenger's Tragedy*, whose immense dramatic power derives not just from the directness and grotesqueness of its imagery but from the fact that it is put at the service of a point of view that is frankly old-fashioned. *The Revenger's Tragedy* refuses to accept that the Court is in any way entitled to put itself forward as the arbiter of values. It is marked by a strong sense of Puritan indignation at sexual licence and infused with a determination to resist innovation in its more sophisticated forms. In *The Revenger's Tragedy* there is never any sense of cultural disorientation or any

expression of the belief that man may be living in a world that is
erratically governed by fortune. On the contrary, the play ensures
both that the wicked are punished and that their punishment is
symbolically fitting. In many Jacobean tragedies the Court seems
all-encompassing. Its claim to define the real is tacitly accepted.
But in *The Revenger's Tragedy* we are always made conscious of a
life beyond its confines and of individuals who remember a world
that was not stained by self-seeking imperatives. When Vindice at
the end of the play says to Antonio

> Your hair will make the silver age again,
> When there were fewer but more honest men

the suggestion that the clock can indeed be put back, the iron age
banished, seems the more plausible, if only because *The Malcontent*
is unable to claim such innocence. Here there seems more than a
glancing reference to the band of Scottish followers whom James
brought with him to the English Court and other allusions confirm
this impression. Lussurio suggests the rapidity with which
reputations could be made at Whitehall when he says

> it is in us
> To rear up towers from cottages,

while Castiza's

> The world's so changed, one shape into another
> It is a wise child now that knows her mother

suggests both anxiety about the rapidity of social change and the
strong pressure at court to conform to a new set of manners,
which is itself a principle theme of the play. It has been suggested
that there is little sense of the political in *The Revenger's Tragedy*
but I find it hard to accept this verdict when, unlike *Bussy
D'Ambois* or *The Malcontent*, it points its accusing finger so directly
at the Duke, as the ultimate source of all the evil that it depicts.
Those who attended James's Court could not but be conscious of
the discrepancy between the stern, august figure depicted on the
frontispiece of his printed works and the rather scruffier and
more disreputable figure that he actually presented. James
undoubtedly was a hypocrite and the King's two bodies were

often very far apart. When the Duke in *The Revenger's Tragedy* confesses:

> It well becomes that judge to nod at crimes
> That does commit greater himself and lives.

this highlights the difficulty of dispensing genuine justice nearer to home at a Court where cupidity and self-indulgence rule. The impeachment of malefactors could scarcely take place given a widespread recognition of the whimsicality and arbitrariness of such proceedings when many others were untouchable. Justice can only be brought about in *The Revenger's Tragedy* by the character of Vindice, who enters the Court from without and who seems to represent some relentless and still active force of retribution in the universe. Like death, whom he seems so close to embodying, Vindice is no respecter of persons.

The Revenger's Tragedy corresponds to Cocteau's demand for a poetry *of* the theatre rather than poetry in the theatre. Its meaning is presented through a series of striking theatrical images, which serve both to constitute the Court as a world of imposture and counterfeit and to annihilate it through the omnipresence and omnipotence of death, the most absolute form of unmasking. *The Revenger's Tragedy* holds up a grotesque Italian mirror to the Jacobean Court in which the punishments are as disproportionate as the crimes. Yet in the play's rage for justice we can never be certain whether Vindice embodies some obscure working of divine retribution or only some imaginative equivalent that has to be called into being precisely because the Heavens have so persistently missed their cue. What Vindice represents is a felt need for retribution in an uncertain and unchanging world, rather than the conviction that such a principle of retribution actually exists. The demand for allegory in *The Revenger's Tragedy* is a demand for meaning and Piato, in styling himself Vindice, seeks single-handedly to restore to the universe whatever is lacking. What makes Vindice so uncanny is that he is simultaneously a completely abstract and remorseless principle of justice, a *deus ex machina* figure, and at the same time a man obsessionally driven by mingled devotion and rage at the fate of his dead mistress. He is both in the game and yet strangely out of it. The skull that Vindice carries at the opening of the play is so peculiarly disorientating because in carrying a symbolic charge it does not cease to be unnervingly particular. Unlike the skull that Hamlet addresses in Act V it prompts not so much general questions and philosophical reflections as precise recollections. It represents simultaneously the evil of the world and the overcoming of that evil in death. Vindice's speech over the skull becomes an act of magical conjuration by which he seeks to guarantee the success of his cosmic mission:

> *Vengeance*, thou murder's quit-rent, and whereby
> Thou show'st thyself tenant to tragedy,
> Oh keep thy day, hour, minute, I beseech,
> For those thou has determin'd: hum: whoe'er knew
> Murder unpaid? Faith, give revenge her due
> Sh'as kept touch hitherto.

In using the phrase 'keep touch' with its sense of 'keep covenant with' and in speaking of revenge as having hitherto kept faith, Vindice thereby introduces the possibility that this may no longer be the case. Like the thunder and lightning which no longer seem unimpeachable signs of wrath, retribution has itself become doubtful. Indeed, what the Italian Renaissance setting precisely designates is a world where policy, frankly and ruthlessly amoral, has every chance of getting away with it. Vindice, in his imprecations to the skull, seeks to become this absent justice and to fill the lack in the world with his own determination. In his compulsive drive to turn each death into a fitting emblem of the sin it represents he will construct an allegorised world so powerful that its truth cannot be doubted. As Howard Felperin has suggested: 'Vindice ultimately refuses to recognise any higher authority or truer authenticity than his own theatrical actions.'[34] Yet in carrying out his self-appointed task Vindice is also vindicating himself. He wants to show that a man who acts out of his own deepest feelings can thereby place himself in harmony with the universe. When Vindice says of his plan to murder Lussurio:

> Ah the fly-flop of vengeance beat'em to pieces! here was the sweetest occasion, the fittest hour, to have made my revenge familiar with him, show him the body of the Duke his father, and how quaintly he died, like a politician, in hugger-mugger, made no man acquainted with it, and in catastrophe slain him

over his father's breast: and oh I'm mad to lose such a sweet opportunity.

We are, of course, reminded of Hamlet's desire not to murder Claudius at prayer but in some act 'That hath no relish of salvation in't', but the difference, we recognise, is that murder itself will not satisfy Vindice unless it can be turned into a morally edifying tableau that will *prove* by its irrefutable vividness that the wicked do not go unpunished.

The Revenger's Tragedy is filled with a terrible rage against the counterfeit. Against the falsity of the world, the elaborately costumed identities of the Court and the whole spectrum of human pretence it opposes the brutal simplicity of death. According to Vindice although ladies can deceive men with 'false forms' they 'cannot deceive worms' and the judge at Junior's trial for rape suggests to the Duke that although greatness may maintain its imposture for a while 'The faults of great men through their cerecloths break.' The Court creates a counterfeit world of day for night, where everything is apparently transposed, as

> last revelling night,
> When torchlight made an artificial noon
> About the court, some courtiers in the masque,
> Putting on better faces than their own,
> Being full of fraud and flattery,

where people are free from any sense of moral responsibility and where sexual licence thrives. By day they display a different artifice in presenting themselves as models of respectability and propriety:

> and in the morning
> When they are up and drest, and their mask on,
> Who can perceive this? save that eternal eye
> That see through flesh and all?

The skull Vindice carries is the ultimate *reductio*. It mocks not only the masks and false faces of the Court but the charade of human existence itself. Everything is articulated in terms of a structural opposition between inside and outside, bone and flesh, death and desire. We see this in Vindice's mocking definition of his profession to Lussurio as a 'bone-setter':

> A bawd by lord
> One that sets bones together.

In this way Vindice also signals the remorseless peripeteias that are to come. In the face of shifting and unstable appearances and uncertain moral standards, Vindice insists, Puritan fashion, on a universe where everything is finally marked. When Vindice confronts Gratiana, his mother, with the charge that she has tried to prostitute her own daughter, both use the symbolically appropriate imagery of disease. Gratiana pleads

> O you heavens!
> Take this infectious spot out of my soul

while Vindice relentlessly focuses on the unpurgeable nature of her pollution:

> Oh you of easy wax, do but imagine
> Now the disease has left you, how leprously
> That office would have cling'd unto your forehead;
> All mothers that had any graceful hue
> Would have worn masks to hide their face at you.

Sin, like disease, cannot be concealed for ever. It will inevitably betray itself by the irrevocable marks that it leaves. For Puritans such as Nicholas Bownd the plague was itself a punishment visited on sexual licence, since those areas where prostitution was carried on were affected most severely. Likewise the punishment of the Duke in Act III in dying of a poisoned kiss from the lips of the skull which Vindice has attired in a mask and clothes is peculiarly apt. Desire brings its immediate punishment. The counterfeit is destroyed by counterfeit. The Duke is further punished by becoming the helpless spectator of the incestuous relationship between his wife and his bastard son. He is thus poisoned both in mind and body, a resemblance that is picked up earlier when Vindice tells Lussurio that Spurio

> like strong poison eats
> Into the Duke your father's forehead

In a play that is full of echoes the incestuous kiss between the
Duchess and her son is as much a dangerous displacement as the
kiss that kills the Duke. For justice to be poetic in such a context,
it must also be forced to undergo the torments of counterfeit
representation. In the concluding masque where the equally
corrupt sons, Supervacuo, Ambitioso, Spurio and Lussurio are
murdered, Vindice insists on the importance of observing the
most precise verisimilitude in the details of the avenger's
costumes:

> The masquing suits are fashioning, now comes in
> That which must glad us all – we too take pattern
> Of all those suits, the colour, trimming, fashion,
> E'en to an undistinguisht hair almost:
> Then ent'ring first, observing the true form,
> Within a strain or two we shall find leisure
> To steal our swords out handsomely,
> And when they think their pleasure sweet and good,
> In midst of all their joys, they shall sigh blood.

This, truly, is to be a dance of death in which pleasure and
punishment, agony and ecstasy will be one. In this final and
absolute unmasking truth can only manifest itself as violence. In
the masque the very care with which the dealers in death simuate
seekers after pleasure proclaims the identity of such apparent
opposites.

In *The Revenger's Tragedy* morality figures as an intruder from
without, but in the tragedies of Webster we are compelled to
experience the life of the Court vicariously from within. Webster
is careful to exclude any possibilities for easy identification or easy
optimism. The characters are offered only very limited options.
Their perception of the world must contend with many others. In
a struggle of all against all, even brother against sister, they must
victimise, or themselves become victims in turn. Yet they run the
risk that they will be caught as much through their own
contrivance as through the plots that are hatched against them:

> Treason, like spiders weaving nets for flies,
> By her foul work is found, and in it dies.

The White Devil begins with a scene that recurs in many Stuart plays, but seldom with such a richness of irony – the announcement of Lodovico's banishment:

Banish'd?
ANTONELLI.   It griev'd me much to hear the sentence.
LODOVICO.   Ha, ha, O Democritus thy gods
                 That govern the whole world! Courtly reward,
                 And punishment! Fortune's a right whore.

Lodovico suggests that the court constitutes a universe of chance and perversity, yet far from wanting to shake its dust from his feet and quit for ever the atmosphere of malice and dissimulation under which he has suffered, he simply cannot wait to return. Like all the others he is irresistibly lured back to the fatal honey-pot and a sticky death in that struggling morass where power and eroticism are so teasingly combined. In a dialogue that reflects the gap between the world and unworldly perceptions in this period, Antonelli offers comfort through a characteristically Puritan trope:

Perfumes the more they are chaf'd the more they render
Their pleasing scents, and so affliction
Expresseth virtue, fully, whether true,
Or else adulterate.

To which Lodovico indignantly replies:

Leave your painted comforts.
I'll make Italian cut-works in their guts
If ever I return.

Lodovico has no use for adversity or for virtue. It is religious consolations that are illusory, not the pleasures and gratification of the Court, which, on the contrary, are all too real. The Court, may have no morality but it does have a code. The participants, like gamblers at a casino, adhere religiously to the conventions and return to the tables again and again in the hope that things will finally go their way. In only about thirty lines of Act V, Scene 3 of *The White Devil* Webster does have his characters speak of 'court promises', 'court honesty' and 'court tears' – the court, by definition, is a world of falsity and counterfeit, where absolutely everything must be suspended, bracketed and subjected to critical scrutiny. The dream that every character has is that of controlling and manipulating all others; to construct a master scenario that will enfold and incorporate everyone else's intentions and plans. Yet for Webster this is the greatest vanity and irony of them all. Webster's subtlety is to suggest that for all their brazenness and guile, his actors are knowingly bent on self-destruction. The very desperation of their designs amounts to a tortured confession of the inner emptiness that they feel.

In Webster the Italian Renaissance comes into its own as the poisoned fount from which all counterfeit representations flow. In dubbing Webster the 'Tussaud Laureate' Shaw wrote more truly than he knew, since he meant that Webster's world was more simulated than real, its horrors counterfeit, whereas it is very much the case that it is the counterfeit that engrosses Webster's imagination and it is the counterfeit in Webster that inspires terror, pity and fear. Unlike his predecessors, Webster makes Roman Catholicism absolutely central to his presentation of the Italian nightmare – which has the effect of making it more treacherous and more dangerous and yet allows the English spectator to feel the more comfortably distanced from such goings on – though in the aftermath of the Gunpowder Plot the threat from Catholicism was far from spent. Both *The White Devil* and *The Duchess of Malfi* cast a cardinal in the role of a principal intriguer and *The White Devil* actually shows Monticelso elected Pope. Although in theory this is peripheral to the main action it makes an enormous impact: in the very scene in which he is elected, against a background in which covered dishes are searched for bribes, Monticelso bribes Lodovico with a thousand crowns to murder Vittoria, whiles ostensibly deploring any such action. Monticelso perfectly exemplifies Flamineo's suggestion that religion is 'commedled with policy' – which is itself one of the principal charges that Protestants level at Rome. But what the play also does is to implicate both in an atmosphere of black magic and witchcraft. Monticelso in his insidious and surreptitious wielding of power figures as a conjuror who calls on familiar spirits to do his bidding. Monticelso keeps an elaborate record of the criminals, spies and informers who can be relied on to serve him and he himself confesses:

> And some there are which call it my black book:
> Well may the title hold: for though it teach not
> The art of conjuring, yet in it lurk
> The names of many devils.

Religion is always a cover for more disreputable activities. Far from suggesting that there is anything untoward or abnormal about this, Webster rather implies that, like the disguise of Lodovico and Gasparo as Capuchin friars, it has been hollowed out into a mere cloak for dissimulation. Witchcraft and Catholicism are linked because Catholicism legitimises all satanic practices by according them a certain reality. Where Chapman and other dramatists of the period were always in danger of being accused of infidelity by presenting magical phenomena on stage, thereby apparently giving credence to them, Webster ingeniously circumvents the problem by having Flamineo address the ghost of the murdered Brachiano as follows:

> I pray speak sir; our Italian churchmen
> Make us believe dead men hold conference
> With their familiars, and many times
> Will come to bed with them, and eat with them

For the appearance of ghosts is much more likely, as Reginald Scot had suggested, amongst people who have been encouraged to believe in them by the Church. Although Flamineo himself says 'This is beyond melancholy', the fact that the ghost fails to rise to his challenge and promptly departs makes it possible for an audience to conclude that the ghost was simply a figment of his imagination – like the ghost of Isabella, which appears to Francesco, but which Webster is careful to present as self-generated:

> Methinks she stands afore me;
> And by the quick idea of my mind,
> Were my skill pregnant, I could draw her picture.
> Thought, as a subtle juggler, makes us deem
> Things supernatural, which have cause
> Common as sickness.

James I, of course, was convinced of the reality of witchcraft and supernatural phenomena, so Webster's stance in relation to ghosts suggests his own more Puritan sympathies. Webster is reluctant to give witchcraft any credence at all; in so far as he does so, he demonstrates how deeply he mistrusts it. The double crime of the murder of Isabella and Marcello, at Brachiano's instigation, is made the more terrible because of the multiplication of the counterfeit. When Isabella is slain by kissing a poisoned picture of Brachiano this counterfeit representation signifies the insincerity of his feelings towards her. Marcello is murdered in a faked accident on the vaulting horse which becomes symbolic of his sexual powerlessness. The black magic at work here appears the more sinister because Isabella is unable to ward off its effects with the white magic of powdered unicorns' horn, which was allegedly able to counteract the poison of a spider. These events are presented to the audience as phantasms summoned up by the power of a conjuror, who specifically dissociates himself from many of the paltry tricks described by Reginald Scot. This, we must believe, is the real thing. Yet it is the reality of counterfeit. The possibilities of fraudulent mimesis that are opened up are disconcerting and deeply disorientating. There is no longer any firm ground in a cognitive sense, just as there is no firm ground in a moral sense either. The play concludes with Lodovico's boast '*I limbed this nightpiece, and it was my best*', thereby asserting his own authorship of the master-scenario, but what the scenarist, Webster himself, presents us with is just such a 'picture' of darkness, whose darkness is the obscurity of the counterfeit. So when Webster, in his conclusion, speaks of 'the true imitation of life, without striving to make nature a monster', what he asks us to believe is that there *is* an imitation that can escape this fraudulent power of the counterfeit and which therefore will not be monstrous. It will be an imitation which pierces the counterfeit and exposes it for what it is.

It is the trial of Vittoria Corrombona in Act III, Scene 2 that foregrounds this issue of counterfeit representation since an audience cannot but be conscious of how much has been omitted from this public spectacle, which represents the most extraordinary travesty of justice. The scenic message is constructed through a ritual in which authority, dressed in elaborate robes, seeks to pillory Vittoria as a whore and to make her the scapegoat for more widespread corruption. The symmetry of the scene is such as to imply that if Vittoria is what they say she is, then contrariwise those, such as Monticelso, who are prosecuting her must be white and pure. Yet whiteness in this sense can scarcely exist in *The White Devil*, since what the white devil designates is the all-pervasive presence of hypocrisy, which only *appears* to be white. Vittoria is not pure, but then neither is Monticelso. The court is a kind of preposterous homage before principles that no longer exist. The proceedings have a distinctly Catholic character. Since the vernacular had superseded the use of Latin and French in English courts, a trial conducted by a cardinal that employed Latin and incomprehensible jargon so that its proceedings would not be understood would be distinctly reminiscent of Catholic ritual. Justice is reduced to meaningless mumbo-jumbo, where a litany of accusation replaces the need for witnesses and evidence. The trial becomes a struggle over the counterfeit. Monticelso insists that Vittoria is not the innocent she may appear to be. He accuses her of counterfeiting the splendours of a prince's court and of being a holy whore, which

> like the guilty counterfeit coin
> Which whosoe'er first stamps it brings in trouble
> All that receive it.

When the English ambassador praises her brave spirit, Monticelso answers:

> Well, well, such counterfeit jewels
> Make true ones oft suspected.

Monticelso's tortuous reply demonstrates the inherent dynamism of the counterfeit, by which it puts absolutely everything in question. The true or the genuine can scarcely exist. Vittoria attempts to turn this rhetoric back on Monticelso and the proceedings of the 'trial' itself. But she is placed in a Catch-22 situation, since the very forcefulness with which she defends herself will only make her appear a shameless, brazen hussy and will therefore serve to confirm the charges against her. As Monticelso says:

> And look upon this creature was his wife.
> She comes not like a widow: she comes arm'd
> with scorn and impudence.

What is significant here is that a contemporary audience, recognising that there could be no objectivity in the trial, would tend to read it in terms of Protestantism's battle against the corrupted might of the Roman Church. One reason why Vittoria and Flamineo tend to emerge more favourably from *The White Devil* than their conduct might seem to warrant is that Webster contrives to present them as if they were Protestants engulfed in a Catholic world, since they persistently refuse to defer to the power of institutional authority. Vittoria turns the language of sexual impropriety back on Monticelso by saying

> Yes, you have ravish'd justice
> Forc'd her to do your pleasure.

She insists that it is his charges and court proceedings that are counterfeit:

> For know that all your strict-combined heads
> Which strike against this mine of diamonds,
> Shall prove but glassen hammers, they shall break;
> These are but feigned shadows of my evils.
> Terrify babes, my lord, with painted devils,
> I am past such needless palsy; for your names
> Of whore and murd'ress, they proceed from you,
> As if a man should spit against the wind,
> The filth returns in's face.

Implicit in this is the familiar charge that since the Roman Church has sacrificed its moral authority through its own corruption it can no longer aspire to pass judgement on others. Rome is the true whore, the Whore of Babylon, and it is Rome that offers counterfeit religion and counterfeit justice. The Protestant gaze can easily penetrate the idolatrous representations of the trial. It is a mockery through and through.

These Protestant connotations are strongly present in the final act, where Vittoria and Flamineo must face the prospect of their death. They are preceded by Brachiano, whose moment of passing is debased and degraded. He falls into 'a strange distraction' in which

> His mind fastens
> On twenty several objects, which confound
> Deep sense with folly.

Lodovico remarks on the ignominy of his condition. He is unable to grasp the significance of his situation. But what, in any event, removes the last vestiges of dignity from the scene is the fact that it is presided over by Lodovico and Gasparo, posing as Capuchins, who complete their mutterings in Latin by strangling him. This demonstrates not merely the scandalous reality of Roman religion but, in English eyes, epitomises the essential hollowness of a faith which in its ritualistic obsessions can leave no space for the individual conscience. In the final scene Webster insists that dying is a private matter, in which each individual must try to come to terms with their actions in life and make a personal settlement of accounts. Flamineo, by his counterfeit death, seeks to expose the treacherousness of women, since Vittoria and Zanche had sworn to die with him, but Flamineo too has erred by his preoccupation with the conduct of others. Finally, for Flamineo and Vittoria, dying becomes a gesture of freedom and independence through which they can belatedly liberate themselves from the corrupt imperatives that govern the courtly life

> *Prosperity doth bewitch men seeming clear,*
> *But seas do laugh, show white, when rocks are near.*
> *We cease to grieve, cease to be Fortune's slaves,*
> *Nay cease to die by dying*

and Flamineo significantly adds:

> I do not look
> Who went before, nor who shall follow me;
> No, at myself I will begin and end.

So, at the last, Flamineo, whose whole life has been dictated by the requirements and the actions of others, finds the courage to face death alone. In this moment at least, before the white seas of death, there can no longer be falsity or space for the counterfeit.

In *The Duchess of Malfi* (1614) the Court asserts itself no less imperiously, but what is significant is that Webster sets against it a private sphere, which, though it vainly struggles to maintain itself in face of the pressure exerted by Ferdinand, the Duke and the Cardinal, nevertheless does represent an alternative centre of values. In *The White Devil* it is hard to think of either Vittoria or Flamineo existing outside the world of the Court. Their destiny is to be used by such as Brachiano and Francisco and their limited autonomy seems epitomised by Brachiano's order that they shall follow him to their death. But Antonio and the Duchess retain much of their innocence and integrity. Their life together in a relationship that is necessarily clandestine figures as a tiny atoll of affection and decency that is at first encircled then extinguished by an irresistible sea of treachery and deceit. In *The Duchess of Malfi* we find a more subtle sense of the counterfeit that is to influence Webster's successors Middleton and Ford, in which the characters are made the helpless victims of the counterfeit appearances that society imposes upon them. They are driven by passion they can only dissimulate, not control. They are forced into a position of falsity that contains within it the seeds of destruction. In consequence, it becomes harder and harder to pass judgement upon them since we see how their lives are hopelessly twisted by the forces that impinge upon them. The flame of independence and free will still burns, but it is like the last flaring up of a candle just as it is at the point of extinction. Yet their desperation testifies to a depth of passion, an emotional veracity, that the Court could never acknowledge. There even a flickering candle is a conflagration in miniature. In a world where everything seems permitted only love is taboo. In *The Duchess of Malfi* the force of this interdiction is demonstrated when the Duchess is compelled to embark on a fake pilgrimage to Loreto in order to find sanctuary; yet it may be that this errand is truer than the purpose it counterfeits. But even at the holy shrine of Loreto there is to be no escape, for it is, after all, only one more face of corrupt ecclesiastical power. The dumb show in which the banishment of the Duchess from Loreto is combined with a ceremony in which the Cardinal divests himself of his religious robes in order to don the uniform of a soldier, offers a symbolic representation of the secularisation of the Church. Policy is all. The pretence of piety is only to be maintained in the determination of her brothers to keep the Duchess a 'holy relic', who at their whimsical behest must continue to signify the purity of womanhood and deny her feelings as a woman. The price of

238   *England's Time of Crisis*

greatness is that those of noble birth must live out their lives in a web of artifice where nothing matters but *raison d'état* and personal independence is necessarily excluded. As the Duchess says to Antonio, in declaring here love for him:

> And as a tyrant doubles with his words,
> And fearfully equivocates; so we
> Are forc'd to express our violent passions
> In riddles, and in dreams, and leave the path
> Of simple virtue, which was never made
> To seem the thing it is not.

While the idea of a natural existence is invoked by the Duchess when she speaks wistfully of

> The birds, that live i'th'field,
> On the wild benefit of nature, live
> Happier than we

it can only seem like some impossible phantasm that lies completely out of reach. At Court everything matters, everything is of consequence: the repercussions of every action must be carefully pondered. So although the Duchess actually is spontaneous at the very moment when she questions the possibility of being so, she is nevertheless right to do so, since there can be no place for it in her life so long as she is being watched over by Bosola. Although the terror of the Court ultimately rests on the very real possibility of violence, its deeper source is the sense each individual has that his or her existence is of absolutely no consequence. For Ferdinand, the Duchess is a widow and must remain so. By offering her the dagger with which he proposes that she should kill herself he simply makes manifest what has been implicit all along – that she lives only on sufferance. Doubtless Ferdinand has some kind of incestuous attachment to her; doubtless he disapproves of Antonio's lowly status; perhaps he fears some threat to his own position through her independence; however, the point is that *any* gesture of independence threatens the Court, whose very foundations are built on flattery, deference, compliance and anxiety. When the Duchess objects to the stratagems that she and Antonio are compelled to resort to in self-defence –

> O misery, methinks unjust action
> Should wear these masks and curtains; and not we

she does so because she believes that she has nothing to hide and that such imposture reduces them to the same squalid level as everyone else. The ultimate absurdity is that Ferdinand and the Cardinal believe they have the right to lecture her on the importance of reputation and the evils of hypocrisy, that inescapable white devil. It is one of the many ironies of the play that Webster places the critique of this perverse obsession with reputation in the mouth of Bosola, the arch-cynic and malcontent:

> Can this ambitious age
> Have so much goodness in't, as to prefer
> A man merely for worth: without these shadows
> Of wealth, and painted honours? possible?

Bosola, of course, knows that it cannot, but his hypothetical enquiry nevertheless sets up wider reverberations since if even he himself is only valued as long as he can be of use and if value depends 'on so changeable a prince's favour', then the struggle on which Court existence is predicated is ultimately meaningless, even for those who are devoted players of the game. Although *The Duchess of Malfi* is in some respects more hopeful than *The White Devil* it is far more pessimistic in its assessment of the Court. The dream of being master of the game, of constructing a scenario that will subjugate all rivals, that of Lodovico in *The White Devil*, now appears as some fantastic dream of reason that could only be conceived in a climate of perversity and madness. In *The Duchess of Malfi* this irrationality is laid bare. For Webster it is necessarily produced by a world of counterfeit since those who live within it in their multiple impostures lose all sense of who they are or why it is that they do the things they do. This diminished sense of reality is already a form of madness.

In Act V, Scene 3 Antonio and Delio walk in the ruins of an ancient abbey, part of which, significantly, has been made over into military fortifications. It is here that the Cardinal has his residence. In this unexpected setting of the open air Antonio speaks of his love of the past:

> I do love these ancient ruins:
> We never tread upon them, but we set
> Our foot upon some reverend history.
> And, questionless, here in this open court,
> Which now lies naked to the injuries
> Of stormy weather, some men lie interr'd
> Lov'd the church so well, and gave so largely to't,
> They thought it should have canopi'd their bones
> Till doomsday. But all things have their end:
> Churches and cities, which have diseases like to men
> Must have like death that we have.

The reflections present a distinctively Protestant view. The ruins serve as an emblem of the vainglory of the Roman Church and of the pride and self-satisfaction of those who sought to guarantee their spiritual redemption by the purchase of indulgences. The proud cities of Renaissance Italy and the still deeply corrupted Church will meet with a similar fate. So Antonio loves the ruins as much for what they represent as for what they actually are. The abbey itself was counterfeit: it represented to all that saw her a promise of glory, spiritual might and eternal bliss that could not be finally honoured. Now it is nothing more than a worthless, crumpled promissory note. In *The Duchess of Malfi* itself we cannot doubt that the state of the world and the state of the Church is now grown infinitely worse. Webster portrays Italy as the domain of the Antichrist where the only role left for religion is to serve as a cloak for evil and immoral purposes. Like all good Protestants of his day Webster believes that it is scarcely possible to convey the depths of depravity to which the Roman Church has sunk, but he nevertheless proffers his audience a striking figure that can stand for it – the scene in which the Cardinal poisons his mistress by asking her to kiss the book that he is holding, a book which we cannot but assume is the Bible. In this transvaluation of values good is always precluded, necessarily suspect. In the nightmare of the counterfeit it is always necessary to interrogate appearances, to disarm and deflect any possible counter-movement which may give the other an advantage. As Bosola points out to Ferdinand:

> Yet take heed:
> For to suspect a friend unworthily
> Instructs him the next way to suspect you,
> And prompt him to deceive you.

This is the Italian Renaissance equivalent of the Golden Mean. Inevitably in such a context the Duchess and Antonio cannot but appear as reckless simpletons who know not what they do. *The Duchess of Malfi* is not a naturalistic play but one which seeks to explore the uttermost limits of the modern as that would then have been understood by an English Protestant audience. The horrors of Act IV, in which the Duchess is psychologically destroyed before she is brutally strangled, involves some of the most grotesque events ever presented on the Jacobean or any other stage, but before rushing in to deliver some pat aesthetic or moral judgement we need to consider very carefully just what they are intended to signify. The attempt to arouse horror is always complex because it is always so much more than a gut reaction and violence pure and simple will not necessarily provoke it. Horror has a metaphysical dimension. We are frightened not just by what we see but by our powerful sense that evil is potentially unlimited; any awareness of its concrete limitations will always cause our reaction to collapse back into laughter. In the emotional torturing of the Duchess, Webster strives for an apotheosis of the counterfeit. Ferdinand torments her first by cold-bloodedly offering a dead man's hand in place of his own. He then shows her lifelike wax effigies of Antonio and her children in order to convince her that they are dead. We must believe that this will induce the most extreme psychological disorientation, intensified to the point of madness by the retinue of madmen who are loosed upon her. Such madness can be seen as having been produced by homology, by an inability to know the true from the false. The scene can be read emblematically. The dead hand signifies Ferdinand's insincerity and the absence of any genuine feeling at Court. The effigies of her husband and children suggest that art is the dehumanising technology of a soulless world. Ferdinand notes with satisfaction:

> Excellent; as I would wish: she's plagued in art.
> These presentations are but fram'd in wax
> By the curious master in that quality,
> Vincentio Lauriola, and she takes them
> For true substantial bodies.

We may also note that such bodies that lack substance are the product of a culture where religion is equally devoid of substantive content. For Webster, Renaissance Italy is precisely such a hollowed-out world. It has become nothing more than elaborate decor. Such a perception also runs through the long-running conflict over the nature of the masque between Inigo Jones and Ben Jonson. For Jonson, speech is the soul of the masque and when it becomes an entirely visual spectacle it becomes a positive moral danger. We must never underestimate the seventeenth-century fear of mimesis. The potential for alienation and dehumanisation that is for us bound up with the development of science, technology and mass production, in the Renaissance is centred on the alarming new developments in the visual arts. The counterfeit produces a loss of certainty about the nature of the world and the human capacity to interpret it. Paradoxically mimesis *derealises* by the confusion it produces in the spectator, by the very havoc it wrecks on his powers of judgement. The whole basis for knowing seems fatally undermined. The counterfeit sucks the individual down into a dizzying vortex of deceitful appearances, in which Machiavellian policy, withcraft and false religion are unnaturally combined. In *The Duchess of Malfi* Ferdinand is associated with witchcraft through Bosola's self-description as the Duke's 'familiar' and through the Cardinal's prophetic suggestion that his hostility to any affair on the part of the Duchess is excessive:

> How idly show this rage! which carries you
> As men convey'd by witches, through the air
> Of violent whirlwinds.

In Act IV Ferdinand stands revealed as an exponent of evil arts. The function of witchcraft in these scenes is that of sympathetic magic: to use simulacra to drive the life out of the Duchess so that she herself becomes an empty shell. When she is shown the waxworks of her family, she says:

> it wastes me more,
> Than were't my picture, fashion'd out of wax,
> Stuck with a magical needle, and then buried
> In some foul dunghill.

When the Duchess subsequently asks her waiting-woman, Carila to describe her wasted appearance, she answers:

> Like to your picture in the gallery,
> A deal of life in show, but none in practice:
> Or rather like some reverend monument
> Whose ruins are ever pitied.

The counterfeit preys on the living. The Duchess of Malfi is now nothing more than a pathetic simulacrum of her original self, which is why she so desperately, yet so triumphantly cries out: 'I am Duchess of Malfi still.' Such scenes refocus painting and sculpture in their traditional folk context as forms of aggression and symbolic destruction. In consequence art is not simply parasitic on a real world but is its deadly, dangerous rival. The true meaning of the counterfeit is death. Pictures in galleries, sculptures on tombs vainly seek to perpetuate life since they are forms of death already. No matter how skilfully they may contrive to imitate, they serve as a continual reminder of mortality. Art can never be more than a *momento mori*. Its function is not so much to celebrate life as to mock it. Yet this mockery can also be seen as an extension of the counterfeit that is practised daily at Court:

> For those whose faces do belie their hearts
> Are witches.

So at the heart of Jacobean tragedy is a sense that earthly existence is nothing more than a macabre dance of death. Yet even the theological implications of such a perception are undermined, for the force of the counterfeit is to display a world that has been emptied of meaning. Even vengeance seems purposeless. When Bosola has presided over the strangling of the Duchess it is hard to discern any redeeming significance in his decision to punish Ferdinand and the Cardinal when his call for a pension is refused. This is not justice but the banality of evil. Bosola's dying words strike the truest note:

> We are only like dead walls, or vaulted graves
> That ruin'd, yield no echo.

The world of *The Duchess of Malfi* is without resonance. The last traces of humanity have been erased.

By comparison with Webster, Middleton's major tragedies, *Women Beware Women* and *The Changeling*, written a decade later, are far less metaphysically anguished and overwrought, yet they are profoundly intelligent. Middleton does not simply take the counterfeit as a given but probes and explores it from every conceivable angle. As I have already suggested the miasma of deceit and evil conjured up by earlier Jacobean dramatists has strong anti-Catholic overtones, but Middleton deliberately avoids this even when he might appear to have powerful reasons for stressing it. For example, *The Changeling* is set in Spain and was written not long before Middleton produced his notorious attack on Spanish foreign policy in *A Game at Chesse* (1624), yet there is nothing specifically Spanish about the play in the way that *The Duchess of Malfi* addresses matters distinctively Italian. Middleton focuses so intensively on personal relationships that the plot might just as well have been set in England. Although the English nobility might not be able to match the intense concern with personal honour and dignity displayed by Vermadero, de Piracquo and Alsemero, they were concerned with it nevertheless – as Donne's misfortunes amply demonstrate. Middleton's real subject is the way in which culture represses and perverts human sexuality. His characters are forced to conceal and dissimulate their real feelings behind a mask of public rectitude. To obtain what they desire they are driven to more and more reckless deceits and impostures until their passions are driven to the surface with all the violent energy of a volcano. For Middleton, the counterfeit is an existential nightmare in which each individual hides his or her emotions from others and is correspondingly compelled to decipher the intentions of others from the enigmatic signs that simultaneously betray and mislead. When Alsemero confesses his love for Beatrice at the beginning of *The Changeling*, Beatrice, instead of responding in kind, gives him this dusty answer:

> Be better advis'd, sir:
> Our eyes are sentinels unto our judgements,
> And should give certain judgement what they see;
> But they are rash sometimes, and tell us wonders
> Of common things, which when our judgements find,
> They can then check the eyes, and call them blind.

As with the mutual glance exchanged between the Duke and the still 'innocent' Bianca in *Women Beware Women*, the eye is the medium through which the soul is filled with irrational, erotic passion. Thus, paradoxically, the eye is always blind because it can never be other than a medium of error through which the individual is led to forget his place in society and the duty and deference that he owes to others. It creates a multiplicity of misrecognitions. Tomazo de Piracquo and Alsemero fail to read Beatrice correctly and Beatrice herself never grasps the depth of passion which her servant, de Flores, feels for her. It always seems to be human nature that produces tragedy in Middleton, yet it is never clear whether this comes about through the perverse arrangements of society or the perversity of a human nature that struggles against it.

Middleton's more complex sense of what is at stake in counterfeit representation stems from his greater understanding and more sympathetic attitude to the predicament of women. Middleton recognises that there will be oppression and inauthenticity in marital relationships when women remain essentially unfree, even when they are fortunate enough to be able to choose their husbands. A woman is a chattel placed in the possession of a man and her sense of oppression will be inescapable not just because the marriage is necessarily loveless, but because the terms of the contract itself set so little store on a woman's freedom, independence or happiness. Marriage, as Middleton so powerfully grasps, is not simply coercive it is demeaning – as Isabella protests in *Women Beware Women*:

> oh the heart-breakings
> Of miserable maids, where love's enforc'd!
> The best condition is but bad enough;
> When women have their choices, commonly
> They do but buy their thraldoms, and bring great portions
> To men to keep 'em in subjection,
> As if a fearful prisoner should bribe
> The keeper to be good to him, yet lies in still,
> And glad of a good usage, a good look sometimes.
> By'r Lady, no misery surmounts a woman's.

Since Middleton is never prone to idealise or gloss over the penalties women suffer under, he is therefore able to show their struggles to resist in a more positive light. It would seem that Middleton's plays reflect the tendency in commercial Puritan culture to acknowledge women as individuals and to treat them with greater respect. However, it cannot be denied that Middleton's general presentation of women tends to reinforce the negative stereotypes of Western culture, where woman is seen as deceitful, false and unreliable, consistent only in so far as she conforms to the eternal pattern of Cressida. The very titles of Middleton's plays, *Women Beware Women* and *More dissemblers besides Women*, minister to this prejudicial view. The image of woman in Middleton is powerfully bound up with a sense of unpredictability and danger, where in the notion of 'a woman's will' the drive for independence and sexual pleasure is linguistically fused. Middleton is, in fact, quite sympathetically disposed to this desire for erotic fulfilment on the part of a woman and is by no means in accord with Leontio's contrary insistence in *Women Beware Women* that Bianca shall meekly

> go after the rate of my ability,
> Not the licentious swinge of her own will.

Middleton is not afraid to present highly sexed women. He recognises that it is they who must bear the brunt of a male-dominated society's hypocrisy and double standards. He grasps very clearly that what is at stake is not just a wanton longing for forbidden pleasures but the desire on the part of a woman to have an existence in her own right. Yet at the same time Middleton remains within the Western tradition of courtly love that implies that it is the taboo itself that creates eroticism. Isabella, Hippolito and Bianca in *Women Beware Women*, Beatrice and de Flores in *The Changeling* are powerfully attracted to that from which they are debarred. Passion, it seems, is necessarily destructive. But Middleton's sense of what *makes* it destructive is infinitely more complex than the assertion might suggest. Middleton recognises that what precipitates catastrophe is not purely passion but the fact that woman always becomes entangled in male assumptions about honour and possession; anything she does is simply re-articulated within a social code that deems men the only possible actors. So although Middleton may effectually reinforce negative stereotypes of women, he nevertheless deeply undermines these stereotypes by his continual and insistent suggestion that women, despite their handicaps, must be regarded as agents on the social scene.

In *Women Beware Women* all the relationships in the play are in some way socially improper. Hippolito conceives an incestuous passion for his niece, Isabella. Bianca's relationship with the Duke is adulterous, as is Livia's subsequent infatuation with Leontio, and the impropriety is intensified by the difference in age and social status. Livia herself admits to the immorality of her advances to Leontio, in terms which recall the amorous widows of Petronius and Chapman:

> 'Tis as unseasonable to tempt him now
> So soon, as for a widow to be courted
> Following her husband's corse, or to make bargain
> By the grave-side, and take a young man there.

Even Leontio's initial marriage to Bianca went against the proprieties, since he virtually kidnapped her in flagrant violation of her parent's wishes. Since the only other marriage proposed in the play is between Isabella and a wealthy idiot, Middleton does nothing to encourage the view that wedlock as currently practised is a very satisfactory arrangement. Its principal function is to serve as a cover for indiscretions since, as Livia points out 'Nothing o'erthrows our sex but indiscretion.' Isabella is herself the child of a man other than Fabritio, her supposed father, who is now using his position to enforce a transaction with a man she utterly loathes and detests. Indeed the whole notion of guardianship is quite crucial to the play. Leontio tries to keep Bianca away and out of sight – 'The jewel is cas'd up from all men's eyes' – while Hippolito is hypocritical enough to draw the line at his sister's relationship with Leontio, while practising incest himself. The whole idea of 'lawful' love becomes hopelessly confused when the Duke decides to legitimise his passion for Bianca by disposing of Leontio, her lawful husband. It is against such a background that we must assess the whole vexed question of Bianca's 'alteration' – "Tis the most sudden'st, strangest alteration' – in abandoning an innocent relationship with Leontio for a scandalous affair with the Duke. The transition occurs on the very balcony where only moments before she bids a fond and tearful farewell to her husband. One devastating glance exchanged with the Duke as he proceeds in state through the town is enough to do the damage and this seems to confirm Bianca's and Middleton's conviction that the eye is inherently unstable:

> what's the eye's treasure
> But change of objects.

It would seem that Bianca has not been the innocent that she appeared to be. Behind the prurient mask she conforms to the anxiety-making stereotype of the lustful and unpredictable woman who will not hesitate to follow her fancy – the rightful prerogative of man. Yet even here the issue is fraught with ambiguity. For although Leontio postulates their love as ideal:

> we embrac'd
> As if we had been statues only made for't.
> To show art's life

the very difficulty of thinking art as life not counterfeit, the way in which his metaphor posits love as frozen immobility rather than authentic emotion, serves to problematise his assertion even in the uttering of it. Middleton implies that Bianca's alteration is more truly to be understood as an assertion of the spirit of freedom in a natural reaction against the unnatural condition of restraint, verging on imprisonment, in which she has been kept. Passion can be seen as potential for self-mutilation, for the consequences are damaging whether it festers in secret or whether it is openly displayed. Hippolito, speaking of his 'strange affection' confesses that he came by it

> Ev'n as easily
> As man comes by destruction, which oft-times
> He wears in his own bosom.

So Middleton's characters inflict injuries on themselves and others through the violence of their emotions, yet given the state of society it can hardly be otherwise. The orgy of killing with which the play ends may seem excessive, even by the standards of the genre, but by its very excess it serves to disclose the depth of feeling that has been culturally repressed:

> Oh how painful 'tis
> To keep great sorrow smothered.

In *The Changeling* Middleton hammers home his insight that the ultimate source of the tragic is society's refusal to come to terms with a woman's need to express her identity and sexuality. The question that Freud posed, 'what do women want?', is one that cannot even be thought; yet even Freud's formulation of it suggests that it is one that declines any realistic answer. It opens up a vista of dismayingly insatiable requirements so that the myth of a 'woman's will' is subtly reinforced. In *The Changeling* disaster stems from the fact that Alonzo, whom Vermadero is determined to have married to his daughter, Beatrice, refuses even to contemplate the possibility that she may be in love with somebody else. Tomazo, his brother, recognising Beatrice's manifest lack of enthusiasm for the match, suggests that he should break off the engagement and try to forget her as soon as possible. For if he is conscious that she really loves somebody else this can only render his life a torment. Alonzo indignantly repudiates this tactful and sensible suggestion:

> I should depart
> An enemy, a dangerous, deadly one
> To any but myself, that should but think
> She knew the meaning of inconstancy,
> Much less the use and practice.

In so speaking Tomazo infringes a whole series of cultural taboos. Women are trapped within the binary sets of constancy and waywardness, chastity and lustfulness, obedience and disobedience, truth and falsity. If they are not the former they must be the latter. Alonzo's words make it abundantly clear why woman is always regarded as inconstant, since for woman to know the meaning of constancy she would have to have no identity at all. There can be no questions concerning feminine independence but only those that revolve around culturally significant questions of masculine honour. Anything that is conceded to woman is taken away from man; more than this – it unmans him entirely. So in the zero-sum game of marriage a woman's freedom is always dearly bought at the cost of disgrace and humiliation to the man. A woman who even so much as thinks of another man whom she loves when forced against her will into a contractual marriage is as good as a prostitute, indeed is a prostitute. Yet even this thought itself cannot be thought. The operation of taboo must be total and complete. For a woman could only crave such love and independence if she were

driven by lustful, insatiable desires. Hence the desire for autonomy
in a woman in inherently shameful. Middleton intimates that the
staid and apparently stable world will always be at risk. Precisely
because it represses it will necessarily be disrupted by the desires
pulsating beneath the deceptive surface. Beatrice and de Flores are
united by a single imperative: their refusal of propriety, their
absolute commitment to desire. Since society cannot openly
acknowledge either love or desire it can only dream of them as
frightening apparitions and it will necessarily encounter the
monsters of which it dreams, as Beatrice and de Flores. So the
paradox of *The Changeling* is that Beatrice and de Flores are
simultaneously sinister representations of boundless evil and
ordinary individuals driven by passions which they cannot control.
Once Beatrice loses her innocence she loses it totally. As a woman
she can never experience her love for Alsemero in the pure and
saintly fashion that Alsemero displays in his opening speech:

> 'Twas in the temple where I first beheld her . . .
> The place is holy, so is my intent.

For no 'intent' on the part of a woman could ever be holy. It would
necessarily be impious and profane. Once Beatrice has
acknowledged the importance of this feeling to her she experiences
a loss of transparency in the world. She is plunged into a nightmare
of counterfeit representation which she can neither escape nor
control. Her discovery of de Flores as a willing, not to say
over-enthusiastic, 'accessory' to her crime is dream-like in the easy
and unobstructed way that all her secret wishes can be led out of
fantasy into a fulfilment in the real world; but, of course, there can
be no such collaboration because of the necessary asymmetry of
desires. It is as if the truth of Beatrice's desiring the saint Alsemero,
who would not welcome such a desire, is that what she gets and
what she really desires and deserves is de Flores, a monster also.

Passion produces the counterfeit because Beatrice and de Flores
must continually and exhaustingly pretend. It is passion that
relentlessly sets in motion a chain of substitutions. The replacement
of Alonzo by Alsemero produces a further replacement of Alsemero
by de Flores. Diaphanta takes Beatrice's place with Alsemero on her
wedding night and de Flores takes Alsemero's place with Beatrice.
What is significant here is the way in which social class and the
counterfeit are linked. Just as a changeling was most often a child of

humble origin substituted for one of high birth, so here there is a comparable glissando down the social scale. The truth of the hankering after forbidden fruit on the part of Beatrice and Alsemero is made disturbingly evident when they are manipulated into an erotic coupling that makes a mockery of all propriety and rank. The servant serves as a signifier of lust. The motif of imposture and sustitution is ironically doubled in the comic sub-plot but this nevertheless emphasises that disguise is innocent (comic) by comparison with the profounder disguise of false appearances. Beatrice's display of contempt for de Flores was a 'black mask' –

> there was a vizor
> Over that cunning face and that became you.

Both Beatrice and de Flores are split in two. Behind the 'honest', compliant de Flores there lurks another who is violent, disrespectful and lustful, just as behind the beautiful and innocent Beatrice, ironically named after Dante, lurks the lascivious Joanna, whom de Flores calls upon with his dying breath. Middleton deliberately refuses to pass moralising judgement upon them. The role of revenger is attenuated. Beatrice and de Flores always hold the attention and they bring judgement upon themselves. In confronting de Flores as her warped and distorted double, Beatrice is tormented by the thought that she may indeed be as deformed as Alsemero says she is, though that deformation is itself produced by a world that cannot acknowledge female sexuality. When Beatrice remorsefully confesses: 'I have kiss'd poison for't, strok'd the serpent' she seems to acknowledge all too nakedly the craving for sexual pleasure that has been the cause of her downfall. When Alsemero is told by de Flores that Beatrice is a whore and he exclaims:

> oh cunning devils!
> How should blind men know you from fair-fac'd saints

he speaks more truly than he knows, for it is this wilful social blindness that generates the treacherousness of the counterfeit.

In this emphasis on the importance of freedom in love John Ford is Middleton's successor, but in Ford's continual desire to soften the contours of his theme his plays veer always toward the sentimental rather than the tragic. Nevertheless the issue of women who are

forced to marry against their will and inclination is central both to
Love's Sacrifice and *The Broken Heart*. With Ford it becomes clear how
much Jacobean tragedy was fuelled by a sense of national paranoia
over Catholicism and foreign innovation, how crucially it depended
on an anxiety about trusting the surface of things. Ford's plays
typically lack this anxiety. In *Love's Sacrifice* and *The Broken Heart*
everything is cleaned up. The dangerous blurring of traditional
moral values to the point even of obliteration is replaced by clear
edges of black and white. Both Bianca, the wife of the duke in *Love's
Sacrifice*, and Penthea in *The Broken Heart* are involved in adulterous
relationships because they are married to men whom they find
antipathetic, but Ford is so concerned to present this as wholly
innocent that he runs the risk of lacking a theme altogether. Penthea
insists that it is her relationship with her husband, Bassanes, that is
adulterous and that she is still 'wife' to Orgilus to whom she had
originally been betrothed. Orgilus, in turn, insists on his own
unspotted virtuousness:

> Time can never
> On the white table of unguilty faith
> Write counterfeit dishonour.

On this reading of affairs, while the duplicity of the Court and the
immorality of its arrangements may indeed present Penthea and
Orgilus in a bad light, this can never affect the way they truly are.
Since the spectator is encouraged to share this confidence the
dangerousness of the counterfeit disappears. Indeed *Love's Sacrifice*
verges on bathetic tearfulness when we are asked to believe that, in
the triangle between the Duke, Bianca and Fernando, the court
favourite, an unlawful kiss would precipitate the death of all three.
Were Italian courtiers ever as tender-hearted as this? But Ford
must have it so, since as a Court dramatist he can never suggest that
this great world is altogether ignoble and corrupt, but must rather
imply that it is imperilled by the presence of one or two bad apples in
the barrel: a D'Avolos, a Ferentes, an Ithocles. Ford reinforces the
taboos surrounding female sexuality whilst appearing to challenge
them because he insists that an impropriety cannot even be thought.
In a symptomatic metaphor Penthea claims that her pathologically
jealous husband, Bassanes, has absolutely no grounds for
suspecting her:

> Sir, may every evil
> Locked in Pandora's box shower, in your presence,
> On my unhappy head, if, since you made me
> A partner in your bed, I have been faulty
> In one unseemly thought against your honour!

So long as a man's rights are absolute, a woman's are non-existent. So long as the issues at stake cannot even surface into discourse then claims for feminine autonomy can never be real. Moreover, Ford's plays would be more challenging if he were prepared to concede that such uncertainty is made inescapable by the whole way in which promiscuity and respectability become mutually legitimising within the courtly milieu. But he cannot make this admission because to do so would be to put in question Charles's great ideal of a purified royal circle. What is always potentially powerful in Ford is his sense of the claustrophobic and oppressive atmosphere at Court, so that even the slightest action will set tremors going through the entire structure and portend an imminent collapse of the whole house of cards; but, conversely, this may also point to the limitations of his theme and suggest Lilliputian gestures that have been magnified to Brobdingnagian proportions. It is a relief to turn to Ford's one indisputably great play, *'Tis Pity She's A Whore* (published with *Love's Sacrifice* and *The Broken Heart* in 1633), precisely because its subject-matter is genuinely, not notionally shocking, so genteel values can gain no effective purchase. *'Tis Pity She's A Whore* authentically reflects the intellectual crisis of the age for it directly raises the question of the pertinence of religious values in an increasingly secularised world. The dilemma is posed in an equivocal statement made by Richardetto, the 'supposed physician':

> All human worldy courses are uneven;
> No life is blessed but the way to Heaven.

an argument which is, of course, directly contrary to the Protestant belief that it is possible to be virtuous and God-fearing in the context of ordinary everyday life. Richardetto suggests that beyond a total dedication to God, a commitment which few are likely to make, there can only be a multiplicity of erratic and irregular courses which will exclude piety altogether. In this way Ford points up in characteristically Protestant fashion the hypocrisy of a Catholicism that notionally insists on the strictest possible moral code which in practice it consistently disregards. It might seem a matter of general consent that the course of Giovanna and Annabella, in incestuously loving one another, is more uneven than most, but since everyone else turns a deaf ear to the moral adjurations of the Friar then why are Giovanna and Annabella obliged to heed them. In fact they listen more than most. The notion of incest is troubling not so much because it is morally wrong as because it is hard to see why it is just about the only thing left that is. Certainly Giovanna and Annabella can find no easy answer. Annabella eventually repents of her sin and Giovanni is wracked by uncertainty and doubt. The clarity and depth of his passion puts all absolutes in question:

> Lost! I am lost! my fates have deemed my death:
> The more I strive, I love; the more I love,
> The less I hope: I see my ruin certain.
> What judgement or endeavours could apply
> To my incurable and restless wounds,
> I throughly have examined, but in vain.
> O, that it were not in religion sin
> To make our love a god, and worship it!
> I have ever wearied Heaven with prayers, dried up
> The spring of my continual tears, even starved
> My veins with daily fasts: what wit or art
> Could counsel, I have practised; but, alas,
> I find all these but dreams, and old men's tales,
> To fright unsteady youth; I'm still the same:
> Or I must speak, or burst.

What gives Giovanni's argument a disquieting force is that it accords so well with the Protestant critique of Catholicism. He suggests that the teaching of the Church on incest may be nothing more than traditional superstition and suggests that his own subjective feelings have the power and the right to question it. Yet the work of interrogation goes in both directions. Giovanni's whole identity becomes problematic because he is caught between a creed that presents his feeling as immoral, false and inauthentic, and a love that unsettles absolutely everything he believes. Giovanni suffers not just because his feelings are incestuous but because he is too *sincere*, too intellectually strenuous. It would never be possible for him to be lulled in the easy hypocrisy of Soranzo or to follow him in the intricate operation of double standards, as 'too double in your dissimulation'. It is Giovanni's passion for truth still more than his passion for Annabella that is socially unsettling. Giovanni asks for reasons that society is simply incapable of providing. Immorality, cruelty and oppression continue their routine, day-to-day functioning. Even cardinals 'think murder not amiss' but the prohibition against incest remains the sole enduring moral absolute, so shocking that even Vasques, Soranzo's paid bully-boy and assassin, can tut-tut: 'O, horrible! to what height of liberty in damnation hath the devil trained our age.' Soranzo is desperate to protect his 'reputation' from the stigma of incestuous infidelity, yet Soranzo's hands are stained with murder and he does not hesitate to dispatch anyone who stands in his path in the most brutal and unscrupulous fashion. Annabella is simply one more victim who can be sacrificed on the altar of his counterfeit virtue. But Annabella courageously and unashamedly mocks Soranzo. Giovanni is determined to resist his ridiculous attempts to present himelf as a model of saintliness and outraged virtue. In killing Annabella with a kiss, Giovanni will save her from the scandalous ritual of public ignominy and shatter all the pretences that sustain it. Giovanni's final appearance is unrepentant, shameless and shocking. Yet the hollowness and insincerity of the public world that he has contested is ironically confirmed even after his death, as the Cardinal orders:

> Take up their slaughtered bodies, see them buried;
> And all their gold and jewels, or whatsoever,
> Confiscate by the canons of the church,
> We seize upon it to the pope's proper use.

Paradoxically it is Giovanni and Annabella who in their incestuous love affirm the claims of the spirit. In *'Tis Pity She's A Whore* at least – right down to its very title, which the Cardinal offers as a wholly unproblematic characterisation of Annabella – the counterfeit retains its menacing, threatening character as an insidious Catholic resistance to Protestant claims to authenticity and truth. But, Ford suggests, these Protestant claims may be unsettling in another way. Certainty and falsity may go down together.

10

The Private World of Donne, Burton and Browne

In the Renaissance we encounter a new mode of consciousness – the *private*. I use the word 'consciousness' advisedly. In Western culture the private has become a form of shorthand for a whole complex system of values that embraces such things as private property, the assumption that certain things will not be shared, the expectation that each person in a family will have their own room, the right not to have one's telephone tapped, the notion of personal space that others should not intrude upon and so on. But in the Renaissance this elaborate system has yet to be constructed in terms of an ethic of privacy. Not only is there very little privacy but it can scarcely even become a value to be desired. It is with the emergence of this value that I am concerned. The great houses of the period were constructed in large suites of rooms where each led directly onto the next. There were no corridors and no specially segregated sleeping areas, which, as Lawrence Stone has pointed out,[1] did not develop until the latter part of the seventeenth century. While the poor inevitably lived in close proximity with one another, the wealthy did not envisage the creation of private spaces in their magnificent dwellings, but were, on the contrary, concerned to have larger and more numerous salons in which to socialise and entertain. Although the private requires financial resources to establish it, it cannot be directly correlated with conspicuous consumption, but stems rather from the psychological need to resist discordant and disquieting social pressures. The private is born in a spirit of anxiety and defence and it is marked by the paradoxical call for a space, even in the mind, where the individual can be allowed to be 'himself'. In *The Family, Sex and Marriage 1500–1800* Lawrence Stone suggests that a significant moment in Elizabethan England for the growth of personal autonomy came when the government drew back from instituting a thoroughgoing religious inquisition:

The first clear sign of the new attitude in official circles occurred in the late sixteenth century when Lord Burghley protested against Archbishop Whitgift's inquisitory procedures to investigate private religious opinions, on the grounds that they were making 'windows into men's souls,' which he regarded as an illegitimate intrusion into privacy.[2]

What is interesting here is that Stone, in raising the matter, has difficulty in writing about it in a manner that will not beg the question – by referring to 'private religious opinions' he automatically invokes a more modern sense of things although he is discussing a situation in which there could be no clear or certain invocation of such a right. Stephen Greenblatt in *Renaissance Self-Fashioning* would locate this articulation of a private sphere even earlier, in the construction of an interior space that could remain insulated from the intense psychological pressures at the Court of Henry VIII:

> With this drastic diminution of self-differentiation and private inwardness, we approach the heart of More's strategy of imagined self-cancellation in *Utopia*, for his engagement in the world involved precisely the maintaining of a calculated distance between his public persona and his inner self. How else could he have sat at Wolsey's table? How could he make his way in a world he perceived as insane and riddled with vicious injustice? Even in his own family he kept back a part of himself from all except, perhaps, his daughter Margaret. His whole identity depended upon the existence of a private retreat; his silences were filled with unexpressed judgements, inner thoughts.[3]

This inner sphere was fortified by the construction of a new building, quite separate from and apart from the main house, containing a library and a chapel, where More would spend long hours in study and private meditation. As has often been observed, More's ideal community in *Utopia* has certain affinities with the medieval monastery and his own retreat has a distinctly monastical feel. Yet More is altogether too prominent and too powerful a figure to make a wholly convincing embodiment of this private consciousness, for it stems rather from a sense of the powerlessness and marginality of the individual who must resist social pressures and who is not, as with More, at the very centre

of the public stage. The private person is more likely to be an
individual who stands outside the very highest ranks of society
and who defines himself through that new phenomenon, the
private collection of books. He is learned, scholarly, sceptical; his
natural habitat is the library. Montaigne is an exemplary and
notable instance. We know from his essays that Montaigne was
utterly dedicated to his library and that it was the place where he
used to spend virtually all of his waking hours. It was located on
the upper floor of a tower overlooking the courtyard, with a
chapel and a chamber where he could rest below and an adjoining
gallery where he could take a stroll. In this private space
Montaigne was completely cut off from the rest of his family:

> The forme of it is round and hath no flat side, but what serveth
> for my table and chaire: In which bending or circling manner, at
> one looke it offreth me the full sight of all my books, set round
> upon shelves or desks, fine rancks one upon another. It hath
> three bay-windowes, of a farre-extending, rich and unresisted
> prospect, and is in diameter sixteene paces void. In winter I am
> lesse continually there: for my house (as the name of it
> importeth) is pearched upon an over-pearing hillocke; and hath
> no part more subject to all wethers than this: which pleaseth me
> the more, both because the accesse unto it is somwhat
> troublesome and remote, and for the benefit of the exercise
> which is to be respected; and that I may the better seclude my
> selfe from companie, and keep incrochers from me: There is my
> seat, that is my throne. I endevour to make my rule therein
> absolute, and to sequester that only corner from the communities
> of wife, of children and of acquaintance.[4]

Significantly Montaigne adds onto this description the admission:
'Elsewhere I have but a verball authoritie, of confused essence.'[5] It
is only there in the private sanctum that Montaigne can be truly
monarch of all he surveys; it is only there that his sense of himself
as lord and master returns to him. In the family, surrounded by
servants, he finds himself diminished in the general hurly-burly.
It is only when he is alone that he can be truly present to himself.
For Montaigne, introspection is a duty and the solitude of the
library is the only place where that task can be suitably carried
out. It is a theatre of self-exploration where he can mull over what
he has read in his books and capture his thoughts even at the

very moment when they come to him, often in a quasi-divine frenzy of inspiration:

> There without order, without method, and by peece-meales I turne over and ransacke, now one booke and now another. Sometimes I muse and rave; and walking up and downe I endight and enregister these my humours, these my conceits.[6]

If Montaigne ever got an important idea when he was not working in his library he would immediately rush over there to write it down, and he was so desperately anxious that he might forget it even while walking across the courtyard that he would ask a member of his household to commit it to memory. The act of writing was uniquely associated with being in the privacy of the library, so that although Montaigne had these techniques of temporising, the crucial work of inscription had to take place there. For it is in the very processes of writing itself that the private man can come to the fore, that Montaigne's latent identity can be triumphantly brought to the surface. Montaigne believes that he lives in an age of flattery and dissimulation, when it is only possible to tell people what they want to hear. So for Montaigne to set down precisely what he thinks in the solitude of his library is to be the servant of truth in corrupted times. In forming his thoughts Montaigne simultaneously formulates himself:

> In framing this pourtraite by my selfe, I have so often been faine to frizle and trimme me, that so I might the better extract my self, that the patterne is thereby confirmed, and in some sort formed. Drawing my selfe for others, I have drawne my selfe with purer and better colours, then were my first. I have no more made my booke, then my booke hath made me. A boke consubstantiall to his Author: Of a peculiar and fit occupation. A member of my life. Not of an occupation and end, strange and forraine, as all other bookes. Have I not mis-spent my time, to have taken account of my selfe so continually and so curiously? For those who onely run themselves over by fantasie, and by speech for some houres, examine not themselves so primely and exactly, nor enter they into themselves, as he doth, who makes his study his worke, and occupation of it: Who with all his might, and with all his credit engageth himself to a register of continuance.[7]

Montaigne is not content to suggest that the self is filled out and completed in the process of introspection and composition that constitute writing, he is actually prepared to argue that there is really no identity until this task has been carried out. To exist in the public world is always to be a shadow. It is only inscription that can give substance to the self. Yet, paradoxically, Montaigne's identity has a public character also: it is only through the incessant labour of writing and of writing under the eye of that hypothetic other who is to be his reader that the Montaigne who will appear before the world takes shape. So at a certain point the private becomes public.

The discourse of privacy is always riddling and enigmatic since it seeks to retain its solitary character even when it is finally published for the world to read. We must think of a secluded recess suddenly illuminated with a burst of light, like a side-chapel of a cathedral that is eventually lit up by the setting sun, rather than of a person deliberately seeking the spotlight. There is no necessary insincerity in the claim of a writer that he does not seek attention since he is always deeply conscious of the perils of publication: his motives for appearing in print will certainly be mistrusted: the writing itself will be open to misreading and the claim he makes to be a serious private person will be imperilled by this very act. Of the English writers discussed here, Donne published virtually none of the poetry by which he is now remembered in his lifetime, even though they were circulated in manuscript. Sir Thomas Browne insisted that *Religio Medici* had never been intended for publication. Burton apologised elaborately for presenting himself before the public at all. By using the alias of Democritus Junior, Burton showed that he intended to retain his own private character. In this way he not only will not comply with the requirements of a public domain he will, on the contrary, positively struggle against it:

> Gentle Reader, I presume thou wilt be very inquisitive to know what antic or personate actor this is that so insolently intrudes upon this common theatre to the world's view, arrogating another man's name; whence he is, why he doth it, and what he hath to say. Although, as he said, *In the first place, supposing I do not wish to answer, who shall make me?* I am a free man born, and may choose whether I will tell; who can compel me? If I be urged, I will as readily reply as that Egyptian in

Plutarch, when a curious fellow would needs know what he had in his basket, *When you see the cover, why ask about the thing hidden?* It was therefore covered, because he should not know what was in it. Seek not after that which is hid; if the contents please thee and be for thy use, suppose the Man in the Moon, or whom thou wilt to be the Author; I would not willingly be known.[8]

Yet, despite this, Burton *did* reveal his name in his Epilogue to the book. What is the point of this masquerade? The modern reader will all too readily dismiss it as a transparent literary device and will be disposed to see it as an attempt to attract attention rather than to deflect it. Such an analysis would be altogether too reductive. In fact Burton asserts his independence as a private man as much in his final gesture of disclosing his name as in his initial demonstration of withholding it. He refuses to allow the reader to appropriate him until the book has appropriated the reader. In this way Burton maintains his identity as a stubborn recluse and suggests that in the case of a work that is the product of many long years of solitary study, publication is to be regarded more as an afterthought than as an original intention. *The Anatomy of Melancholy* thus seeks to establish its private character. Although the book mediates between the public and the private it can neither resolve nor eliminate the tensions and contradictions of which the book is itself the conscious product. The work endlessly crosses and recrosses the threshold that both connects and divides them. Although the book is indeed in the world it does not thereby confess to being of it. In facing the world the writer becomes the more deeply conscious of the gulf that separates him from it. As Francis Barker has written of that definitive instance of the private text in the seventeenth century, Pepys's *Diary*, where publication was never even envisaged:

The *Diary* for all the fulness of its days, despite being so richly populated with others and with the furniture of gossip and events, is thus the record of a terrible isolation. At the moment when the soul reaches out to appropriate the outer world, the very gesture reinforces the division by which it is other than what it seeks to apprehend.[9]

The degree to which the private text figures as intensely

antagonistic to a public world is evident in Sir Thomas Browne's *Religio Medici*. Browne composed the text in 1836 and it circulated in many manuscript copies. One of these was used by the London publisher, Andrew Crooke, as the basis of an unauthorised edition, but Browne forgave the offence and supplied a partial revision of the text, which appeared in 1643. The tortuous nature of Browne's motives is apparent both from his introduction and from his actual decision to co-operate with Crooke. He may well have been flattered at the extent of the interest that had been shown in his text and he may also have thought that he might as well make the best of a bad job, especially since his own integrity in the matter could not be questioned. Browne's enforced involvement in the act of publication becomes both a symptom of the corruptness of the times and, at the same time, a forceful blow struck against all such doubtful tendencies, a public intervention that nevertheless insists on its private character. Indeed, the very transparency and unclouded truthfulness of Browne's private religious meditations can by their very authenticity expose the carelessness that characterises the public domain. Browne's gesture of supplying amended copy points up the necessity for such cleansing acts of rectification. As we enter the world of *Religo Medici* Browne asks us to meditate on the ubiquity of evil and urgent need for each individual to make a stand against it. The fate of *Religio Medici* somehow epitomises the state of the world *circa* 1643:

> Certainly that man were greedy of life, who should desire to live when all the world were at an end; and he must needs be very impatient, who would repine at death in the society of all things that suffer under it. Had not almost every man suffered by the presse; or were not the tyranny thereof become universall; I had not wanted reason for complaint: but in times wherein I have lived to behold the highest perversion of that excellent invention; the name of his Majesty defamed, the honour of Parliament depraved, the writings of both depravedly, anticipatively, counterfeitly imprinted; complaints may seeme ridiculous in private persons, and men of my condition may be as incapable of affronts, as hopeless of their reparations. And truly had not the duty I owe unto the importunitie of friends, and the allegeance I must ever acknowledge unto truth prevayled with me; the inactivities of my disposition might have made

these sufferings continuall, and time that brings other things to light, should have satisfied me in the remedy of its oblivion. But because things evidently false are not onely printed but many things of truth most falsly set forth; in this latter I could not but thinke my selfe engaged: for though we have no power to redresse the former, yet in the other the reparation being within our selves, I have at present represented unto the world a full and intended copy of that Peece which was most imperfectly and surreptitiously published before.[10]

Browne characteristically ties the reader up in 'nots'. The whole passage is couched in the form of an extended negation – for private man is nothing if not *against*. Yet, though always engaged, Browne declines to actually be of the conflict; his commitment manifests itself rather as a reluctance to get involved, a distinct obstreperousness about letting things be dragged out into the open. Though Browne has made his 'secresie publike' we know that *Religio Medici* was 'a private exercise directed unto myselfe' not just by the stylistic idiosyncrasies which Browne is convinced mark it as unimpeachable utterance but still more by the tenacity and doggedness with which he worries at his own peculiar bone.[11] As a private man Browne recognises that his protestations may seem unconvincing if he has no public reputation to maintain but the dilemma of the private person is that once privacy has been lost, privacy cannot be the remedy. The cure must partake of the poison of which it is to be the antidote for it to be efficacious. The private seeks to master an alien public world with which it is perennially and necessarily at odds through the intrinsic power of that which it is compelled to disclose. Surrounded by intimations of disaster it always foresees a final victory. From this perspective to write is necessarily to negate.

Of our three authors, Donne, Burton and Browne, Donne seems by far the least convincing instance of a consciousness wedded to privacy. Unlike Burton or Browne, Donne, as Dean of St Paul's for the last decade of his life, was a conspicuous public figure and even in the *Songs and Sonets*, where publication was not envisaged, he seems to hog a spotlight of his own imaginative fabrication. It is hard to think of Donne as a reclusive person, despite many evidences that he was one. He seems always a devotee of glitter, greasepaint and tinsel, longing for a captive and captivated audience. All this I would certainly not want to deny. However, I would want to argue that Donne always sought to shelter and guard his identity from the world; to insist that even in the midst of advancement and conformity he always saw himself as being at odds. Donne always felt himself to be a man apart because of his upbringing in a traditional Catholic family, at a time when to persist in such practices meant continual anxiety about the possibility of betrayal or detection, the risk of imprisonment, torture or death. Too much should not be made of the actual beliefs themselves. Although certain Catholic influences continue to make themselves felt in Donne's writings there is no reason to doubt the sincerity of his conversion to Anglicanism, despite its evident convenience. In Anglicanism he found a homely, ramshackle spiritual mansion very like the old, where there was still a good deal of space for intellectual manœuvre and this manœuvring was something which Donne actually relished. It had the added attraction of being free from the fanaticism and intolerance of the Jesuits, whom Donne never ceased to blame for the many and multifarious sufferings which the Catholic faith had inflicted on his whole family. Donne believed that the Jesuits' aggressive posture had done much to create an atmosphere of fear and hostility in England. In their zeal for the struggle they had no hesitation about turning run-of-the-mill Catholics like his uncles, mother and brother into yet more martyrs for the cause. So, for that very reason, Donne was attracted to the idea of a spirituality that lay primarily in the individual's own personal relationship with God. He had seen all too clearly how faith could be distorted as it was used instrumentally to further political, personal and institutional ends. In Donne's morbid preoccupation with death, articulated through an imperious imagery of putrefaction and decay, in his conviction that he was living in a world that is drawing to a close, in his belief in the worthlessness of man without an infusion of God's grace, above all in his sense of the desperate uncertainty and volatility of human existence, it is difficult to discern anything but the anguished Protestant. What was significant for Donne about having been a Catholic was his conviction that he would always be a marked man, despite his act of apostasy. The stigma could never be entirely removed. All his life Donne was engaged in a desperate endeavour to make himself acceptable to others, and on the way he suffered setbacks and unforeseen reversals that came near to psychologically destroying him. Finally, after many unhappy years on the periphery he finally came to command the centre. As Dean of St Paul's, basking in royal and popular acclaim, he finally belonged. Yet in his heart Donne was always *other*. This private Donne could never be accessible to the world.

Donne, in the depths of his interior being, was permanently scarred by the experiences of his youth. For all his parade of bravado and high spirits he was a genuinely melancholy man, in an age when melancholy was as much a literary affectation as a depressive state of mind. Though he constantly sought to lift the pall of gloom that lingered over him by the thousand and one fresh starts that he made in his own mind, he was always brought back to the underlying reality of his situation. When T. S. Eliot said that for Donne a thought was an experience, he wrote more truthfully than he knew. For in the bleakest periods of his life Donne put so much of his emotional energy into the writing of poetry that it was as if he struggled to create freedom and hope out of a context in which they were perennially denied. Donne was always in sympathy with the notion of suicide not so much because it was something that he directly contemplated as because it was a possibility that was constantly in his mind – and one that seemed neither ignoble or morally wrong. For those whose lives always seem to run against the grain of the world, like the Catholics of Donne's time, the question as to what is suicidal can only seem a matter of nice distinctions. For those in power and authority, or in the dominant majority, suicide will always seem wilful, arbitrary, morally unjustifiable; for those who risk persecution anyway it must seem to lie in the will of heaven whether a person consciously seeks and achieves martyrdom, or collaborates with those who do, or who is made guilty by association, or who finds release from such a predicament in self-destruction. In such circumstances there is no easy way of avoiding self-destructive action. Even conversion may be a suicide of a kind. The writing of *Biathanatos*, a justification of suicide under certain very particular circumstances, was an enterprise dear to Donne's heart, both because it brought to the foreground the problems of living within an adversarial and persecuted culture and because, in an age of radical simplifications and severe alternatives, it served to demonstrate that action is always difficult and *always* complex. Donne strongly identified with the early Christian fathers who lived under the Roman Empire because he well knew what it was to be regarded as an outcast and as the internal enemy. The contradiction of *Biathanatos* is that the text as a whole is dedicated to interminable casuistical distinctions, yet it is introduced by the frankest confession imaginable:

> Beza, as a man as eminent and illustrious in the full glory and noon of learning, as others were in the dawning and morning, when any least sparkle was notorious, confesseth of himself that only for the anguish of a scurf which overran his head, he had once drowned himself from the Miller's bridge in Paris, if his uncle by chance had not come that way. I have often such a sickly inclination; and whether it be because I had my first breeding and conversation with men of a suppressed and afflicted religion, accustomed to the despite of death and hungry of imagined martyrdom, or that the common enemy find that door worst locked against him in me, or that there be a perplexity and flexibility in the doctrine itself, or because my conscience ever assures me that no rebellious grudging at God's gifts, nor any other sinful occurrence, accompanies these thoughts in me, or that brave scorn, or that faint cowardice beget it, whensoever any affliction assails me, methinks I have the keys of my prison in my own hand, and no remedy presents itself so soon to my heart as mine own sword.[12]

This passage is rich in ironies created by its context. Donne can validate the experience of a persecuted Catholic minority in England by appealing to the Protestant authority of Theodore Beza, the French follower of Calvin, who was exposed to the same persecution in reverse. Beza was saved by the chance interposition of his uncle, whereas Donne's uncles, both Jesuit priests, lured him in the direction of a suicidal martyrdom which he nevertheless managed to evade. For Donne the world was always a prison and never more so than at the time of writing *Biathanatos*, yet the remedy that presented itself was not so much suicide as the idea of writing a book about it. In justifying the possibility Donne created space in his own mind to step around the actual desire to implement it. In constantly fingering the handle of his sword Donne was thereby able to leave it in its scabbard and achieve some reconciliation of his contradictory and wayward feelings.

Donne's pessimism about life in general was shaped not only by his status as a Roman Catholic and by his subsequent and attendant personal misfortunes, it was also deeply conditioned by his sense that the world was in a state of progressive deterioration and decay. The best-known advocate for this view in Donne's time was his fellow ecclesiastic, Bishop Godfrey Goodman, who published *The Fall of Man* in 1616, but Donne had formed his views independently at a far earlier date than this under the influence of the writings of St Cyprian. Cyprian, one of the early Christian fathers and martyrs, was bishop of Carthage in the third century AD and was a contemporary and disciple of the celebrated Christian polemicist, Tertullian. The period from the death of Marcus Aurelius in AD 180 was one of the darkest and most confusing in Roman history, marked by threats from without and instability within. The Christians themselves, by their refusal to worship the Emperor, played an important role in this destabilising process and they were therefore systematically persecuted. For Gibbon this was the century in which the Roman Empire definitively and irrevocably entered into its long drawn-out period of decline. For Christians it was the darkest hour before the dawn, preceding the institutionalisation of Christianity under Constantine. St Cyprian regarded this political disorder as simply part of a much larger process of deterioration in the physical universe that foreshadowed the end of the world. If the world was in such a terrible state and if it was coming to an end anyway, then suicide for the devoted Christian was simply a rational way of entering the promised afterlife without further suffering or delay. In his conclusion to *Biathanatos* Donne alludes to Cyprian's 'encouragement' to suicide:

> who, out of a contemplation that the whole frame of the world decayed and languished, cries to us, *Nutant parietes* – the walls and the roof shake, and wouldst not thou go out? Thou art tired in thy pilgrimage, and wouldst thou not go home?[13]

For Donne the call continued to be a powerful one precisely because he accepted the cosmological assumptions that underpinned it. In Donne's writing, from his earliest Satires to his later sermons, there is a constant reference to this decay of the world as an ineluctable fact. In this third Satire on religion he warns against the dangers of worldliness and insists that

as
The worlds all parts wither away and passe,
So the worlds selfe, thy other lov'd foe, is
In her decrepid wayne, and thou loving this,
Dost love a withered and worne strumpet.

In *The First Anniversarie* on the death of Elizabeth Drurie, published
in 1611, and one of the few works of Donne to appear in his
lifetime, he describes a whole host of symptoms that would seem
to demonstrate beyond any possibility of contradiction that the
world is in decline. Human life is short. Illness is widespread and
people are afflicted by malignant new diseases like syphilis.
People are smaller and have diminished intellectual and physical
powers. The world is become inharmonious, marked by confusion
in the planets, earthquakes and civil wars. There has been a loss
of beauty, proportion and colour in the universe. Virtue itself is
dead. In *The First Anniversarie* Donne seems to deplore this state
of affairs but in his later sermons he suggests that in order that we
should fix our minds on eternal things God has deliberately made
the world into a gigantic sign of impermanence as a perpetual
warning:

As the world is the whole frame of the world, God hath put
into it a reproofe, a rebuke, lest it should seem eternall, which
is, a sensible decay and age in the whole frame of the world,
and every piece thereof. The seasons of the yeare irregular and
distempered; the Sun fainter, and languishing; men lesse in
stature and shorter-lived. No addition, but only every yeare,
new sorts, new species of wormes, and flies, and sicknesses,
which argue more and more putrefaction of which they are
engendered. And the Angels of heaven, which did so familiarly
converse with men in the beginning of the world, though they
may not be doubted to perform to us still their ministeriall
assistances, yet they seem so far to have deserted this world as
that they do not appeare to us, as they did to those our Fathers.
S. Cyprian observed this in his time.[14]

Since Donne was himself continually plagued by serious
illnesses which brought him many times to the point of death,
these words, from a sermon of 1625, were spoken from the heart
Faced with such an unrelenting roll-call of indicators of the

ephemeral nature, not just of human existence but of the world itself, we are suitably humbled: 'Lest the world . . . should glorifie it selfe, or flatter, and abuse us with an opinion of eternity.'[15] It is likely that in the very last years of his life Donne gave up these views, since George Hakewill in the second edition of his *An Apologie of the Power and Providence of God* of 1635 cites Donne as a convert to his own more optimistic perspective, and Hakewill needed all the support he could get in his struggle with the insufferable Bishop Goodman.[16] But the fact remains that for most of his life Donne espoused a radical pessimism, which was not simply a cast of mind but a whole metaphysics.

Paradoxically it was the very difficulties that Donne experienced as a Catholic that imbued him with what we might otherwise want to regard as a Puritan sense of the treacherousness and difficulty of the world – but for long the Puritans were in a minority just as the Catholics were and Elizabethan policy often bracketed them together. It was out of the risks, dangers and many false steps of his personal odyssey as he struggled from the wilderness of exclusion towards the Promised Land of social acceptance, that Donne became convinced that man's passage through life could never be anything other than a desperate journey. In one of his late sermons he even suggested that were this not necessary for salvation it were better not to have ever lived at all:

> If there were any other way to be saved and to get to Heaven, then by being born into this life, I would not wish to have come into this world. And now that God hath made this life a *Bridge* to Heaven; it is but a giddy, and a vertiginous thing, to stand long gazing upon so narrow a bridge, and over so deep and roaring waters and desperate whirlpools, as this world abounds with.[17]

As Donne looked back over his life he could not but be conscious that the misfortunes he had suffered, great as they were in his own mind, paled into insignificance when compared with the disasters that he had so very narrowly averted. Under the intense pressure of circumstance Donne's personality was reshaped many times over. In his early youth he was part of a community at bay, the associate of fugitives, outcasts and conspirators. In manhood he was a rake, a man about town, a soldier-adventurer and an investigator into the corruptions of the legal system. For a long time, after his rash clandestine marriage to Ann More, he was once more a social outcast, a man utterly dependent on the crumbs of charity and patronage that he received from others. Finally he became respectable – the divine who preached God's word before the King himself. For this very reason Donne knew what a complex and variable thing character could be. Donne constantly compared men to sponges. He saw them as light, empty, hollow: simply there to soak up and assimilate any influences to which they were exposed. He knew that a person was not fixed and unchangeable but an identity always in a process of flux, process and transformation. He was conscious of the split between his private self and his many public roles, yet he also knew that his life was built up out of many contradictory and scattered fragments. In one of his sermons he suggested that it was precisely the task of Christian faith to reassemble man out of the many diverse things that he had been. The sinner Donne invokes is clearly autobiographical:

> And truly, in our spiritual raising of the dead, to raise a sinner putrified in his own earth, resolv'd in his own dung, especially that hath passed many transformations, from shape to shape, from sin to sin, (he hath beene a Salamander and lived in the fire, in the fire successively, in the fire of lust in his youth, and in his age in the fire of Ambition, and then he hath beene a Serpent, a Fish, and lived in the water successively, in the troubled water of sedition in his Youth, and in his age in the cold waters of indevotion) how shall we raise this Salamander and this Serpent, when this Serpent and this Salamander is all one person, and must have contrary musique to charme him, contrary physick to cure him? To raise a man resolv'd into diverse substances, scattered into diverse formes of severall sinnes is the greatest worke.[18]

Scattering is always a powerful notion for Donne because he sees it as a pervasive tendency in the universe in general which only religion and faith can resist. The dispersion and diffraction of the spirit is a tendency that is homologous with the decay and dissolution of the body and the physical universe. For this reason Donne is intensely preoccupied with figures that can stand for an integrative or restorative function, whether he is referring to 'that subtle knot, which makes us man' in 'The Extasie' or the magical act whereby he seeks to preserve himself from the possibility of change by scratching his name in glass in 'A Valediction of my name in the Window'. Indeed it can be argued that Donne's poetry continually aspires to the condition of sorcery, that in the act of writing he seeks to retrieve the personality that he is always on the point of losing. This battle between good and bad magic is expressed in *Witchcraft by a Picture* where he fears the dissolution of his identity in the multiplicity of images of himself that are reflected in his lover's eyes, but her tears at his departure wash away his uncertainty and convince him that she retains a single pure image of him in her heart. Although this poem deploys the distinction between the truthful and counterfeit representation it also communicates Donne's deeply felt anxiety about his possession of a stable identity.

In the *Satires* Donne exposes the contradictions and conflicts in his mind. As a sometime Catholic he perceives himself as belonging neither with those who have kept faith with Rome nor the unruffled courtiers with whom he comes in contact, yet he knows that he will have to try and make his way in the world despite this ambiguous situation. Already we see in action the rhetorical method that becomes so powerful and so complex in the *Songs and Sonets*: Donne continually ironises secular pursuits by enveloping them in religious imagery, yet he maintains an underlying seriousness of tone because the tropes that he uses are still rich in connotations and because he has already grasped that all life's pilgrimages are ultimately one. In the fifth Satire, as in the second, Donne's target is the law, whose abuses he had enquired into when assistant to Thomas Egerton, the Lord Keeper. Yet the Kafkaesque vanity of struggling against an impervious and wholly corrupt legal system also suggests the difficulties that Donne himself faces, as an ex-Catholic, when trying to pursue a career:

> Where wilt thou appeale? powre of the courts below
> Flow from the first maine head, and these can throw
> Thee, if they sucke thee in, to misery,
> To fetters, halters; But if the injury
> Steele thee to dare complaine, Alas, thou goest
> Against the stream, when upwards: when thou art most
> Heavy and most faint; and in these labours they,
> 'Gainst whom thou should'st complaine, will in the way

Become great seas, o'r which, when thou shalt bee
Forc'd to make golden bridges.

This sense of being in a labyrinth from which there is no
conceivable exit is one that recurs often in Donne's writing. His
mocking suggestion that since judges are Gods it is necessary to
plead with the voice of Angels (gold coins) of course deploys a
familiar Elizabethan pun, but it also demonstrates the degree to
which high and low have become hopelessly confused as one is
constantly referred from one to the other. Since Donne's whole
life was spent trying to swim against the current he was naturally
able to empathise with those who sought to obtain justice through
a system that was precisely designed to deny it. There is always a
note of desperation in Donne, yet it can take many diverse forms,
from the frantic, sepulchral rhetoric of the sermons to the
mocking, sardonic humour of the secular poems. Donne is never
altogether at ease with things as they are no matter how
energetically he tries to comply.

In his early ventures in satire Donne is as much preoccupied
with his own pretensions to be a satirist as with the follies and
abuses that he would criticise. He knows that he cannot offer the
authoritative point of view of the well-established insider. He is
equally well aware that his own bid for attention by the very act
of writing makes him cut as dubious a figure as any swaggering
gallant of the Elizabethan *beau monde*. His equivocal feeling about
the whole enterprise are reflected in the opening of Satire I,
where a fashionable acquaintance importunes him to forsake the
authentic, altogether private, environment of the library:

Away thou fondling motley humorist,
Leave mee, and in this standing woodden chest,
Consorted with these few bookes, let me lye
In prison, and here be coffin'd, when I dye;
Here are Gods conduits, grave Divines; and here
Natures Secretary, the Philosopher;
And jolly Statesmen, which teach how to tie
The sinewes of a cities mistique bodie;
Here gathering Chroniclers, and by them stand
Giddie fantastique Poëts of each land.
Shall I leave all this constant company,
And follow headlong, wild uncertaine thee?

Thus, even in the act of abandoning his sager counsels for a more erratic guide Donne implies that he is probably getting in deeper than he knows and that in abandoning his role of the reclusive scholar, in order to mingle with the flamboyant company of the streets, he may consequently lose all perspective upon the world. Donne purports not to take his role as satirist entirely seriously. Although he will satirise, he affects to be largely uninterested in what he is writing about and can therefore only pursue his ill-assorted role rather half-heartedly. Donne begins Satire II in seemingly abject mood:

> Sir, though (I thank God for it) I do hate
> Perfectly all this towne, yet there's one state
> In all ill things so excellently best,
> That hate, towards them, breeds pitty toward the rest.
> Though Poetry indeed be such a sinne
> As I thinke that brings dearths, and Spaniards in,
> Though like the Pestilence and old fashion'd love,
> Ridlingly it catch men; and doth remove
> Never, till it be sterv'd out; yet their state
> Is poore, disarm'd like Papists, not worth hate.

The ironies proliferate immediately. Donne humorously alludes to the Puritan claim that the poor harvests of the 1690s and the Spanish Armada of 1688 were God's punishment on England for her sins and suggests that there can be no sin greater (in Puritan eyes possibly not!) than that of being a poet. So Donne himself is a sinner – but, like the Papists, not worth the hate. Donne, who is asking not to be hated as a poet, asks also not to be hated as a Papist. In craving attention as a poet he also asks the favour of being permitted to remain unnoticed. His satire can be the more abusive because it is to be discounted in advance. Its strenuousness is only a mock strenuousness; it is only vitriol and water. It parades its superficiality even when it is written from the heart. Yet in Satire III, on religion, this seriousness of purpose can no longer be concealed. Here Donne speaks out, insisting that truth in religion must be a matter for the individual conscience and that therefore it can never be a matter of compulsion or for the exercise of worldly authority:

> Foole and wretch, wilt thou let thy soule be tyed

> To mans lawes, by which she shall not be tryed
> At the last day? Will it then boot thee
> To say a Philip, or a Gregory,
> A Harry, or a Martin taught thee this?

Donne impartially cites Philip of Spain and Pope Gregory on one side, Henry VIII and Luther on the other, all of whom attempted to legislate the faith of the individual, to dramatise his own conviction that the public cannot rule the private. By this light *cuius regio eius religio* and papal fiat are equally an anathema. Donne argues that under such official coercion men are actually much more likely to be damned than saved – an argument with which Milton would have agreed:

> As streames are, Power is; those blest flowers that dwell
> At the rough streames calme head, thrive and do well,
> But having left their roots, and themselves given
> To the streames tyrannous rage, alas are driven
> Through mills, and rockes, and woods, and at last, almost
> Consum'd in going, in the sea are lost:
> So perish Soules, which more chuse mens unjust
> Power from God claym'd, then God himself to trust.

Here we catch not only the enunciation of a moral principle but a flash of Donne's own bitterness at his experience of having been caught between the Jesuits on one side and the Elizabethan State on the other. If his religious convictions were to be determined by *force majeure* they could have no inner authenticity. Moreover, his greater fear was that, as the result of it all, he would be damned anyway. Donne's famous metaphor:

> on a huge hill,
> Cragg'd, and steep, Truth stands, and hee that will
> Reach her, about must and about must goe;
> And when the hills suddennes resists, winne so

was no abstract, universal metaphor but a vindication of his own situation: Donne hoped that his circuitous path from Catholicism to the Church of England, far from damning him, might nevertheless enable him to attain salvation, in the face of any doubtful auspices and despite the gloomy prognosis. The pursui of truth became a personal and private pilgrimage in which redemption would be won not through affiliation to one Church or another but through the intensity of his own commitment to it.

All this is a long way from satire but it is to satire that Donne returns in the fourth of the poems in which he addresses the vices of the Court. Donne jests by saying that his sin is to have been in Purgatory, that is to say to Court, which implies that since there is no Purgatory for Protestants there can be no sin in being at Court either. Donne ironically presents himself as a Christian martyr, who for his pains must endure interminable anecdotes concerning the fashionable and the prominent:

> Toughly and stubbornly I beare this crosse, But th'houre
> Of mercy now was come; He tries to bring
> Me to pay a fine to scape his torturing.

Nevertheless, coming from one who has been a Catholic, this figure can scarcely elicit an easy laugh. Catholics *were* tortured, and in Satire V Donne refers to the Puirsuivants who robbed and persecuted Catholic families, who were obliged to pay for being in receipt of these disagreeable services. It is not so much that Donne is satirising as that he is using satire to free himself from all that is burdening his conscience. When Donne writes:

> At home in wholesome solitarinesse
> My precious soule began, the wretchednesse
> Of suiters at court to mourne, and a trance
> Like his, who dreamt he saw hell, did advance
> It selfe on mee, Such men as he saw there,
> I saw at court, and worse, and more; Low feare
> Becomes the guiltie, not the accuser; Then,
> Shall I, nones slave, of high borne, or rais'd men
> Feare frownes? And my Mistresse Truth, betray thee
> To th'huffing braggart, puft Nobility?

the contrast between private truth and public hell is at its sharpest. Donne knows that he does not belong there and that his presence is a betrayal: the hell and emptiness that he sees there is his own. In seeking advancement Donne was forced to deny his deeper feelings and in consequence he tortured himself on a multiplicity of levels. Even the conclusion to this Satire is deeply ironic.

Donne offers it to the reader 'With Macchabees modestie' but at the same time asks that it should be esteemed as 'canonical'. As the book of Maccabees is part of the Apocrypha, whose authenticity is denied by Protestants, in the same way Donne concedes that as he, as a sometime Catholic, only enjoys apocryphal social status, but in writing a satire he hopes to become canonical, that is accepted into society. So the poem is a rejection of society dressed up as a bid for approval, a gesture of recalcitrance that purports to be inoffensive. Donne plays the fool to disguise the fact that he is in earnest, yet the imposture never quite convinces. And he *does* want to be accepted just the same.

Late in the year 1601 Donne secretly married Ann More, the teenage daughter of a wealthy Surrey landowner, who had been living in London under the protection of Donne's patron, Sir Thomas Egerton. This reckless action shaped the rest of Donne's life, though doubtless not in the way he had envisaged. Donne certainly miscalculated. He must have imagined that the father would eventually condone the match out of regard for his patron and that the marriage would establish him in a secure social position. George More did relent in the end, but by then it was too late, and it was Egerton himself who was implacable. Donne was dismissed from his service and thrown into prison. There could have been no greater humiliation, but a more protracted torment was to come: until Donne became ordained in 1615 his years were spent in the wilderness, living from hand to mouth and abjectly begging for patronage.

Donne's action in marrying Ann did not simply involve romantic infatuation but was a deliberate gesture of rebellion and independence, as Sir Thomas Egerton well recognised. At bottom he deeply resented the steps he had had to take to establish himself and he loathed his position of dependence. He despised the peacocks of the Court, and still felt himself to be in an internal exile. Much of the complexity of the *Songs and Sonets* stems from Donne's rueful awareness that while he would not sacrifice everything for religion, he had quite unwittingly sacrificed all for love.

If Donne was driven to celebrate his love in verse this was not so much because the blessings were self-evident as that they were often in doubt. Ann was to die in her early thirties after bearing him twelve children, only seven of whom survived. They lived in straitened circumstances and were daily reminded of the extent to which they were utterly dependent on the charity and goodwill of others. Donne was a man completely adrift. He lacked a role of any kind. As a Catholic he had at least experienced the loyalty and mutual devotion of a group under threat; even in the face of fear, persecution and hatred it must have seemed that every action he took was charged with immense significance, for good or ill. But now everything he did was inconsequential; he mattered to no one. It was as if he had ceased to exist. He was now excluded from all worlds, whether Protestant or Catholic. He had burned his bridges on all sides. He now had to face the prospect that, unlike many other hangers-on at Court, he might never again be restored to favour. The depth of his disgrace was such that even when Donne acquired quite influential patrons they were able to do very little for him. In the wilderness Donne's life was blighted by constant illness but, as he himself recognised, his sickness was as much of the mind as of the body and therefore almost beyond either diagnosis or remedy:

> If I knew that I were ill, I were well . . . of the diseases of the mind there is no criterion, no canon, no rule, for our own taste and apprehension and interpretation should be the judge, and that is the disease itself. Therefore sometimes when I find myself transported with jolity and love of company, I hang leads at my heels, and reduce to my thoughts, my fortunes, my years, the duties of a man, of a friend, of a husband, of father, and all the incumbencies of a family; when sadness dejects me either I countermine it with another sadness, or I kindle squibs about me again, and fly into sportfulness and company: and I find ever after all, that I am like an exorcist, which had long laboured about one, which at last appears to be the mother, that I shall still mistake my disease.
>
> And I still vex myself with this, because if I know it not, nobody can know it.[19]

Donne was not merely tortured by the sense of his own insignificance in the eyes of the world but by guilt and remorse at the suffering he had imposed on his wife and family. Yet it seemed that there was no action he could take which would enable them to find a way out of this collective misery, and even if there was he would hardly be in any position to take it in his current state of debility. Donne's very sanity was at risk as he struggled like a drowning man to rise to the surface of his depression. The writing of some of the *Songs and Sonets* may have been part of an infinitely protracted and only partial cure. In a letter to Sir Henry Goodyer of 1609 Donne endeavoured to make the best of his lot by suggesting that his life was now steadier and more stable than that of any typical denizen of the Court:

> In that life one is ever in the porch or postern, going in or out, never within his house himself: it is a garment made of remnants, a life ravelled out into ends, a line discontinued, and a number of small wretched points, useless, because they concur not: a life built out of past and future, not proposing any constant present; they have more pleasures than we, but not more pleasure; they joy oftener, we longer; and no man but of so much understanding as may deliver him from being a fool, would change with a madman, which had a better proportion of wit in his often *lucidis*.
>
> You know that they which dwell farthest from the sun, if in any convenient distance, have longer days, better appetites, better digestion, and longer life: and all these advantages have their minds which are well removed from the scorchings and dazzlings and exhalings of the world's glory: but neither of our lives are in such extremes; for you living at court without ambition, which would burn you, or envy, which would divest others, live in the sun, not in the fire: and I live in the country without stupefying, am not in the darkness, which is not no light, but a pallid, waterish, diluted one.[20]

Donne's mode of writing, though doubtless sincere, is full of unconscious ironies. For in his desire to convince himself that his lot is not all bad he projects onto the Court everything that makes him despondent about his own situation. It is he whose destiny it has been to be Phaeton, scorched and driven to destruction in his ambitious bid to drive the chariots of the sun. It is Donne whose life seems fragmentary and pointless. He is truthful mainly in saying that he would not wish for the lucid intervals of the madman, since it is insanity that he most fears. Although Donne feels evident relief at having escaped the perpetual instability and anxiety of life at Court, just as a man in jail consoles himself with the thought that nothing worse can happen to him, what he has exchanged it for is the certainty of unbroken depression. Donne had wagered everything in his desire to bask in the sun of social acceptance. Now in darkness, or in the thickening twilight, he longs for illumination once more.

There can be little doubt that the majority of the poems for which Donne is best remembered were written in these wilderness years, though it may be, as Helen Gardner suggests, that they were concentrated between 1607 and 1614.[21] In any event, Donne's *Songs and Sonets* are significantly misconstrued by the almost universal determination to read them as poems of love. This may seem a harmless enough assumption but that is just the trouble. We are asked to take these poems as somehow exemplary and to take their extraordinary intellectual virtuosity as if it were nothing more than the means to a very worthy end. Although the *Songs and Sonets* have been unfailingly admired in the twentieth century I nevertheless feel that they have suffered by being forced to lie in this Procrustean bed. My objection to much contemporary criticism of Donne is not that it is so anxious to tie the poems down to specific 'experiences', or that it feels bound to argue that Donne is capable of being sincere, as that love is the home key and dominant to which all critical discussion relentlessly returns. This romantic interest dominates as much when Helen Gardner praises Donne for his 'greatness and originality as a poet of love' as when she criticises 'The Extasie' because 'It smells a little of the lamp.'[22] It is there as much when Wilbur Sanders praises 'The Anniversarie' and 'A Valediction Forbidding Mourning' because 'one is prompted to talk more about the quality of the love celebrated than about the condition of the celebrating mind',[23] as when Robert Ellrodt speaks of 'le narcissism de l'amant'.[24] In my opinion the subtlety and complexity of the poems that Helen Gardner has classified as 'Songs and Sonets II' stems from the fact that they cannot be regarded as love poems pure and simple: that they are generated by the condition of depression and spiritual isolation which he had experienced for so long and that therefore they need to be seen as being therapeutic as much as they are expressive. We need to think of the *Songs and Sonets* as a collection like Baudelaire's *Les fleurs du Mal* in which specific circumstances of time and place matter less than the overall mood which they project. Donne, like Baudelaire, for a long time lived in a spiritual vacuum in which he had to struggle against a sense of his own worthlessness. For many years, at Mitcham and the Strand, Donne also was the king of a rainy country, who could find nothing to distract him or lift his gloom. His poems are, quite legitimately, as much concerned with creating a sense of value in himself as they are with valuing anyone else. They are a way of combating through hyperbole and verbal 'squibs' the sense of emptiness and guilt that menaced his whole existence; they are exotic flowers carefully tended over idle, protracted days. In a sermon of 1620 Donne describes a sense of overpowering helplessness and futility such as must have affected his mind at this time:

> But in such an extension, such an expansion, such an exaltation, such an inundation of woe, as this in our text, *Vae mundo*, woe to the world, a tide, a flood without any ebbe, a Sea without any shoare, a darke skie without any Horizon; That though I doe withdraw my selfe from the woeful uncertainties, and irresolutions, and indeterminations of the Court, and from the snares and circumstances of the City; Though I would devest, and shake off the woes and offences of Europe in Afrique, or of Asia in America, I cannot, since whereever, or howsoever I live, these woes, and scandals, and offences, tentations, and tribulations will pursue mee, who can express the wretched condition, the miserable station, and prostration of man in this world? *vae mundo*.[25]

Looking back he could now acknowledge, as he had not been able to in his letter to Goodyer, that he had been unable to live in tranquillity when cut off from the Court, but that he had looked into the very abyss of despair. The poetry of the *Songs and Sonets* was a temporary carnival for the spirit, a desperate, mocking attempt to exalt the private world over the public world that had so decisively rejected him.

In the *Songs and Sonets* Donne produces an imaginary transvaluation of all values in which the mighty are brought low as the insulted and the injured are raised. Donne literally makes the private universe of the lovers everything, the public world nothing. If a cloud still continues to hang over him because he has once been a Catholic, very well, then he will go all the way and canonise himself and his mistress as saints of love in the face of Protestant indignation and disbelief. This posture is not entirely a joke since Donne needs all the faith he can get. Instead of thinking like an underdog he will think himself a king. The tone of the poems is complex because Donne manages to combine ridicule of the social world with a celebration of love, yet mingle with all of it more than a touch of irony at his own expense. Yet Donne manages to swagger along this awesome tightrope with contemptuous ease. He is a performer and relishes being one. Donne finds the basis for imaginative reversal in those intellectual currents of his time that call in question the power and authority of the centre. As the result of the discoveries of explorers it is no longer possible to think of the world as centred on the Mediterranean. The new philosophy suggests that the earth, instead of being a still centre, surrounded by revolving crystalline spheres, may itself move around the sun. Protestants deny that religion must be centred on Rome and on the figure of the Pope. Similarly Donne questions in a contemptuous way the centrality of King and Court by making preposterous, but by no means trivial, claims for himself. In 'The Sunne Rising' Donne makes a virtue of his enforced idleness by mocking the self-important business of polite society and the sun that dances attendance upon it. The lovers inhabit a timeless eternal realm that is free from all customary and ritual obligations. The honours and wealth struggled over by courtiers are essentially counterfeit. Only their love is real. The delight of the poem lies in the insouciant way in which quite disparate things are brought together; so that Donne in mocking and chiding the sun, which in a waning world is becoming progressively more exhausted by its task, is able, almost in passing, to put king, court-huntsmen and country ants on the same level. Donne uses the idea, which frequently recurs in his sermons, that the qualities of things in the universe are always for the use of others, to suggest that the sun will have performed a moral duty in warming them. Donne accepts the idea that the whole world must dance to somebody's tune, of which the sun's rising is the epitome, and asks only that that tune shall be his. 'The Sunne Rising' is a dream of power that is not altogether in jest. In Jacobean England Donne is Gulliver in Brobdingnag, but in his verse at least, he can be Gulliver in Lilliput.

In 'The Canonisation' Donne tries a slightly different tack. Here he is quite frankly prepared to admit all his disabilities from his poor health and greying hair to the disastrous state of his fortunes. Donne nevertheless insists that he is indifferent to all other worldly pursuits since he is perfectly content with the vocation of love. In the second stanza Donne comes completely clean and jokingly concedes his objective insignificance in the world. His tears, sorrows and repeated illnesses have left no mark on the world whatsoever. Public and private are totally isolated from one another. The world goes on as usual 'Though she and I do love'. Though sexual love is self-destructive and ephemeral it nevertheless offers the prospect of immortality as the lovers, extinguished by the power of their own lust, are nevertheless reborn from their own ashes and immortalised in verse. But again Donne concedes that they cannot actually live by love. It is only in the death they are so eagerly pursuing – since folklore has it that each act of love shortens life by a day – that they will by their very constancy and dedication to erotic pleasure be immortalised as saints of love. Instead of copying the fashions of others, as men do at Court, the lovers will diminish the world until it is no more than that which they see reflected in each other's eyes and they will themselves be model and example for all others to imitate. Unnoticed in life they will be conspicuous only in death.

In a 'Valediction to his booke' Donne is equally ready to admit to failure. Their book of love will be construed 'To anger destiny, as she doth us.' Donne will struggle against his ignominious fate on earth by carefully compiling manuscripts recording their love by which they can ultimately be vindicated. Given further invasions by the barbarian infidel – an undoubted hazard at a time when the Turkish advance into Europe was giving rise to considerable alarm – true learning will only be able to survive so long as a faithful record of their love remains. Donne can be ironic at his own expense –

> In this thy booke, such will their nothing see,
> As in the Bible some can finde out Alchimy –

for just as authority for magical practices can even be looked for in sacred texts, so even the most ephemeral and illusory activities will find confirmation in Donne's book of love, since it is after all the true and absolute summation of nothing, the quintessence of dust! In 'The Relique' Donne rises to his greatest impiety and makes sacrilegious use of his erstwhile faith: his lover will be Mary Magdalen to his erotic Christ, their very bones will become the object of idolatrous veneration. The poem itself can serve as an affidavit of the miracles of love which they have performed. Yet, equally ironically, Donne implies that what has made this love miraculous is precisely its spirituality, the fact that it has been liberated from bodily appetites. The paradox of the poem is that it asks that physical tokens shall be taken as signifiers of the spiritual. Since Protestants believed that the age of miracles was past, Donne insinuates that it is only in later ages that the miracle of their love will finally be accepted for the miracle that it is.

However, it is in 'The Anniversarie' and 'A Valediction Forbidding Mourning' that Donne develops the most powerful validation of their love. In each case the master trope is grounded in Donne's long-held belief that the terrestrial world, indeed the whole universe, is in a process of decay and decline. From this universal tendency only their love is exempt. In 'The Anniversarie' Donne uses the occasion to pour scorn on the transitoriness of Courts, kings and favourites. Though Donne himself was at one point to entreat Lord Hay, one of the King's early homosexual passions, to be of service to him, he here abolishes all such worldly considerations. When kings and princes are everywhere unsure of their position their love, in contrast, will remain absolutely secure since there is no one else who can betray them. Even the sun itself is subject to deterioration through time, yet their love will persist. In all this hyperbole Donne is partly serious. He well knew how fleeting and how fluctuating reputations could be at Court, so to suggest that love could be infinitely more enduring was perfectly reasonable. Donne's period of exile forced him to scrutinise every aspect of his life, to examine critically all the varying values that he had tried to live by and to concentrate on the things that mattered. In the future he would be equally fanatic. Then religious spirituality supplants a spirituality of love as his main concern, but he opposes both to the materialism of a secular world – while trying to make his way in it all the same.

In 'A Valediction Forbidding Mourning' Donne asserts that his love is a spiritual mystery, beyond the power of ordinary human understanding. It does not depend on the ordinary tokens of presence and physical contact; in parting, far from being attenuated and subject to loss, it positively expands and grows. In this poem Donne posits Ann More – to whom it is surely addressed – as the centre of stability in his life and admits to the wayward and peregrine side of his own nature. Donne becomes the celebrant of his own invisibility. Their love is miraculous precisely because it leaves no sign or mark, because it is a subtle attuning of the spirit in which the lovers are always conscious of each other even though the world knows nothing of what they experience. Donne rejects the courtly world, clotted with symbols of majesty, opulence and power in order to rejoice in the infinitely more potent force of love.

Yet 'The Extasie', surely Donne's most subtle and ingenious poem, gives one further twist to the argument in a complex synthesising of Platonism with Christian doctrine. In a letter to Sir Thomas Lucy, Donne described letter-writing as 'a kind of ecstasy, and a departure and secession and suspension of the soul, which doth then communicate itself to two bodies'.[26]

In the poem Donne and his lover lie thus suspended like statues while their souls mingle together to create a new unity. However, this experience is not offered to the reader for its own sake but rather as a figure that is to be used in contemplation. Donne makes an ironic distinction between the way in which the doctrine of the transmigration of souls could be grasped by an adept or initiate into such mysteries and the way in which it could be understood by a lay public. The sage neo-Platonist will already be so completely refined in spirit and so utterly disembodied that he will have no difficulty in perceiving the ecstasy and will depart yet further purified by the vision which he has spiritually apprehended. But, says Donne, it is unfair of us to neglect our bodies since they are the medium that makes spirit possible and unless there is a return to the body it will be impossible to instruct ordinary human beings in these secret rituals of love:

> To'our bodies turne wee then, that so
> Weake men on love reveal'd may looke;
> Loves mysteries in soules doe grow,
> But yet the body is his booke.

So Donne climaxes the poem with a subtle irony at the expense of both the Protestant and Catholic faiths: it is their love that is the real presence, the real thing – yet others can only hope to grasp it at second hand through images or books. The physical dimension of their love is only necessary so that more fallible spirits may have the possibility of grasping it. So the poem moves between a private, actually incommunicable love and a public domain that will be impoverished if it is not vouchsafed a glimpse of it even in some subtly debased form.

In such poems Donne endeavours to banish all thoughts of the negativity of existence by such virtuoso flights of language and perverse logic, but melancholy thoughts were never very far away. In particular, it is characteristic that the poems are strangely obsessed with the idea of death, not simply in those poems that take it as the central idea, such as 'The Funerall', 'The Relic', 'The Dissolution' and 'A Feaver', but even in those which seem less obviously concerned with it. There is the introductory reference to the mild passing away of virtuous men in 'A Valediction Forbidding Mourning', the mention of separate graves for the lovers in 'The Anniversarie', the trope by which so many of the poems conclude by invoking death as in 'A Valediction of Weeping', 'The Good-morrow', 'A Valediction of my Name in the Window' and 'The Dreame'. In reading these poems it is hard not connect them with the Donne of *Biathanatos*, who knows that he carries the key to his prison in his own hands. Donne's sense of himself is always fragile. In 'A Valediction of my Name in the Window' he scratches his name as a talisman against absence, dissolution and time, yet even this is a 'ragged bony name' reminiscent of his 'ruinous Anatomie' – it is the trace of a trace. In 'A Valediction of Weeping' his tears have no value in themselves but can only be currency because

> thy face coines them, and thy stampe they beare,
> And by this mintage they are something worth.

This is, of course, humorous self-mockery but it does point to a deeper truth since Donne lost value in his enforced withdrawal from social circulation. He always felt that he needed some sort of external validation. If he were to acquire any credibility or legitimacy it could only be through the intervention of others. In one of his letters he asks to become the friend of a prominent person on the grounds that 'There is some of the honour and some of the degrees of a Creation to make a friendship of nothing'.[27] This language is doubtless the hyperbole of deference but it is a strikingly worded testimony all the same. As Jonathan Goldberg has pointed out:

> running through the *Letters to Severall Persons of Honour* is the recurrent motif of Donne's need to have a place in the world if he is to be anything and his complete dependence on others if this is to happen. . . . Donne's letters function as testaments to

his own 'impotencie' and nothingness; their role is to keep his name in circulation.[28]

Although there may have been some intimacy between Donne and the Countess of Bedford, who was for a while his friend and patron, it is likely that 'Twicknam Garden' reflects Donne's sense of frustration at being unable to retain the Countess's favour in either the private or the public sense because of his low social status. The Countess enjoyed a prominent position at Court and might have been able to help him if she had a mind to. The poem reflects Donne's mixed feelings on his visits to the Countess's residence at Twickenham. On the one hand, his friendship with the Countess seems to be the one ray of sunshine and hope on his otherwise oppressive existence and offers him the prospect of a more worthwhile future; on the other, because Donne has allowed himself to become emotionally involved with her, his visits there have become a torment. This potential Paradise is destroyed for him by the humiliation of rejection perhaps – but it seems more likely that Donne himself recognised that any relationship was necessarily precluded by his marginality and lack of social position. So Donne, as always, is drowning in a sea of lacks. Surely what 'mocks' Donne is not any outright rebuff but rather his own constant desire to return to Twickenham Garden, even while recognising how hopeless and pointless this is, as every visit intensifies his sense of the status discrepancy between himself and the Countess. Donne's expressed desire to be 'a stone fountain weeping out my year' reflects his desire not to be excluded altogether from the felicity of being accepted in the very best social circles for which the necessary price would be that his love should become completely petrified. He can obtain neither love nor advancement because love is out of the question, while his agitated emotions make it impossible for him to endure the role of congenial place-seeker any longer.

It is tempting to connect 'A Nocturnall upon S. Lucies day being the shortest day' with the Countess of Bedford, since Lucy was her Christian name, but I am more inclined to believe that the poem expresses a general sense of emptiness and negativity in Donne's life as the result of the disgrace of his marriage and would rather want to connect the poem with the illness of Donne's wife in 1611. The extinction of light on the darkest darkest day of the year is a fitting moment for Donne to contemplate the extinction of his own hopes and to meditate on the terrible price he has paid for love:

> For his art did expresse
> A quintessence even from nothingnesse,
> From dull privations, and lean emptinesse:
> He ruin'd me, and I am re-begot
> Of absence, darknesse, death; things which are not.

Here Donne sardonically reverses the thrust of his rhetoric elsewhere in order to suggest that the alchemy of love, far from cancelling the world, only has the power to make his sense of nothingness even more intense. Ironically by invoking the doctrine of 'The Sunne Rising' – that the beneficial qualities in all things are always for others – Donne suggests that he alone cannot profit from this state of affairs. He can gain nothing whatsoever from the external universe but can only become a still more intensified nullity. Donne's sense of severance in a private sphere of his own has no triumphal overtones here. He is not even a shadow. He is without either future or consequence. For the thought of Ann's death must have made Donne think that all his sacrifices had been for nothing. Face to face with the reality of death, he could no longer transfigure it.

This was the darkest hour before the dawn; but the dawn itself was to be a death of another kind. Donne, finally stamped with the seal of the King's approval, became Dean of St Paul's. The old, uncomfortable, disgraced and disgraceful Jack Donne was finally spirited from the scene. Donne was now a respectable, indeed eminent, public person. Yet Donne in his public role focused indefatigably on spirituality as a wholly private, personal matter. He never criticised the rich and powerful. He never directed his sermons at social abuses. On all controversial matters he kept his silence. Just as all Inigo Jones's masques were designed to be seen from the position occupied by the king, so all Donne's sermons were addressed, actually or hypothetically, to the ear of the king. Having risked all once, Donne could never take any risks again. But there can be little doubt that he remained just as ambivalently contemptuous of the fashionable world as he had before. After the death of James I, to whom he owed a personal loyalty, he became a little more outspoken, if always guarded and circumspect. In an open-air, popular sermon

delivered at Paul's Cross on 22 November 1629, two years before
his death, Donne stressed the fundamental contradiction between
the values of the Christian religion and the vain, pleasure-seeking
ambience of the Court in a way that smacks more than a little of
Puritanism. Worldly and carnal men, said Donne, with more than
half an eye on the present, had always found Christianity
scandalous:

> They were offended in Christ that he induced an inglorious, a
> contemptible Religion, a Religion that opposed the *Honours* of
> this world; and a sooty, and Melancholique Religion, a Religion
> that opposed the *Pleasures*, and the delights of this world; and a
> sordid, and beggarly Religion, A Religion that opposed the
> Gaine and the Profit of this world.[29]

In so saying, Donne openly conceded that the kind of
establishment, worldly, comfortable faith that he himself had
come to epitomise could never really be authentic. His guilt over
his own situation fuelled the tortured, mesmerising sermons of
his later years. Like Hawthorne's Dimmesdale, Donne sought to
cancel his own bad faith by being, despite it all, a true witness for
Christ. Yet in the private sphere Donne was more openly critical.
John B. Gleason[30] has shown that Donne annotated his copy of
More's *Utopia* with contemporary allusions, criticising ship money,
the soap monopoly and those who used every pretext to insist on
the king's prerogative, which in practice meant not only more
centralised power but more corruption. So Donne was a covert
radical who was in public reduced to a craven silence. Both
Donne's greatness and his weaknesses stem from this deep split
in his existence between the public and the private.

Donne was always the intellectual. His life was a perpetual
struggle between self-assertion and self-abasement, for, on the one
hand he loved to give free rein to the sharpness of his mind and
the sophistication of his intelligence, yet to some extent he
distrusted this side of himself, partly because it often got him into
trouble and partly because he feared its unsettling, destabilising
influence. He worried about spiritual pride, but he worried still
more about the doubts that his ever-questioning mind created –
as he himself said:

The mind of a curious man delights to examine it self upon

Interrogatories, which, upon the Racke, it cannot answer, and to vexe it selfe with such doubts as it cannot resolve. . . . He shall suspect his religion, suspect his Repentance, suspect the comforts of the minister, suspect the efficacy of the Sacrament, suspect the mercy of God himselfe.[31]

Donne's whole life was a prolonged interrogation of himself, his motives, his faith, the nature of existence itself, even his own desire to always probe more deeply. In the Holy Sonnets Donne is at once able to problematise his own role: 'But whom am I, that dare dispute with thee', and yet at the same time to object to the unfairness of a situation in which of the all creatures in the universe, man is the only one who has to face the prospect of eternal damnation. And Donne had certainly faced it. All his life Donne was torn between a desire to attract attention and a fervent wish to blend into the wallpaper, and this is there even at the end as Donne at once gives his personal relationship with God a melodramatic importance and yet asks for nothing more than to be a nothing:

> Batter my heart, three person'd God; for you
> As yet but knocke, breathe, shine, and seeke to mend;
> That I may rise, and stand, o'erthrow mee, and bend
> Your force to breake, blowe, burn and make me new.

From a divinity that is itself multiple, Donne looks for a divine power that will reassemble all his multiple identities and weld them into a new and pristine being that is no longer subject to division.

Burton, like Donne, was a frustrated place-seeker and like Donne he became demoralised and embittered by the sheer difficulty of trying to keep himself in a state of reasonable financial solvency and by the infinitely protracted uncertainty of all his attempts to obtain patronage. For many long years Burton was a poor scholar at Christ Church, Oxford, and it was not until the 1630s that Burton finally obtained the living of Segrave in Leicestershire, by which time he was well into his fifties. In his 'Digression of Air' inserted into the fifth edition of 1638, Burton, an inveterate grumbler, felt obliged to insert some sort of favourable reference to the place. He frankly described it as 'more barren than the villages about it', yet went on to praise it for the fact that 'no place likely yields a better air'.[32]

For this salubrious climate, if salubrious it was, Burton was indebted to his patron, Lord George Berkeley, to whom *The Anatomy of Melancholy* was dedicated. Our reading of *The Anatomy of Melancholy* is subject to considerable distortion because we are inclined to take the sixth and final edition as a single, composite work and are consequently disposed to imagine that the work's rambling, digressive style and its character as a repository of arcane and curious learning are absolutely *sui generis*. It becomes hard to see the book as anything other than a revelation of Burton himself and the reader will tend to conclude that the topics he treats are of interest, like the essays of Montaigne, largely because of the insights they afford into the nature of the author's personality. Certainly in the process of the revision and expansion of *The Anatomy* over a 20-year period we witness the development of a more self-consciously self-dramatising writing, in which Burton more and more emerges from behind his stacked arrays of sources to command centre stage in his own right – like the first violin of a small chamber orchestra who is finally persuaded to mount the rostrum and to direct operations with a baton rather than with a bow. However, what I do simultaneously want to insist on is that the very first version of *The Anatomy of Melancholy* is a rather different cup of tea. For while, even there, we can discern the lineaments of the crochety and eccentric misanthrope which Burton eventually became, Burton at 44 is an angry, indignant and deeply serious man whom we should not presume to patronise. *The Anatomy of Melancholy* of 1621 is an extended treatment of the subject of melancholy which both offers a comprehensive survey of medical and philosophical thinking on the subject but which also goes far beyond any textbook intention to launch a thoroughgoing attack on contemporary society. As a young man Burton was clearly a malcontent at a time when it was still fashionable to be one. The heyday of the malcontent can be assigned with some precision to the period from 1595 to 1610 – Webster's *The Duchess of Malfi* (1610) suggests that the pose is becoming unfashionable. Where Burton was unusual was that for him, like Marston, being a malcontent was rather more than just a pose and because he persisted in it long after all the others, Marston included, had given up. The first edition of *The Anatomy of Melancholy* turns a posture into a philosophical critique. It is only later that affectation creeps in. The earlier Burton, though always learned and digressive, writes forcefully and to the point. We should note that in 'Democritus to the Reader' Burton characterises himself as follows:

> I put forth what my genius dictated, out of a confused company of notes, and writ with as small deliberation as I do ordinarily speak, without all affectation of big words, fustian phrases, jingling terms, tropes, strong lines, that like Acestes' arrows caught fire as they flew, strains of wit, brave heats, elegies, hyperbolic exornations, elegancies, &c., which many much affect. I am a water-drinker, drink no wine at all, which so much improves our modern wits, a loose, plain, rude writer, & as free as loose, I call a spade a spade, I write for minds, not ears, I respect matter, not words.[33]

The reader, although certainly acknowledging the colloquiality of Burton's style, will more than likely be somewhat baffled by his robust claim that this has neither Euphuism or affectation in it and will either assume that it is ironically intended or that it is to be taken with a massive pinch of salt. Yet the 1621 *Anatomy* is serious and does not pull its punches. Burton's insistence that he writes for minds not ears testifies to a clarity and integrity of purpose that subsequently becomes blurred as Burton endlessly dilates the section on love melancholy and piles misogyny on misanthropy. The difference can be measured by comparing the flamboyance of Burton's later critique of contemporary fashions in the opening of 'Democritus to the Reader' with its piled-high enumerations of infamy with the earlier version where it is abundantly clear that Burton is not simply grumbling, that he really does want to change the world and is frustrated by his inability to do so:

> I have confusedly tumbled over many Authors in our Libraries, with small profit, for want of art, order, memory, judgement. I never travelled but in a Map or card, in which mine unconfined thoughts have freely expatiated, as having ever beene especially delighted with the study of *cosmography*. *Saturne* was Lord of my geniture, culminating, &c., and Mars principall *significator* of Manners, in partile conjunction with mine *Ascendant*; both in their houses, &c. I am not poore, I am not rich; *nihil est, nihil deest*; I have nothing, I want nothing; all my Treasure is in

Minerva's Tower. Preferment I could never get, although my friendes providence, care, alacrities and bounty was never wanting to doe me good, yet either through mine owne default, infelicity, want or neglect of opportunity, or iniquitie of times, preposterous proceeding, mine hopes were still frustrate, and I was left behind, as a dolphin on shore, confined to my Colledge, as *Diogenes* to his tubbe. Saving that sometimes as *Diogenes* went into the citty, and *Democritus* to the Haven to see fashions, I did for my recreation now and then walke abroad, and looke into the world, & could not choose but make some little observation, not as they did to scoffe or laugh at all, but with a mixed passion

> Bilem saepe, iocum vestri movere tumultus   Horace

I did sometimes laugh and scoffe with *Lucian,* and satyrically taxe with *Menippus,* weepe with *Heraclitus,* sometimes againe I was

> petulante splene cachinno   Persius

and then againe

> urere bilis ecur   Horace.

I was much moved to see that abuse which I could not amend.[34]

In this statement Burton's writing is far less pyrotechnically dazzling but it does make a lot more sense of his claim to be direct. What comes across is both the pathos of Burton's situation as the lonely, impotent scholar and the corresponding intensity of his moral indignation, which, in revision, is subtly dissipated by the omission of the image of himself as a stranded dolphin, by the alteration of 'weepe' to 'lament' and by the substitution of thanks offered to his 'noble and munificent Patrons' for the frank acknowledgement of failure and discontent at the iniquity of the times. The changes in *The Anatomy of Melancholy* necessarily reflected the changes in Burton's own situation as the unknown malcontent became a well-publicised author, whose book went through edition after edition.

Any initial reading of *The Anatomy* will almost certainly produce the conclusion that Burton is a fatalistic writer who sees little prospect that the world could be other than it is; who is convinced that melancholy is not only the only possible, but the only rational response to a world that is as black as he paints it; who, after surveying the entire human predicament from every possible angle, is forced to the conclusion that we have no alternative but to endure it as best as we can. Burton seems to acknowledge the vanity of all intellectual endeavours, perhaps especially his own, when he likens himself to 'a mired horse that struggles at first with all his might and main to get out, but when he sees no remedy, that his beating will not serve, lies still',[35] but even an allusion such as this undergoes sea-change in the passage from first to sixth edition. In 1621 this metaphor follows on directly from Burton's acknowledgement that he has utterly failed to gain any advancement: 'I was once so mad to bussell abroad, to seeke about for preferment, tire myself, and trouble all my friends and had my projects, hopes and designes, amongst the rest',[36] whereas it is subsequently interlarded with so many Latin interpolations, quotations and references to generous benefactors that much of the forcefulness of the original is lost. Changes such as this may seem to represent nothing more than an expansion of the original argument but the difference is actually quite significant. In the original version Burton is simply saying that he personally has given up on the rat race, whereas this subsequently becomes a response to the human condition in general. It is the distance between a man who is bitter and disillusioned about the state of English society but who still thinks critically about it and a man who no longer cares one way or the other. In the first edition it would be quite inappropriate to use this quotation to characterise the work as a whole – indeed it would fly in the face of a good deal of evidence to the contrary – whereas in Burton's final text it does have a certain plausibility. In Burton's revisions there is a consistent tendency to change passages that are forceful, direct and based on personal experience into more general philosophical disquisitions. For example when Burton is describing the miseries of the scholar in seeking preferment and the corresponding misery he must endure when he actually gets it he writes:

If after long expectation and much and earnest suit of our selves and friends, we obtaine a small benefice at last: our misery begins afresh, we light upon a crackt title, or stand in

feare of some precedent lapse, or some litigious people, that
will not pay their dues without much repining, or compelled by
long suit; all they think well gotten that is had from the Church
and by such uncivill, harsh dealings, they make theire poore
minister a weary of his place, if not of his life: and put case they
bee quiet honest men, make the best of it, as often it falls out,
hee must turne rusticke, and dayly converse with a company of
Idiots and Clownes.[37]

Here the sense of the humiliation, frustration and tedium
experienced by the scholar is vividly communicated. It is clearly
based either on Burton's own personal experiences or on that of
friends whom he knew were experiencing similar problems. It
directly relates, as does much else, to the England of 1621. But if
the reader will turn up the concluding pages of 'The miseries of
scholars' in the widely disseminated sixth edition all he will find
is a lengthy digression in Latin that proclaims: 'Quod tot Resp.
malis afficiatur, a nobis seminarium' [We are the nursery in which
those ills are bred with which the state is afflicted],[38] and a
passing reference to the awkwardness of falling among 'peevish
puritans, perverse Papists, a lascivious rout of Atheistical
epicures'.[39] The style is humorous and whimsical. A disposition to
eloquence has taken over even in the alliteration. Burton is no
longer the struggling underdog, but the all-knowing, crotchety
sage.

It is necessary to insist, somewhat pedantically, on the subtle,
yet pervasive significance of these changes because they condition
our sense of the overall direction and trajectory of the work and
specifically offer clues as to how we should take Burton's
introductory 'Democritus Junior to the Reader'. For this
introduction is itself a virtuoso performance in which Burton
alternately irritates and disarms and summons to battle or truce
his greatly perplexed addressee. So that since the introduction
already poses conundrums which are beyond its power to resolve
we are naturally tempted to scan the body of the text for some
kind of resolution. But Burton's expansion of *The Anatomy of
Melancholy* by as much as half has the effect of diminishing the
significance of this otherwise inordinately lengthy prelude and
of reinforcing his role as a latterday Democritus who seeks only to
laugh at human madness and folly. Whereas Burton has initially
suggested that, faced with the evils of poverty, war and extensive

moral corruption and injustice prevalent in the contemporary world, not only was laughter scarcely an adequate response, but even moral indignation would have to be completed by a suitable programme of action.

If we look at Burton in the context of his time what is evident is that what he calls 'melancholy' (which in his terminology is no longer simply one of the four humours that determine human personality but a complex shorthand by which to designate the manifold evils of earthly existence), we have to recognise that it is not just Burton's contemptuous estimate of the world that is contentious, for at the time there would be few who would disagree, but rather his sense, expressed somewhat tentatively in his prefatory remarks, that something can actually be done about it. It is certainly to the point to compare Burton with his Puritan contemporaries, with whom he certainly did not see eye to eye, but with whom he nevertheless has certain curious affinities. Like the Puritans, Burton distrusted the world: he described it as

a maze, a labyrinth of errors, a desert, a wilderness, a den of thieves, cheaters &c., full of filthy puddles, horrid rocks, precipices, an ocean of adversity, a heavy yoke, wherein infirmities and calamities overtake and follow one another, as the sea waves.[40]

It is fickle, deceptive, invariably menacing. However, unlike them, Burton sees an intense religious commitment not as a solution but as itself part of the problem. He does not perceive a rejection of this world as inescapably involving a quest for redemption in the next. Rather, Burton was deeply preoccupied with the state of things on earth and anxious that others should share in his concern. For Burton, spiritual health is not simply something for the individual to strive toward in an ongoing internal dialogue with God, for he is deeply conscious of the multifarious ways in which men are conditioned and shaped by a whole range of forces operating in the universe of which God is only the very distant, if ultimate source. Where Burton does have common ground with the radical Puritanism of a later generation is in his expressed desire for a general reformation of the world:

We had need of some general visitor in our age, that should reform what is amiss. . . . . It were to be wished we had some such visitor, or (if wishing would serve) one had a ring or rings, as Timolaus desired in Lucian, by virtue of which he should be as strong as 10,000 men, or any army of giants, go invisible, open gates & castle doors, have what treasure he would, transport himself in an instant to what place he desired, alter affections, cure all manner of diseases, that he might range over the whole world, and reform all distressed states and persons, as he would himself.[41]

The fact that Burton calls for a solution in magical terms does not mean that he was any the less serious than those who looked for a remedy in the return of Christ in earth in fulfilment of the prophecies in the Book of Revelations. Burton would doubtless have scoffed at such apocalyptic views as the empty speculation of ignorant men, but Burton was often demoralised and discouraged by the cynicism of the times. It is by no means impossible that a somewhat younger Burton, beginning rather than ending his speculations in 1640, might have been encouraged by the more widespread atmosphere of Utopian speculation. Even some of the more radical sects might have been on his wavelength. But in any event he would certainly have put forward his proposals in less diffident mood. For Burton's tone is influenced not so much by his lack of faith in Utopia as in his justified sense, in 1621, that he was not likely to be taken very seriously by those who took the Duke of Buckingham as their chronometer. Unlike the radical Puritans, what Burton lacked was the sense of belonging to a strongly committed and closely knit group. He had no conviction that his words would find an echo.

To most twentieth-century eyes Burton is a dotty antiquarian, who will piously and uncritically reproduce the views of interminable ancient 'authorities', quite regardless of the fact that they never fail to contradict one another, without any attempt on his part either to adjudicate their claims or to sift the evidence. However, in his own day Burton had some claim to be considered as a 'modern'. Admittedly Burton harks back to the classical past with a nostalgia that would be quite foreign to George Hakewill, his contemporary, but he does believe that the modern era offers a potential for knowledge that far exceeds the ancients and to that end cites perhaps the most celebrated of all modernising tags:

Though there were many Giants of old in Physick and

Philosophy, yet I say with Didacus Stella, A dwarf standing on the shoulders of a Giant may see farther than a Giant himself: I may likely add, alter, and see farther than my predecessors.[42]

It is in just such a spirit that *The Anatomy of Melancholy* is conceived. Burton believes that by laboriously collating and assembling as many diverse opinions as possible on the subject of melancholy he will put the contemporary reader in the position of obtaining an overview of the whole subject for the very first time. What Burton has done is to compile a data base from which further enquiry can proceed. Moreover, Burton, though by no means in tune with all the objectives of experimental philosophy, was well acquainted with the cosmological speculations of such figures as Galileo, Tycho Brahe, Copernicus and Kepler. Burton did not simply reproduce existing ideas on melancholy. In his analysis it expands into a pervasive mental condition that is produced by such a wide variety of causes that this in turn calls for analysis of human society in general. Burton thinks not as a doctor but as a cultural determinist. Following Boterus, Burton argues for a pathology of particular cultures; an argument which is embryonically sociological and which implicitly contradicts an assumption which he at other times seems to make, that melancholy is a universal phenomenon. For poverty, unhappiness and discontent are generated by very specific social conditions and can be tackled by a programme of measures directed towards eliminating the circumstances that produce it:

> but whereas you shall see many discontents, common grivances, complaints, poverty, barbarism, beggary, plagues, wars, rebellions, seditions, mutinies, contentions, idleness, riot, epicurism, the land lies untilled, waste, full of bogs, fens, deserts, &c., cities decayed, base and poor towns, villages depopulated, the people squalid, ugly, uncivil; that kingdom, that country must needs be discontent, melancholy, hath a sick body, and had need be reformed.[43]

In this way the tacit medical analogy can have more radical implications. In 1621 Burton's analysis would have been given additional impact just by the fact that, from the features he enumerates, England would be a prime candidate for such a reform. So while *The Anatomy of Melancholy* may well be an expression of melancholy, we also need to bear in mind that Burton's vast project is ultimately intended to *combat* melancholy: 'I write of melancholy, by being busy to avoid melancholy.'[44] Burton's intention in compiling the book was not simply to enable his readers to while away an idle hour. In the context of a personal life that had for the most part been deeply frustrating Burton saw *The Anatomy* as a work that could serve a beneficial social purpose: 'I will therefore spend my time and knowledge, which are my greatest fortunes, for the common good of all.'[45]

I therefore find it difficult to accept Stanley Fish's claim, in *Self-Consuming Artifacts*, that Burton's Utopia in 'Democritus Junior to the Reader' is not seriously intended, and that it scarcely even exists. That,

> The Utopia is just one more barrel, one more false promise, one more substanceless hope of sanity and order, and, like the others, it surfaces for a few brief moments before the advancing tide of melancholy rises to overwhelm and obliterate it.[46]

To begin with, Burton's is *not* a completely abstract Utopia and it would be wrong to project our modern understanding of what is at stake back into a period when the term is much less fully articulated and ideologically loaded. Moreover, Burton is *very conscious* of practical conditions and his analysis goes far beyond the general parameters established by Plato and More. Burton is well aware that the good society cannot be achieved without economic prosperity and a great many of his proposals are formulated with this particular objective in mind. If Burton's Utopia was merely the froth on a day-dream and the vain speculations of an idle moment, if he was solely concerned with elaborating an ideal but necessarily impossible model, there would be scarcely any point in his saying of egalitarian communities: 'Utopian parity is a kind of government to be wished for rather than effected, the Christianopolitan Republic, Campanella's City of the Sun, and that New Atlantis, witty fictions, but mere chimeras.'[47] The fact that he does say it indicates that he is bothered about practicalities and that he is concerned with implementing reforms that are actually feasible, as when, for example, he concedes that it is not really possible for usury to be banned: 'I will tollerate some kind of usury. If we were honest, I confess, we should have no use of it, but being as it is, we must necessarily admit it.'[48] To say this is not, of course, to deny the undoubted fact that Burton does incorporate into his text a number of dismissive statements, which can be taken as a frank confession of the futility of all such speculative models. In particular he observes:

> These are vain, absurd, and ridiculous wishes not to be hoped: all must be as it is, Bocchalinus may cite Commonwealths to come before Apollo, and seek to reform the world itself by commissioners, but there is no remedy, it may not be redressed, *desinent homines tum demum stultescere quando esse desinent*, so long as they can wag their beards, they will play the knaves and fools.
>
> Because therefore it is a thing so difficult, impossible, and far beyond Hercules' Labours to be performed; let them be rude, stupid, ignorant, incult, *lapis super lapidem sedeat* and as the Apologist will, *resp. tussiet geaveolentia laboret, mundus vitio*, let them be as barbarous as they are, let them tyrannise, epicurize, oppress, luxuriate, consume themselves with factions, superstitions, law-suits, wars and contentions, live in riot, poverty, want, misery; rebel, wallow as so many swine in their own dung. with Ulysses' companions, *stultos jubeo esse libenter*.[49]

But this passage cannot be simply cited, as Fish does, to produce the bald conclusion that there can be no remedy. For the question as to whether you think there is a remedy or not depends on a multiplicity of things. Burton's very indignation is itself calculated to arouse the reader and to force him to question in his own mind whether the state of things as they are really has to be accepted. Burton knew very well that there were remedies, which he had long and deeply pondered. What he doubted was whether the will was there to take effective action. *The Anatomy of Melancholy* oscillates between two poles; between the belief that the sources of melancholy can be eradicated by addressing the forces that produce it, and the view expressed elsewhere, in 'Remedies for Discontents' that there are various ways in which it can be alleviated in the mind of the individual. Doubtless as he grew older Burton became more and more fatalistic, a mood that is reflected in many of his revisions, but 'Democritus Junior to the Reader' still retains the forcefulness of its original critique. I would further want to point out that Fish, in citing the above passage, cuts it off after the reference to the Labours of Hercules, which significantly alters its tone. When it is cited in full it becomes quite clear that Burton is railing at his audience – saying, if all these absurdities don't bother you, very well, carry on as you are – but his invective is designed to shock his readers out of their complacency, to make them recognise that, actually, something really *ought* to be done about it.

Moreover, it has to be remembered that at the time when Burton was writing, authors had to be very circumspect about what they wrote. There was the very real possibility that they might incur the royal displeasure and be put in jail. Again, most authors wrote either to gain patronage or maintain it, as a perusal of the preliminary pages of almost any seventeenth-century publication that is not a Puritan pamphlet will certainly show. While by this time gaining a patron may no longer have been Burton's sole objective, he was obviously not unmindful of blessings which he so conspicuously lacked and to that end he would have tried to avoid giving obvious grounds for offence. Though Burton was a scholar of Christ Church his social status was relatively low – far lower, for example, than that of George Hakewill, whom, as I pointed out earlier, was obliged to lean over backwards to be deferential in his controversy with Godfrey Goodman, the blinkered but powerful bishop. So Burton has to offset his determination to be forthright with diplomatic concessions to the reader, as when he says in conclusion:

> I owe thee nothing (Reader), I look for no favour at thy hands, I am independent. I fear not.
>   No, I recant, I will not, I care, I fear, I confess my fault, acknowledge a great offence,
>
> – motos praestat componere fluctus –
>
> I have overshot myself, I have spoken foolishly, rashly, unadvisedly, absurdly, I have anatomised mine own folly.[50]

In the same way Burton incorporates flattering references to James I, even though he knows that James is the source and centre o. the whole patronage system that he castigates and although James is responsible for the proliferation of monopolies which he quite explicitly criticises. Burton is deeply concerned at the general state of English society but he knows that he must mask the obvious thrust of his critique. In this sense sketching a Utopia is itself a diversionary measure, since it implies that Burton is not necessarily concerned with the here and now. So I would want to argue that Burton's Utopia, far from being trivially meant, is actually a code through which he can speak out against what he sees as an unjust, unfair and incompetently run society.

Although Burton's analysis of contemporary evils is often positively vertiginous in its impact, he nevertheless focuses his attention on a number of major issues. To his credit, Burton was horrified by the barbarity of contemporary warfare and while he did not believe that it could be abolished altogether he did think that it could be conducted in a much more humane fashion. Here again his sense of outrage was always tempered by a spirit of realism. Burton was especially concerned with analysing problems of agriculture and trade. His researches had convinced him that no major civilisation has ever persisted for any length of time without having either an assured supply of food or prosperous cities engaged in trade. On both these counts the condition of England gave cause for concern. Burton was shocked by the expensiveness, partiality and blatant corruption that was endemic in the legal system. He was equally concerned at that notable sign of the times, the congregation in towns and cities of large, disorderly bodies of masterless men, who lacked regular employment. In his belief that this constituted a serious social problem Burton was certainly right. He was also appalled at the unscrupulous way in which the struggle for advancement and preferment was carried on at Court, especially since the ostentatious forms of cultural display that characterised it were carried on against a general background of poverty and conspicuous suffering. Burton could not regard all this with equanimity. Burton believed, or certainly did believe in 1621, that a more just, equitable, peaceful and prosperous society was possible and in thinking about possible alternatives the examples of the Low Countries and China were very much in his mind. Burton wanted to see a determined effort to improve the level of food production and promote trade on the lines of the Dutch and he felt that this could be combined with an honest, efficient bureaucracy which would run all the activities of the state on the model of China. But in proposing such an analytic approach to the problems of English society Burton was well ahead of his time. He also wanted to see a greater concern for the general welfare, which would involve such things as the construction of hospitals and almshouses, the erection of bridges, the provision of theatres and schools, the introduction of fire precautions, the development of markets and places of recreation. He appropriately cites the Latin tag: *'non nobis solum nati animus'* [We are not born for ourselves alone].[51] Burton's proposals were eminently practical. Although we may wish to highlight the self-interested nature of his wish for a society in which scholars like himself would have an important place, the fact remains that the Stuart kings could have benefited greatly by considering both the evils he drew attention to and the remedies he proposed. Burton knew that you could not hope to run a country simply on the basis of bribery. There would have to be a strengthening of the role of the state, an improvement in living conditions, a better legal system, a greater sense of common purpose.

It may seem paradoxical that, in a chapter devoted to the emergence of a private world, as the inner psychological space that can resist the pressures, conformities and mendacities of the public sphere, I should have largely concentrated on validating the seriousness of Burton's reforming intentions. For is not the private Burton that well-known scholarly, misanthropic recluse, and, if this is the case, am I not, in attempting to redraw his image, at the same time abolishing my subject? However, it is an essential part of my argument that Burton's sense of himself as a private person is something that progressively develops over the many years in which he wrote and revised his *Anatomy*. Clearly to be private in this way is not simply a form of consciousness, it is also a matter of social positioning. The private person belongs to the educated classes and has a certain social standing, but he is located on the margins of the dominant cultural groupings and his effective exclusion from real power or influence means that he tends to be disillusioned with many of the values and attitudes of his day. He has few illusions about his actual importance in the great world but for that very reason he wishes to establish a certain distance from it and to articulate his own perspective, whether or not this goes against the grain. Indeed, just to set his opinions down on paper may have a certain therapeutic effect. Writing becomes a kind of alternative to the public role. Thus, in 'Democritus Junior to the Reader' Burton set out his views knowing that it is highly unlikely that they will be gratefully received. He hopes perhaps that they will find an echo somewhere – from some other private individual. At the same time he has already psychologically prepared himself for indifference. He is ready to shrug it off and perhaps even secretly welcomes it – since this only confirms him the more fully in his chosen role as Democritus Junior, the one man who can perceive the whole world's folly. Although confirmation and recognition would be welcome they nevertheless have the effect of sucking the individual back into a public world which he has already abjured and of once more exposing him to the hazards, risks and disappointments that were his very reason for turning his back upon it. There is much to be said for remaining a private repository of clarity, authenticity and truth. For Burton, as for the radical Puritans, the truth of private conscience is absolute and it is not to be tempered to suit the exigencies of a corrupt public world. Although they are anxious to be heard, they are also apprehensive that in the general process of dissemination and diffusion the purity of the original word will be lost. Both write under the aegis of the Reformation ethic in which the Catholic Church is the master instance of a general tendency in the world to adulterate, ameliorate, pervert and directly falsify. They fear a loss of meaning all over again. So the private is also a kind of shorthand for a possibility of truth in the world that is always threatened by powerful institutional forces. It is noticeable that in his revisions to *The Anatomy of Melancholy* Burton lays an increasing emphasis on his own unimpeachable status as a private person, that he insists upon it and is conscious of this as a significant category in a way that was not evident on the occasion of the work's first appearance. It is only at a later date that he makes his proud boast: 'I had as live be still Democritus junior, and a *prius privatus* [private person] *si mihi jam daretur optio, quam talis fortasse Doctor, talis Dominus* [as a Doctor of Divinity or bishop].'[52]

We cannot fail to note the irony of this. Burton can now revel in his status as a private person just because he has become something of a celebrity and his whole identity is closely bound up with the literary persona of Democritus Junior. Burton has managed to make himself into a kind of signifier of private man and of everything that such a man is capable of representing. Scholar that he was, Burton could not be unaware of the extraordinary value placed on fame in the Italian Renaissance. Yet Burton made himself famous not by winning the favour of kings

and princes but by propelling himself into the limelight from the
seclusion of his study. This extraordinary feat was only possible
because *The Anatomy of Melancholy* was always something more
than a compendium of learning: it was a vivid essay in self-
dramatisation in which Burton was able to suggest that only he
could be a true critic of the world because only he had had the
determination to turn his back upon it. He can be trusted because
he has no particular axe to grind and because he is able to keep
his distance. Privacy becomes an extraordinary virtue, a talismanic
power that can carry the individual through a corrupted world
unscathed. In the process of amplification and revision many of
Burton's original motives for writing the book are lost sight of as
he increasingly strives to impose his personality on the reader
through stylistic exuberance and a kind of manic discursivity in
which the reader feels himself sinking under a veritable torrent of
babble. Burton is the disc jockey of early print culture. Whereas
for the earlier Burton being a private person was still something of
a problem, since he was still angry and irritated enough to feel
that the world had left him in the lurch, he subsequently turned it
his very *raison d'être*. The Burton we now recognise is the one who
launches this extraordinary self-justifying tirade:

> I live still a Collegiate student, as Democritus in his garden, and
> lead a monastick life, *ipse mihi theatrum*, sequestered from those
> tumults & troubles of the world, *et tamquam in specula positus*,
> (as he said) in some high place above you all, like Stoicus
> Sapiens, *omnia saecula, praeterita presentiaque videns, uno velut
> intuitu*, I hear & see what is done abroad, how others, run, ride,
> turmoil, & macerate themselves in court and country, far from
> those wrangling lawsuits, *aulae vanitatem, fori ambitionem, redere
> mecum soleo*: I laugh at all, *only secure lest my suit go amiss, my
> ships perish*, corn and cattle miscarry, trade decay. *I have no wife
> nor children good or bad to provide for*. A mere spectator of other
> mens' fortunes and adventures, and how they act their parts,
> which methinks are diversely presented unto me, as from a
> common theatre or scene. I hear new news every day, and
> those ordinary rumours of war, plagues, fires, inundations,
> thefts, murders, massacres, meteors, comets, spectrums,
> prodigies, apparitions, of towns taken, cities besieged in *France,
> Germany, Turkey, Persia, Poland*, &c., daily musters and
> preparations, and such like, which these tempestuous times

afford, battles fought, so many men slain, monomachies, shipwrecks, piracies, and sea-fights, peace, leagues, strategems, and fresh alarms. A vast confusion of vows, wishes, actions, edicts, petitions, lawsuits, pleas, laws, proclamations, complaints, grievances, are daily brought to our ears. New books every day, pamphlets, currantoes, stories, while catalogues of volumes of all sorts, new paradoxes, opinions, schisms, heresies, controversies in philosophy, religion &c. Now come tidings of weddings, maskings, mummeries, entertainments, jubilees, embassies, tilts and tournaments, trophies, triumphs, revels, sports, plays: then again, as in a new shifted scene, treasons, cheating tricks, robberies, enormous villainies in all kinds, funerals, burials, deaths of Princes, new discoveries, expeditions; now comical then tragical matters. Today we hear of new Lords and officers created, to-morrow of some great men deposed, and then again of fresh honours conferred; one is let loose, another imprisoned; one purchaseth, another breaketh; he thrives, his neighbour turns bankrupt; now plenty, then again dearth and famine; one runs, another rides, wrangles, laughs, weeps &c. That I daily hear, and such like, both private and publick news. Amidst the gallantry and misery of the world; jollity, pride, perplexities and cares, simplicity and villany; subtlety, knavery, candour and integrity, mutually mixing and offering themselves, I run on *privus privatus*; as I have still lived, so I now continue, *statu quo prius*, left to a solitary life, and mine own domestick discontents.[53]

This highly self-dramatising presentation of himself as a man who has mercifully escaped most of the aggravations of the world, by comparison with which his own domestic discontents must look trivial indeed, now utterly overshadows the original Burton, who actually found his marginal situation demoralising and oppressive. Now he is contented with his solitary lot and he offers his book to the reader as a haven of calm and tranquillity, far from the stormy seas of seventeenth-century conflict. Innovation, instability and perils are everywhere. But *The Anatomy of Melancholy* is now a kind of bulwark against confusion, a prophylactic against the times. Burton sees his century as an infernal scene of multiplication, but the paradox is that no one is more a part of this than Burton himself, with his relentless enumeration of possible sources of melancholy: anything and everything can be a cause. The ampersand becomes, for Burton, a key expressive device: it articulates his whole sense of a world that is getting more and more out of control so that only a book that is itself interminable can stand against it. Yet the strangest osmosis of all is that *The Anatomy of Melancholy*, a book that takes all the world and all human history for its province, is somehow transformed into a celebration of private man – of Democritus Junior in his study.

Nevertheless this self-construction as a private person was not without costs, either for Burton or for Donne. They felt that they were outcast from society. There was always difficulty and tension in the role. With Sir Thomas Browne, on the contrary, we are always conscious of a mind at ease with itself and with the world. While Donne had to learn to live in world that revolved around the person of the King and while Burton saw himself as inhabiting the margins of a universe subject to an ever-increasing confusion, Browne seems almost oblivious of the discord around him, like the still centre of a hurricane. When Browne speaks, as he often does, of his 'solitary and retired imagination'[54] we sense a man who finds it congenial to disengage himself from the hustle and bustle of daily life,

> Annihiliating everything that's made
> To a green thought in a green shade.

With Browne we are seldom made conscious of the pressures of circumstance. Apart from the querulous note struck in his preface to the authorised edition of *Religio Medici* he is not easily disturbed. A more genuinely private man than either Donne or Burton, who surely relished the celebrity they ultimately acquired, Browne seems untouched by everything, as securely enclosed in his own private world as if it were a crystalline sphere – or a belljar. He is always serene and untroubled. Although Donne once advised Sir Henry Wootten

> Be thou thine owne home, and in thy selfe dwell;
> Inne any where, continuance maketh hell,
> And seeing the snaile, which every where doth rome,
> Carrying his owne house still, still is at home.
> Follow (for he is easie pac'd) this snaile,
> Bee thine owne Palace, or the world's thy gaole

it was not advice that he was personally able to take. The snail and the tortoise were favourite Puritan emblems, representing steadfastness and tenacity in adversity, yet the Puritans were always more strenuous and more mentally anguished than their putative model. More than anyone it was Sir Thomas Browne who kept himself to himself and continued in his own easy-paced, unruffled way, carrying his own house on his back in the form of the unpretentious yet durable carapace of the opinions that he set forth in *Religio Medici*.

With *Religio Medici* there is the ever-present danger of succumbing to the spell of timelessness which the book itself so insistently weaves. Browne's experience of the seventeenth century could not be more different from that of his contemporaries, Milton and Clarendon, discussed in the following chapter, although the three men were born within a few years of one another. We need to remind ourselves occasionally that *Religio Medici* was written before his thirtieth birthday by a rather bumptious and self-important young man, who had just returned to England from his medical studies abroad and who no doubt wished to acquire a reputation among his genteel acquaintances for wisdom, piety and learning. It was written at a time when Laud's mastery of the English Church seemed absolute, when to a man of High Church Anglican sympathies, like Browne, it must have seemed that the gap between Canterbury and Rome could easily be narrowed in the course of a few solemn conclaves. If there was one thing that Browne was never quite able to grasp it was that religion was no longer a matter for adjudication by élites. For Browne, religion is unquestionably important but he believes that the time has come for the well-educated layman to step forward to defend it as much from the abstruse speculations of theologians as from the vulgar enthusiasms of the masses. The particular contribution a doctor can make is to bring a cool head and a well-balanced judgement to the controversy, reminding the excited participants that they are in danger of losing sight of how much, as Christians, they have in common, in their furious concentration on the issues that divide them.

Yet, for all that, *Religio Medici* is an extraordinarily narcissistic and self-regarding work, which over the centuries has contrived to irritate almost as many readers as it has comforted and edified. Dr Johnson gave Browne's capacity for wonder short shrift. He acidly commented: 'The wonders probably were transacted in his

own mind: self-love, co-operating with an imagination vigorous
and fertile as that of Browne, will find or make objects of
astonishment in every man's life.'[55] In Dr Johnson's characteristic
linguistic inflection 'own mind' reduces Browne's sense of wonder
to a solipsistic fiction. To insist on one's own particular sense of
things is both to trivialise and to exaggerate. It is to deny the
universality of human experience. J. B. Masterman, writing in
1897, has spoken of Browne's 'artless and fascinating egoism',
while more recently Stanley Fish has complained that *Religio
Medici* is self-indulgent, lacking in humility and over-eager for
applause.[56] Yet Browne's profound sense of his own importance
can itself be as much an object of wonder as an occasion for
disparagement or glancing condescension. The unswerving and
somewhat haughty eye that gazes out of his portrait seems to
epitomise his own sense that he is equal to every human problem
and every human dilemma, that he, in his capacity as a private
individual, can bring every issue to trial before the bar of his own
judgement. Browne did not hesitate to adjudicate some of the
most complex and contentious religious issues of his day. If he
often appears to equivocate and temporise, this is only a strategy
that enables him to assert himself the more forcefully in his self-
appointed task of disposing of problems. Yet it goes without
saying that biblical interpretation in the seventeenth century was
no light matter. It called for the most strenuous sifting of every
single word of the text, even just in the everyday practice of the
sermon, where an hour or more would be devoted to the exegesis
of a single verse, in the course of which a whole sheaf of parallel
and related citations would be assembled and further expounded.
Anyone who has studied William Gouge's commentary on St
Paul's letter to the Hebrews and pondered the implications of the
exhaustive treatment he devotes to one of the shortest books in
the whole Bible – so that it becomes a veritable Mississippi delta
by comparison with its source – will stand astonished at the
casual insouciance with which Browne performs his pirouettes on
a dance-floor made up of so many venerable tomes. Although
Browne never wore his learning lightly, he was certainly not
disposed to allow it to become a burden to the spirit. For all his
parade of scepticism Browne was never deeply troubled by the
conflict of interpretations. He believed that the intellectual
confusion that had been created by the conjunction of the printing
press with the Reformation could be undone by the simple device

of specifying a few canonical texts, as the medieval Church had done:

> 'Tis not a melancholy Utinam of mine owne, but the desires of better heads, that there were a general Synod; not to unite the incompatible difference of Religion, but for the benefit of learning, to reduce it as it lay at first in a few and solid Authors; and to condemne to the fire those swarmes and millions of *Rhapsodies*, begotten onely to distract and abuse the weaker judgements of Scholars, and to maintain the Trade and Mystery of typographers.[57]

The idea of an *Index* was congenial to Browne. Though he himself delighted in diverse and curious learning, he distrusted it as soon as it became contentious. Like a good medical man he wanted a few set texts, a basic syllabus, in which the equivalent of Galen and Aristotle would be taught to all students. This was the ready and easy way to close Pandora's box.

For all its engaging style, the matter of *Religio Medici* is highly provocative. Certainly Puritans, such as Alexander Ross, one of his earliest critics, could have found much in it that was objectionable. Browne delights in religious ceremony and ritual for its own sake. He believes in miracles and denies that the age of miracles is at an end. He boasts that he has never been afraid of Hell and prides himself on his own lack of pride. He seems to take it for granted that he is to be among the elect yet is also disposed to deny that any notion of the elect can be meaningful. He is prepared to concede that the world is in its last days but then perversely insists that there is nothing new in this and that it has actually always been the case: 'That generall opinion that the world growes neere its end, hath possessed all ages past as neerely as ours.'[58]

It is characteristic of Browne that he is not really very bothered whether this statement is true or not. From a Christian point of view, Browne's somewhat boastful claim that he has tried to follow Seneca's injunction 'to be honest without a thought of Heaven and Hell', and that he has discovered within himself 'an unbred loyalty to virtue'[59] is somewhat disconcerting. Although Browne insists that this means a struggle against the frailty of his nature and thus against original sin, his invocation of virtue in this sense is tantamount to denying that man can only be saved through God's grace. To many seventeenth-century readers Browne's suggestion that he would be happy to bring up the rear in Heaven would have seemed a good deal less than modest. It is all rather like a Finals student saying that he would be quite contented with an unstarred First. The question of Christian discipline is also crucial. Browne claimed to be a loyal member of the Church of England. As such he would be expected to profess its doctrines and subject himself to its authority. Yet Browne seems to arrogate to himself the final decision in all matters of faith, thereby opening the door to a dangerous eclecticism. As Sir Kenelm Digby noted in his *Observations upon Religio Medici*:

> Yet I cannot satisfie my doubts, how hee maketh good his professing to follow the great wheele of the Church in matters of *Divinity*: which surely is the solid basis of true *Religion*: for to doe so, without jarring against the conduct of that first mover by Eccentricall and irregular motions, obleigeth one to yeeld a very dutifull obedience to the determinations of it without arrogating to ones selfe a controlling ability in liking or misliking the faith, doctrine and constitutions of that *church* which one looketh upon as their North starre: *Whereas if* I mistake not this author approveth the Church of *England* not absolutely but comparatively with other reformed Churches.[60]

Here, Sir Kenelm Digby alludes to a passage early in *Religio Medici* where Browne professes:

> In Philosophy where truth seemes double-faced, there is no man more paradoxicall then my self; but in Divinity I love to keepe the road, and though not in an implicite, yet an humble faith, follow the great wheele of the Church, by which I move, not reserving any proper poles or motion from the epicycle o my owne braine.[61]

Sir Kenelm Digby's *caveat* 'if I mistake not' is certainly called for by the peculiar nature of Browne's style. It is not merely that Browne prefers to assert himself through qualified negations and that he guards his more pontifical utterances with strategically located disclaimers and with abrupt switches of argumentative focus, even his most unequivocal statements are typically undermined by confessions he makes elsewhere. This particula sentence, which seems to constitute one of the few really solid planks in the whole ramshackle structure of *Religio Medici*, rapidly gives way if there is any attempt to place any weight upon it. While Sir Kenelm Digby has acutely sensed the relativistic implications of Browne's whole mode of arguing, he can hardly be correct in thinking that Browne sees the Church of England as merely somewhat better than other reformed Churches. For Browne has very little interest in reform, is clearly hostile to Puritanism and in general treats the Reformation as if it is effectively over. What is equally worth pondering is that it is by no means certain that what Browne has in mind here in speaking of 'the Church' is the Church of England. It is of course true that Browne is a member of it and that since he speaks of 'keeping the road' he would seem to be speaking of adherence to the 39 articles. Yet one would have to add that this statement occurs in a general context in which Browne has been insisting on the common faith of all Christians and his reluctance to divide himself from any man in religious dispute – any stress here on a singular set of beliefs would run counter to the thrust of his whole argument. When he subsequently levels criticism at 'those of my religion'[62] he means this not in any exclusive sense, but only Christians as opposed to Mahometans, Jews and pagans. Moreover, he insists that the distinctive feature of Christianity as a religion is that it is not exclusive: 'It is the promise of Christ to make us all one flock.'[63]

So although Browne may well have had the Church of England in mind as the focus of his 'humble faith', it is actually very hard to believe that Browne believes that he is very firmly committed to anything if the reader simply follows the thrust of his own reasoning. We might certainly be inclined to believe that Digby has carelessly misread Browne or turned his own argument against him by attributing 'Eccentrical and irregular motions' such as Browne in this passage specifically disclaims by denying that he reserves 'any proper poles or motion from the epicycle of my owne braine', yet Browne seems almost immediately to contradict himself by going on to speak for his sometime belief in three heresies: the saying of prayers for the dead; mortalism, the belief that the soul dies with the body; and the notion that God will not persist in his vengeance against the wicked for ever, which 'could never have been revived, but by such extravagant and irregular heads as mine'.[64] Admittedly Browne now claims that these

heresies have extinguished themselves from his mind, but he
goes on to suggest that there will always be heresies and heretics
and that one reason for this is that 'men of singular parts and
humors have not beene free from singular opinions and conceits
in all ages'.[65]

Clearly Browne puts himself in this category. He undoubtedly
is of the conviction that there is nothing wrong with having
singular opinions provided this remains an essentially private
matter. They only cause trouble when they are aggravatingly
presented as a challenge to the existing order with some
deliberately subversive intent. So at the very moment when
Browne is to all appearances proclaiming his unswerving allegiance
to the Anglican faith he is also reserving for himself the right to
think as he likes without being stigmatised as a heretic. A further
irony in this is that by questioning notions of heresy and the idea
that it is possible to become a martyr for the faith Browne renders
his own self-definition as a member of the Church of England still
more problematic. Of John Hus he writes: 'The Councell of
Constance condemnes *John Husse* for an Heretick, the Stories of his
owne party stile him a Martyr; He must needs offend the Divinity
of both, that says hee was neither one nor the other.'[66] The
general thrust of Browne's argument here is to devalue the idea
of martyrdom in general, and Protestant martyrdom in particular.
His target is clearly Foxe's *Book of Martyrs*, one of the founding
documents of the Elizabethan Church. Now in 1635 Foxe is no
longer as definitive of the Church as he had been, since Laud, the
one man who now epitomises it, was strongly opposed to
everything that Foxe represented. But for the majority of those in
the Church of England, nourished on memories of the Marian
persecutions and gunpowder treason, Browne's laid-back attitude
to martyrdom would have seemed quite shocking. What should
be stressed here is the *private* character of Browne's allegiance. If
he proclaims it and believes it, that is all that remains to be said.
He does not grant others the right to judge the quality of his
belief, the genuineness of his protestations or the specificity of his
commitment. Yet it is impossible to convict him of laxity and
impiety anyway, since he concludes the first part of *Religio Medici*
by conceding that, while there may be in his belief 'many things
singular, and to the humour of my irregular self',[67] he is prepared
to disown them if challenged. So we are still left with the puzzle
as to why Browne thinks it worthwhile to set down this faith of

his, as a doctor, if not to bring out its distinctiveness and singularity, when at one and the same time he implies that his opinions are dispensible and certainly not worth fighting for. Browne's strategy here is defensive. Since his vanity is such that he does not hesitate to place the whole world in brackets and find it all 'but a dreame, or a mockshow'[68] he will allow the reader to place his own work under erasure. The beauty of this strategy is that through the very contract of reading that Browne establishes it seems very unreasonable to respond to his parade of tolerance and conciliatoriness with cries of 'heretic', 'papist' or 'traitor'. For all his insistence on loyalty and tradition, Browne is an innovator and a splitter. As Sir Kenelm Digby divined, he makes religion not a grandly contested matter of public truth, but a question of individual and private taste. Browne, finally, is answerable to no one but himself.

The seventeenth century was a period in which there was an eager and widespread interest in the prophecies contained in the book of Revelations. From Napier, the inventor of logarithms, to Newton, the inventor of calculus, many powerful minds devoted themselves to the arduous task of calculating the year in which the world was most likely to come to an end. On the basis of such authoritative studies as Joseph Mede it was anticipated that this could be expected to occur before the end of the century. Yet Sir Thomas Browne, who confessed to an obsession with the 'secrete Magicke of numbers',[69] remained strangly untouched by these speculations. In 1635, when Browne was composing *Religio Medici*, Samuel Hartlib, the Utopian reformer and disciple of Paracelsus, returned to England from Leyden and immediately began a correspondence with Joseph Mede in which he reported that Mede's privately circulated *Clavis Apocalyptica* was eagerly sought after there.[70] Yet Browne, who had been studying medicine in Leyden only two years earlier and who must have been exposed to similar influences, refers to such ideas in *Religio Medici* only to reject them decisively: 'Now to determine the day and yeare of this inevitable time, is not only convincible and statute madnesse, but also manifest impietie.'[71]

At a time when many of his contemporaries sought to use the Bible as the key to world history, Browne remained sceptical and aloof, not just because he distrusted prophecy, but because he distrusted history. Browne, the physician, believed that the natural world offered man direct access to the works of God and afforded

him gratifying confirmation of a serenely functioning, elaborately
structured universe, whereas the irreconcilable conflicts of biblical
interpretation, of which the prophecies in Revelations were only
one instance, could serve to create uncertainty and confusion. So
Browne was an early spokesman for natural religion: 'Surely the
Heathens, knew better how to joyne and reade these mysticall
letters, than wee Christians, who cast a more carelesse eye on
these common Hieroglyphicks, and disdain to suck Divinity from
the flowers of nature.'[72] Browne worried about history because he
believed that it was always written for self-serving, opportunistic
ends and that therefore the narratives thus produced were not to
be relied upon. A consistent tone of disparagement of such erratic
memorials runs through Religio Medici. He defends prayers for the
dead on the grounds that they are 'far more noble than a
History',[73] and he speaks of himself as 'not caring for Monument,
History or Epitaph'.[74] He allies himself with his fellow Protestants
in suspecting religious relics because of 'the slender and doubtful
respect I have always held unto Antiquities',[75] and speaks of his
sense of 'what counterfeit shapes & deceitfull vizzards times
present represent on the stage things past; I doe believe them
little more than things to come'.[76]

Although Browne professes to accept the Bible in a spirit of
total faith, in practice he treats it as yet another dubious narrative.
There are many biblical stories that are as fanciful as those that he
is anxious to expose in Pseudodoxia Epidemica – 'there are in
Scripture stories that doe exceed the fables of Poets'[77] – and if
there is no certainty in scripture as to whether or not Judas
committed suicide then there must be many other places in the
Bible where certainty is equally hard to come by. These arguments
cannot really be resolved by a determination to believe in the
Bible, since as long as the Bible is subject to interpretation then
different sects will continue to believe different things. So it is
clear that although Browne dare not come right out and say so, he
does not believe that the Bible can be made the sole basis of
Christian faith. Browne has a further reason for distrusting the
historical, which is that it serves as a perpetual reminder of the
frailty and fragility of human existence. The trasitoriness of
empires, the brevity of human life are made the more intolerable
when, far from it being probable that they will be remembered,
there is a positive certainty that they will not. Browne seeks to

evade the diachronic which brings with it only confusion, difficulty and pain through a mysticism of the synchronic. Nowhere is this more clearly evident than in Browne's joint publication of *Hydrotaphia* together with *The Garden of Cyrus*. Urn burial was a subject of more than passing interest for Browne – the question 'who knows the fate of his bones'[78] was one that, in a morbid age, genuinely did concern him. The use of funerary urns as a proud and solitary bid to outface the passing of time evidently captured his imagination even as he recognised that it was ultimately doomed: 'In vain do individuals hope for Immortality, or any patent from oblivion, in preservations below the Moon. . . . There is nothing strictly immortal, but immortality; whatever hath no beginning may be confident of no end.'[79]

It is only in the cancellation of time, in the annihilation of its depradations under the eye of eternity that Browne can find comfort or satisfaction. Hence Browne turns aside from the prophetic number 6 in the Book of Revelations to pursue the synchronic ramifications of the mystical number 5, the quincunx, as it endlessly repeats itself through the whole order of nature and human customs. Six betokens an ominous finality, whereas 5, in its perpetual recurrence, is the type of eternity. There is no terror in Browne's conception of predestination precisely because, in his vision of it, it is as fixed and stable as the creation itself. In the eye of eternity time and the future are abolished:

> *Predestination*, which hath troubled so many weake heads to conceive and the wisest to explaine, is in respect to God no prescious determination of our estates to come, but a definitive blast of his will already fulfilled, and at the instant that he first decreed it; for to his eternitie which is indivisible and altogether, the last Trumpe is already sounded, the reprobates in the flame, and the blessed in *Abrahams* bosom.[80]

Doubtless the fact that Browne, in his mind's eye, saw himself bashfully bringing up the rear in Heaven helps to explain why the doctrine of predestination never really bothered him, but in this instantaneous moment the whole trepidation of waiting is abolished. In the mire of history it is the very uncertainty of human destinies that oppresses, whether in this world or the next, but it is the very splendour with which the doctrine cancels all sense of temporality that Browne finds aesthetically satisfying. To conceive of existence as 'but one permanent point without succession, flux or division'[81] is to be a god oneself.

It is Browne's profound sense of a divinity within, his faith in the essential mysteriousness of each and every person – 'Wee carry with us the wonders, we seeke without us: There is all *Africa*, and all her prodigies in us'[82] – that underpins his sense of the importance of private man. Browne takes quite literally the notion that man is the microcosm. He believes that every question can be settled by a simple recourse to oneself. Sir Kenelm Digby was quite taken aback by Browne's readiness to ramble on about himself in an inconsequential yet self-important way: 'As when he speaketh of the soundness of his body, of the course of his dyet, of the coolness of his blood at the summer solstice, of his age, of his neglect of an *Epitaph*.'[83] He was even more astonished that Browne should, in describing himself as contemporaneous with three Emperors, four Grand Signiors and as many Popes, effectively make 'such great *Princes* the land-markes in the Chronology of himselfe'.[84]

Thus private man can effortlessly turn the tables on the pretension of public greatness. Almost unassumingly Browne makes himself the measure of all things and takes it for granted that he is the axis around which the whole world revolves. He can perform this feat the more readily since the world is a pattern of analogies and figures that he himself has deciphered. It is precisely because Browne is so confident of this that he feels no great eagerness to engage in the dust and heat of battle along with Milton, Lilburne, Overton and myriad warring Puritan voices. In *Religio Medici* he criticises Democritus and, therefore by implication, Burton for railing against the vices of the age. For only a few can be virtuous and virtue is not a public matter. In its original context Browne's position can seem complacent and narrowly self-regarding, but not a few who might once have scorned him eventually came around to something very like his point of view. For example, Joseph Salmon, who was a leading figure amongst the feared and subversive Ranters, was also conscious of 'some quickenings of the divine principle within me',[85] but this took the form of believing, with Abiezer Coppe, that any inward monitions toward swearing, drunkenness and sexual promiscuity, since they came from God, could not be regarded as unclean. Salmon

initially set out to challenge and to shock. He was proud of the
hostility the Ranters provoked for this seemed to prove that they
had been chosen by God to be the instrument of a wider
redemption. But after such discouragement and a few spells in gaol
Salmon became less and less interested in controversy. In *Heights
in Depths and Depths in Heights* (1651) Salmon wrote: 'I cannot
inveigh against any form, party of religious interest: it becomes
not my sweet silence, to bawl and brawl with the unquiet spirits
of men.'[86] By comparison with the sense of unity and tranquillity
that he was able to discover within himself, he found the world
full of confusion: 'If we look upon the Temporary, or more
outward state of things; good Lord how subject is it to revolutions
and vicissitudes? what is it that we can call certain, but only
uncertainty.'[87]

Although Salmon offers his reflections to the reader in the hope
that he will be able to profit from his experiences and in a spirit of
self-vindication from public calumnies, he has really given up on
the whole social scene. The work is more a dialogue with himself,
an inward meditation, in which he tries to reach a private
settlement of accounts:

> Truly for my part, as I sit still and behold how the over-busie
> world is acted; so I can quietly let them alone, to roul in their
> confused labyrinth: but because in many things I have offended;
> and the froward spirits of men are not easily courted to a
> pardon: I have here thought meet, to cite a small parcel of the
> most crying errors of the times; and (before I withdraw into my
> sweet and safe retires) spend a little time in sweeping them
> from my door: so that the evil of error, may not lie in the porch,
> to disquiet my blessed rest, and disturb the sweet slumbers of
> my silent mansions.[88]

Salmon no longer sallies forth into the world in order to arouse
and convert and rather seeks to preserve his own little corner of it
inviolate from the moral pollution of others. This private discourse
is always on the point of lapsing into silence since it is only
uttered under the pressure of some inner moral necessity and not
with any strong expectation that anyone is actually listening. Like
George Herberts's well-swept room, it clears a virtuous space in
which all that matters is that the action itself should be sincere

and well intentioned. In the private world there is always the possibility of truth, which somehow always gets lost in the process of public communication. In a way the auditor is an embarrassment.

11

The Public World of Clarendon, Hobbes and Milton

In the seventeenth century, as even a cursory glance at the *Oxford English Dictionary* will demonstrate, there is a greatly increased sense of a public world that carries with it a complex set of public responsibilities. Just what connotations a word such as 'public' carries can only be decided by an analysis of contemporary usage, but undoubtedly what is most decisive is a developing consciousness that the political does not consist solely of matters to be determined by the reigning monarch – a conviction that all power ultimately stems from the people and that therefore their welfare and interests need to be considered. But, at the same time, 'public' is obviously coupled with 'private' in a binary opposition, where 'public' may designate a certain altruism as opposed to the pursuit of selfish 'private' interests; it may equally suggest a sense of patriotic duty that the compels the individual to give up the tranquillity of 'private' life. The first and most obvious source of this notion of a public world is the literature of classical antiquity. Plays that were based on such sources could readily invoke a language that was customary in Greece and Rome and apply it implicitly to somewhat different contemporary sources. Thus Philotas in the Samuel Daniel's play of that name insists on his concern for the general welfare and deplores the fact that all those in the circle around Alexander are only concerned with pursuing their own interests. 'And none at all respect the publike good.' However, Chalisthenes characteristically suggests that such sentiments must necessarily be bogus:

> Philotas, all this publike care, I feare,
> Is but some priuate touch of your dislike.

This questioning of Philotas's credibility is obviously founded on

the belief that whatever the word purports to designate is essentially
unreal, and this doubtless reflects Daniel's own sense of the
difficulty of speaking such a language at the palace of Whitehall.
However, this sense of a public world was greatly strengthened by
the revival of a common-law tradition by Sir Edward Coke and his
associates. In this way the identity of the nation was associated with
a network of precedents which served to protect the rights of
Englishmen from any kind of 'alien' encroachment. It was this
rather than the person of the king that was at the root of all political
authority and it suggested the possibility of a political framework
based on negotiation, bargaining and compromise, where a variety
of interests would have to be taken into consideration. As J. G. A.
Pocock has pointed out:

> The cult of customary antiquity was a peculiarly English brand of
> legal humanism, and the great Jacobean antiquaries, who
> asserted it as they began undermining it, were humanists of a
> very special sort; and, however remote from civic humanism in
> the republican and Florentine sense, it was, unmistakably and
> post-medievally, a species of civic consciousness. It defined, in
> traditionalist terms, a public realm and a mode of action therein.[1]

What was perhaps even more significant was that this whole
method of arguing tended to suggest that any notion of the public
interest would have to be defined in opposition to the king, perhaps
even that it is this public interest that the king cannot represent.

The arguments of the Puritan preachers may have been even
more influential in developing a sense of the English people as a
community, one whose interests must be both advanced and
defended. The preachers were in principle opposed to the power of
the bishops and they believed that the ecclesiastic hierarchy was
using its position to frustrate reforms in defiance of God's will and
the wishes of the people. Their resistance to the bishops meant that
they had to produce a definition of the Church that was as
all-embracing as possible so that progressively it becomes natural to
speak as if Church and people were one. This identification is
evident in Cromwell's celebration of the battle of Marston Moor in
1644: 'Truly England and the Church of God hath had a great favour
from the Lord, in this great victory given unto us, such as the like
never was since this war began.'[2]

Whereas arguments from the common-law tradition tended to be
defensive, the Puritan preachers, with the Old Testament tradition

in their minds, went on to the offensive. God had made a Covenant with his people that was binding upon them and he would tolerate no half measures, no delay in the bringing about of his kingdom. In their addresses to Parliament they insisted that Members had a clear duty to implement all the necessary changes and for them it simply went without saying that it was Parliament which was sovereign. In his address *The Song of Moses* Stephen Marshall stressed that God, the people and the people's representatives must be welded together indivisibly in the pursuit of their common cause:

> I hope you purpose according to your Covenant, and what God requires and expects at your hands, to stick close to Christ and his Cause, to sink and swim with the Church, and the Cause of Christ, with singlenesse of heart, and unwearied resolutions, to carry on the work of God, to value yourselves onely as his instruments, and let him do by you, and with you, what is good in his own eyes.[3]

In this style of argument Parliament has an indisputable mandate to govern but one which has to be continually underwritten by God and the ministers who speak for him if it is to have any continuing validity. However, the argument that it was through the people that the voice of God would be manifested could be set out in still more uncompromising terms. In Thomas Goodwin's *A Glimpse of Sion's Glory*, the traditional notion of *vox populi, vox dei* is asserted with more than its customary force. He admittedly goes on to argue, very much in the manner of Stephen Marshall that, in the final analysis, all the important decisions will have to be taken by Parliament, but he does begin by insisting that the groundswell of popular feeling against popery flows from an impulse that is truly divine:

> You that are of the meaner rank, common People, be not discouraged; for God intends to make use of the common People in the great Worke of proclaiming the Kingdome of his Sonne; the Lord *God* omnipotent reigneth: the Voice that will come of *Christs* reigning, is like to begin from those that are in the Multitude, that are so contemptible, especially in the eyes, and account of *Antichrists* spirits, and the *Praelacie*, the vulgar Multitude, the common People; what more contemned in their mouths than they? and yet it is from them that this Voice doth come; The Lord God omnipotent reigneth.[4]

For those who opposed the king, the right that was on their side was always implicitly divine. The flow of legitimacy was now reversed. It was with the people that you had to begin. Nevertheless once the rebellion was underway the notion of a public interest was no longer solely a matter for those who supported Parliament. The Royalists were, of course, clear that their duty lay in fighting on the side of King, but they were also obliged to advance arguments as to why supporting the King was also in the general interest and to show that those who invoked it were actually acting against it. Thus Clarendon said of Pym: 'No man had more to answer for the miseries of the Kingdom, or had his hand or head deeper in their contrivance.'[5]

While on the one hand Fairfax, in an ultimatum, calling on Prince Rupert to surrender Bristol to the Parliamentary forces in 1645, could insist that it was the King's duty to heed the advice of Parliament 'in which multitude of Councellours lys his safety, and his people's interest',[6] it was equally possible, in 1659, for the future Charles II to offer General Monck a sweetener of £100,000 p.a. to abandon Parliament with the words: 'the good I expect from you will bring so great a Benefit to your country and to yourself that I cannot think you will decline my Interest'.[7] The circumstances of Civil War generated a sense of a public world in which each individual was obliged to arrive at his own personal interpretation of how the interests of the community could best be served. So many of the critical events of the period between 1640 and 1660 hinge on the decision of particular individuals to act in ways that may not be obviously justifiable or strictly legal but which they believe are for the public good: Sir John Hotham's resistance to the King's attempt to seize the arsenal at Hull; Holles's determination to disband the army in 1647; Pride's Purge instituted by Ireton; the seizure of Charles I by Cornet Joyce; the Restoration of Charles II by General Monck. This was now the framework within which political action had to be assessed.

Although Clarendon, Hobbes and Milton were deeply committed to this world of public affairs, the vicissitudes of fortune were such that they were compelled to lead lives that were as reclusive as those of Donne, Burton and Browne. Although Clarendon enjoyed two great moments of political influence – as a leading adviser to Charles I from 1640 to 1643 and as Charles II's chief minister for the first seven years of the Restoration – he spent the rest of his mature years, nearly two decades in all, in exile and for much of that time he was engaged in writing his history of 'the rebellion'. Hobbes was a fearful and melancholy scholar, very much in the mould of Burton, who sedulously steered clear of trouble and who also lived in exile for many years. Milton was actively involved in the events of the Civil War, both as a pamphleteer and as Latin Secretary to the Council of State, but much of his greatest poetry was written in blindness and internal exile after the Restoration. Yet for all that, their lives were crucially dominated by the great events of their time and they made it a lifetime task to try to comprehend why things had turned out as they did. It would be easy to explain the pessimism that colours their writings in terms of their own personal anxieties and the instability of the times in which they lived, but it is to be more decisively understood in terms of the explanatory models they developed in response. For Hobbes and Clarendon the task was to explain how it was that such a shocking and unforeseen event as the rebellion could ever have taken place; for Milton it was try to understand the equally scandalous miscarrying of the revolution, the catastrophe of the Restoration. From either side of the Civil War the course of events from 1640 to 1660 seemed unpredictable, erratic, beyond reason – and yet, there *must* be a key.

Clarendon's account of the Civil War period aspires to be an objective and critical history in the manner of his mentor, Thucydides. The task he sets himself is to explain the course of events, to offer a balanced picture of the leading figures on both sides and to provide a narrative that is substantive, authorative and detailed. Yet for all that it is a deeply personal work that often reads much more like a lament, prolonged over many books, at the parlous state that the English nation has been brought to. Although Clarendon's story has a happier ending than that which Thucydides had to tell, since it concludes with the Restoration of the monarchy under Charles II, it is driven by an equally powerful sense of the way in which there arose out of apparently trivial and inconsequential beginnings, when compromise was not only possible but seemingly inevitable, an irreconcilable conflict in which both sides were to be the losers. Indeed, for Clarendon, pondering the example of his great predecessor, the English catastrophe must have seemed even more perverse, since the rivalry between Athens and Sparta was long-standing, whereas the two sides of King and Parliament scarcely existed in their latter-day sense before 1640. After that date they polarised so rapidly that Clarendon's attempts to mediate were becoming impossible almost from the very moment that he began. Writing with hindsight it seemed to Clarendon that the events of those years were like a cataclysmic eruption that had virtually obliterated all sense of the national past. Although Clarendon longed for the return of Charles II and although he fervently hoped that the old order could be restored as it once was or as he imagined it to have been, in his heart he knew that nothing would ever be quite the same again. Such an emphatic, such a prolonged repudiation of royal authority must inevitably leave its mark. Clarendon nostalgically and unrealistically idealised the decade before the war when England had 'enjoyed the greatest calm and fullest measure of felicity that any people in any age for so long time together have been blessed with; the wonder and envy of all the parts of Christendom'.[8]

Certainly, if nothing else, it does demonstrate what a gloomy view Clarendon, along with many of his contemporaries, was disposed to take of world history if the age of Laud's persecutions was to be seen as the nearest thing yet to the Golden Age. From his point of view this was not a rash judgement. He was careful to argue its superiority over the reigns of both Elizabeth and James I, on the grounds that at this time England no longer faced the threat of foreign invasion or internal sedition. For Clarendon, England in the 1630s was a little island of calm in a Europe dominated by the Thirty Years War – the very last place conflict was to be expected. Undoubtedly to claim this argues a certain wilful blindness on the part of a man who had, after all, set out to be the Civil War's great interpreter, but it was integral to his whole conception to claim that crisis suddenly loomed up out of the blue, like a collision at sea in the thickest fog. Looking back from his periods of repeated exile, Clarendon ceaselessly invoked the good old days and 'the good old frame of government'[9] that had served England so well. What made Clarendon pessimistic was the violence, the unpredictability, the sheer unnecessariness of it all. It seemed almost beyond belief that Charles I, the legitimate king, could ever have been brought to such a desperate pass; that for many years almost every conceivable royalist project should have ended in abject failure; that Charles, his son and heir, should have had to wander Europe for many years in a state of humiliating dependence on the alleged goodwill and manifest bad faith of his fellow monarchs. For Clarendon and his prince, the biblical question, 'How long, O Lord, how long?' was all too apposite. It was one of the strange ironies of Clarendon's situation that the very man who scorned Puritan attempts to use the Bible as the key to contemporary history should have himself perceived the Royalists as Israelites in the wildnerness and should have earnestly scanned the Psalms of David for clues that might afford either consolation or illumination. The most surprising aspect of Clarendon's history is the fact that, despite its retrospective orientation, it nevertheless retains much of the character of a diary, poignantly conveying a sense of the agonies, frustrations and disappointments which the Royalists experienced over such a prolonged period. Here, above all, Clarendon is truthful. First his hopes for reconciliation were dashed, then his hope that Charles I could win. In exile he fondly imagined that the revolution would founder in conflict and discord amongst all the emergent parties, but he was confounded by Cromwell's appearance as an all-powerful Machiavellian prince, a man feared and respected throughout Europe. The good old days seemed further away than ever. Although the Restoration was a miracle brought about just when he least expected it, it could not wholly alleviate the pain that the war had caused. To Clarendon the rebellion was an act of such astounding perversity that it virtually defied any attempt at rational explanation.

What Clarendon desired with every fibre of his being was to restore the status quo, both in a literal and a symbolic sense. In killing the King the Commonwealth had also severed, or seemed to sever, all the legitimating strands of authority that were united in his person, like a rope twisted out of many fibres. So the purpose of Clarendon's history is not simply to vindicate himself, the King and Royalist cause, in that order, but to project his own deeply felt conviction that in the dark time from 1640 to 1660 the person of the King is like a taper burning steadily through the encircling gloom, so that although it may occasionally splutter and seem on the verge of extinction, it nevertheless holds out an enduring promise of clarity, stability and order. The monarchical presence that has been so radically eclipsed in the actual passage of history by Parliament and Cromwell, will in his narrative always persist as powerful and authoritative. In language the King will be restored to fullness and plenitude and it will seem as if the gap that opened up in reality actually never was, or that it will be like a fissure produced by volcanic activity that is reclosed by the same remorseless power that originally brought it into being. In serving as the memorialist of the rebellion, Clarendon paradoxically seeks to dematerialise it. As

B. H. Wormold has pointed out in his classic study of Clarendon, the perspective from which he wrote was 'the angle and point of view of the King'.[10]

Given the fact that Clarendon became the leading politician on the Royalist side and given that he embarked on his history with the specific intention of describing events from a Royalist standpoint, such an approach might seem entirely predictable, but the implications of this strategy go far beyond mere partisanship. Clarendon wrote both to show where Charles I had acted misguidedly and also to vindicate him, an approach which would seem to guarantee balance, at least in so far as it might lead to a sober assessment of the rights and wrongs of the way in which the Royalist case was handled. Clarendon was, after all, a lawyer. With hindsight, Clarendon strongly identified with the King in all the perplexities and the difficulties that he faced in a way which he recognised had not been possible for him at the time. Whereas Clarendon had earlier been annoyed when the King would not follow his advice, now he could not but sympathise with the plight of a monarch who had been led astray by the evil counsel of less scrupulous advisers than himself. But if, at least as far as the King was concerned, to understand all was to forgive all, he did not extend this charitable principle to his erstwhile Parliamentary colleagues. In Clarendon's self-righteous and sanctimonious mind the King became fused together with himself in a composite model of conciliatoriness, rectitude and fortitude: they represented a citadel of reason that was only overthrown by the combination of shortsightedness and venal self-interest on the part of those who served the King, and by the malice, irrationality and deceit of those who had influenced Parliament. In his conception of it 'the King' becomes an idealised gold standard of authority, legitimacy and truth that can never be tarnished by time, a figure that can transcend all the trials and tribulations of circumstance and all actual deviations and infractions of the norm. The King will continue to define reality even when there is no King. The King will always be the centre even when he has been decisively relegated to the margins. Such is the faith of a Royalist. What disturbed Clarendon about the 19 Propositions was precisely that they would leave 'only the shadow and empty name of the King'[11] or, in the words of the royal reply to them, that he might be 'but the sign of a King'.[12]

What Clarendon understands by and invests in the idea of a king becomes something very like the idea of God: a numinous, intangible but pervasive presence which serves as a guarantee that there is order and meaning in the universe. Clarendon never ceases to believe in God and never ceases to believe in the King. He must continue to think well of the King against all the odds and in the face of the most compelling testimony to the contrary. The King, whether Charles I or Charles II, is always more than the particular personages who bore that name and to whom Clarendon owed his loyalty: it is the name for a principle of stability in a world that inescapably lacks it. Even without a King, the idea of one would still be necessary because once that notional point of anchorage is lost there is no alternative but to confront a perennially open and perpetually fluctuating public world, where anything is possible and where the past, instead of serving as some authoritative court of appeal, can abruptly recede, like a familiar shoreline on a boat that is headed towards the open sea.

There is a rhetoric to Clarendon's invocation of the idea of a King which may once have seemed quite natural, but which now provokes mingled wonder and astonishment at the sheer doggedness that underpins it. Clarendon concludes Book XI of his history with a description of the execution of Charles and of the shameful and treacherous purchase of the royal treasure by Cardinal Mazarin and the King of Spain, yet Clarendon unblinkingly begins Book XII by referring to 'the King'. Now certainly it is a well-known principle that 'The King is Dead! Long Live the King!' but Charles I did not die peacefully in his bed but in a manner unprecedented in European history – on the scaffold. Moreover, his son had never been a king himself. Nor was there any certain expectation at that time that he would become one. Indeed, most of Clarendon's subsequent pages, right up to the very eve of the Restoration, chronicle the progressive waning of such hopes, as Clarendon is forced to acknowledge that Charles's pretensions, far from being seen as possessing an overwhelming moral force, are regarded by most of the crowned heads of Europe as nothing more than an irritating distraction from the important task of promoting better relations with Cromwell. Even kings could learn from Machiavelli. Of course, the fact that Charles does eventually and miraculously become King serves to validate this language retrospectively, so that Charles is always implicitly King and his coronation can be seen simply as authenticating and confirming a status that was always God-given and beyond any real necessity for human validation. Yet for all this Clarendon might have in some small way conceded that, for the time being at least, Charles was a prince, albeit with a clear title to the throne. Clarendon was determined to avoid equivocating or temporising on this issue not just because he wanted to demonstrate his loyalty, but because in this way the Civil War would be symbolically diminished. It could only figure as a temporary interruption of a natural state of affairs, a chimera, a bad dream. Thus there is ultimately no obligation to search and sift 'the rebellion' as events that carry a meaning of their own. On the contrary, it must remain forever aberrant, unjustified and unjustifiable. In Clarendon's view of things reason is at first exiled and then restored. The sources of such an event necessarily lie beyond the compass of reason itself.

Clarendon is one of the earliest of conspiracy theorists. Though he well knew that in the events leading up to the war there continued to be urgent discussions both on the Royalist and Parliamentary sides, he draws a clear distinction in his own mind between the uncertain and divided counsels that habitually surround the King and the manipulation and intrigue that he invariably associates with Parliament. The King necessarily always acts in good faith – though Clarendon was fully aware that there were often compelling grounds for putting that good faith in question. The King's opponents are designated 'the factious and schismatic party'[13] in order to suggest that, far from having genuine grievances or strongly held convictions, all those that fall under that rubric must have no other end in view but to cause havoc and confusion. Doubtless a reading of Thucydides may have helped to firm up such an interpretation. At the very most Clarendon is prepared to concede that both James I and Charles I were too hasty in dissolving Parliaments when their discussions grew inconvenient, but in his rather absurdly protracted account of the stewardship of the Duke of Buckingham he tried to shift most of the responsibility for this onto a figure who was safely out of the way.

Had Clarendon devoted even half the space he allocates to the Duke to an analysis of the religious background to the conflict – which scarcely emerges with any greater clarity in his account of Laud – his narrative would have acquired a greater breadth and depth. But in asking Clarendon to explain the Civil War we are, of course, making a peculiarly modern demand and one which he is by no means anxious to comply with. Yet Clarendon's blindness on the issue of Church reform really does seem quite extraordinary when one considers that it was Lord Falkland, one of his closest friends, who had launched a devastating attack on the bishops for their unremitting persecution of Puritan clergy and Puritan values.

Clarendon, hardly suprisingly, was an élitist and his decision to write his history through biographical sketches of eminent notables and gentlemen reflects this. He is happy with the idea that sensible and judicious conclusions can be mutually agreed on by men of great parts and noble pedigree, especially when they are eminently counsellable and of sober judgement. He regards reason as the prerogative of the gentleman. He cannot but regret that the rebellion brought onto the stage of history persons whom he did not regard as suitable to grace its august boards: the likes of John Lilburne, who before the war had nothing but 'a poor bookbinder',[14] or those members of the Barebones Parliament, who were 'inferior persons, of no quality or name, artificers of the meanest trades, known only by their gifts in praying and preaching'.[15] It is not altogether surprising that Clarendon should be hostile to the Puritan preachers, at whose door he, correctly, laid much of the blame for civil war, or that in his account of them, even in so exhaustive a work, he should have little more to say of them other than that 'under the notion of reformation and extirpating of Popery' they 'infused seditious inclinations into the hearts of men against the present government of the church, with many libellous invectives against the State too'.[16]

However, in the case of Falkland, a person of superior status and a member of his own set, the situation is rather different. He is one person who we might expect Clarendon to take seriously. But all he can say is that his late friend should be exonerated from the unfair charge that he is hostile to bishops. If there is any substance to the charge at all it is only because Falkland unhappily developed a dislike of Archbishop Laud. This was quite understandable, if regrettable, since Laud *did* have a rather unfortunate manner, even though his bark was considerably worse than his bite – or so, at least, it seemed to Clarendon, whose position was not that of a Puritan minister but that of one who was both a protégé and personal friend of Laud. So in any way it all comes back to the personalities of the great. But the deeper reason for Clarendon's almost deliberate obtuseness is that he is determined to present the rebellion as an irrational and unwarranted event, wantonly fanned by a tiny minority of cunning and unscrupulous malcontents:

> It will be wondered at hereafter, that, in a judging and discerning state, where men had, or seemed to have, their faculties of reason and understanding at the height, in a kingdom then unapt and generally uninclined to war, (how wantonly soever it hath since seemed to throw away its peace,) those men who had the skill and cunning out of froward and peevish humours and indispositions to compound fears and jealousies, and to animate and inflame those fears and jealousies into the most prodigious and boldest rebellion that any age or country ever brought forth.[17]

Clarendon actually has a vested interest in *not* understanding it.

Nevertheless we must acknowledge that for Clarendon, as for many of his contemporaries, the unforeseen and unpredictable events of his time did pose extraordinarily daunting problems to the understanding. All attempts to probe the obscurity seemed either vain or partial. There was no single key to the riddle. Clarendon's pessimism was not simply the product of his own personal misfortune or even of some Job-like sense of bafflement at the heaviness of God's hand. It was rather the product of a deep perplexity in his mind as he weighed, pondered and vacillated between sacred and secular systems of interpretation. There was, of course, no question of his adopting a wholly human and social perspective; rather, the difficulty lay in deciding what fell within the province of human reason and what should be attributed to the action of divine Providence, in so far as that could be understood. At least one reason why the most comprehensive and detailed contemporary account that we have of the Civil War is written from a Royalist point of view is that the Royalists had rather more to explain, even though, as I have already indicated, such an explanation was always likely to be problematic and even might seem to be no explanation at all. On the Parliamentary side the case was clear: the King was usurping new powers and the Church and people were oppressed; God had justified the revolution by many an extraordinary sequence of successes both on and off the battlefield. Only the Restoration posed a problem, but even this, unpalatable as it was, could be seen as God's judgement on the excesses of the revolutionary period. Clarendon was much more reluctant to invoke the action of divine Providence directly even though this still served its turn as an overall interpretative framework. Clarendon believed that a fair and mutually acceptable settlement between King and Parliament *had* been possible and that, therefore, this phase of the struggle could only be discussed in terms of the motives and reasoned arguments of the participants. But what he finally saw as the abjuration of reason could not itself be explained altogether in rational terms; over and beyond the malice and bad faith he perceived in the Parliamentary leaders lay yet darker forces in the popular mind, what he designated 'this strange wildfire among the people'[18] and 'that rage and madness in the people of which they could never since be cured'.[19]

Clarendon believed, like Pitt, that you should let sleeping dogs lie. As he saw it, matters could have been settled without too much difficulty so long as they remained within the circle of the rational élite, but as the circles of agitation and interest relentlessly spread outward, events necessarily got out of hand. At the same time, especially in the later sections of the narrative, where Cromwell figures so prominently, Clarendon is drawn towards a system of explanation based on the politics of Machiavelli. Faced with Cromwell's remarkable record of success Clarendon is predictably reluctant to explain it, as Cromwell himself did, as the wonderful blessings of Providence that have been showered on God's own people. His assessment is that Cromwell and his associates succeeded by keeping their intentions secret, by manipulating others in so far as it was possible to do so and finally, when they were brought to it, by imposing their will by force. Cromwell was undeniably effective both because he was 'the greatest dissembler living'[20] and because of the clear-sighted ruthlessness with which he carried through his plans. Clarendon only invokes the action of divine Providence in respect of a handful of Royalist successes, such as the King's escape in a tree at Worcester, but above all in the miracle of the Restoration, which, on God's part, was 'such a prodigious act of Providence as he hath scarce vouchsafed to any nation since he led his chosen people through the Red Sea'.[21] Despite this, Clarendon could not altogether evade the disturbing possibility that the rebellion itself might have been inspired by the divine will. Early on in his narrative he even voiced the heretical thought – no doubt inspired by his reading of the Old Testament in exile in Jersey – that God might be 'angry with and weary of the government by kings and princes'.[22] Charles I's misfortunes were so spectacular and so consistent that whilst Puritan claims to favour could not be entertained there nevertheless was the distinct possibility, probability even, that his fate did represent some kind judgement on the nation: 'There were so many miraculous circumstances contributed to his ruin, that men might well think that heaven and earth conspired it, and that the stars designed it.'[23]

Clarendon, like his chronicler predecessors, is careful to offer this as no more than widely held popular opinion and he also does not offer an explanation. However, there can be no doubt but that Clarendon was deeply disturbed by such a concatenation of circumstances and that it was this that lay at the root of his pessimism. For if Charles had made mistakes he was nevertheless essentially well meaning; if he was 'the worthiest gentleman, the best master, the best friend, the best husband, the best father, and the best Christian, that the age in which he lived produced',[24] then the cruel fate suffered by such an exemplary figure was as inexplicable as it was excessive.

Under the relentless pressure of adverse circumstance Clarendon was more and more thrown back on a posture of resignation and stoical passivity, believing, like Milton, in his later years that 'They also serve who stand and wait.' Like his adversaries, he combed the Bible for sources of comfort and consolation and found it above all in the Psalms of David, which seemed to offer the assurance that if only men could steadfastly endure adversity they would finally live to see their enemies punished. Although Clarendon had criticised the Puritan ministers for using the Old Testament to interpret contemporary history, he nevertheless became convinced that the Psalms did offer a clue to events in his own times, and it was as the result of reading the Psalms that he acquired the faith to believe in the possibility of the Restoration:

the more I read and revolved the Subject Matter of those Psalms, the inevitable Judgements pronounced upon prosperous Wickedness, Pride and Oppression; and the Protection and Exaltation promised to those who suffer unjustly, and are not weary of their Innocence, not depart from it upon any Temptation, I found Cause enough to believe, that both the one and the other might possibly fall out, and come to pass in this World, as it must unavoidably do in the next. Methought found so many lively descriptions of our selves, and our Condition, and so many lively Promises of Comfort and Assistance, as if some of them had been Prophecies concerning it, and intended to raise and Preserve our souls from Despair.[25]

For the Royalists the prospect of unending exile abroad was a fate more bitter than we can even begin to imagine and it was only natural that examples from the Old Testament of a similarly outcast and defeated people should constantly spring to mind. It was simply impossible to believe that the verdict of 1649 could be final. But this faith made Clarendon even less inclined to play politics. At bottom he did not see how the situation could be retrieved purely through human agency, and the failure of so many Royalist schemes only served to confirm him in this opinion. He showed little interest in developing new political alliances or in hatching plots for restoration. He seemed either to be acting like a dog in the manger or to have given up the struggle altogether. As R. W. Harris points out:

Hyde's attitude during these years must have been very difficult to understand, and this has much to do with the hostility he incurred from so many royalists. For to them he appeared always to be opposing other men's point of view, opposed to those who favoured an alliance with Presbyterians, or the expeditions to Scotland, or understandings with the Levellers, or assassination plots, or the political manœuvres of the queen and the Louvre party. It seemed a natural inference that he wished to keep the reins of power entirely in his own hands. There was truth to this, for the king was often beset by hare-brained schemes of courtiers which could only do harm. But beyond this there was in Hyde's mind a conviction which few men understood, that the restoration of the monarchy was ultimately inevitable, because it lay in the logic of history, or in different terminology, because it was the will of providence. Men might help or hinder the process, but they could not direct it, because they could never be certain of the consequences of anything they did.[26]

Providence and the 'logic of history' are clearly two rather different things. It was precisely because Clarendon had so little faith that the King could be restored by ordinary methods that he put his faith in some miraculous divine intervention. He did not believe the Restoration was inevitable in the sense that it would be dictated by the course of circumstances. Moreover, he had a still stronger reason for distrusting action. He became convinced that in the modern age to act at all was to act by the lights of Machiavelli and to be prepared to countenance evil provided that the cause was just. This was why he suspected the opportunism of so many Royalist schemes. Although he recognised that men could not simply sit back and wait for a miracle and that they were under a moral and religious obligation to pursue worthy ends, he nevertheless feared a total fall into the world of *policy*, which might be both morally corrupt and presumptuous in the eyes of God. Clarendon believed in a public world, but he never for one moment thought that it could be governed by wholly secular considerations. The person of the King was the last bastion against this and therefore God could not permit such a state of affairs as the Commonwealth to endure for long. The only safe and morally sound course was to wait on God's judgement:

> There cannot be a more mischievous Position, than that we should be doing and endeavouring to help ourselves. He that hath lost his Way in a dark Night, and all the Marks by which he should guide himself, and know whether he be in the Way or not, cannot do so wisely as to sit still till the Morning; especially if he travel upon such uneven Ground and Precipices, that the least mistake in Footing may prove fatal to him: And it will be the same in our other Journey; if we are benighted in our Understandings, and so have no Path to tread in but where Thorns and Bryars and Snakes are in our Way; and where the least deviation from the right Track will lead us into Labyrinths, from whence we cannot be safely disentangled: it will become us, how bleak and stormy soever the night is, how grievous and pressing soever our Adversity is, to have Patience till the Light appears, that we may have a full Prospect of our Way, and of all that lies in our Way. If the Malice and Power of Enemies oppress us, and drive us to those Exigents, that there appears to us no Expedient to avoid utter Ruin, but submitting and concurring with their Wickedness: we ought to believe that either God will convert their Hearts or find some other as extraordinary Way to deliver us; and if he does not, that then

our ruin is necessary, and that he will make it more happy to us than our Deliverance would be.[27]

Clarendon, the once active man of affairs and the earnest seeker after conciliation and compromise, now suspects all efforts on the part of men to secure their own deliverance. The whole domain of public affairs that had opened up in the crisis between King and Parliament seems at one and the same time to have thrown up perplexities beyond the power of human reason to calculate. To try to shape the course of events was like trying to ride a tiger.

Along with Clarendon in the exiled community of the Court was Thomas Hobbes, mathematics tutor to the future Charles II, but a man better known, indeed notorious, for that ungodly work *Leviathan*. For a long while Hobbes's reputation was easily eclipsed by that of Clarendon, who could be seen as the prime instigator of a more reasonable and conciliatory spirit in politics. Now, 'Clarendon' lies on a musty shelf whilst the pages of *Leviathan* are intently scrutinised. Hobbes appears as one of the brightest intellectual stars of his age, Clarendon as a planet in eclipse.

Both Hobbes and Clarendon were deeply marked by this period of exile. It was disturbing enough to be an outcast from one's own country but their alienation was greatly intensified as the Commonwealth movement was continually protracted and there never seemed to be any light at the end of the tunnel. Had Parliament been able to patch things up with the King after the early skirmishes, the Royalists would still have been deeply scarred by the whole turn that events had taken. Indeed it was the King's recognition that he was trying to close the door after the horse had already bolted that made him so intransigent and so difficult. It was hard to see that one course of action might be a whole lot worse than another when it seemed that the worst had already happened. The King's authority and credibility were in ruins. Unlike Clarendon, Hobbes was not prepared to sit things out indefinitely. He returned to England in 1651 when Cromwell was firmly in power, a circumstance that has given rise to speculation that Hobbes's justification of absolute sovereignty was offered as a vindication of Cromwell's unshakeable military power.

But for Hobbes, as for Clarendon, the Civil War had been an unthinkable catastrophe, which should never have occurred and which must never be repeated. The difference lay in the fact that Clarendon believed that agreement could have been reached between King and Parliament if both sides had been disposed to compromise, whereas for Hobbes the whole idea of mixed monarchy and of reconciling different interests was precisely the cause of the trouble. Sovereignty was indivisible. Charles I had been quite wrong to try to reach terms with the Parliamentary leaders. His concessions led to a breakdown in authority and the confusion which ensued was, for Hobbes, tantamount to a dissolution of the whole Kingdom. It was Act I of *King Lear*. Moreover, as Hobbes saw it, the debate over the constitution itself had been deeply muddled. Each side had attempted to justify its position by an appeal to various historical precedents and traditions. Hobbes could see no point in fishing in such murky waters. Nothing could be decisively settled in this way. The evidence was confused and inconclusive and in the final analysis quite beside the point. Moreover, the whole discussion had been muddied still further by a careless and irresponsible use of language by those who had sided with Parliament so that it was almost impossible to discern what the fundamental issues were. What was needed was a text that would cut through all this irrelevant verbiage to the very heart of the matter, that would argue clearly and decisively from first principles, without any irrelevant appeals to what might or might not have happened in the past – what was needed was *Leviathan*.

Hobbes is resolutely and defiantly modern – perhaps the only true modern of his age – in his belief that there is absolutely nothing to be learnt from the past. Although the example of Euclidian geometry hovers constantly before his eyes, Hobbes is very much the self-righteous Protestant in his rejection of the intellectual corruptions of the Middle Ages and in his refusal to bow the knee before such pagan authorities as Aristotle. For Hobbes the past is full of cobwebs. So long as the past is reverenced the minds of men will be attics filled with intellectual clutter and they will neither be able to think for themselves or be able to formulate the problem with sufficient clarity to make a solution even thinkable. *Leviathan* is only separated from the final edition of *The Anatomy of Melancholy* by some ten years, yet in mental attitude they seem centuries apart. Burton copiously and relentlessly cites authorities which he knows cannot be reconciled and whose diversity he positively relishes, whereas Hobbes cites absolutely no 'authorities' whatsoever and refers to other authors, if at all, only to confute them. Had Hobbes pondered the history of the English monarchy more carefully he might have been brought to recognise that the problem of authority was by no means reducible to the ideas of sovereignty which he formulated. But it would not have been congenial for Hobbes to entertain the thought that authority has always been contested and that therefore the sovereignty he so authoritatively brandishes before the reader is something of a chimera, for the whole object of the exercise is precisely to establish it as an absolute. Hobbes's state is like the lines that have length but no breadth and the points that have position but no magnitude in geometry. They must not have their clarity of outline sullied by the introduction of irrelevant contingencies. Hobbes believes that if you think through the problem of the State from first principles you will be brought inexorably to the stage of recognising that at some point a simple but vital choice has to be made between order and chaos, between unquestioned sovereignty and perpetual contestation. However, once you start dragging in the past the evidence becomes subject to endless manipulation and a clear-cut issue becomes hopelessly obscured as the grounds of the argument are continually shifting:

> they appeale from custome to reason, and from reason to custome, as it serves their turn; receding from custome when their interest requires it and setting themselves against reason, as oft as reason is against them: Which is the cause that the doctrine of Right and Wrong is perpetually disputed, both by the Pen and the Sword: Whereas the doctrine of Lines and Figures, is not so; because men care not, in that subject what be truth, as a thing that crosseth no man's ambition, profit, or lust.[28]

Once politics becomes a subject in its own right, based on rigorous and careful argument that begins with definitions and proceeds by careful stages from elementary and self-evident propositions to more complex conclusions, this will finally put an end to all such amateurishness, special pleading and wishful thinking. Amazingly, this is a politics beyond any special interest. *Leviathan* simply outlines the fundamentals. Its conclusions may be unpalatable, but they cannot be disputed. Since they cannot be disputed they can serve as the unshakeable foundation of political order.

The virtue of Hobbes's hypothetical state of nature is precisely that it lies outside history. Man in the savage state, such as the American Indians whom Hobbes so much enjoys disparaging, and whose discovery on distant shores seemed to lend such weight to his arguments, can have not history since they have no settled civilisation or political order. Contrariwise, European man, who is so fortunate as to be able to take all this for granted, has lost sight of the circumstances that dictated it and with them a reverence for a blessing that he is once more in danger of losing. With Hobbes, the whole Paradise trope is decisively reversed. In Hobbes's myth of history there is the prospect of a cyclical pattern in which, without the elixir of sovereignty that has transformed anarchy into order, anarchy will once again ensue. Like the cooking, which for Lévi-Strauss marks the division between nature and culture, Hobbes finds in the moment of the social contract a crucial crossing of divides, where man, in a single sublime moment, is able through self-discipline to realise a higher destiny for himself, in unquestioning obedience to the law. So, for there to be sound government, it is not only necessary to be ruled by a sovereign whose authority is undisputed but to recover the original piety and reverence that men once displayed before institutions that afforded them security and protection. Hobbes believes that modern man has become blasé and that he must recover the wisdom of ancient society, but that he must be brought to a recognition of this necessity through the most modern methods of scientific reasoning. Yet the state of nature which Hobbes hypothesised and the motives of the agents who acted within it were very closely based on Hobbes's own experience of the seventeenth century. The Civil War itself to Hobbes's mind was such a state of nature. Any form of government would be better than this:

> and that the greatest, that in any forme of Government can possibly happen to the people in generall, is scarce sensible, in respect of the miseries, and the horrible calamities, that accompany a Civil Warre: or that dissolute condition of masterless men, without subjection to Lawes, and a coercive power to tye their hands from rapine, and revenge.[29]

Since he also wrote that 'amongst masterless men there is perpetuall war, of every man against his neightbour',[30] it is clear that Hobbes was greatly concerned at the large number of able-bodied vagrants who wandered about the countryside and who, by congregating in large towns such as London, posed a very real threat to the maintenance of law and order. As a potential source of tumult and a focus of social discontent they represented to Hobbes a relapse into pre-civilised modes of existence, and what exacerbated the problem was that, instead of being disciplined and taught obedience, they were encouraged to greater indiscipline by careless and irresponsible talk about liberty. Yet Hobbes's actual analysis of human behaviour is based not so much on lowly vagabonds as on the conduct of their betters at Court. It is at the Courts of Elizabeth, James and Charles that men struggle all the more desperately for position and status because it is through the mechanism of the Court that influence grounded in localised power and tradition is being progressively devalued. It is at Court that 'men are continually in competition for Honour and Dignity',[31] and it is at Court that what Hobbes posited as the inclination of mankind in general: 'a perpetual and restless desire of Power after Power, that ceases onely in Death'[32] is most conspicuous.

Indeed, Hobbes at the Court in exile must have been struck by the degree to which the desire could persist even when the power itself was demonstrably lacking. Hobbes's sense of man in motion has a special relevance to courtly society, where a cultivated instability is the order of the day, since it is this that enhances the power of the monarch. Not even the greatest noble in the land can imagine that his status is inalterable. What is so eagerly sought after is not status *per se*, which no longer exists, as the esteem which goes with the possession of influence – but this is something that is itself continually varying, so that every individual is advancing or retiring, never at rest. Everyone must strive for more influence and edge ever forward just so as not to be jostled out and excluded for ever. Hobbes absolutises all this in his definition of felicity, which was not as quaint old monks had once assumed 'the repose of a mind satisfied' but 'a continual progress of the desire, from one object to another'.[33]

There are no satisfied minds at Court. Here Hobbes's thinking runs in a circle: the state of nature is predicated on such a psychology and such a psychology is confirmed by the state of nature. Yet Hobbes subsequently warns us that we must beware of those who claim to know best what happiness or felicity is:

> And consequently men had need to be very circumspect, and wary, in obeying the voice of man, that pretended himself to be a Prophet, requires us to obey God in that way, which he in Gods name telleth us to be the way of happiness. For he that pretends to teach men the way of so great felicity, pretends to govern them; that is to say, to rule, and reign over them; which is a thing, that all men naturally desire, and is therefore worthy to be suspected of Ambition and Imposture; and consequently ought to be examined and tryed by every man, before hee yeeld them obedience; unlesse he have yeelded it them already, in the institution of a commonwealth, as when the Prophet is the Civil Sovereign, or by the Civil Sovereign Authorised.[34]

Is Hobbes himself such a prophet? Well he is and he isn't. By the final twist of his argument he admits that he may be beginning to look rather as if he were one. He may seem to be ambitious because he seeks to place his work in the hands of the King as a guide to action. But he seeks no power for himself. He has no special axe to grind. He cannot be secretly claiming to know better than others and thus obtain power over them because he only defends the power that is there already. To speak for the status quo is to be genuinely disinterested in a way that no other point of view can be, for Hobbes will change nothing. There is no glimmering of *Utopia* in *Leviathan*. Yet there is a paradox about Hobbes's claim to reason from first principles since what truly confirms reason as reason is not so much the internal laws of its own rationality as the fact that it functions on behalf of authority. At the pinnacle of his ratiocinative structure and at the centre of power Hobbes places an all-powerful sovereign, who will legitimise Leviathan just as Leviathan legitimises him. In such a mutually supportive relationship all the old destructive conflicts disappear. But one of the puzzles about the Hobbesian monarch is that his role will be to abolish all the vices generated by the courtly society. *Leviathan* is an intervention in an emergent public domain whose purpose is to abolish it. The age of controversy will be brought to a close.

Although Hobbes's mind was exacerbated by the prospect of a struggle of all against all, he was ever more deeply disturbed by the conflict of interpretations. The tremendous hermeneutic endeavours of the age were undertaken in the belief that the truth could be arrived at through a careful study of the relevant documents, but though it was truth that was aimed at, it was often discord and scepticism that resulted. Hobbes was genuinely worried about this gigantic explosion of interpretative activity and one of the primary objectives of *Leviathan* was to try to put a stop to it. Hobbes believed that the study of the Greek and Latin classics and the undue deference paid to the opinions of such pagan authors had led to an undue preoccupation with nebulous ideas of freedom and a corresponding fear of tyrants who would allegedly infringe it, whereas all that a man could possibly ask was that he would receive life and security in return for unquestioning obedience to his sovereign lord. Hobbes was also greatly irritated by the attempts of lawyers to interpret those historical documents pertaining to the relationship between King and Parliament since he believed that it was for the present to decide the past, not for the past to purport to decide the present. Lawyers deliberately, and for their own benefit, introduced needless complications into the interpretation of the law, when such contested questions were matters for the sovereign arbitrarily to decide – just as Alexander the Great had cut the Gordian knot. The problem arose primarily because the effect of interposing commentaries between the reader and the text is to produce infinite delay and uncertainty: 'For Commentaries are commonly more subject to cavill, than the text; and therefore need other Commentaries; and so there will be no end to interpretation.'[35]

Hobbes was equally troubled by the activity of the clergy in interpreting the meaning of the Bible. Had their subtle discussions of the significance of biblical texts been purely of a theological nature and been conducted solely within the schools, as with the medieval disputations that were conducted in Latin, Hobbes would not much have minded but he *was* concerned when they drew contemporary political inferences and stirred up the people. This was tantamount to a usurpation of political authority;

> when the spirituall power, moveth the Members of a common-wealth, by the terrour of punishments, and hope of rewards (which are the Nerves of it), otherwise than by the Civill Power (which is the Soule of the Common-wealth) they ought to be moved; and by the strange and hard words suffocate their

understanding, it must needs thereby Distract the people, and either Overwhelm the Common-wealth with Oppression, or cast it into the fire of a civille warre.[36]

Hobbes was not in much doubt that the safety of the commonwealth was too serious a matter to be put at the mercy of people who spoke of hell-fire. He likened this affliction of the body politic to the convulsions of epilepsy, where a man who loses control of his senses may helplessly fall into water or flames. Doubtless Shakespeare's Menenius Agrippa would not have envisaged such complicated ailments, but in the aftermath of Civil War a more sophisticated pathology is called for. For Hobbes this outbreak of interpretative activity was an alarming phenomenon for three reasons: it used or purported to use reasoning to undermine sovereignty when all valid reasoning must begin with a recognition of the inevitability of sovereignty; it produced endless irresolvable disputes whose consequences were socially disruptive; since its starting point was the interpretation of texts it was arguing from authority and not from first principles and therefore could not be truth:

> Nor that which is gotten by Reasoning the Authority of Books; because it is not by Reasoning from the Cause to the Effect, nor from the Effect to Cause; and is not Knowledge, but Faith.[37]

Paradoxically the very man whose materialist opinions made him one of the most dissonant voices on the jukebox of the new print culture was also one of its most fervent critics.

Just as Clarendon in his darkest hours continued to think of the King as being at the centre of affairs, even when kingship itself had become problematic, so in Hobbes's system of things the sovereign becomes the new guarantee of absolute certainty. Hobbes's claims for politics as the new master discipline are precisely grounded in the fact that, since religion has become a socially destabilising force instead of one that upholds authority, the power which the Pope has hitherto claimed as vice-regent of God on earth must now be claimed by kings. Henry VIII was right. From his own day to this, Hobbes has been accused of being an atheist, but while such a conclusion can legitimately be drawn from the general analysis of man which Hobbes presents in Book I of *Leviathan*, it is somewhat misleading to stress this without recognising that Hobbes is instituting a State religion that is a religion of the State. The assurance that medieval man found in the idea of an harmonious universe of crystalline spheres presided over by a wide and all-powerful God is replaced by Hobbes with the idea of a harmonious and well-ordered State presided over by a wise and all-powerful sovereign who can exclude all the risks of interpretation by resolving every issue by his own personal and immediate fiat. As there were, or should have been, no arguments in Heaven, so there will be no arguments on earth. The state itself is to be thought of in religious terms – Hobbes speaks of the moment when the people yield up their independence to their sovereign as 'the Generation of the great LEVIATHAN, or rather (to speak more reverentially) of that *Mortall God*, to which wee owe under the *Immortall God*, our peace and defence',[38] and defines sovereignty as 'the soule of the Commonwealth'.

However, whereas an immortal God can give rise to endless controversy, this mortal God will put a stop to it. In his discussion of such purified sovereignty Hobbes adopts the language of an enraptured and intoxicated Protestantism. He believes that this new faith, purged of errors and superstitions that have accumulated over the centuries, will really work. Religion's traditional task of instilling obedience will be revivified and reclaimed as the State itself becomes the object of a reverential awe. In true swingeing Protestant fashion Hobbes stigmatises all those who disagree with him as inhabitants of 'the Kingdom of Darkness' and he presents all threats to the stability of the realm (faith) as forms of black magic. Hobbes alleges that the activities of popular and ambitious men who stir up rebellion against the State 'may be ressembled to the effect of witchcraft'.[39] Their claims are inherently fraudulent and illegitimate. In some strange way Hobbes resembles the eighteenth-century thinker John Brown who believed that at one time the role of prophet and king had been one and the same. Hobbes believes that the king is the only authentic prophet and if he is not regarded as such there can no limit to the chaos and disorder into which men will be thrown:

they must either take their owne Dreames, for the Prophecy they mean to be governed by, and the tumour of their own hearts for the spirit of God; or they must suffer themselves to bee lead by some strange Prince; or by some of their fellow subjects, that can bewitch them, by slaunder of the government, into rebellion, without other miracle to confirm their calling, then sometimes an extraordinary successe, and Impunity; and by this means destroying all laws, both divine, and humane, reduce all Order, Government, and Society, to the first Chaos of Violence, and Civill warre.[40]

If the sovereign is taken as the focus of religion, then religion can acquire the substance and stability that are lost when it comes an issue contested by a thousand prophesying voices. Despite his alleged atheism Hobbes read his Bible with considerable care and the thing that particularly struck him was that there were some seventy other prophets at the time of Moses, yet only Moses exercised effective political power. Yet Moses would have had a much easier time and there would have been no dancing round the Golden Calf if he had had no rivals at all. Although Hobbes talks a great deal about force and coercion, in practice he believes that the way to maintain the authority of the state is through relentless ideological pressure. Men are to be instructed in the duty of obedience. There must be no dissonant voices to unsettle their minds:

> the Common-people's minds, unless they be tainted with dependence on the Potent, or scribbled over with the opinions of their doctors, are like clean paper, fit to receive whatsoever by Publique Authority shall be printed on them.[41]

The public domain will be necessarily monologic. Indeed, Hobbes reverses the whole terms of the discussion. Only the king can represent the public world and no private judgement can ever be urged against him. There can be no basis for dissention. The word will be restored to the purity that it once possessed – in the beginning. Thus, the tables are unexpectedly turned and any notion of the modern in the seventeenth century becomes more and more perplexing. For now it is Burton, with his frank enjoyment of diversity and confusion, who seems the more advanced, while Hobbes begins to look like some contemporary of Thomas Aquinas who, like Rip Van Winkle, overslept!

Although Clarendon and Hobbes were directly concerned with affairs of state, their sense of a public world was always very narrowly construed. For them the political universe always firstly

centred on the person of the King and, secondly, on the role of
royal counsellor, which Clarendon held on two separate occasions,
but to which Hobbes only aspired. As they understood it,
problems or difficulties in the State were always to be approached
from the standpoint of the King. His own interest was always
paramount. This focus on the monarch was so habitual that it
virtually went unnoticed. The sovereign was the State long before
Louis XIV definitively announced it. So in considering the extent
to which Milton's whole life was profoundly influenced by his
decision to involve himself in public affairs and to work for the
public good, as he understood it, we need to consider just what a
radical step this was. Milton felt that in this he was only doing his
duty, but very few of his contemporaries could have grasped the
significance of such an act of dedication – there was one's duty to
God and King, but that was as far as it went. Duty was
synonymous with loyalty, obedience and compliance. Milton's
sense of public obligation was grounded in his reading of the
classics. What he most admired was the public-spiritedness that
led such men as Cincinnatus, the elder Cato or Tiberius Gracchus
to devote themselves to the well-being of their fellow-citizens
even at the price of unpopularity and the sacrifice of a life of
peace and tranquillity. In some sense this might be described as
Milton's humanism, but in so saying we must also recognise that
the Italian humanists were always the servants of princes so that
they never drew the conclusions that Milton drew. Machiavelli
was an Italian patriot, but his thinking here was always
subordinated to the idea of a prince. Milton was almost unique in
his determination to see to it that the values of classical antiquity
should not simply be preserved as effigies in a museum but that
they should be made to come alive again in his own day. Milton's
imaginative relationship to the past was so powerful that he was
able to see the present in the light of antiquity, and antiquity in
the light of the present. The Bible and the classics were a guide to
action for him. As he saw it, England in the 1630s was in danger
and therefore he must devote all of his efforts to the struggle for
religion and against the tyranny of Charles I:

> I saw that a way was opening for the establishment of real
> liberty; that the foundation was laying for the deliverance of
> man from the yoke of slavery and superstition; that the
> principles of religion, which were the first objects of our care,

would exert a salutary influence on the manners and constitution of the republic; and as I had from my youth studied the distinction between religious and civil rights, I perceived that if I ever wished to be of use, I ought at least not to be wanting to my country, to the church, and to my fellow Christians, in a crisis of so much danger; I therefore determined to relinquish the other pursuits in which I was engaged, and to transfer the whole force of my talents and my industry to this one important object.[42]

What is significant here is not just the strength of Milton's commitment, which leads him to drop everything else, or his sense of urgency, but the way in which his loyalty is redefined so that neither king nor magistrate is so much as mentioned and the fact that the cause which Milton throws himself into is essentially insurrectionary and revolutionary. Such an act of clarification and emancipation will necessarily involve a radical transformation in the state. But as such it makes comparable demands on the individuals. From being a poet, Milton becomes wholly dedicated to pamphleteering and political agitation – a radical step about which he was initially very apprehensive. In *The Reason of Church Government* he spoke of having to 'leave a calm and pleasing solitariness, fed with cheerful and confident thoughts, to embark in a troubled sea of noises and hoarse dispute'.[43] Milton gave up the best years of his life, from his early thirties to early fifties, to be at this centre of conflict and confusion, but he never once doubted that this was for the best. He would be England's champion – in print.

Yet in reflecting on Milton's intervention in the public sphere at this critical moment in English history, we must beware of distorting the nature of his concerns by attempting to subsume them under some general notion of the 'political'. Precisely because modern political theory traces itself back to the controversies of this period and because Victorian ideas about the development of the constitution still cast a shadow over its historical interpretation, we need to think more carefully about the ideas of those who cannot so readily be seen as forerunners of the modern. We need to recognise that many of those who were most active in the struggle against King and Church establishment were not really interested in politics at all. Their minds were focused exclusively on what we would call 'religious' questions but which therefore unconsciously attributes to them a narrowness and specificity of concern which would be altogether alien to their own perception of things. As they saw it, these were matters of vast, not to say cosmic, import where the fate of whole nations was at stake as the Apocalypse loomed on the horizon and as the final struggle with the Antichrist was ushered in. Hobbes and Milton are intellectually far apart, but what is instructive about their divergence is that Hobbes reduces all religious issues to the political, whereas Milton reduces all political issues to the religious. What this meant in practice for the young Milton, reflecting on the fate of the Church in the 1630s, a Church from which he felt himself to be so much at variance that he could not possibly serve in it as a minister, was that he believed that when you got right down to it the cause of virtually all the evils that afflicted the kingdom could be traced to the existence of Bishops. This was not at all an unreasonable proposition at the time when Milton wrote. Archbishop Laud had established himself as Charles's all-powerful minister. Laud was endeavouring to strengthen the Church hierarchy by placing his own protégés in all the leading positions and by using them to drive out the preaching Puritan ministry. Such men were an anathema to Laud because they persistently undermined and challenged authority by their own precept and example; they insisted on standards of piety, godliness and dedication to which the bishops themselves could not possibly adhere. For the Laudian Church, for all its talk of the beauty of holiness, credibility must always flow from status not godliness. For Milton it was the gravest possible indictment of the Church, and indeed of the state of the country in general, that those Puritans who were the most sincere and dedicated Christians in the land were being persecuted and driven from the country and were being compelled to seek refuge on the inhospitable shores of America:

> Let the astrologer be dismayed at the portentous blaze of comets, and impressions in the air, as foretelling troubles and changes to states: I shall believe that there cannot be a more ill-boding sign to a nation (God turn the omen from us!) than that when the inhabitants, to avoid insufferable grievances at home, are enforced by heaps to forsake their native country.[44]

This does not mean that Milton did not take such astrological omens seriously. As Christopher Hill has rightly emphasised, Milton studied at Christ's, Cambridge, the college of Joseph Mede, whose interpretation of the Book of Revelations in its relation to the course of world history deeply influenced a whole generation of Protestants and encouraged them to believe that the Apocalypse was at hand.[45] Indeed Milton's *Of Reformation in England*, from which this statement comes, was written under the influence of precisely such a conviction. This Puritan emigration is an ominous sign that England, once the leading light of the Reformation, is in danger of becoming the domain of the Antichrist: 'If the splendour of gold and silver begin to lord it once again in the church of England, we shall see Antichrist shortly wallow here, though his chief kernel be Rome.'[46]

Here, surely, Laud himself is punningly named as the architect of a policy that is deliberately calculated to suppress Christian virtue and independence in favour of empty formality, gorgeous spectacle and a servile compliance; a policy that will be ruthlessly enforced through the ecclesiastical courts. Like many of his contemporaries, Milton was greatly concerned that England was tarrying in the work of completing the Reformation. The Elizabethan settlement had only been a half-way house. What was now needed was to press on even further to eliminate both the status hierarchy and the quasi-magical aura that surrounded the activities of the priest as he presided over mysterious rituals at the upper end of the church. Christian worship must be based on genuine piety and fellowship. It must never become a method of manipulating ignorant congregations into obsequiousness and deference towards the powers that be. As Milton damningly wrote in *The Reason of Church Government*:

> Thus we see again how prelaty, falling in opposition to the main end and power of the gospel, doth not join in the mysterious work of Christ, by lowliness to confound height; by simplicity of doctrine, the wisdom of the world; but contrariwise hath made itself high in the world and the flesh to vanquish things by the world accounted low, and made itself wise in tradition and fleshly ceremony, to confound the purity of doctrine which is the wisdom of God.[47]

For bishops to entertain such ideas, Milton recognised, would be a contradiction in terms. So long as the temptations of advancement, power and of multiple benefices were dangled over the head of the priesthood it would be the corrupt clergy who would be rewarded. Little by little the zeal for reform was waning. The whole impetus for reform was in danger of being lost and the responsibility for this was not purely Laud's but must be laid at the door of the episcopacy in general:

> And still it is episcopacy that before our eyes worsens and slugs the most learned and seemingly religious of our ministers, who no sooner advanced to it, but, like a seething pot set to cool, sensibly exhale and reak out the greater part of that zeal and those gifts which were formerly in them, settling in a skinny congealment of ease and sloth at the top: and if they kept their learning by some potent sway of nature, it is a rare chance; but their devotion most commonly comes to that queasy temper of lukewarmness, that gives a vomit to God himself.[48]

For a long time reformers within the Church of England had been forced to bide their time. After receiving some dusty answers from Elizabeth they had hoped for better things from James I but had met with an instant rebuff from that quarter also. Now under Charles I the position had deteriorated still further. The violence of Milton's language expresses not only his anger and impatience at the endemic Laodiceanism of the Church, but also a recognition that this is not simply a question of rekindling a mood of spiritual fervour as of confronting a structural phenomenon that cannot be so readily altered. The pre-eminence of Laud demonstrated not only how thoroughly the Church had been corrupted by its relation with the State, but it also showed what a powerful weapon a corrupt Church could be in the hands of a tyrannical ruler, such as Milton believed Charles to be. It was now crystal clear that the Church had become far too useful an instrument for enforcing compliance for it ever to be dispensed with and that, therefore, its institutional forms would have to remain unaltered, since the authority of bishops was crucial to the maintenance of such a role. Moreover, it was not enough that there should be powerful bishops. It was also essential that they should be worldly: if they were to use their position to promote a genuine spirituality their roles would at once become positively subversive. Milton saw the Church as a community of believers, mingling and worshipping in a free, open and democratic manner, united by a common faith in God, the Bible and a determination to search out the truth. It must be made up of the serious and the dedicated rather than the self-seeking and the superficial. A Church must necessarily be progressive. It will be driven from within, not restrained from without. Milton knew that Christianity itself had been a revolt against the religion of the Scribes and Pharisees and he wanted to bring back the simple, direct faith of the early Church. For a modern bishop to embrace that would be like trying to square the circle:

> But he that will mould a modern bishop into a primitive, must yield him to be elected by popular voice, undiocesed, unrevenued, unlorded, and leave him nothing but brotherly equality, matchless temperance, frequent fasting, incessant prayer and preaching, continual watchings and labours in his ministry; which what a rich booty it would be, what a plump endowment to the many-benefice-gaping-mouth of a prelate, what a relish it would give to his canary-sucking and swan-eating palate, let old bishop Mountain tell me.[49]

The combination of personal laxity and licence with a repressive and intolerant attitude towards others was a positive anathema to Milton. He loathed the 'church masquers' and 'dancing divines' who postured and paraded as England's hour grew still more belated and desperate; he despised and deeply resented 'this impertinent yoke of prelaty, under whose inquisitorial and tyrannical duncery, no free and splendid wit can flourish'.[50]
But the source of the evil lay deeper than the undoubted vices of the ecclesiastical hierarchy: it was rooted in the interdependence of Church and State. It followed that the Church as a body of believers must be freed not only from the bishops but from the shackles of the State as well. Whereas for Hobbes the maintenance of an undivided sovereignty was such an overriding good that all else must be sacrificed to it, for Milton the issue was quite the reverse. It was the liberation of the Church that was of paramount importance and the State would simply have to put up with the consequences. Indeed, the implication of Milton's position at this time is that a strong, dedicated and united national Church is a community in itself, which actually has no need of any external authority. For Milton, Church discipline, conceived of as a common desire and collective pressure to lead a wholly Christian

life, makes the whole business of political coercion redundant. He still sees a role for the civil magistrate, but it is very much a residual and back-up function and one suspects that Milton would ideally have liked to dispense with it altogether. For the very existence of the political as a brutal source of power and authority serves to undermine everything that the Church represents. So it is scarcely any wonder that Milton should have grounded his religious faith and epic manifesto in a representation of the Garden of Eden, whose continuance as a happy garden State depends only on man's capacity for self-discipline.

Milton believed that there was a second Fall, which was very nearly as bad as the original expulsion of Adam and Eve from paradise, when the original authenticity of the Christian faith was utterly lost when it became the State religion of the Roman Empire under Constantine. The price of this 'success' was that the values to which it was originally dedicated were fatally compromised in their subordination to *raison d'état* and political expediency. Needless to say, Milton's assessment of Constantine in *Of Reformation in England* is utterly at variance with the view that Hobbes expressed in *Leviathan* some ten years later; but Hobbes could only have confirmed Milton's sense of the correctness of his views, since Hobbes uses the example of Constantine to 'prove' that religion must be and has always been subject to the power of civil authority. Milton's belief that Constantine's reign had been a disaster was as much a humanist view as it was a Protestant, supported as it was by his reading of Dante and Petrarch. As Milton saw it, the task of reformation was essentially to undo the ill that Constantine had originally wrought and for which he, rather than his papal successors, was primarily responsible. From being the creed of the poor and the despised, Christianity was elevated to assume an official role in which, decked out with great pomp and ceremony, it became assimilated to the pagan creeds that had preceded it. 'Christianity' came to epitomise everything that the early Christian fathers has so desperately struggled against. The reformed present, guided by Wycliffe, Luther and Calvin, must pronounce stern judgement on this decadent past, and never permit itself to be intimidated, overawed or led astray by any deceitful appeal to 'tradition':

How should the dim taper of this emperor's age, that had such need of snuffing, extend any beam to our times, wherewith we might hope to be better lighted, than by those luminaries that God hath set up to shine to us far nearer hand? And what reformation he wrought for his own time, it will not be amiss to consider. He appointed certain times for fasts and feasts, built stately churches, gave large immunities to the clergy, great riches and promotions to bishops, gave and ministered occasion to bring in a deluge of ceremonies, thereby either to draw in the heathen by a resemblance of their rites, or to set a gloss upon the simplicity and plainness of Christianity; which, to the gorgeous solemnities of paganism, and the sense of the world's children, seemed but a homely and yeomanly religion; for the beauty of inward sanctity was not within their prospect.[51]

The damage was profound, not just because the Church hierarchy only paid lip-service to the faith they supposedly represented, but because in its institutionalised diffusion the real spiritual message of Christianity was never grasped at all. Milton was especially irritated by the attempt in ecclesiastical tradition to present Constantine as the saviour of the Church. Of course, it was understandable that those who embodied Christian worldliness should revere a man whose innovations sanctioned them in their enjoyment of luxury and privilege but it was nevertheless scandalous, indeed positively impious, to suggest that the fate of God's Church lay in the hands of a secular ruler. It was very much the reign of Constantine that Milton had in mind when he wrote, many years later, in *Paradise Lost*:

> Then shall they seek to avail themselves of names,
> Places and titles, and with those to join
> Secular power, though feigning still to act
> By spiritual, to themselves appropriating
> The Spirit of God, promised alike and given
> To all believers; and from that pretence
> Spiritual laws by carnal power shall force
> On every conscience.

In such a manner religious truth and inner conviction are transformed into a deference exacted through political domination. Christianity is destroyed within and from within.

Milton's indignant critique of the state of English society showed a strong anti-authoritarian and anti-institutional bias and in reading his publications at this time we can see that 'No bishop no King' is no longer just an argumentative scarecrow to warn off the reformers but a position the logic of which is so compelling that Milton sees no alternative but to embrace it. It is bishops and kings together, working hand in hand, who bar the way to any practical implementation of Christ's teaching. There can be no hope of any significant improvement so long as this collusion continues. Milton purposefully argued that Charles I's behaviour was so high-handed, insensitive and intolerant as to be consistent with any notion of a tyrant and that therefore he had quite justifiably been deposed. But Milton had actually got to a point where it seemed to him that bishops and kings would have to go, whether amiable and responsive or not. The price of keeping them was simply too high. We can estimate the radicalism of Milton's approach by recalling Clarendon's sincerely held opinion, which was, after all, far better informed than Milton's, that a compromise between King and Parliament would have been possible. But, of course, for Clarendon and for many latterday historians, the Church simply did not enter into it at all. Milton could never have accepted any compromise that left the bishops still in position, nor could he have accepted the implication, so universally accepted since Henry VIII, that the King had some sort of right to rule and regulate the Church. On the contrary, it was this pretence which was at the root of the trouble. Milton, like Hobbes, began his analysis not from the actual state of human society, but from an analysis of human nature. Whereas Hobbes stressed man's supposedly insatiable drive for power, Milton insisted on the human capacity for freedom and self-realisation. Milton simply ridiculed those, like Hobbes, who argued that people should submit themselves unconditionally to the domination of a single man. He simply could not believe that they could be 'so strangely in love with slavery'.[52]

Whereas Clarendon and Hobbes started from the standpoint of the King and reasoned from there, Milton refused to accept that any one person could enjoy rights at the expense of a whole people. Far from seeing a beneficent and enduring political order that was now threatened by the prospect of anarchy, Milton saw the self-realisation of a free and godly community as being thwarted and obstructed by the corrupt tyrannical figures of Laud, Strafford and Charles himself. Milton was never one to exonerate Charles from responsibility through the fiction of a man led astray by evil counsellors, nor did he believe that Charles possessed some special magic that must be preserved at all costs. The King would have to be tackled along with the rest. The time had come for the English people to take their destiny into their own hands. As far as Milton was concerned, the idea that the people were not ready for political responsibility was all one with the argument that they could not be allowed to reason and think, with the Catholic claim that the mysteries of faith were too complex for their understanding, with a Bible in Latin. Statesmen spoke of the risks of political disorder, bishops of the dangers of schism, but Milton was willing to take these risks, if risks they were, because he believed that the proferred alternative, a continuation and intensification of the evils of the status quo, was a disaster infinitely worse – as he wrote in *Eikonoclastes*:

> It were a nation miserable indeed, not worth the name of a nation, but a race of idiots, whose happiness and welfare depended on one man. The happiness of a nation consists in true religion, piety, justice, prudence, temperance, fortitude, and the contempt of avarice and ambition. They in whomsoever these virtues dwell eminently, need not kings to make them happy, but are the architects of their own happiness; and, whether to themselves or others are not less than kings.[53]

Those who spoke of the benefits of political order were guilty of fetishism and actual impiety since they put mere political and worldly goods before religious truth and the salvation of Christian souls. Such had been the story of the long perversion of the Christian faith in the hands of the Roman State and the Roman papacy. But this evil empire, as Mede and others taught, was finally coming to its end. And it was a Christian's duty to struggle against it. For faith that is not completely free is no faith at all – as Milton wrote in *De Doctrina Christina*:

> For if our personal religion were not in some degree dependent on ourselves, and in our power, God could not properly enter into a covenant with us; neither could we perform, much less swear to perform, the conditions of that covenant[54]

for,

when the magistrate takes away this liberty, he takes away the gospel itself; he deprives the good and bad indiscriminately of their privilege of free judgement.[55]

So, for Milton, political authority had everywhere and at every time subverted man's divinely given capacity for freedom and stifled his capacity for moral self-realisation. But now, after an immensely long period of exile, God's people would assume command of their own destiny. Yet, in the beginning, this would be difficult since they had become unfit for freedom – the result of having been kept in a state of acquiescent and mindless subjection. Milton feared that men were still too timorously overawed by the trappings of status and the power of tradition to move boldly forward:

> I fear yet this iron yoke of outward conformity hath left a slavish print upon our necks; the ghost of linen decency still haunts us. We stumble and are impatient at the least dividing of one visible congregation from another, though it be not in fundamentals; and though our forwardness to suppress, and our backwardness to recover, any enthralled piece of truth out of the gripe of custom, we care not to keep truth separate from truth, which is the fiercest rent and disunion of all.[56]

As far as Milton is concerned all this talk of schism is mere opportunism, designed to keep bishops in their comfortable benefices, to preserve them in luxury from which the gospel will always be kept at arm's length. If the vicious old mechanical conformity, analogous to the automatic bowings and bendings of the knee of Catholicism, was to be swept aside it was inevitable that there *would* be differences and disagreements, that was what freedom was all about. Nevertheless it was essential to grasp the opportunity in both hands and take that risk because only in this way could Christianity be awakened from its long sleep of death. Milton wanted a thousand flowers to bloom. Against the bishops who flattered themselves on their efforts to forestall 'schism', Milton wrote:

> With as good a plea might the dead-palsie boast to a man, It is I that free you from stiches and pains, and the troublesome feeling

of cold and heat, of wounds and strokes: if I were gone, all these would not molest you. The winter might as well vaunt itself against the spring, I destroy all noysome and rank weeds, I keepe downe all pestilent vapours; yes, and all wholesome herbs, and all fresh dews, by your violent and hide-bound frost: but when the gentle west winds shall open the fruitful bosome of the earth, thus overgirded by your imprisonment, then the flowers put forth and spring, and then the sun shall scatter the mists, and the manuring hand of the Tiller shall root up all that burdens the soile without thanks to your bondage.[57]

Milton could only see good coming from the experiment, for it would be an active process of seeking the truth rather than a sterile and rigid system of precluding it. It has become almost axiomatic for modern critics of Milton to complain that his protestations of freedom and tolerance are insincere, by modern standards, since he will not extend this principle to Catholics. But Milton's inevitable response would be that the Roman Church was precisely the obstacle – how could an organisation that had suppressed the truths of the gospel for more than a millennium possibly play any part in the process of their recovery? How could an organisation that imposed a rigid conformity on its members participate in an open-ended and free enquiry? Milton genuinely believed that liberty was the best school of virtue. He was convinced that truth must be sought through conflict, exploration and trial. It could not just be handed over as something signed, sealed and delivered. In *Areopagitica* Milton spoke of truth as having been torn to pieces like the mangled body of Osiris and suggested that the task of piercing it together would continue until the Second Coming:

> Suffer not these licencing prohibitions to stand at every place of opportunity forbidding and disturbing them that continue seeking, that continue to do obsequies to the torn body of our martyred saint.[58]

The radical implication of all this is to suggest that Jesus has been martyred at the hands of his own Church and that the task of reassembling the doctrines that have been so recklessly scattered on the winds of time is one that may well continue indefinitely. Milton, like Emerson, saw himself as an endless seeker, but he did so admittedly in the belief that the Apocalypse was imminent and that with it all man's troublesome questions would be answered once and for all.

If Milton remained undisturbed by the prospect of conflict and disagreement this was very much because he was committed to a dynamic interpretation of history in which truth itself was no longer something that was static and fixed but was bound up with the ongoing process of man's intellectual and moral development. A humanity freed from monastic shackles and committed to the re-establishment of the Christian faith would be on its way towards becoming reunited with God. The centuries old alienation of man from his Creator was now coming to an end. In the shadow of the Last Judgement the divine and the human would once more converge. In *Areopagitica* Milton used the metaphor of the building of the temple, so beloved of Puritan ministers, to suggest that perfection would not consist of uniformity, but rather that a symmetrical and harmonious whole could be built out of a mass of moderately diversified materials. For a moment Milton begins to sound like an apologist for the Church of England, but for him the crucial difference would be that while the Church of England, under its corrupt regime, of bishops is always temporising and tarrying, the new unity would be genuinely grounded on Reformation principles and forged out of a collective sense of purpose. If Milton was to experience one especially keen feeling of disappointment under a commonwealth that had so many achievements to its credit, it was that this deeper sense of national purpose and unity never really emerged. In *Of Reformation* Milton deplored the politician's art of attempting to perpetuate a state of affairs that has become irrelevant to the needs of the people, where the sole concern is 'how to solder, how to stop a leak, how to keep up the floating carcass of a crazy or diseased monarchy or state, betwixt wind and water, swimming upon her own dead lees',[59] and he contrasted this with what he believed was the true alternative, a nation infused with a sense of collective identity and Christian faith: 'a commonwealth ought to be put one mighty Christian personage, one mighty growth and stature of an honest man, as big and compact in virtue as in body'.[60]

Sadly, the Rump and Barebones Parliaments never came remotely close to realising such an ideal. The unparalleled opportunity of the revolution threw up an incredible diversity of views as the result of which England was more divided and fragmented than ever before. The unity and solidarity of England depended solely on the person of Cromwell and on the existence of the New Model Army. Despite this, Milton was sustained by the deep conviction that England had been uniquely chosen as an instrument of the divine will to lead in the last days and to serve as a shining example to other lands. Milton, like Winstanley, insisted that England, as the redeemer nation, was not to be measured or judged by the standard of others that were still shrouded in sinfulness and ignorance. England was already on a far higher plane. Winstanley, in *A New-Yeers Gift* of 1649, had warned army and Parliament: 'Look not upon other lands to be your pattern, all lands in the world lie under darkness. So doth England yet, though the nearest to light and freedom of any others; therefore let no other land take your crown.'[61]

Similarly, Milton in his *A Defence of the People of England* of the following year rejected Salmasius's raking together of a host of precedents drawn from world history as quite beside the point: 'For the English think they need not allege the examples of foreigners for their justification . . . they were born free, they stand in need of no other nation, they can make what laws they please for their own good government.'[62] In a defiant spirit Milton rejected all normative modes of argument. England was about to rewrite the rulebook. In *Areopagitica* Milton interpreted England's rejection of a king as a sign of divine favour, which implicitly placed them above the Jews as a theocratic nation since the Jews had rejected God and incurred his anger in order to have a king. In such an exhilarated mood all such internal divisions as existed could seem relatively inconsequential. Moreover, these were the years when Milton himself played a glittering part on the national and international stage as the leading defender of the revolution. His belief in England's special destiny as the most favoured nation of God was matched, if not surpassed, by Cromwell. In considering the extraordinary elation which Puritans experienced at this time we need to remember that they had believed that God was with them even as they faced the pressures of extreme adversity under Laud; now, by contrast, the astonishing successes of the revolution seem to demonstrate unequivocally, and in a manner almost unparalleled in world history, that God *had* decisively intervened on their side. According to Cromwell:

in the king's first going from the Parliament, in the pulling down of the Bishops, the House of Peers, in every step towards that change of the government, I say there is not any 'one' of these 'things' thus removed and reformed, but there is an 'evident' print of Providence set upon it, so that he who runs may read.[63]

Cromwell proclaimed that the truth of this was confirmed irrefutably by the fact that God's engagement on the side of Parliament was acknowledged even by those who had sided with the King – as we have already seen, Clarendon admitted as much. But Cromwell went even further. His prodigious record of military success was such, the marks of divine favour so unparalleled, that he was convinced that God's 'appearances and providences amongst us are not to be outmatched by any story'.[64] Even the Jews, the chosen people, had not been similarly favoured. Indeed, by all biblical accounts the Jews as a people had been distinctly unsuccessful. So England was fortunate indeed.

In a speech before Parliament on 23 January 1657 Cromwell described the English people as 'A people of the blessing of God, a People under his safety and protection. . . . And you have of this no parallel, no, not in all the world! You in the midst of your glorious things.'[65] But if this meant, as it surely did, that God was watching over England to defend the achievements of the revolution, then that divine guardianship was soon to be withdrawn. Only a year later Cromwell was dead. Under Cromwell's son, Richard, the old tensions between Parliament and the Army resurfaced and Richard became a ruler without any authority. On 30 December 1659 General Monck crossed over from Scotland into England with his forces and invited Charles to return. On 8 May Charles was proclaimed King of England and on 29 May he had his triumphal return to London. For Milton this turn of events was nothing less than a catastrophe. As the author of the abusive and contemptuous *Eiconoklastes*, and a celebrated defender of both the commonwealth and the act of regicide, he was a marked man, whose claim to be executed was as strong as any. Yet Milton somehow survived and, by an enormous effort of will, was able to create out of his latter days of blindness, isolation and despair, a titanic poetic achievement. Yet Milton's physical blindness, which he had suffered since 1652, was almost a lesser blow than the terrible intellectual obscurity into which he was now so unexpectedly hurled. How could God have done such a thing!? There could be absolutely no doubt that the cause for which they had striven had been just and that God himself had given them innumerable signs of his continued regard and favour. How was it that God, who had singled England out to be the vanguard nation in the work of Reformation, to rinse away all the decadent and irreligious practices that had sullied the pure waters of true religion, how was it that he could be so unpredictable and unjust as to now turn his back abruptly on those who had sought to live in conformity with his will and bring back in self-righteous triumph the very forces of darkness against which they had so bitterly struggled? Doubtless many of those on the Parliamentary side had acted selfishly and irresponsibly. Perhaps they had been hasty in assuming that the Puritan revolution would be a final settlement of accounts, in the last days of the world. Clearly that time had not yet come. Even so Milton was left with a powerful sense of betrayal. He had envisioned a world in which men exercising their own inner spiritual freedom would, at one and the same time, be doing God's will. He had conceived of history as a kind of collaboration between God and man and he held tenaciously on to such an optimistic vision of things even in the dark days of the writing of *Paradise Lost*. But for the moment Milton was badly shaken. It was as if the Calvinists, whose determinism he had rejected, had been right all along. William Perkins, the leading English exponent of Calvinist theology, had written in *A Treatise Tending unto a Declaration, Whether a man Be in the Estate of Damnation, or in the Estate of Grace*:

> Neither must any thinke it to be cruelty in God to forsake his creature which he hath made: for he is sovereign Lord over all his works: and for that cause he is not bound to any; and he may doe with his owne whatsoever he will. And thus his will is not to be blamed: for men are not to imagine, that a thing must first bee just and then afterward that God doth wil it: but contrariwise, first God wils a thing, and thereupon it becomes just.[66]

In this tradition of Reformation theology, which can be traced back to William of Ockham, God's freedom is so absolutely prioritised that nothing whatsoever can be permitted to stand as a limitation upon it. God is not obliged to be either loyal or just in the eyes of men, for to make this stipulation would be to presume to know better than God and restrict his necessarily infinite possibilities of action. God can do as he likes and men will just have to live with the consequences – concluding that God may indeed be just but that the principles of his justice are too hard for human reason to grasp. But Perkins's doctrine is undoubtedly a hard saying and Milton had always found it so. Now this right of God to be whimsical tormented him.

Yet Milton retained his high sense of the role of the poet, as both visionary and prophetic. The poet's task, like that of the Old Testament prophets, was to recall his people to order and to infuse them with an enthusiasm for the heroic tradition of which they are a part. They must be reminded of their destiny even in the face of circumstances that seem to put this in question. When Milton wrote *The Reason of Church Government* and there presented one of his most elaborate expositions of the poet's role, he saw it as being very much akin to the task undertaken by Foxe in his *Actes and Monuments*:

> to sing Victorious agonies of Martyrs and Saints, the deeds and triumphs of just and pious Nations, doing valiantly through faith against the enemies of Christ; to deplore the general relapse of Kingdoms and States from justice and God's true worship.[67]

That Milton still adhered to this view that poetry should be at once celebratory and admonitory is evident from his subsequent writing of *Paradise Regained* and *Samson Agonistes*. But with *Paradise Lost* the greater difficulty he faced was that while the Restoration unquestionably represented such a period of relapse, it nevertheless must, in some obscure way, represent the deliberate decision of divine providence. So the poet's task of justifying the ways of God to man was an urgent one, since God's unpredictable, unforeseeable and incomprehensible action could undermine the faith of precisely those who were most deeply committed to him. Like Dante's *Divine Comedy*, Milton's poem begins in darkness and ends in light, but the parallel is rather misleading since God's whole relation to illumination has become infinitely more obscure. Dante is in no doubt that there is light and that he can move progressively towards it, whereas for Milton God's intentions are shrouded in darkness, yet only God can shine a light into the darkness which he himself has made. Milton must presume to understand God's thinking and he must believe, as no Calvinist would, that such an understanding is possible and that God himself would wish it, yet his starting-point is the fact that he does not understand it at all. Milton simply cannot believe that God could be so ruthless and insensitive as to keep his own people in an impenetrable darkness as to his purposes when they depend for their very existence on the illumination that only he can grant them. So the very writing of the poem, as a series of flashes of inspiration that permit Milton to outline progressively the unfolding of God's purpose in world history, will itself serve as a demonstration that enlightenment *can* be achieved. Just because Milton felt that there was some justice in the charge that God had not done enough to keep him and his fellow Puritans fully informed, he was particularly careful to show, in *Paradise Lost*, that God had absolutely leaned over backwards to make sure that Adam was kept in the picture at all times. Yet Milton is conscious that a gap *has* opened up between God and the saints who have endeavoured to be the instruments of his will, and the task *Paradise Lost* sets itself is to close this gap by delivering a series of revelations that will shed light on God's design in the universe and man's place within it. Milton's wager is that God will want to dispel the darkness, indeed his very request 'what in me is dark / Illumin' is only made because Milton is sure that it will be answered.

Milton's vast endeavour in *Paradise Lost* is to offer his readers a vision of the universe, which, whilst not shirking any of its difficulties, will always be comprehensible. If man can understand, then this will also demonstrate that God is good. For Milton would most definitely have had his doubts about the goodness of a God who did not give a damn one way or another. In effect God has to rise to the new demands of seventeenth-century reason. Milton refuses to accept the idea of a God who prefers to keep the faithful in a state of benighted and monkish ignorance. If God has let man down it is absolutely imperative that man should be told the reason why.

Nevertheless the shock of the Restoration put in question Milton's original faith that God was to be identified with a continuous, progressive, restorative force in the universe and that he would give his unqualified support to all those who threw themselves into the struggle against the Antichrist. In the euphoria of the revolutionary period, conceived of as one decisive moment that would cancel once and for all the accumulated iniquities and impieties of history, it had been all too easy to overlook the fact that God himself had presided over a world whose practices for so long had been radically at variance with his will and the teaching of Christ in the gospels. On the one hand there was the question, 'Why had God done so little about it?'; on the other the still more disquieting, 'Why, having decided to do something about it, had God suddenly backed down, without giving his followers any warning?' What seemed so particularly unfair was that not only was he punishing the faithful but he was actually rewarding the sinful and reprobate. It was as if he had lost sight of what the conflict was really about, as if he had somehow lost interest. For many of the enterprises which were most precious to God had now cruelly foundered on the rocks of circumstance. The achievements of the Commonwealth were to be thrown away. Nothing had been done about the bishops. Paradise had been closed down as an experiment almost before it had begun. Yet God seemed to assume no responsibility for all this, but had simply sat back and washed his hands of the whole affair, like Pontius Pilate. Admittedly this might be a very narrow and shortsighted view of the matter, and no doubt God had his reasons – which, being God, would certainly be very good ones – but the fact that God had a serious communication problem could hardly be evaded. As Milton experienced the terrible fear, anxiety and loneliness of the outcast and contemplated the awesome spectacle of an all-powerful Charles II, who was exacting retribution by bringing to the scaffold such leading figures in the rebellion as Hugh Peters and Sir Henry Vane, he must have thought of the proposition of Salmasius which he indignantly rejected in *A Defence of the People of England*: 'We spit out your second point and would have your blasphemous mouth stopped for calling God the greatest of tyrants because, as you keep saying, he is spoken of as King and Lord of tyrants.'[68]

God's behaviour seemed very unreasonable. For if he had foreseen the defeat of the revolution, as he undoubtedly had, then he had been deliberately leading the saints up the garden path. As William Empson has shrewdly pointed out,[69] though without drawing the full political conclusion from it, Satan suggests in Book I of *Paradise Lost* that God deliberately egged the rebel angels into a rebellion, which they would never have been drawn into had they known the true facts of the situation:

> But he who reigns
> Monarch in Heav'n, till then as one secure
> Sat on his Throne, upheld by old repute,
> Consent or custome, and his Regal State
> Put forth at full, but still his strength conceal'd,
> Which tempted our attempt, and wrought our fall.

What makes these lines all the more interesting is that the language Milton uses clearly implies a parallel between the eating of the apple in Paradise and the downfall of Satan, and what links them is the suggestion that God deliberately set the whole thing up and actually made it easy for angels or men to indulge in gestures of disobedience and defiance which he had all along determined to punish with the utmost ruthlessness. In such a light God appeared not so much as a wise and all-powerful creator as a petty and vengeful tyrant. This would, of course, be to take the worst possible view of God's behaviour and to look at the matter from a Satanic standpoint. Arguably God foresaw it all but his commitment to the existence of freedom meant that he had no alternative but to allow events to take their course. But clearly God's knowingness as contrasted with everyone else's ignorance puts both men and angels at a very considerable disadvantage. Is it reasonable to expect them to act wisely if they know so little of what is going on? God appears to make no distinction between those who act in good faith and those who do not, between those who wish to serve him and those who are disobedient. On not a few occasions in *Paradise Lost* God begins to seem like a Stuart monarch, who surrounds himself with spineless and obsequious flatterers, while the fallen angels in Hell who will pay any price rather than go along with so much empty pageantry and ceremony seem much more like the outcast Puritans in

> preferring
> Hard liberty before the easie yoke
> Of servile pomp.

Milton was sure that God could provide a convincing rebuttal to these and other criticisms and it was obviously impossible to form a judgement if one was not in possession of all the facts, but he nevertheless felt that from the human point of view, perhaps especially from the Puritan point of view, there *was* a case to answer. *Paradise Lost* puts God on trial and the charges against him do eventually surface even if they are presented somewhat obliquely. It is after the Fall in Book IX that Milton allows Adam to set out his most serious grievance against God, albeit attributed hypothetically to Satan, that God is erratic, whimsical, unpredictable and therefore always ultimately destructive:

> Nor can I think that God, creator wise,
> Though threatening, will in earnest so destroy
> Us his prime Creatures, dignified so high,
> Set over all His works, which in our Fall,
> For us created, needs with us must faile,
> Dependent made; so God shall uncreate,
> Be frustrate, do, undo, and labour loose,
> Not well conceaved of God, who though his power
> Creation could repeate, yet would be loath
> Us to abolish, lest the Adversary
> Triumph and say; Fickle their State whom God
> Most Favours, who can please him long? Me first
> He ruind, now Mankind; whom will he next?

The picture of God that emerges here is not a pretty one. It seems that God has made a botched job of the whole creation of mankind and is already bored with it. He would really prefer to forget the whole thing and turn to the creation of yet another world; and the only reason why he cannot bring himself to do so is that he is unwilling to admit to another failure and fearful that Satan's accusation of unreliability will seem to be well founded. So God has to be patient with man just to keep up his image.

In all his writings Milton laid a quite remarkable emphasis on God's perfection and self-sufficiency, which therefore implied that there was no necessity for God to embark on the creation of the universe or anything else. Referring to the passage in *Paradise Lost* where Adam draws a distinction between his mortal frailty, which requires a companion, and the divine perfection, which does not:

> Thou in Thy secrecy although alone,
> Best with thyself accompanied, seek'st not
> Social communication

Arthur O. Lovejoy observes:

> But what is clearest about this passage is that Milton the
> theologian saw in the juncture of his narrative to affirm once
> again that a self-absorbed and unproductive God would be not
> less, but, if possible more divine, and that there is no necessity
> and, indeed, no reason for the existence of any creature.
> Milton's zeal for this thesis is the more curious because his
> theology here seems out of harmony with his ethical creed and
> moral temper.[70]

Lovejoy's point that such a doctrine seems a somewhat unlikely
one for Milton to hold is highly perceptive, but there were very
pressing reasons why Milton was determined to insist on it. If
God was actively involved in the course of human affairs and if he
had some sort of vested interest in the way that turned out, this
then led almost inescapably to the conclusion that he must finally
be blamed for the general state of the world and for its persistent
refusal of the truths of the gospel. On the other hand, if God had
had no need to create man and the world, if perhaps he had even
embarked on such a course with some misgivings, then instead of
seeming callous and indifferent he appeared rather to be patient
and long-suffering. In his younger days Milton had believed that
God was actively involving himself in human affairs, but now he
believed that God deliberately held back from any such
involvement, much as he might have wished it. A further
implication was that since God's gesture of creation was essentially
a gratuitous one, he was by no means obliged to concern himself
with it. Man should really be flattered if God thought about him
at all. If one revised one's premises in this way then it would once
more be possible to feel a sense of gratitude towards him.

Far from wishing to blame God for everything that had happened,
Milton was anxious to save him from any possible reproach.
Instead of positing God and man working together in harmony,
which was scarcely possible any longer, Milton sought to close
the gulf that had opened up between them by insisting that what
they still shared was a common concern with freedom and that

God had always insisted on preserving man's independence of action even when the consequences caused him intense grief and disappointment. If humanity has suffered, so has God. If man has often been baffled, baulked and frustrated, so too has God. Man has been waiting for God to deliver the goods when he should rightly have recognised that God has been waiting for mankind to do the same. In this misunderstanding it is God, predictably, who has right on his side since any attempt on his part to alter or directly influence the course of events would devalue the priceless gift of freedom that he has bestowed on his erring and ungrateful progeny. The conjuncture of *Paradise Lost* with Newtonian mechanics produced a vision of the world in which God was only Maker and first cause of the universe. Having once set things in motion there was no further obligation or necessity for him to interfere. The particular advantage of Milton's view was that it absolved God from any responsibility for the Restoration. While it is possible that God disapproved of some of the excesses of the revolutionary period and may conceivably have passed judgement upon them, the greater likelihood is that he left England and the saints to work out their own destiny. Consequently they should now have the humility to make the difficult admission: 'We blew it'. Indeed, Milton now recognises that the Calvinist belief in predestination had significantly contributed to the whole turn of events. It had been all very well for people, Cromwell included, to attribute their successes to God when things were going well, but all this had led to a progressive erosion of moral responsibility and a failure to weigh sufficiently the consequences of each course of action. Milton felt that the revolution had lost its way both through Parliamentary vacillation and radical excesses. What for the most part had been lacking was unity, clearly thought-out objectives and a determination to see them through to the end. The saints would have to blame themselves before they tried to blame God. In Hell, Milton's greatest contempt is reserved for Belial, who imagines that all avenues are closed and that there is no possibility for action whatsoever. According to Belial a 'fate inevitable / Subdues us' and they are doomed to impotence:

> we are decreed,
> Reserv'd and destin'd to Eternal woe.

Despite this, the fallen angels both agree on a policy and decide

to implement it immediately, which – as Milton ironically
insinuates – was something that Parliament was never able to do.
The vanity of discussions about predestination is demonstrated
by the case of those who

> reason'd high
> Of Providence, foreknowledge, Will and Fate,
> Fixt Fate, free will, foreknowledge absolute,
> And found no end, in wandring mazes lost.

Freedom, as far as Milton was concerned, was essentially a mental
category – the existence of mind was itself a guarantee of freedom.
Man had been created in order to choose and this was a privilege
that could never be taken away. As Milton continued his great
work under the adverse circumstances of the Restoration this
precious gift became even more vivid for him than it ever had in
the palmy days of pamphleteering. The writing of *Paradise Lost*
was itself a great denial of the times and a gesture of freedom and
independence against the grain. It is impossible to miss the note
of pride with which Milton announces his poetic mission at the
beginning of Book VII:

> Standing on Earth, not rapt above the Pole,
> More safe I Sing with mortal voice, unchang'd
> To hoarce or mute, though fall'n on evil dayes,
> On evil days though fall'n, and evil tongues;
> In darkness, and with dangers compast round,
> And solitude; yet not alone, while thou
> Visit'st my slumbers Nightly, or when Morn
> Purples the East: still govern thou my Song,
> *Urania*, and fit audience find, though few.

Paradise Lost affirms the meaningfulness of the world and the
meaningfulness of the Puritan commitment as much by its
perverse existence in unpropitious times as by what it actually has
to say. It affirms the importance of continuing to struggle against
the pressures of circumstance. The flame of resistance that was
lit by Richard Sibbes and others before the revolution will go on
burning after it.

In the aftermath of the revolution what disturbed Milton was
the sheer ephemerality of that period. For two triumphant decades

the Commonwealth had not only survived but it had prospered. It had successfully seen off every challenge the Royalists could throw at it. The Commonwealth had become an inescapable fact of life, at home and abroad. Yet suddenly the Commonwealth was abruptly dissolved and dispersed, and as Charles II endeavoured to restore his own idea of normality and legitimacy it was almost as if the whole momentous experience had never happened. It was as if it had been completely stricken from the record. Little wonder that the earlier instance of Paradise seemed to flicker with a similarly unreal vividness, for that too had been a living actuality, if a fleeting one. By making Paradise live once more in the imagination of his readers as a radiant historical moment, Milton would shame them into a recognition of how deeply they had fallen. For in England also there had momentarily glimmered a vision – and a realisable vision – of a spiritually purified and morally regenerated world, purged of the sinful corruption of bishops and royal Court, yet in the vital hour they had proved unworthy of it. For Milton, the parallel between Paradise and the Commonwealth was neither fanciful nor sacrilegious but very close. They were both experiments presided over by God, which he had followed with the highest hopes and expectations, but which had both gone badly wrong. Milton believed that it was England's task to carry the blazing torch of truth that would light the way for others. England, set apart from continental Europe, had a unique mission and Shakespeare's description of her as 'this other Eden' could by no means be regarded as hyperbole. So England's failure inescapably brought one back to the Fall, of which it was the type.

Moreover, Paradise itself is the most compelling instance of the transfiguration of values to which the Reformation is dedicated. In Paradise there were no kings, no Courts, no hierarchy, no struggles for pre-eminence (though there were in Heaven!). Love was natural and unashamed, quite unlike the decadence of

> Court amours,
> Mixt dance, or wanton Mask, or Midnight Bal.

Adam and Eve are honest, open and straightforward and their sense of dignity and self-possession is attributable to this rather than to any notion of social position. When Milton says of Adam:

> in himself was all his state,
> More solemn than the tedious pomp that waits
> On Princes, when their rich Retinue long
> Of Horses led, and Grooms besmeared with gold
> Dazles the croud, and sets them all agape

this is directly uttered in rebuke of Court ceremonial, but, of course, it is equally levelled at the Church establishment, which has transformed simple ceremonies of piety and good fellowship into elaborate rituals in which the medium becomes the message and where even the communion table is made unequal. Paradise, by contrast, is a place where even men and angels can sit at the same table. Paradise is a vision of all that life could be if all the oppressive power structures, that divide man from man and man from God, were to be swept away. Milton's sense of a world grown old, which still longs to be regenerated by a return to first principles is, paradoxically, expressed most compellingly through the character of Satan. It is Satan we recognise

> As one who long in populous city pent,
> Where houses thick and sewers annoy the air

who enters Paradise like a Londoner walking out into the surrounding countryside, and it is Satan who is momentarily struck dumb, who becomes 'Stupidly good, or enmities disarm'd' when confronted with the innocence of Eve. Milton intends that his readers should be so disturbed by this perverse identification with the Prince of Darkness that he enforces this point – both by what they have lost and by the fact that they are apparently separated from such felicity by as small a distance as separates the Strand from open fields. Milton well knew that this step back into Paradise was not actually possible but he wanted to highlight dramatically the perversity of the circumstances by which mankind had become alienated from all that it represented. Humanity has become historically inured to a more complex existence in which the sense of freedom has atrophied and with it the self-discipline that should accompany it. As Milton had actually foreseen, there were bound to be problems when men were unexpectedly liberated from the mental fetters in which they had so long been confined. Yet in Paradise, paradoxically and despite God's prohibition, humanity was still in charge. Satan's mocking question, 'for what God after better worse would build?' when referring to the creation of Eden after Heaven, has a still more alarming pertinence to the history of the world since then. The question of blame is nowhere more acute than here. For although mankind may have merited misfortune by its catalogue of past errors, by its persistence in religious forms that are unpleasing to God and by its abiding obsession with status and class which would now make a return to the simplicity and innocence of Paradise virtually impossible, the consequences seem too severe, the woes too lasting. Eve seems justified in questioning Adam's suggestion that dire consequences may follow if they separate:

> Let us not then suspect our happie State
> Left so imperfect by the Maker wise,
> As not secure to single or combin'd.
> Fraile is our happiness, if this be so,
> And Eden were no Eden thus expos'd.

Why did God make Paradise so fragile? Did he really give humanity a proper chance – either in Eden or in England?

It can, of course, be argued that it was not Paradise that was fragile but Eve herself. In his retelling of the Christian myth Milton does not merely reproduce the ancient determination to make woman the scapegoat for all the wrongs of the world, but actually intensifies it by making Adam a relatively innocent and generally reluctant participant in the whole proceedings. The disparagement of woman in *Paradise Lost* can hardly be evaded but it should be emphasised that Milton does give this pivotal moment of the Fall a larger and more complex contemporary meaning. Milton takes the Fall to signify that most agonising dilemma confronting seventeenth-century culture, the difficulty of adjudicating a whole series of conflicting truth claims, not only in respect of the Bible, but in the development of scientific knowledge and in the tension and inconsistency between Christian thought and the classical tradition. Burton could live with contradiction, Hobbes sought to eliminate it, but for Milton there were no easy solutions. Unlike many of his fellow Puritans, who were disposed to reject pagan literature completely, Milton had immersed himself in it and was powerfully committed to it. Yet for that very reason he was deeply conscious of an asymmetry between the two traditions. If, as Milton believed, the Christian faith had been progressively corrupted through its incorporation into the political structure of the Roman Empire and through the assimilation of its beliefs to the model of already established religions, then the classical world of Greece and Rome must bear some responsibility for this. On the other hand, it could be argued, with equal if not greater conviction, that the Renaissance and Reformation shared a common drive towards clarification and enlightenment, in which long-forgotten truths would be reclaimed and in which ancient texts would be purged of the corruptions and debasement to which they had been subjected. For the most part Milton sought a reconciliation between Reformation principles and humanism, but at the very moment of the Fall he finds himself unable to sustain this harmony and leans the other way, for he stresses that Satan, in his clinching peroration that brings about Eve's downfall, draws on all the dangerous powers of classical rhetoric:

> As when of old som Orator renound
> In *Athens* or free Rome, where Eloquence
> Flourishd, since mute, to som great cause addrest,
> Stood in himself collected, while each part,
> Motion, each act won the audience ere the tongue,
> Sometimes in highth began, as no delay
> Of Preface brooking through his Zeal of Right.
> So standing, moving, or to highth upgrown
> The Tempter all impassiond thus began.

As I have noted elsewhere, the Puritan preachers distrusted the use of gesture which they associated with the theatricality of Roman religion. The Christian faith requires no elaborate acts of persuasion precisely because it is true. As Satan in the body of a snake endeavours to persuade Eve, he attempts in sinuous writhing motions to raise himself to a full height – but what this symbolically demonstrates is the actual inability of rhetoric ever to attain the stature of rational truth. Milton's use of this figure at such a point is significant since it implies that it was through the pagan arts of rhetoric and sophistry that the original simple faith was lost, as when Adam says to Raphael in Book VIII:

> How fully hast thou satisfi'd me, pure
> Intelligence of Heav'n, Angel serene,

> And freed from intricacies, taught to live,
> The easiest way, nor with perplexing thoughts
> To interrupt the sweet of Life, from which
> God hath bid dwell far off all anxious cares.

As Christopher Hill has suggested,[71] Eve's belief in her god-like powers after eating of the Tree of Knowledge recalls the Ranters' self-intoxicated sense of their own divinity, but it also needs to be stressed that Satan's speech which outlines these powers recalls both the extravagant claims made for Renaissance medicine and science by such figures as Paracelsus, Bruno and Cardan, but also the general argument on behalf of human greatness urged by such Italian humanists as Ficino and Pomponazzi. So Milton is conscious of the dangers of an extreme humanistic emphasis and of the potential and actual discord that is generated by the attempt to listen to the Bible and the classics simultaneously, like two Charles Ivesian brass bands. The freedom that Milton had argued for in *Areopagitica* was essential for the spiritual development of the individual, but with it came a heavy moral responsibility and the possibility of making serious misjudgements. This, for Milton, was what the Fall was all about.

It is in the aftermath of the Fall that the parallel between Eden and the Commonwealth becomes most significant and it is only at this point that we begin to understand why Milton is so anxious to make a distinction between Adam and Eve. For Adam represents the Puritan saints, who were more betrayed by the course of the revolution than guilty of any betrayal in their own right. Like Adam they were reluctant fellow-travellers. Like Adam they feel they have been unfairly treated: 'Inexplicable / Thy justice seems.' They have done their very best to obey God's command but they are now regarded as sinners not so much because of anything they have done themselves, but through guilt by association – because they are regarded as having endorsed actions which were actually conceived and initiated by others. So Milton suggests Adam did not really have any option but to go along with Eve after the deed was done, just as he himself had to vote the straight ticket of the revolution without being in a position to repudiate many of the things that were done, or were not done, in its name. It may seem strange that at the opening of Book IX Milton should speak of his long deliberation over the subject of a heroic poem and his rejection of

a state of affairs in which war was regarded as the only possible
subject,

> the better fortitude
> Of patience and heroic martydom
> Unsung

for although he had described martyrdom as one of the most
suitable subjects for poetry as far back as *The Reason of Church
Government*, it is far from evident that this is the subject of *Paradise
Lost*. But we need to remember that Milton was always much
more concerned with God's treatment of the saints, those who
had faithfully honoured and served him, than he was with the
state of the world in general. So Adam becomes typical of the
saints in general; the patience and fortitude with which he
endures an interminable and well-nigh incomprehensible chronicle
of sufferings, punishment and pain is exemplary for God's
servants in any age and in any time. If it is especially hard to
grasp why the world should continue to be 'To good malignant, to
bad men malign', it is important to grasp that it is only to the
saints that the perpetual postponement of the Second Coming is a
burden. They naturally long for purity of faith, truth and justice
in a way that the ordinary careless person does not. It is they who
cry out, 'How long, O Lord, how long?' So, while it is difficult for
them to be patient, it is essential that they rise to the moral
challenge that this state of affairs represents. They have God's
guarantee that eventually all this evil will be transformed into
good and with this they must be content. They must try to see
things from God's point of view. But their existence in the world
will always be a form of martyrdom, a long drawn out crucifixion
on the cross of history.

While the impression of confidence in *Paradise Lost* cannot
altogether mask the depths of Milton's disillusionment, in *Samson
Agonistes* the reverse is true: the torments of Samson are once
again to be seen at the darkest hour before the dawn and thereby
announce the revival of Milton's hopes. Milton had always
believed that the Stuart Court was an artificial excrescence on the
body of the English nation and therefore he could not accept that
it would be possible for the Restoration settlement to endure – an
intuition that proved to be correct. What is most significant is that
in *Samson Agonistes* he reaffirms his commitment to a public role,

to the importance of continuing to act in the general welfare, even
if the people themselves seem indifferent to the course of events.
As a young man Milton had made a distinction in his own mind
between the public duty of fighting for freedom and reformation
and the more private and personal vocation of being a poet. In
the years of isolation and disappointment after the Restoration,
when Milton was completing *Paradise Lost*, that distinction was
seemingly confirmed. But in *Samson Agonistes* he reaffirms his
commitment to his original role as the people's champion and
implicitly suggests that the writing of the poem can be as
exemplary as Samson's own actions in reminding his readers of
their own responsibility to the Commonwealth. Samson, like
Milton, has to recover his faith that great actions are still possible
and by his own renewed commitment he will keep the fires of
public-spritedness burning even when they seem on the point of
being extinguished for good. Although the opportunity of the
revolution has been recklessly squandered – Samson describes
himself as one

> Who like a foolish pilot have shipwrecked
> My vessel trusted to me from above,
> Gloriously rigged

– the disaster is not as irrevocable as it seems, for if the English
people have proved that they are ready to stand up for their
rights they can do so again. *Samson Agonistes* is thick with
intimations of public responsibility and although Delilah is the
focus of much bitterness and hostility directed against women, it
is significant that Milton nevertheless gives her a forceful case to
argue. Delilah insists that although her own private loyalties were
to Samson it was impressed on her that it was her *duty* to betray
Samson: 'To the public good / Private respects may yield.'

Since the Philistines in their devotion to sports, festivals and
popular entertainments clearly embody the values of the Royalists
and of the Restoration, what this debate brings out is the way in
which those who have supported the King now habitually resort
to a discourse of public responsibility. The case for the monarchy
is no longer argued in terms of divine right, the indivisibility of
sovereignty or tradition, but on the grounds that it is beneficial to
the nation at large. Needless to say, Milton cannot accept this
argument and Samson in rebuttal insists that those who gave

Delilah such instructions had no legitimacy and no right to do so:
they are

> an impious crew
> Of men conspiring to uphold their state
> By worse than hostile deeds, violating the ends
> For which our country is a name so dear;
> Not therefore to be obeyed.

Milton here returns to the arguments that he had formerly used.
England, as the elect nation of God, like the Jews, cannot be
served or deflected from her righteous course by a corrupt élite of
Royalists that stands in the way. He denies that there can be
political legitimacy for a regime that is indifferent to this higher
purpose. So Samson himself, though ostensibly a private person,
must reaffirm the importance and validity of the mission with
which he was originally entrusted:

> I was no private but a person raised
> With strength sufficient and command from heaven
> To free my country.

In his heroic and self-destructive gesture of bringing down the
temples of the Philistines, Samson demonstrates that the structures
of power and authority can always be destroyed by those who are
sufficiently dedicated and determined to resist them. With *Samson
Agonistes* Milton proclaims that the spirit of the Commonwealth
lives on.

Notes

Notes to Chapter 1: England's Time of Crisis

1. John Foxe, *Actes and Monuments of these latter and perilous dayes touching matters of the Church*, with a life by the Rev. G. Townsend (New York, 1965) vol. I, p. xxxv.
2. Robert Greene, *Life and Complete Works*, ed. A. B. Grosart (New York, 1964) vol. v, p. 256.

Notes to Chapter 2: This Luckless Kingdom

1. Edward Hall, *Union of the Two Noble and Illustre Families of Lancastre and Yorke* (London, 1809) p. 1.
2. Ibid.
3. John Foxe, *Actes and Monuments of these latter and perilous dayes touching matters of the Church* (New York, 1965) vol. III, p. 229.
4. Ibid., vol. III, p. 581.
5. Ibid., vol. III, p. 702.
6. Ibid., vol. II, p. 85.
7. Holinshead, *Chronicle* (London, 1807) vol. I, pp. 737–8.
8. *Fast Sermons to Parliament*, with notes by R. Jeffs (London, 1970) vol. 7, p. 2.
9. See Robert Ornstein, *A Kingdom for a Stage* (Cambridge, Mass., 1972) pp. 1–32; S. C. Sen Gupta, *Shakespeare's Historical Plays* (London, 1966) pp. 1–29; Wilbur Sanders, *The Dramatist and the Received Idea* (London, 1968) pp. 72–109; John Wilders, *The Lost Garden* (London, 1978) p. 71. See also J. W. Lever, 'Shakespeare and the Ideas of his Time', in *Shakespeare Survey 29*, ed. K. Muir (Cambridge, 1976) pp. 79–91.
10. E. M. W. Tillyard, *Shakespeare's History Plays* (London, 1962) p. 42.
11. Ibid., p. 44.
12. Ibid., p. 40.
13. E. M. W. Tillyard, *The Elizabethan World Picture* (London, 1958) p. v.
14. Tillyard, *Shakespeare's History Plays*, p. 152.
15. Ibid., p. 153.
16. Ibid., p. 201.
17. Ibid., p. 49.
18. Ibid., pp. 190, 202, 154, 209, 144.
19. Hall, *Union*, p. 264.
20. Ibid., p. 276.

21. See Henry A. Kelly, *Divine Providence in the England of Shakespeare's Histories* (Cambridge, Mass., 1970) pp. 109–37.
22. Hall, *Union*, pp. 374 and 415.
23. Ibid.
24. Ibid., p. 426.
25. Ibid., p. 431.
26. Tillyard, *Shakespeare's History Plays*, p. 64.
27. Quoted in ibid., p. 84.
28. See *The Mirror for Magistrates*, ed. Lily B. Campbell (New York, 1960) p. 178.

Notes to Chapter 3: The Corrupted Church

1. *Puritan Manifestoes*, ed. W. H. Frere and C. E. Douglas (London, 1954) p. 86.
2. Ibid., p. 92.
3. Ibid., p. 84.
4. Ibid., p. 113.
5. Ibid., p. 99.
6. Ibid., p. 93.
7. Edward Dering, *Two Godly Sermons* (Middleburg, c. 1590) pp. 31–2.
8. Ibid., pp. 14–15.
9. *Cartwrightiana*, ed. A. Peel and L. H. Carlson (London, 1951) pp. 141–2.
10. Patrick Collinson, *The Elizabethan Puritan Movement* (London, 1967) p. 125.
11. Quoted in Peter Lake, *Moderate Puritans and the Elizabethan Church* (London, 1982) p. 127.
12. Quoted in ibid., p. 128.
13. *Marprelate Tracts* (London, 1843) p. 25.
14. Ibid., p. 39.
15. Ibid., p. 16.
16. Ibid., p. 55.
17. Ibid., p. 198.
18. Ibid.
19. Ibid., p. 199.
20. Richard Hooker, *Of the Laws of Ecclesiastical Polity* (London, 1963) vol. I, p. 190.
21. Ibid., vol. I, p. 98.
22. Ibid., vol. I, p. 97.
23. Ibid., vol. I, p. 132.
24. Ibid., vol. I, p. 264.
25. Ibid., vol. I, p. 229.
26. Ibid., vol. I, p. 427.
27. Ibid., vol. I, p. 429.

Notes to Chapter 4: London: the Corrupted City

1. Fernand Braudel, *Capitalism and Material Life, 1400–1800,* trans. M. Kochan (London, 1973) p. 375.
2. A. L. Beier, *Masterless Men* (London, 1985) p. 40.
3. Ibid., pp. 39–40.
4. Paul Slack, *The Impact of the Plague in Tudor and Stuart England* (London, 1985) p. 152.
5. Quoted in Paul Seaver, *Wallington's World* (London, 1985) p. 49.
6. Thomas Nashe, *Works,* ed. R. B. McKerrow, repr. ed. F. P. Wilson (Oxford, 1958) vol. II, p. 158.
7. Thomas Dekker, *A Knight's Conjuring* (1607), ed. L. M. Robbins (The Hague, 1974) pp. 82–3.
8. Ibid., p. 156.
9. Nashe, *Works,* vol. II, p. 28.
10. Ibid., vol. II, p. 29.
11. Ibid., vol. II, pp. 131–2.
12. Ibid., vol. II, p. 142.
13. Thomas Nashe, *The Unfortunate Traveller,* ed. J. B. Steane (London, 1972) p. 91.
14. Henry Smith, *Works* (Edinburgh, 1866) vol. II, p. 49.
15. Ibid., vol. II, p. 158.
16. Ibid., vol. I, p. 247.
17. Ibid., vol. I, pp. 175–6.
18. Ibid., vol. I, p. 366.
19. Ibid., vol. II, p. 266.
20. Ibid.
21. Thomas Dekker, *The Wonderful Yeere 1603,* ed. G. B. Harrison (Edinburgh, 1966) pp. 34–5.
22. Nicholas Bownd, *Medecines for the Plague* (London, 1604) p. 80.
23. Ibid., p. 82.

Notes to Chapter 5: The Corrupted Court

1. Quoted in Linda Levy Peck, *Northampton: Patronage and Policy at the Court of James I* (London, 1982) p. 146.
2. Barnabe Riche, *The Honestie of this Age* (London, 1614) p. 12.
3. Francis Bacon, *The Essays,* ed. J. Pitcher (London, 1985) p. 130.
4. Sir William Cornwallis, *Essays* (London, 1610) unnumbered.
5. Norbert Elias, *The Court Society,* trans. E. Jephcott (Oxford, 1983) p. 94.
6. Quoted in Charles Richard Cammell, *The Great Duke of Buckingham* (London, 1939) p. 115.
7. Jonathan Dollimore, *Radical Tragedy* (Brighton, 1984) p. 48.
8. Cornwallis, *Essays,* unnumbered.
9. Ibid., unnumbered.
10. See Anne Barton, *Ben Jonson, Dramatist* (London, 1984) pp. 312–13.

11. See I. Lotman, 'The Decembrist in Daily Life', in *The Semiotics of Russian Cultural History*, ed. A. D. and A. S. Nakhimovsky (Ithaca, NY, 1985) esp. pp. 112–19.
12. *Letters of King James VI and I*, ed. G. P. V. Akrigg (Berkeley, Calif., 1984) p. 388.
13. Quoted in Charles Richard Cammell, *The Great Duke of Buckingham* (London, 1939) p. 166.

Notes to Chapter 6: The Corrupted World

1. Robert Burton, *The Anatomy of Melancholy*, 6th edn (London, 1660) p. 19.
2. Ibid., p. 27.
3. Ibid., p. 3.
4. George Wither, *Britain's Remembrancer* (New York, 1967) p. 28.
5. George Wither, *A Collection of Emblemes (1635)*, introduction by Rosemary Freeman with bibliographical notes by C. S. Hensley (Columbia, SC, 1975) Preface to the Reader, unnumbered.
6. Rosemary Freeman, *The English Emblem Book* (London, 1948) p. 127.
7. William Drummond, *Poems and Prose*, ed. R. H. Macdonald (Edinburgh, 1976) p. 167.
8. Francis Quarles, *Complete Works*, ed. Rev. A. B. Gosart (Hildesheim, 1971) vol. I, p. xviii.
9. Ibid., vol. I, p. 139.
10. Ibid., vol. I, p. 61.
11. Sir Walter Ralegh, *Works* (New York, 1964) vol. II, pp. 149–50.
12. Godfrey Goodman, *The Fall of Man* (London, 1616) p. 210.
13. Ibid., p. 386.
14. George Hakewill, *An Apologie of the Power and Providence of God* (London, 1627) p. iv.
15. Ibid., pp. iv–v.
16. Ibid., p. 2.
17. Ibid., fourth page of Preface, unnumbered.

Notes to Chapter 7: A Great Hazard: the Coming of Civil War

1. Sir Benjamin Rudyerd, *Memoirs*, ed. J. A. Manning (London, 1861) p. 162.
2. Thomas Brightman, *A Revelation of the Revelation* (Amsterdam, 1615) p. 390.
3. Quoted in Christopher Hill, *Puritanism and Revolution* (London, 1965) p. 264.
4. Quoted in ibid., pp. 124–5.
5. Richard Sibbes, *The Bruised Reed and the Smoking Flax* (1630) (Menston, 1973) pp. 204–5.

6. Ibid., p. 252.
7. Ibid., pp. 312–13.
8. Ibid., p. 322.
9. Ibid., pp. 339–40.
10. Ibid., pp. 324–5.
11. Ibid., p. 233.
12. Patrick Collinson, *The Religion of Protestants* (London, 1982) p. 230.
13. Richard Bernard, *The Isle of Man* (London, 1630) pp. 156–7.
14. Ibid., p. 158.
15. William Prynne, *Histriomastix* (New York, London, 1974) p. 854.
16. Ibid., p. 321.
17. Ibid., p. 322.
18. William Gouge, *Commentary on the Hebrews* (Grand Rapids, Mich., 1980) p. 376.
19. Quoted in Christopher Hill, *Intellectual Origins of the Puritan Revolution* (London, 1980) pp. 257–8.
20. See Hugh Trevor-Roper, 'The Fast Sermons of the Long Parliament', in *Religion: The Reformation and Social Change* (London, 1984) pp. 297–344.
21. *Cobbett's Parliamentary History*, vol. II (London, 1807) p. 447.
22. *Fast Sermons to Parliament*, with notes by R. Jeffs (London, 1970) vol. III, p. 159.
23. Ibid., vol. VI, p. 39.
24. Ibid., vol. III, p. 237.
25. Ibid., vol. III, p. 268.
26. Ibid.
27. *The Letters and Speeches of Oliver Cromwell*, with elucidations by Thomas Carlyle, ed. S. C. Lomax (London, 1904) vol. II, p. 275.
28. Ibid., vol. III, pp. 11–12.
29. Henry Burton, *For God and the King* (London, 1636) p. 89.
30. Ibid., p. 56.
31. Ibid., pp. 99–100.

Notes to Chapter 8: Shakespeare and the Crisis of Authority

1. Michel de Montaigne, *Essays*, trans. John Florio (New York, 1967) vol. II, p. 302.
2. Ibid.
3. Ibid., vol. III, p. 154.
4. Ibid.
5. See *Woodstock: A Moral History*, ed. A. P. Rossitter (London, 1946) pp. 47–8.
6. Unamuno, *Our Lord, Don Quixote*, trans. A. Kerrigan (London, 1967) p. 213.
7. Miguel de Cervantes, *Don Quixote*, trans. J. M. Cohen (London, 1982) p. 149.
8. Ibid., p. 410.

9. Ibid., p. 530.
10. See Roland Mushat Frye, *The Renaissance Hamlet* (Princeton, NJ, 1984) pp. 102–10.
11. G. Wilson Knight, *The Wheel of Fire* (London, 1949) p. 168.
12. E. M. W. Tillyard, *Shakespeare's History Plays* (London, 1962) p. 316.
13. Ibid., p. 315.
14. Quoted in ibid., p. 317.
15. L. C. Knights, *Some Shakespearean Themes* (London, 1959) p. 142.
16. Keith Thomas, *Religion and the Decline of Magic* (London, 1971) p. 480.
17. Richard Marienstras, *New Perspectives on the Shakespearean World*, trans. J. Lloyd (London, 1985) pp. 11–39.
18. Plutarch, *Lives of the Noble Greeks and Romans*, trans. Thomas North (New York, 1967) vol. VI, p. 53.
19. Ibid., vol. VI, p. 57.
20. Ibid., vol. VI, p. 61.
21. Quoted in Alan G. R. Smith, 'Constitutional Ideas and Parliamentary Developments in England 1603–1625', in *The Reign of James VI and I*, ed. Alan G. R. Smith (London, 1973) p. 166.
22. Jonathan Dollimore, *Radical Tragedy* (Brighton, 1984) p. 228.

Notes to Chapter 9: Counterfeit Representations: Tragedy at the Stuart Court

1. Vasari, *Lives of the Artists*, selected and trans. G. Bull (London, 1965) p. 259.
2. John Melton, *Astrologaster* (London, 1620) p. 59.
3. Richard Carpenter, *Experience, History and Divinitie* (London, 1642) p. 129.
4. Ibid., pp. 124–5.
5. Sir Thomas Browne, *Works*, ed. G. Keynes (London, 1964) p. 35.
6. Ibid., p. 243.
7. Hugh F. Kearney (ed.), *Origins of the Scientific Revolution* (London, 1964) p. 102.
8. Edward Worsop, *A discoverie of sundrie errours* (London, 1582) pp. 36–7.
9. Francis Bacon, *The Advancement of Learning and the New Atlantis*, ed. A. Johnson (Oxford, 1974) p. 42.
10. Sir Thomas Browne, *The Major Works*, ed. C. A. Patrides (London, 1977) p. 141.
11. Ibid., p. 149.
12. Andrew Willett, *Tetrastylon Papisticum* (London, 1593) p. 92.
13. Robert Burton, *The Anatomy of Melancholy*, 6th edn (London, 1660) p. 27.
14. *The Sermons of Edwin Sandys*, ed. Rev. J. Ayre (Cambridge, 1841) p. 66.
15. Andrew Willett, *Synopsis Papismi* (London, 1592) p. 137.
16. *The Sermons of Edwin Sandys*, p. 11.

17. Ibid., p. 12.
18. William Wilkinson, *A Confutation of Certayne Articles Delivered unto the Familye of Loue* (London, 1579) p. 44.
19. Ibid., p. 28.
20. Ibid., p. 32.
21. Lacey Baldwin Smith, *Treason in Tudor England* (London, 1986) p. 4.
22. Sydney Anglo (ed.), 'Reginald Scot's Discoverie of Witchcraft: Scepticism and Sadduceeism', in *The Damned Art* (London, 1977) p. 109.
23. Reginald Scot, *The Discoverie of Witchcraft* (Arundel, 1964) p. 382.
24. Ibid.
25. Richard Bernard, *A Guide to Grandjurymen* (London, 1627) p. 99.
26. Ibid., pp. 99–100.
27. William Crashaw, *Sermon at Pauls Cross* (London, 1608) p. 170.
28. Quoted in John Morgan, *Godly Learning* (London, 1986) p. 141.
29. Quoted in J. W. Blench, *Preaching in England* (London, 1964) p. 306.
30. Peter Smart, *The Vanities and Downe-Fall of Superstitious Popish Ceremonies* (Edinburgh, 1628) p. 24.
31. Stephen Greenblatt, 'Shakespeare and the Exorcists', in *Shakespeare and the Question of Theory*, ed. P. Parker and G. Hartman (New York, 1985) p. 171.
32. Samuel Harsnet, *A Declaration of Egregious Popish Impostures* (London, 1603) p. 148.
33. Stephen Gossen, *The School of Abuse* (London, 1841) p. 50.
34. Howard Felperin, *Shakespearean Representation* (Princeton, NJ, 1977) p. 168.

Notes to Chapter 10: The Private World of Donne, Burton and Browne

1. See Lawrence Stone, *The Family, Sex and Marriage in England, 1500–1800* (London, 1977) pp. 253–4.
2. Ibid., pp. 229–30.
3. Stephen Greenblatt, *Renaissance Self-Fashioning* (Chicago, 1980) p. 45.
4. Michel de Montaigne, *Essays*, trans. John Florio (New York, 1967) vol. III, p. 48.
5. Ibid., vol. III, pp. 48–9.
6. Ibid., p. 48.
7. Ibid., pp. 400–1.
8. Robert Burton, *The Anatomy of Melancholy*, 6th edn (London, 1660) p. 1.
9. Francis Barker, *The Tremulous Private Body* (London, 1984) p. 10.
10. Sir Thomas Browne, *The Major Works*, ed. C. A. Patrides (London, 1977) p. 59.
11. Ibid.
12. John Donne, *Biathanatos*, ed. M. Rudick and M. Pabst Battin (New York, 1982) p. 39.

13. Ibid., p. 192.
14. John Donne, *Sermons*, ed. E. M. Simpson and G. R. Potter (Berkeley, Calif., 1953–62) vol. 6, p. 323.
15. Ibid., vol. 4, p. 327.
16. See George Hakewill, *An Apologie of the Power and Providence of God*, 3rd edn (London, 1635) p. 378.
17. John Donne, *Sermons*, vol. 7, p. 339.
18. Ibid., vol. 4, p. 327.
19. John Donne, *Life and Letters*, ed. E. Gosse (London, 1899) vol. I, p. 184.
20. Ibid., vol. I, p. 219.
21. See John Donne, *The Elegies and the Songs and Sonnets*, ed. H. Gardner (Oxford, 1975) pp. xlvii–lxii.
22. Helen Gardner, 'The Argument about "The Exstasy"', in *Elizabethan and Jacobean Studies Presented to F. P. Wilson*, ed. H. Davis and H. Gardner (Oxford, 1959) p. 306.
23. Wilbur Sanders, *John Donne's Poetry* (Cambridge, 1971) p. 25.
24. See Robert Ellrodt, *Les Poetes Metaphysiques Anglais* (Paris, 1960) vol. I, pp. 106–16.
25. Donne, *Sermons*, vol. 3, pp. 167–8.
26. Donne, *Life and Letters*, vol. I, p. 173.
27. Ibid., vol. I, p. 181.
28. Jonathan Goldberg, *James I and the Politics of Literature* (Baltimore, Md, 1983) p. 211.
29. Donne, *Sermons*, vol. 9, p. 115.
30. See John B. Gleason, 'Dr Donne in the Court of Kings: a Glimpse from Marginalia', *Journal of English and Germanic Philology*, vol. 66, 599–612.
31. Donne, *Sermons*, vol. 2, p. 84.
32. Burton, *Anatomy*, 6th edn, p. 261.
33. Ibid., p. 11.
34. Robert Burton, *The Anatomy of Melancholy*, 1st edn (London, 1621) pp. 4–5.
35. Ibid., p. 420.
36. Ibid.
37. Ibid., pp. 185–6.
38. Burton, *Anatomy*, 6th edn, p. 139.
39. Ibid.
40. Ibid., p. 107.
41. Ibid., p. 59.
42. Ibid., p. 8.
43. Ibid., p. 47.
44. Ibid., p. 5.
45. Ibid., p. 6.
46. Stanley J. Fish, *Self-consuming Artifacts* (Berkeley, Calif., 1972) p. 329.
47. Burton, *Anatomy*, 6th edn, pp. 62–3.
48. Ibid., p. 66.
49. Ibid., p. 60.
50. Ibid., p. 78.

51. Ibid., p. 61.
52. Ibid., p. 136.
53. Ibid., pp. 3–4.
54. Browne, *The Major Works*, p. 72.
55. Ibid., pp. 487–8.
56. J. H. B. Masterman, *The Age of Milton* (London, 1897) p. 149; and see also Fish, *Self-Consuming Artifacts*, pp. 353–73.
57. Browne, *The Major Works*, p. 92.
58. Ibid., p. 119.
59. Ibid.
60. Sir Kenelm Digby, *Observations on 'Religio Medici'* (London, 1644) pp. 6–7.
61. Browne, *The Major Works*, p. 66.
62. Ibid., p. 93.
63. Ibid., p. 73.
64. Ibid., p. 66.
65. Ibid., p. 61.
66. Ibid., p. 94.
67. Ibid., p. 132.
68. Ibid., p. 112.
69. Ibid., p. 73.
70. See Katherine R. Firth, *The Apocalyptic Tradition in Reformation Britain, 1530–1645* (Oxford, 1979) p. 226.
71. Browne, *The Major Works*, p. 118.
72. Ibid., p. 79.
73. Ibid., p. 68.
74. Ibid., p. 110.
75. Ibid., p. 96.
76. Ibid., p. 97.
77. Ibid., p. 87.
78. Ibid., p. 263.
79. Ibid., p. 312.
80. Ibid., pp. 72–3.
81. Ibid.
82. Ibid., p. 78.
83. Digby, *Observations*, p. 53.
84. Ibid., p. 54.
85. Nigel Smith (ed.), *A Collection of Ranter Writings* (London, 1983) p. 210.
86. Ibid., p. 215.
87. Ibid., p. 208.
88. Ibid., p. 218.

Notes to Chapter 11: The Public World of Clarendon, Hobbes and Milton

1. J. G. A. Pocock, *The Machiavellian Moment* (Princeton, NJ, 1975) p. 351.

2. *The Letters and Speeches of Oliver Cromwell*, with elucidations by Thomas Carlyle, ed. S. C. Lomax (London, 1904) vol. ɪ, p. 176.
3. *Fast Sermons to Parliament*, with notes by R. Jeffs (London, 1970) vol. 6, p. 43.
4. Thomas Goodwin, *A Glimpse of Syons Glory* (London, 1641) pp. 5–6.
5. Clarendon, *The History of the Rebellion*, ed. W. D. Macray (Oxford, 1958) vol. ɪɪɪ, p. 321.
6. John Wilson, *Fairfax* (London, 1985) p. 83.
7. Maurice Ashley, *General Monck* (London, 1977) p. 160.
8. Clarendon, *History*, vol. ɪ, p. 159.
9. Ibid., vol. ɪᴠ, p. 75.
10. B. H. G. Wormold, *Clarendon: Politics, History, and Religion, 1640–1660* (Chicago, 1976) p. 154.
11. Clarendon, *The Life of Edward, Earl of Clarendon* (Oxford, 1759) vol. 2, p. 61.
12. Quoted in R. W. Harris, *Clarendon and the English Revolution* (London, 1983) p. 100.
13. Clarendon, *History*, vol. ᴠ, p. 133.
14. Ibid., vol. xɪᴠ, p. 50.
15. Ibid., vol. xɪᴠ, p. 15.
16. Ibid., vol. ᴠɪ, p. 39.
17. Ibid., vol. ᴠ, p. 150.
18. Ibid., vol. ᴠɪ, p. 39.
19. Quoted in Wormold, *Clarendon*, p. 31.
20. Clarendon, *History*, vol. x, p. 170.
21. Ibid., vol. xᴠɪ, p. 77.
22. Ibid., vol. ᴠɪ, p. 186.
23. Ibid., vol. xɪ, p. 243.
24. Ibid.
25. Clarendon, *A Collection of Several Tracts* (London, 1727) p. 370.
26. Harris, *Clarendon and the English Revolution*, p. 252.
27. Clarendon, *A Collection*, p. 125.
28. Thomas Hobbes, *Leviathan*, intro. K. R. Minoghue (London, 1973) pp. 52–3.
29. Ibid., p. 96.
30. Ibid., p. 113.
31. Ibid., p. 88.
32. Ibid., p. 49.
33. Ibid., p. 49.
34. Ibid., p. 233.
35. Ibid., p. 148.
36. Ibid., p. 175.
37. Ibid., p. 364.
38. Ibid., p. 89.
39. Ibid., p. 177.
40. Ibid., p. 235.
41. Ibid., p. 180.
42. John Milton, *Complete Prose Works*, vol. ɪᴠ, ed. D. M. Wolfe (New Haven, Conn., 1965) p. 622.

43. Milton, *Complete Prose Works*, vol. I, ed. D. M. Wolfe (New Haven, Conn., 1953) p. 821.
44. Ibid., p. 821.
45. See Christopher Hill, *Milton and the English Revolution* (London, 1977) pp. 33–4.
46. Milton, *Prose Works*, vol. I, p. 590.
47. Ibid., pp. 829–30.
48. Ibid., pp. 536–7.
49. Ibid., pp. 548–9.
50. Ibid., pp. 820 and 829, and *Complete Prose Works*, vol. III, ed. Merritt Y. Hughes (New Haven, Conn., 1962) p. 195.
51. Milton, *Prose Works*, vol. I, p. 556.
52. Ibid., vol. IV, p. 472.
53. Ibid., vol. III, p. 542.
54. Milton, *Complete Prose Works*, vol. VI, ed. Maurice Kelley (New Haven, Conn., 1973) p. 398.
55. Ibid., p. 541.
56. Milton, *Complete Prose Works*, vol. II, ed. Ernest Sirluck (New Haven, Conn., 1953) pp. 563–4.
57. Milton, *Prose Works*, vol. I, p. 785.
58. Ibid., vol. II, pp. 549–50.
59. Ibid., vol. I, p. 572.
60. Ibid.
61. Winstanley, *The Law of Freedom*, ed. Christopher Hill (Cambridge, 1983) p. 199.
62. Milton, *Prose Works*, vol. IV, p. 533.
63. *The Letters and Speeches of Oliver Cromwell*, vol. II, p. 276.
64. Ibid., vol. II, p. 405.
65. Ibid., vol. III, p. 12.
66. William Perkins, *Works* (Cambridge, 1603) p. 496.
67. Milton, *Prose Works*, vol. I, p. 817.
68. Ibid., vol. IV, p. 367.
69. See William Empson, *Milton's God* (Cambridge, 1981) p. 47.
70. Arthur O. Lovejoy, *The Great Chain of Being* (Cambridge, Mass., 1936) p. 161.
71. Hill, *Milton and the English Revolution*, p. 397.

Index